MAIMONIDES AND ST. THOMAS ON THE LIMITS OF REASON

SUNY SERIES IN PHILOSOPHY

GEORGE R. LUCAS, JR., EDITOR

MAIMONIDES AND ST. THOMAS ON THE LIMITS OF REASON

IDIT DOBBS-WEINSTEIN

STATE UNIVERSITY OF NEW YORK PRESS

B
759
.M34
D62
1995

Published by
State University of New York Press, Albany

Printed in the United States of America

For information, address State University of New York Press,
State University Plaza, Albany, N.Y. 12246

Production by M. R. Mulholland
Marketing by Dana E. Yanulavich

Library of Congress Cataloging-in-Publication Data

Dobbs-Weinstein, Idit, 1950-
    Maimonides and St. Thomas on the limits of reason / Idit Dobbs
-Weinstein.
        p.   cm. — (SUNY series in philosophy)
    Includes bibliographical references and indexes.
    ISBN 0-7914-2415-4 (alk. paper). — ISBN 0-7914-2416-2 (pbk. :
alk. paper)
    1. Maimonides, Moses, 1135-1204. 2. Thomas, Aquinas, Saint,
1225?-1274. 3. Philosophy, Medieval. 4. Faith and reason.
I. Title. II. Title: Maimonides and Saint Thomas on the limits of
reason. III. Series.
B759.M34D62 1995
181'.06—dc20   94-3369
                                                                    CIP

10 9 8 7 6 5 4 3 2 1

In Memory of my Father
Ephraim (Alfred) Weinstein
(1910-1984)

CONTENTS

APOLOGIA AND ACKNOWLEDGMENTS

In a manner of speaking, this book has its origin in my early childhood or, more precisely, in my first encounter with the Disaster (*Shoah*). My continued preoccupation with the history of philosophy, or with philosophy's appropriations and suppressions of its history, is, quite simply, the manifestation of an attempt to understand the irreducible tension between reason and ethics, the true and the good or just, precisely in the face of Modernity's attempt to conceal such a tension by reducing truth to certainty and justice to its practical application. Modernity's failure to accomplish its theoretical promise or fulfill its practical end, freeing "Humanity" from its dogmatic slumber and theologico-political bondage, when it is coupled (as it should be) with the triumph of the progressive, instrumental rationality manifest in this century's "Disaster," demand a response. Indeed, numerous responses have been forthcoming. Ironically, most, if not all, of them, "Analytic" as well as "Continental," subscribe to Modernity's judgment about medieval philosophy and, hence, either ignore it altogether or ignore significant, non-Western, silenced aspects of it, including those whose influence upon the Christian, Latin tradition are necessary for understanding the Western philosophical tradition. Rather than attempt either to escape reason's disastrous consequences into some other, more humane discourse, "create" an entirely new philosophy, or persevere in a belief in an as yet to be fulfilled progress, in this book I seek to retrieve reflections on the limits of reason and their consequences for the possibilities of knowledge and action by two, major medieval philosophers, Moses Maimonides and St. Thomas Aquinas. Rather than being idiosyncratic, the choice of retrieving the "dialogue" between the non-Western, Jewish Maimonides and the Western, Christian Aquinas renders possible an appreciation of the importance of occluded aspects of the premodern philosophical tradition for understanding the Western tradition and for "discovering" its silenced possibilities.

Owing to the long history of the book gestation, I owe debts of gratitude to more individuals than I can probably recall, especially to former teachers, colleagues and students. To the late John Brückmann I am indebted for his encouragements to pursue graduate work in medieval philosophy, in general, the influence of Maimonides on Thomas Aquinas, in particular. To the late Frank (Ephraim) Talmage and to James P. Reilly, Jr., I am indebted for their dedicated supervision of my advanced graduate work. To the late David Rapport Lachterman, I am indebted for many long, inspiring conversations and extensive comments on an earlier draft of the book. To Tom Gaskill and Julie R. Klein, I am indebted for their probing questions in graduate seminars and conversations on medieval philosophy.

I would like to thank my senior colleague, John Lachs, for his support and encouragement in the final, hence, agonizing preparation of the book for publication. I also want to thank the philosophy department's secretaries, Judy Thompson and Stella Thompson for their extensive help and patience.

Finally, my debt to my daughter, Sophia Bella Dobbs, for twenty-one years of loving patience, and to my friend, Emily Whitcomb, for her loving encouragement, is greater than I can express.

ABBREVIATIONS

With the exception of the following abbreviations of scholarly journals, series, and publishers' names, all abbreviated titles are provided in the first reference noted in the text.

CCSL   Corpus Christianorum Series Latina
CCARJ   Central Conference of American Rabbis' Journal
PAAJR   Proceedings of the American Academy of Jewish Research
PIMS   Pontifical Institute of Mediaeval Studies

INTRODUCTION

Topics 101b3-4: τοῦτο δ᾽ ἴδιον ἢ μάλιστα οἰκεῖον
τῆς διαλεκτικῆς ἐστίν· ἐξεταστικὴ γὰρ οὖσα πρὸς
τὰς ἀπασῶν τῶν μεθόδων ἀρχὰς ὁδὸν ἔχει.

Topics 104b19-20: θέσις δέ ἐστιν ὑπόληψις
παράδοξος τῶν γνωρίμων τινὸς κατὰ φιλοσοφίαν

Topics 104b35-105a2: σχεδὸν δὲ νῦν πάντα τὰ
διαλεκτικὰ προβλήματα θέσεις καλοῦνται.
διαφερέτω δὲ μηδὲν ὁπωσοῦν λεγόμενον· οὐ γὰρ
ὀνοματοποιῆσαι βουλόμενοι διείλομεν οὕτως αὐτά,
ἀλλ᾽ ἵνα μὴ λανθάνωσιν ἡμᾶς τίνες αὐτῶν τυγχάνουσιν
οὖσαι διαφοραί.

An exquisite irony is manifest in the dialectical movement between philosophical language and its popular appropriations. Socrates and Nietzsche were its keenest observers and practitioners, the former when he exposed the majestic deception of the written word, the latter when he described himself as a philologist. With the exception of the word "*philosophy*," nowhere is the irony of language manifest more acutely than in the word *reason*. The reduction of the robust sense that reason/*logos* had for the ancient Greek philosophers to a narrowly circumscribed demonstrative rationality was accompanied, on the one hand, by a proliferation of philosophical vocabulary that was needed to replace all the other senses of *reason* and, on the other, by a popular appropriation of the polysemy of *reason*. The popular, looking-glass images of *reason*, however, like Humpty-Dumpty's vocabulary, are without reason or unable to give a reasonable account. Following both Plato and Aristotle, Maimonides and Aquinas keenly appreciated the ironies inherent in language, especially in the context of dialectical, paradoxical problems, of which providence is an exemplary instance. For, by means of discursive reason the investigation of providence calls demonstrative reason into question and indicates that a recognition of its limits is a necessary condition for understanding.[1]

In addition to the difficulties inherent in the study of any paradoxical problem and its strange language, the contemporary reader of Maimonides' and Aquinas' philosophical investigations of such problems encounters difficulties that arise from the radical changes that have taken place between the premodern and modern philosophical idiom and comportment.[2] Given the twofold layers of difficulties and given that these difficulties concern *paradoxa*, it is not surprising that the greatest tensions between premodern and modern philosophy lead to charges of self-contradiction and inconsistency against many premodern philosophers. Since the philosophical study of the limits of reason as they become manifest in Maimonides' and Aquinas' discussions of the questions underlying the "problem of providence" is a study of *paradoxa*, it must confront both of these difficulties, withholding both judgment and assent. Rather than attempt to resolve or dismiss difficulties and contradictions, rather than translate "strange notions" into modern idiom, in the following study I hope to show the central role they play in Maimonides' and Aquinas' "ethical pedagogy."

Since Moses Maimonides and St. Thomas Aquinas occupied preeminent positions in medieval philosophy, both thinkers are numbered among the few medieval philosophers who have not been ignored by the philosophers of the succeeding centuries. The attention they have received, even when grudgingly, suffices as testimony for the relevance of their thought to the understanding of subsequent philosophical discussions. For, we can no more understand Spinoza's thought without Maimonides than we can understand Descartes' without Aquinas. Unfortunately and ironically, however, the willingness to acknowledge the importance of their contribution often led to the uncritical appropriation of some essential elements of Maimonides' and Aquinas' teachings irrespective of their tension with other, equally essential elements. These latter elements were either ignored or dismissed, even when they served as fundamental, or ontologically prior, principles for the former and, hence, were necessary for understanding the discourses based upon them. Paradoxically, other contemporary scholars deny the validity, even the intelligibility of Maimonides' and Aquinas' metaphysical[3] and ontological principles, the very principles that, for them, serve as the originative principles of all other philosophical discourses. The rejection of the primary principles of their thought is often based upon the assumption that there exists a fundamental conflict between revelation and philosophy; medieval metaphysics is merely apologetics dressed in philosophical garb. The result of this "enlightened" bias is not only the distortion of Maimonides' and Aquinas' thought, but sometimes also the incorporation of some of their teachings into systems of thought comprising other elements directly in conflict with them.

Modern appropriations notwithstanding, for both Maimonides and Aquinas, philosophy is synonymous with harmony and can neither encompass *irreconcilable* tensions nor conflict *essentially* with other modes of knowing.[4] Admittedly, their writings exhibit an affirmation of revealed principles that is a habit foreign to contemporary philosophical discourse. Nevertheless, they also manifest a bold courage which makes possible their appreciation and admiration for pagan philosophy, its desire for truth, and its ability to have attained to the understanding that rendered possible further knowledge. Above all, they identified the excellence of ancient philosophy as an exemplary mode of the human compulsion to know. The belief that human perfection was intellectual perfection and that its culmination was knowledge of God when coupled with the concomitant beliefs in the truth of revelation and in the sensible origin of human knowledge led both Maimonides and Aquinas to seek ways of exhibiting the harmony between philosophy and revelation. The principle of harmony or cosmos through which aspects of truth are disclosed should not be confused with the assumption that there can exist only one source of human knowledge, let alone one mode of its expression, if sensible experience is not to be denied meaning and if dogma is to be avoided. For human knowers do not even possess simultaneous knowledge of the visible world, let alone of its principles.

Since human knowledge depends upon the multiplicity of experience, and since "[a]ll teaching and learning through thinking (*dianoetike*) proceeds from prior knowledge,"[5] or tradition of inquiry, in order to avoid both redundancy and the demonstrated errors of others, the immediate sources of human knowledge have to be distinct from its unifying principles. Yet, although a multiplicity of discourses may manifest contradiction and error, it neither does so necessarily nor are all contradictions necessarily erroneous; rather, it may reflect different foci, distinct disciplines, distinct ways of knowing. Only from a Modern perspective is a single unifying discourse the necessary condition for genuine knowledge. Consequently, only to an "ignorant" reader are paradoxes and contradictions hindrances to understanding. In contrast to the "*moderni*," Maimonides and Aquinas underlined the differences between orders and types of discourse, investigated the differences and relations between modes of knowing without reducing them into a single mode and, accordingly, adopted diverse approaches to interpretation which are exemplary instances of philosophical practice.

I

If we can characterize the perennial philosophical pursuit, at least until the end of the nineteenth century, as the most profound (often tragic, sometimes nihilistic) human expression of an enduring desire for immortality, the possibility of fulfilling this enduring desire was considered by Maimonides and Aquinas to be attainable only through the perfection of the human intellect, the nearest one could come to an imitation of God. Since their accounts of the nature of the activities constituting *imitatio Dei* are based upon their respective understanding of the nature of the universe, the human place in it, and above all, God's relation to it, the question of providence seems to me to provide the best focus from which to begin an examination of Maimonides' and Aquinas' thought as exemplary instances of the engagement with the *aporiae* that manifest both the extent and the limits of human knowledge. The question of providence, i.e., of God's relation to the universe, is the best impetus for an investigation of human knowledge precisely because it questions the possibility of human knowledge of God, the archaic *aporia*. For, if human perfection consists in *imitatio Dei* of which the manifestation is free activity, or the actuality that resembles absolute divine actuality most closely, and if knowledge is the condition for human freedom, then the question of providence is a question of human rather than divine knowledge.

Since, by definition, the concept "providence" signifies some ordered relationship(s)[6] between God and the world and between the human being and God, it immediately manifests the interrelationship among the discourses of metaphysics, ontology, psychology, noetics, and ethics, inherent in medieval thought, and necessary for understanding it. For even if we wish to appropriate or retrieve some elements of Maimonides' and Aquinas' philosophy, while rejecting others, we cannot do so successfully—that is, without creating an insurmountable tension, or a barrier to further understanding, within our own enterprise—unless we first understand the implicit principles giving rise to a particular insight that we find attractive.[7] Since their thought was formed in dialogue with their predecessors and contemporaries, understanding their unique contributions to a given topic requires familiarity with their sources.[8] If I were to choose but one instance exemplifying the uncritical appropriation of each thinker's writings, I would immediately point to the "esoteric-exoteric" problem in Maimonides' writings, especially in the *Guide of the Perplexed*,[9] and to the attempts by contemporary natural law/natural rights theorists to reduce their arguments to those of Aquinas.

As I shall argue in some detail in Chapter 1, the radical separation and surmised opposition between layers of meaning in Maimonides' writings entirely ignores the aim of the work. Ironically, this type of opposition renders impossible the appreciation of the epistemic role of contradictions in his works. Whereas Maimonides exhibits the harmony between reason and revealed knowledge in the very act of interpreting their divergent discourses, his interpreters attempt to establish a radical separation between layers of meaning by means of the *Guide*. With respect to Aquinas, the legitimation of liberal conceptions of natural law theories with Aquinas' writings overlooks the context of his discussion, ignoring the fact that the natural law argued for in the *Summa Theologiae*,[10] pertains, *inter alia*, to an internal state of original justice that is modified considerably after the Fall and that in no way indicates the human possession of some primordial "rights." In addition, even though Aquinas' twofold ontology and, especially, the causality of the Good may lend greater force to a natural law theory based upon Aquinas' thought, it is generally ignored. Consequently, in order to preserve some meaning, any argument for natural law based upon Aquinas' teachings must also take into account the existential consequences of the Fall, although it need not accept its historical facticity. Furthermore, on the basis of Aquinas' discussions, no immediate transition from natural law to natural rights is possible nor could be made possible. On the other hand, if it is the ontological foundation of natural law that is accepted, then the entire ontological system of which it is a constituent part must be taken into consideration. For, unlike Maimonides and Aquinas, we live in a world where the God of revelation is radically absent from philosophy. We can no more return to the medieval city than to the Athenian *polis* of which the cosmology and *paideia* are neither our own nor can become ours by means of a direct appropriation. Consequently, in order to guard against anachronistic misrepresentations, the appreciation, let alone appropriation, of some of Maimonides' and Aquinas' insights require not so much their translation into a familiar idiom, but rather the development of a careful philosophical hermeneutics[11] conscious of its own presuppositions even and precisely as it attempts to understand theirs.

The purpose of the present study is twofold: First, by means of a comparative philosophical examination of discussions of diverse questions concerning providence in the thought of Maimonides and Aquinas, I seek to determine the degree of philosophical compatibility between them, and where disagreement is evident, its origin, nature, and philosophical consequences.[12] Second, I hope to retrieve some occluded aspects of Maimonides' and Aquinas' thought that (a) render possible a better understanding of each thinker and (b) may provide us with a richer philosophical vocabulary for discussions of the limits of "reason," the consequent inevitable limits of language and interpretation, and above all, the relation between knowing and acting.

In addition to making manifest a far greater kinship between Maimonides' and Aquinas' thought than has been generally recognized,[13] the comparative study will render possible an understanding of how and why, even though they adopt some radically different ontological principles, Maimonides and Aquinas reach strikingly similar conclusions concerning the existential dimensions of human life, especially the possibilities and modes of knowledge and the actions consequent upon them. The comparative nature of the study provides a twofold advantage. First, I believe that it is precisely in virtue of the comparison, that is, in virtue of retrieving the dialogue between them and engaging in dialogues with them, that light can be shed upon aspects of their thought that are otherwise occluded. It is only in this manner that each thinker's distinct contributions can, in turn, be appreciated. Second, the comparison brings into sharp relief the dialogical nature of Maimonides' and Aquinas' thought and, thereby, also shows how and why for them (and for me) philosophical understanding is never completed or always on the way to knowledge.

By characterizing the study as a dialogue *with* Maimonides and Aquinas as well as one between them, I seek underline the fact that I bring to it contemporary concerns and sensibilities that inevitably "color" my conclusions. The very choice of emphasis upon the existential dimension of providence as well as the selection of the *topoi* I consider necessary for understanding it constitute decisive determinations of what and how aspects of their thought will be disclosed. The central role I assign to *paradoxes*, contradictions and ironies clearly shape the discussions in a particular way. My only "apology" is that I consider Maimonides' and Aquinas' thought exemplary instances of the engagement with philosophical questions that I find compelling and that they have helped me clarify. Of these questions, the ones that highlight the uses and abuses of reason, the ones that undermine, on the one hand, the conflation of knowledge with *techne* and, on the other, the separation between knowledge and action, and above all, the ones that underline pedagogy and interpretations as ethical comportments of resistance against dogma, paradoxically, seem to exhibit "strange" contemporary sensibilities.[14]

II

The most significant reason for the general reluctance to investigate the question of providence in Maimonides and Aquinas is succinctly indicated by David Burrell, who argues that it manifests "collective prudent counsel, for the history of each tradition records, one after another, the shipwrecks of those who essayed it, as well as bitter aftermaths in their respective religious communities. The more bitter as certain stages of this inquiry lead one to dilemmas so harsh that atheism alone could offer plausible rest to the spirit."[15] Paradoxically, philosophers shy away from the question because they believe that it is intelligible only to the pious, whereas theologians avoid it for fear that it may lead to disbelief. The theologians' reticence, in fact, seems to vindicate the philosophers' conclusion that providence ought not be regarded as a question but rather must be affirmed *sola fide*. With respect to providence, neither the philosophers nor the theologians seem to be willing to entertain the possibility that a certain degree of uncertainty, whether it is skeptical or agnostic, is a prerequisite to both knowledge and examined belief and that the "failure" of rational skepticism may result in an "ignorance" of a kind radically different than the skeptical. Unlike the "*moderni*," both Maimonides and Aquinas considered the question of providence to be the locus for exhibiting the fact that belief without understanding is no belief at all, nor is demonstrative reason alone sufficient for understanding.

Another major reason for the reluctance to study the question of providence (even by believers) is based upon the assumption—fully justified in view of the balance of scholarship on the subject—that its most fundamental problem is the possibility of affirming temporal human freedom in the light of eternal divine knowledge. However, not only can we examine the significance and role of providence with respect to human existence as a question independent of the nature of divine knowledge, but also, inasmuch as both Maimonides and Aquinas understood the order of knowledge to be inverse to the order of being, they considered the study of the human place in the order of being to be temporally prior to the study of God.[16] That is, since human knowledge of divine attributes is, at best, analogical, more often radically equivocal, understanding the metaphysical, ontological, and noetic aspects that form the human relation to providence is a prerequisite for even the most limited understanding of the nature of divine knowledge.

By examining a range of questions necessary for understanding the relations between providence and human perfection, I wish to show that, despite the differences between them, for both Maimonides and Aquinas, the necessary—though insufficient—condition for human perfection is an intellectual[17] assent to revealed principles that is consequent upon intellectual pursuit. The study attempts to show both the necessity for demonstrative reason and the necessity for recognizing its limits as a condition for further knowledge. In this light, irrespective of how we name non-demonstrative knowledge, whether it is called *revealed*, *extra-natural*, or *a-rational*, its significance consists in showing the dangers and consequences of "hubris" both with respect to knowledge and with respect to action.

The study is so structured that, although some of its individual chapters, especially, Chapters 1 and 2, can be read independently from what follows, each chapter also explores a different aspect of the same question, namely, the limitation of human knowledge, and serves as a background for what follows.[18] Chapter 1, "Maimonides and Aquinas as Interpreters," is addressed primarily to methodological questions. By first reviewing the historical background of the development of biblical exegesis, I outline some of the general problems inherent in the attempt to provide a rational systematic account of 'the eternal word of God' in its temporal, varied modes of human transmission. This brief examination brings to light a medieval climate open to and willing to abide with language as essentially ambiguous, a climate whose attitudes both thinkers share, albeit in different ways. Second, through a review of the scholarship addressed to Maimonides' and Aquinas' methodological procedures, I address the general difficulties inherent in interpreting their works and the need to examine their works more synthetically, as instances of thinking on the way. Third, I examine their "methodological" procedures in order to show how and why their works constitute instances of interpretation as philosophical practice in which individually contextualized judgments, rather than rules, hold sway.

Chapter 2, which is a study of Maimonides' and Aquinas' explanation of providence in the context of their commentaries on the Book of Job, is thus also a study of the application of their hermeneutics to a biblical text. Given that *Job*, a revealed text, addresses the problem of providence independently of revelation,[19] it offers an occasion for a philosophical inquiry concerning the nature and scope of sublunar providence and, especially, of its significance to actual human existence. Since the text raises the question of the relation between rational and revealed knowledge, it also presents an occasion for examining the harmony between philosophy and revelation as it is understood by Maimonides and Aquinas unhindered by the principles of either mode of cognition. However, unlike other texts addressing the same question, Job also brings into relief the tension between speculative and practical perfection and outlines the difficulties in, as well as the possibility of, establishing a harmony between them. By challenging the truth and reality of divine justice in the light of a seeming injustice intentionally willed by God upon a just man, the text seems to present a paradoxical situation that inverts the biblical order of justice and presents the human being as the true measure of things. Moreover, insofar as Job's moral probity is not denied but rather is contrasted with his imperfect knowledge, the text seems to suggest that moral perfection is either irrelevant to true perfection or an imaginative human fiction. Consequently, both Maimonides and Aquinas consider the biblical text as an occasion to explain the manner in which the failure of natural reason to recognize its limits, which is emphasized in the biblical story, constitutes not only a speculative but also a moral deficiency, which must be overcome if we are to understand providence.

The combined purpose of the first two chapters is to establish the "methodological" and "conceptual" boundaries for the detailed inquiry into a philosophical study of the role of providence in human perfection. Since the meaning of concepts is reconstituted at every historical stage according as they reflect upon what is accepted—explicitly or implicitly—as the purpose of existence,[20] by investigating, in the preliminary chapters, the threefold relation between language, meaning, and purpose, I establish both the range and the limits of the meaning of the concept "providence." Consequently, in Chapters 3, 4, 5, and 6 I investigate each essential constitutive subject separately in order to examine their combined consequences in the final chapter and present a mode of understanding providence strictly in the context of human existence.

Chapter 3 addresses the question of the origin of the universe. For the very notion of providence consists of three moments, namely, that there exists a provider or providers, that there exist beings who are provided for and who may, in turn, also provide, and that there are some conditions prerequisite for the continuous (even though not contiguous and even if changing) ordered relations between the provider(s) and those provided for. The examination of the status of origin or the primordial, least present, condition for providence, the question of the origin of the universe will determine the possible scope of what can be known and said about the relation between the provider(s) and those provided for.

After the philosopher demonstrates the existence of the first and final cause following Aristotle,[21] the possible relations between the cause of causes and the things caused remains to be understood. If the first cause, or god, can bring about a fundamental change only as the result of the eternal necessity of (its) nature and only out of coexisting eternal entities, or if the divinity is the range of necessary natural forces, the relations between the divine and the world of change would, at best, be a relation of an ordering principle to its consequences. In order to safeguard the integrity of the first cause, on the one hand, and posit a unifying principle that can account for the permanence of the universal changing order, on the other, Aristotelian metaphysics[22] also requires that the first cause be indifferent to this world. Consequently, if the entities eternally coexisting with it are principles of change, or of natural corruption, then the human being may be doomed to what Dante described as life in longing without hope.[23] But, since the origin is either indemonstrable (Aristotle and Maimonides) or unknowable (Aquinas), how can it give rise to knowledge? On the other hand, since *true* desire without hope was unintelligible for both Maimonides and Aquinas, each thinker attempted to establish that creation *ex nihilo* was as *likely an opinion*[24] as the Aristotelian argument for eternity, an attempt that was philosophically possible precisely because Aristotle himself claimed that demonstration cannot be had with respect to the question of the origin of the universe.[25] Only after such a probability is established, is it possible to argue that God had created the world out of absolute nothing and, hence, that His relations to it are not limited by anything nor is the possibility of human perfection limited by any principles other than those decreed by the divine "will" and "wisdom."[26]

After examining the principles underlying human existence in Chapter 3, in Chapter 4 I analyze their primary consequences for sublunar, materially determined individual existence. By focusing upon the concepts "form," "prime matter," and "privation," the three principles required not only for generation and corruption but also for the actualization of the human soul, I can delineate the nature of the relations between the material and the immaterial dimensions of human existence, its determinations and indeterminacies, and the possibilities of perfection consequent upon them. In addition to investigating the relation between matter and form in the composition of natural substances, I emphasize the distinction between matter and privation, especially in view of the Neoplatonic attribution of evil to matter, since it is necessary to understand the conceptual difference between these principles before determining what can be said about the nature and possibility of human perfection. Insofar as Chapters 3 and 4 discuss principles of natural composition rather than determinate natural entities, they explore the possibility of knowing indeterminate "things" or "things" that have no existence *in se* but can be said to *exist* only *in alio*. Both chapters show that no inference can be made from an actual determination to that which renders all determinations possible. Once the epistemic status of first principles is questioned, all human categories based upon them are disclosed as human constructions. Thus, it becomes clear that the primary principles that underlie the possibility, scope and meaning of human perfection, cannot be known through what is traditionally called *natural reason*.

Chapter 5 addresses the nature of the human soul and its operations, the means for attaining perfection, and especially, the nature of the internal relations within the intellect. The investigation of intellectual operations exhibits both what human judgments consist of and the natural limits of rational operations, limitations that render necessary the epistemic role of divine law in human perfection, both theoretical and practical. Chapter 6, follows the consequences of the discussion of epistemic psychology to philosophical ethics and explores the simultaneous role of divine law in moral and intellectual perfection. Although, as I shall point out throughout the study, with respect to metaphysics and ontology Maimonides and Aquinas differ in some essential premises and conclusions, nevertheless, Chapters 5 and 6 indicate why and how, with respect to their understanding of the nature of human existence and the actual possibility of attaining final perfection, many and significant aspects of concurrence can be found between them.

Since true human perfection consists equally of speculation and action and since right action requires an intellectual desire for the true as the good, speculative perfection is in some respects a prerequisite for moral perfection. However, since the sensible origins of human knowledge render knowledge of some intelligibles disproportionate to rational operations so that these intelligibles cannot be held with demonstrative certainty and since the relationship between the true and the good is far from evident,[27] let alone can be known with certainty, neither speculative nor moral perfection can be attained fully without extra-natural/rational aid. Consequently, both Maimonides and Aquinas argue that so long as the individual does not recognize the full extent of natural human limitations, he or she cannot attain true human perfection since he or she is also unable to apprehend the true meaning of divine law. Human relations to the law, or obedience, which is first addressed in Chapter 6, is explored further in Chapter 7. These relations can take one of two distinct forms; namely, the individual can either be subject to the will of an external legislator or be a participant actualizing the apprehended—that is, internalized—principles of divine law by means of his or her own will. The human relations to the law, which are but manifestations of one's actual being, are, in fact, also the manifestation of one's place in the providential order.

In a manner of speaking, the tension between speculative and practical perfection mirrors the seeming conflict between reason and revelation. The mirror image, which is but an instance of the inverse relations between the order of being and the order of knowledge, clearly reflects the limitations of human knowledge and the consequent necessity of divine law for attaining human perfection. The recognition that there exists an essential harmony between reason and revelation establishes all acts of knowing as direct articulations of particular modes of being and becoming. Consequently, the resolution of the tension between reason and revelation within the order of knowledge becomes the condition for attaining the concurrence between theory and practice; human moral actions are the manifestation of what an individual is, namely, an intellectual being. And insofar as the harmonization of reason and revelation makes evident that the perceived tension between them was but a seeming tension, it also discloses that the perceived tension between speculation and action was merely the result of human ignorance.

Once the scope and limits of natural human knowledge are defined, and after it is established that the human relations to divine law vary in proportion to the degree of their theoretical and practical perfection, I focus directly upon my primary concern and elaborate the dimensions of providence in human existence, with respect to both knowledge and action. Naturally, both of the last two chapters, but especially the final one, have to address the question of human freedom. However, apart from providing a brief explanation of the significance, in fact, the absolute necessity, of affirming human freedom within the entire philosophical enterprise constituting both Maimonides' and Aquinas' works, I do not address the question of divine knowledge of particulars since, as I have indicated and as will become evident, it does not belong properly within the discourses of philosophy nor is it necessary for understanding the concept of providence as it pertains to human existence.

After I rethink the most significant conclusions of the study as well as indicate the aspects that I consider to open up possibilities for rethinking Maimonides' and Aquinas' works in particular, and (I hope) other premodern thinkers, I explain the manner in which divine law is the means by which individuals can choose freely to transform themselves from passive subjects to active participants in divine providence. I argue that so long as divine law is obeyed as an extrinsic principle of action, individuals remain merely bound subjects of providence and, irrespective of whether they obey out of fear or unaided natural reason, neither their knowledge nor their actions are proportionate to their true end. Since these two classes of human beings, the ignorant and the strictly rational, obey something the true reality of which they do not apprehend, they are related to providence as to blind fate. Thus, for both Maimonides and Aquinas, without divine law, not only is it impossible to bridge the dichotomy between speculation and action, but also the human being is indeed subject to blind fate, or lives in "longing without hope."

In order to become an active participant in divine providence, in order to be free to actualize one's longing for knowledge and freedom, the limitations of natural reason must first be recognized. However, in contradistinction to many

philosophical schools, for both Maimonides and Aquinas the recognition of
relative human ignorance does not imply a resignation to a hopeless longing for
immortality. Rather, such a recognition is the condition for permanence or
freedom from change. Although Aristotle recognized the limitations of rational
demonstration with respect to metaphysics as well as the indemonstrability of
the first principles of every science, he did not recognize a mode of human
knowledge in excess of the finite. Since the Aristotelian individual could fully
apprehend only the realm of change, he or she was 'doomed' to remain in it.[28]
The closest the philosopher could come to *imitatio Dei*, or to overcoming the
human finitude, was by indifference to it, an indifference that was ultimately
tragic since it manifest the failure to actualize a natural desire or end. As a
response, in an attempt to safeguard revelation from derision and philosophy
from religious condemnation, many of Aristotle's religious epigones, attempted
to demonstrate the indemonstrable, an attempt vehemently criticized by both
Maimonides and Aquinas.

By questioning the extension of rational demonstration further than
Aristotle did, that is, by encouraging philosophical skepticism, divine law, for
Maimonides and Aquinas, not only renders possible greater knowledge but
also transforms the philosopher's indifference to a political[29] compulsion to
teach. Moreover, the emphasis placed by both Maimonides and Aquinas upon
the limits of natural reason is the condition for overcoming the separation
within knowledge, rather than the resignation to the inherent radical dichotomy
between modes of cognition. Once revealed knowledge is internalized, it refines
the conclusions reached previously by unaided reason, and thus, it also extends
the domain of rational demonstration. The enhanced apprehension of the true
reality of the sensible universe is also the true understanding of providence
and of the properly human—that is, free—active role within it. The activity of
the provident individual, which is true *imitatio Dei*, resembles neither that of
Aristotle's moderate moral person nor that of his indifferent philosopher.
Rather, *imitatio Dei* is characterized by the excess received from divine overabundance that communicates being to, and confirms it in, changeable creatures. Paradoxically, with respect to knowledge of God the excess leads to
genuine *agnoia*, with respect to action it is manifest, on the one hand, as a
compulsion to communicate it to others in speech, the compulsion to teach, and
on the other, in great reticence. I conclude Chapter 7 with a brief indicative
examination of the manifestation of the excess in the language of the *via negativa*; namely, as the contradictions, negations, and remotion that displace the
authority of demonstration.

1

MAIMONIDES AND AQUINAS AS INTERPRETERS

The Development of Philosophical, Biblical Exegesis

The quest for a systematic, coherent account of revelation began as soon as diverse existential experiences came into tension with the unique and seemingly univocal promise of revelation. Persecution and exile seemed to defy the fundamental principles of the Torah. The defeats, loss of kingdom, and constant humiliations suffered by the 'chosen people' at the hands of idol worshippers challenged not only the belief in the omnipotence and omniscience of God, but also the beliefs in creation, providence, and prophecy. The personal loving relationship between God and his people depicted in the early biblical stories required refinement by the post-exilic prophets, receiving its most comprehensive treatment in the Book of Job. Thus, the separation between the physical and spiritual ecumene necessitated intellectual reflection on the Bible and led to the first attempts at biblical exegesis.

Two major currents are evident in early Jewish biblical interpretation, Hellenistic-philosophical and rabbinic.[30] Despite great dissimilarities between them, both approaches manifest an absence of a unified doctrinal systematization and hence lead to no single accepted tradition.[31] Moreover, irrespective of whether or not Philo had exerted any philosophical influence on later Jewish thought, no such influence can be discerned in the biblical exegesis, prior to Maimonides. The absence of a systematic or philosophical unity evident in pre-Maimonidean interpretation, however, does not signify an anti-intellectual tendency in early Jewish thought. Rather, scholarly pursuit and the acquisition of knowledge were seen as the vehicle for human perfection as early as the pre-Maccabean period.[32] The polysemy of the Torah not only became an early commonplace of Jewish thought but also led directly to the concomitant truism regarding its hierarchical levels of meaning, accessible to progressive degrees of knowledge.[33] Moreover, despite later attempts to separate radically between the letter of the Torah and its more profound layers of meaning and to legitimize this practice by reference to the revered scholars of the tradition, the various levels of meaning are understood to be interrelated until the thirteenth century. In fact, the more speculatively inclined the interpreter was, the more concerned he[34] was with establishing a relation between the external and the internal levels of meaning, rather than with invalidating the former. Sa'adia Gaon, the tenth century Iraqi thinker composed works ranging from a philosophical commentary on creation, through a biblical dictionary and an Arabic translation of the Bible, to a work that develops principles of biblical interpretation in the light of reason.[35] Abraham Ibn 'Ezra, whose religious piety has been doubted and whose philosophical thought has been considered often to approach pantheism,[36] was also a cautious biblical commentator who, as exegete, commented on his text verse by verse and "limited his horizon to the text or to the immediate context, especially if his intention was, at least in principle, to make his text express what, in his opinion, it signified literally."[37]

The preceding brief overview of the Jewish tradition of biblical interpretation clearly suggests that, apart from the strictly legal teachings of the Torah and the Talmud of which the possible interpretations are limited, Maimonides inherits an exegetical tradition that is neither systematic nor dogmatic, but rather can be characterized as an attitude of *open* reverence to the text as a living historical tradition.[38] In his systematic explanations of Jewish teachings, both legal and philosophical, Maimonides' main concern is to establish the truth contained in the Torah through a clearer articulation, rather than to adhere reverentially to a word that is seemingly unfitting and, hence, may lead to perplexity. Just as the Sages openly and vigorously disagreed with one another in their interpretations of the Torah,[39] so Maimonides disagrees with authorities, both past and present, when he deems it necessary. Rather then demonstrating a radical break with a dogmatic tradition, the very fact of questioning, even in its most vehement expression, exhibits Maimonides' firm membership in the Jewish tradition.

Christian biblical exegesis can be said to originate with Christ's rebuke of Jewish literalism. The distinction between the law of the heart and the law of the members, which is repeated often in the New Testament[40] and is reinforced by the understanding of the Old Testament as a prefiguration of the New, led to a heightened interest in interpretation and necessitated its systematization, especially when faced with the Jewish denial of the validity of the new teachings. In addition, from its very inception, Christianity had to contend with the competing claims to universal truth of both Greek philosophy and the mystery cults, whose accounts seemed to rest upon spiritual principles similar to its own and whose possession of a physical ecumene supported their claims even if they belied their spiritual substance. Thus challenged by those who shared in its monotheism, on the one hand, and by those who seemed to share in its spiritual claims, on the other, Christianity had to develop rapidly an approach to interpretation that took both into account. It is not surprising, therefore, that

Christian biblical exegesis adopts philosophical language from the beginning.

Since its challenge to Judaism rested upon the distinction between the letter and the spirit of revelation, the first principle of Christian exegesis immediately called for an account of the relation between the two aspects of language as layers of meaning. Against its philosophical background, it was inevitable that the account of the relation between letter and spirit initially would be associated and then closely linked to the understanding of the relationship between body and soul. Given the Alexandrian, Neoplatonic roots of Christian biblical exegesis, the separation of the literal or carnal meaning from the spiritual resulted in the diminution of the value of the letter; just as the body was the necessary tomb of the soul from the confines of which it strove to be liberated, so the exegete strove to free the spirit of Scripture from its necessary literal garb. Although the letter was rarely discarded completely, its importance became evident progressively as Christian exegesis developed its own synthesis of rabbinic and philosophic (Philonic) interpretation.[41]

This development culminated with Augustine, who "gave the letter a concrete chronological reality which it had never had before. . . . Augustine accepted the historical truth of the letter more wholeheartedly than St. Jerome. We must believe in the fact; then and then only may we seek its spiritual meaning."[42] The fact, however, must be understood in its historical context. When the context is changed, as in the case of customs, or when the letter seems to conflict with charity, the literal meaning must be discarded.[43] Augustine's sensitivity to the nature of language, to the distinction between sign, signifier, and signified, led to a keen awareness of the immanent possibility of error and, hence, to a development of a language theory and a hermeneutic that not only dominated the Middle Ages, but also did not meet its equal until the twentieth century. In *De Doctrina Christiana*, Augustine clearly designated four levels of meaning—literal, allegorical, moral, and anagogical; he outlined the causes of error; he enumerated tools for their remedy; and finally, he set norms for instruction. For all that, Augustine's sensitivity to language and his openness to non-Christian traditions did not extend to the Hebrew language of the Old Testament to which he preferred the Greek Septuagint.[44] It is noteworthy that Augustine's instruction concerning the Hebrew language is the only one completely disregarded by later Christian exegetes.[45]

While St. Gregory's exegesis embodied the teachings of Augustine, his emphasis on the moral and spiritual senses of the Bible set these as the focus for succeeding exegetes until the thirteenth century.[46] Although Augustine emphasized the importance, indeed necessity, of secular learning for interpreting the Bible, the decline of learning in the West limited the early medieval scholar to the few tools available to him, restricting the development of biblical exegesis. Abiding by another Augustinian dictum about the utility and immediate applicability of biblical wisdom and, as it was, closely associated with the monastic schools, medieval biblical interpretation is *de facto* more Gregorian than Augustinian, with the letter of Scripture discarded more often than it is heeded. The renaissance of learning in the twelfth century that witnessed the revival of lay education also led to the separation between scholar and monk.[47] Greater sophistication led to the keen awareness that "[t]o despise the literal sense is to despise the whole of Scripture"[48] since the literal sense does not represent the word alone, but also its meaning without which no further explanation is possible. Notwithstanding the progressive systematization of interpretation and the limitations it placed upon possible excess, the moral and spiritual senses continued to be the focus of the exegete, whose understanding of God and the universe is still Augustinian and, hence, rests upon a fundamental separation of body and spirit. Only with the rediscovery of Aristotle can Christian biblical exegesis overcome the distrust of the letter. The essential relations between body and soul, one of the principles of Aristotelian philosophy, and the impossibility of human knowledge apart from the sensible universe which it teaches made possible a systematic philosophical interpretation of the Bible that could reunite its letter with its spirit.[49]

Although Aquinas is heir to a tradition of interpretation more systematic and more defined than Maimonides', Beryl Smalley's *Study of the Bible* makes abundantly clear that it is not a rigidly fixed tradition. Despite the emphasis on the spiritual meaning of Scripture, the Christian tradition before Aquinas is greatly varied, with no two writers manifesting full agreement except on fundamental doctrinal decrees. Consequently, like Maimonides, Aquinas heeds the letter of the tradition only when he deems it to be the best and clearest expression of the truth contained in the Bible. And it is precisely in this practice that he is also following the tradition. Rather than a dogmatic adherence to authority, Aquinas' exegesis is reverential to its spirit, that is, to the pursuit of truth.[50] Following Augustine's teachings, Aquinas fully avails himself of secular knowledge and puts it at the service of Scripture, not only because he wishes to exploit philosophy, but especially because he believes in the fundamental unity of truth.

Maimonides' and Aquinas' Approaches to Interpretation

The voice is Plato's voice, but the hands are the hands of Aristotle.

My paraphrase of Genesis 27:22 is an abbreviated description of both the 'method' and substance of Maimonides' and Aquinas' approach to interpretation. Since truth is one and error the cause of multiplicity,[51] since language and comprehension are historically conditioned, and since the concurrence between sign, signifier, and signified is problematic, it is both fitting and desirable to combine whatever available tools there are in order better to understand the singular truth. Consequently, both Maimonides and Aquinas perceive a consonance of ends, that is, an essential compatibility, not only between Plato and Aristotle, but also between philosophy and revelation. Whereas Smalley claimed that the Aristotelian influence on biblical study and its consequent recognition of theology as a speculative science resulted in a desirable liberation of theology from exegesis and vice versa,[52] it seems to me that this recognition changed these disciplines and modified their relations rather than radically separated them. Moreover, it seems to me that, in the case of both Maimonides and Aquinas, we cannot and ought not draw rigid boundaries delimiting their individual writings or subjects. Both Maimonides and Aquinas can be viewed as examples par excellence of medieval philosophical exegesis precisely because they combined the best tools of the exegete, the philosopher, and the theologian.[53]

The importance of the intimate relations between the fitting (*conveniens*) modes of interpretation and understanding for both Maimonides and Aquinas cannot be exaggerated.[54] Both thinkers preface every single work with a statement designating its purpose, its audience, and above all, the proper procedure required by the subject matter in general; both preface new subjects within each work; and each dedicates a section of his *magnum opus* to the question of interpretation.[55] Had many of their interpreters been as careful when reading them, most of the controversies surrounding their thought would not have seen the light of day. Likewise, as will become clearer in the discussion of Job in the following chapter, paying closer attention to their letter can resolve many seeming disagreements, both methodological and substantial, between Maimonides and Aquinas and consequently can facilitate comparative studies of their thought.[56]

Two major, closely related, broad questions merit close attention when focusing upon Maimonides' and Aquinas' writings as interpretations, namely, the nature of individual expositions and the relations between distinct works. The general tendency in Maimonidean scholarship has been to distinguish radically between his 'legalistic exoteric' works and the 'esoteric' *Guide of the Perplexed*, and in the latter work, the exoteric from the esoteric layers of meaning, especially in those subjects designated by him as secrets of the Torah.[57] In fact, reflecting this radical division, Maimonidean scholarship is polarized to such an extent that the scholars at each extreme often seem to be discussing two different thinkers. At one end are those scholars, who, themselves unable to harmonize faith and reason, project their skepticism onto Maimonides and read him as a prudent dissimulator of his true opinions.[58] Those maintaining this position often read Maimonides as an Aristotelian philosopher in all realms except for political philosophy, where he is understood to follow al-Farabi's Plato.[59] Consequently, apart from *The Treatise on [the Art of] Logic*, a very early work that is also his least original, they do not consider any of Maimonides' works to be properly philosophical, the *Guide* being a theological work and thus dialectical rather than demonstrative.[60] At the other end are scholars whose respect for the master is so great as to diminish seeming inconsistencies in Maimonides' writings by justifying a problematic position as, in fact, consistent with a traditional interpretation.[61] The graduated middle in Maimonidean scholarship is occupied primarily by mitigated versions of the two positions outlined above and by scholars evaluating Maimonides' thought through a Neo-Kantian lense,[62] with the notable exception of those scholars who attempt to read Maimonides with as little 'prejudice' as possible.[63] It is hardly surprising that both polarized positions often agree that there are two Maimonides, a theologian and a philosopher: the former Maimonides represents the 'we' of the tradition, the latter upholds the 'I' of the philosopher that is expressed rarely, and always in a veiled form, precisely because the 'I' and the 'We' positions often conflict.[64] Nor is it surprising that those scholars attempting to withhold preconceptions, or cognizant of their 'biases', see Maimonides' works as complementary rather than contradictory, although, at times, 'falling short' of the philosophical consistency and rigor promised by him.[65]

The diversity of readings encapsulated above is neither unwarranted nor readily resolvable. The most controverted subjects, those designated by Maimonides as secrets of the Torah, are also those subjects exceeding demonstrative reasoning, according to him.[66] Moreover, Maimonides does not elaborate a systematic theory of knowledge (let alone an epistemology) by means of which the interpreter can develop a comprehensive account adequate for bridging knowledge reached by demonstration and revealed knowledge without engaging in extensive interpretation. Consequently, the interpreter's philosophical 'biases' cannot be left out of the interpretation entirely.

Maimonides, in contradistinction to his interpreters, describes the relation between the exoteric and the esoteric layers of meaning and, hence, of interpretation as that of an apple of gold to the filigreed casing protecting it and insists not only that revealed non-demonstrative knowledge is true and that some revealed knowledge is superior to the philosophic, but also that demonstrative reasoning is a prerequisite for prophetic knowledge. In addition to his discussion of interpretation in the *Guide*, the content of Maimonides' other writings gives the lie to an understanding of Maimonides as a prudent writer of fiction. A brief look at the 'Book of Knowledge', the Preface to his most legalistic (hence 'exoteric') *Mishneh Torah*,[67] either should dissipate such a radical distinction among his works or, indeed, lead to dangerous perplexity. Under principles of the Torah, Maimonides discusses not only the unity, the simplicity, and the incorporeality of God, but also composition, the four elements, the soul as the human form, the spheres, and the relation between the Account of Creation and the Account of the Chariot. Admittedly, the discussion of each topic is brief, pre-philosophical or propaedeutic; nevertheless, no subject is concealed, notwithstanding its difficulties. Consequently, it seems to me that by heeding Maimonides' letter as well as his spirit, by attempting to understand and uphold the *intentio auctoris*, and by granting a coherence to the latter, if not always to the former, it is possible to discover a multifaceted account of knowledge consistent with Maimonides' thought that can reconcile apparent contradictions, understand real ones and can, in fact, harmonize two modes of cognition. As will become evident in the following chapters, Maimonides' account of providence affords the starting point for such an attempt.

Although the terminology differs, Thomistic scholarship manifests a tendency to a twofold division similar to the one found in Maimonidean scholarship. That is, the *Summa Theologiae*, especially I^a Pars and I^a-II^{ae}, and the commentaries on Aristotle are the texts upon which the philosophers focus, whereas the biblical commentaries are seen as the almost exclusive domain of the theologians;[68] the philosophers interpreting Aquinas as a Christian Aristotelian, the theologians primarily as a Christian Neoplatonist.[69] In addition, certain works, especially commentaries such as *De Divinis Nominibus* and *De Hebdomadibus*, are neglected almost entirely because they do not lend themselves easily to classifications within either disciplinary approach since, although they are primarily philosophical, they are also clearly Neoplatonic.[70] Given these tendencies to divide Aquinas' writings, it is not surprising that Thomistic scholars generally can be distinguished into those who are predominantly Aristotelian and 'metaphysicians' who recognize Neoplatonic elements in Aquinas' thought. In contradistinction, Aquinas recalls his biblical commentaries as often as he refers to the Philosopher, the *Platonici*, and so on.[71]

An additional difficulty arising out of Aquinas' writings and leading to conflicting interpretations surrounds the status of the commentary. The general question raised is whether the commentator's own thought ever is evident in his expositions on the thoughts of others. This question becomes more critical when the text commented upon is a revealed text, especially when Aquinas designates the exposition as a literal one, as he does in the case of Job. Those scholars who claim that the expositor's own voice cannot be discerned in commentaries thereby indirectly also judge the work philosophically insignificant and delimit its sphere of interest to historical evidence. In judging the expositor to function only as a glossator or a literal translator in the strictly Modern, post-Reformation sense, they also contradistinguish the works into distinct, unrelated disciplines.[72] However, the opinion that an exposition is more than merely a translation into present day idiom is not devoid of difficulties. For if one accepts the validity of the claim that an expositor, in this case Aquinas, *de facto*, "oversteps the explanation of the word of God" for spiritual purposes, despite his insistence that "the literal sense alone be adhered to,"[73] it remains to be asked what "spiritual purpose" can be in tension with the "word of God," what criteria can be used to distinguish the "word" and "spirit" of divine revelation when Aquinas denies such a radical distinction, except one imposed by the interpreter?[74]

The resolution of these problems can be found first by heeding Aquinas' letter, second by paying closer attention to historical evidence, and finally by interpreting his works according to his own instructions. First, I shall address the former questions since these can be resolved by direct evidence and without interpretation; subsequently I shall treat the question of interpretation in the following section, when outlining Maimonides' and Aquinas' approaches.

Both in the *Summa* and in *Quodlibet* VII Aquinas states clearly that the three senses distinct from the literal are all contained within the literal sense and are dependent upon it.[75] Moreover, he maintains that the literal sense does not manifest a correspondence between the signifier and the object signified, but rather is a sign of the latter's substance, "[f]or when scripture designates the arm of God, the literal sense is not that there is a corporeal member of this kind in God, but that which is signified by this member, namely, the operative power."[76] The testimony of William of Tocco, repeated by Bernard Gui in the *Vitae Sancti Thomae de Aquino*, both provides historical evidence supporting and explaining Aquinas' exegetical procedure and brings his approach to exposition into the sharpest focus: "He wrote . . . on Job *ad litteram* which no doctor had attempted to explain literally on account of the profundity of the literal sense which no one was able to discover."[77] Both the text quoted from the *Summa* and Aquinas' witnesses suffice to overcome the gulf between the aforementioned positions. The inadequacy of language for representing incorporeal concepts and objects necessitates the explanation of the full range of meanings contained in the letter of the Bible.[78]

Interpretation as a Philosophical Practice[79]

Prior to an examination of Maimonides' and Aquinas' specific approach to interpretation, a few preliminary remarks are called for in order to guard against interpreting the terminology that this inquiry requires according to its modern connotation.

As Gadamer points out, the conceptual history of hermeneutics makes evident that with respect to knowledge, the opposition between theory and practice is an odd modern phenomenon, "for the classical opposition ultimately was a contrast within knowledge, not an opposition between science and its application."[80] For Aristotle, whose definition of philosophy is accepted generally by both Maimonides and Aquinas, both theoretical and practical philosophy involve, indeed are, practice. Only with the modern conflation of practice with production is practice no longer understood as the actualization of life, since production is defined by set *necessary* rules, the application of which requires only the acquisition of a skill. However, for premodern philosophers, in contradistinction to animal life, which is actualized by an externally determined necessity, the actualization of human life is characterized by the choice and freedom consequent upon understanding or the intrinsically determined human act. When this definition is applied to interpretation, and hermeneutics is understood to belong to philosophical practice, as it is by Maimonides and Aquinas, it cannot connote simply the application of set rules to a clearly defined topic. Rather, it implies judgment about the fittingness of general principles and their subsequent, continuous adaptation to particular contexts that are not immediately evident. Moreover, since the specific context is not immediately apparent, the principles informing philosophical interpretation themselves are the result of theoretical practice. When the given text is a commentary on another difficult text, in particular a biblical one, great caution must be exercised by the modern reader. We cannot assume that we can understand a given text of either Maimonides or Aquinas by a direct application of the general set of rules articulated in their *magna opera*, nor by the application of a combination of those rules with the rules specific to the topic under consideration. Least of all can we assume, if we heed either thinker, that a one-to-one correspondence between rules and text can ever be found. Rather, we must accept that, in each instance of articulation, distinct judgments occurred that are implicit in the text. Consequently, prior to unraveling the range of meanings embodied in a given articulation, we must attempt to understand the nature of the judgment involved in its composition. Indeterminate as such an approach may be, the task is not as awesome as it initially seems. First and foremost, the fundamental, or more precisely guiding, principles informing medieval philosophy are defined explicitly; Maimonides and Aquinas were no exception to the general rule. Second, both thinkers are quite explicit when their interpretation of general principles departs from those of the respective traditions by which they are informed.[81] Hence, the interpretation of these texts demands of the modern reader the suspension not so much of judgment as of disbelief. The last 'rule' is important when dealing with any text written in an idiom either occluded by the progressive "Westernization" of philosophy or, in the West, no longer in practice; it is especially relevant when dealing with concepts "discredited" by modern science and discarded by philosophy, as is the case with many biblical ideas, if understood literally. Rather than providing their readers with the definitive doctrine, both Maimonides and Aquinas are instructing them by example in the practice of interpretation as a philosophical activity.

The Preface to the *Guide* is Maimonides' *apologia* for composing the work. As such, it is an occasion for the author not only to justify the need for the work, delimit its scope, designate its audience, and so forth, but most important, it allows him to express his own opinions as yet unhindered by the limits of a given subject. The Preface is written as a personal communication to an absent student whom Maimonides had instructed previously, in person, and hence whose preparation for advanced instruction he could assess, as well as for the few other students who meet the same requirements.[82] Although no rules are outlined in the Preface, by explicitly stating the conditions prerequisite to the study of the *Guide*, Maimonides not only delimits its audience clearly and informs the generic 'student' about the nature of the work, he also counsels caution. In fact, Maimonides clearly criticizes undue haste and disordered procedure, thereby indirectly rebuking Joseph and those who have taught him without due preparation. "As I also saw, you had already acquired some smattering of this subject from people other than myself; you were *perplexed*, as stupefaction had come over you; your *noble* soul demanded of you to *find out acceptable words*."[83]

However, responsibility for Joseph's perplexity cannot be attributed to his other tutors and to him in an equal measure. Whereas they are not said to possess noble qualities, Joseph is said to possess a noble soul, a soul capable of attaining wisdom by nature. Having been able to discern the impropriety or undesirable nature of the *words* used to instruct him, Joseph's noble soul as well as Maimonides' repeated counsel should have curbed his unruly desire for knowledge.[84] "Yet I did not cease dissuading you from this and enjoining upon you to approach matters in an orderly manner. My purpose in this was that the truth should be established in your mind according to the proper methods and that certainty should not come to you by accident."[85]

From Maimonides' address to Joseph as rabbi,[86] as well as from statements about his piety, we learn that, prior to seeking Maimonides' help, he has studied the Torah and the Talmud and hence already had attained the rank of 'jurist' and held true opinions on the basis of authority.[87] We also learn that he has studied the *art* of Kalam. In itself, this preparation would not have qualified him for further study, had he not exhibited in addition a strong desire and longing for speculative knowledge. Moreover, according to Maimonides, the strong desire for knowledge is not necessarily proportionate to the capacity for it and, hence, must be tested through instruction in the preliminaries to the natural sciences, that is, in mathematics. Although guidance was necessary in the preliminary stages of study, once the capacity proved to be equal to the task, the student could be left to pursue it alone, "knowing where [he] would end."[88] Having established the student's capacity for mathematics, astronomy, and logic, Maimonides cautiously began to reveal to him the secrets of the prophetic books by means of "certain flashes" and "certain indications." However, despite Joseph's desire, Maimonides did not judge these preliminaries to suffice for full instruction in divine subjects nor for the determination of the nature of the art of Kalam. The order of study outlined thus far, the progressive mastery of these subjects, and a strong desire for additional knowledge are clearly the 'tools' prerequisite to reading the *Guide*; however, these are not the principal reasons for its composition, a specific type of perplexity is.

In the Preface, Maimonides indicates but does not elaborate upon the causes of perplexity. From his remarks about the preliminary nature of mathematics and from his certainty about its conclusions we know that by themselves the natural sciences do not lead to dangerous doubt. These subjects require *merely* the acquisition of an art, a skill, in order to ensure their proper pursuit. We also learn from the Preface that inordinate haste, untimely pursuit, and improper instruction in divine matters are the causes of that type of perplexity which is the principle reason for the composition of the *Guide*. Maimonides also alludes to a relation between the intentions and the methods of the Mutakallimun and the perplexity of the student. This type of perplexity originates in the inquiry whether their methods are demonstrative and what the nature of their *art* is. The art of Kalam, then, is distinct from the arts propaedeutic to philosophy.

The Preface is the occasion to pose the problems, it is not the appropriate context, however, for their resolution. In a manner of speaking, the entire *Guide* is a preparation for the resolution of questions set out in the Preface, as well as the active acquisition of the virtue required for the continued pursuit of these and similar questions.[89] Only upon reading, and rereading the text does one become aware of the fact that the central or most difficult problem posited in the Preface is also the problem least apparent. The relative obscurity of the problem cannot be attributed to prudent intent at dissimulation; rather it exhibits responsible pedagogical caution. Since the intended audience of the *Guide* are the perplexed who are potentially, rather than actually wise, and who are seeking certainty, questioning the limitations not only of the demonstrative methods, but especially of all language as well as of natural human reason, could lead only to greater perplexity and hinder the actualization of any degree of knowledge. Prior to raising these type of doubts in the minds of the perplexed, the prudent teacher both begins to dissolve minor doubts and establishes primary principles for inquiry into more obscure subjects. The introduction to Book 1 and the lexicographical chapters constitute the preparatory stages for overcoming the perplexity consequent upon the first confrontation between philosophy and revelation through recourse to the teachings of both traditions.

The opening lines of the Introduction immediately identify the origin of perplexity as the radical ambiguity of language and thereby indicate that all instances of perplexity are also instances of error about language.[90] The opening statement is thus also an indication that adherence to the letter of the *Guide* will lead to error. That is, the opening statement discloses that the practice of interpretation can never be separated from "theoretical philosophy," if *theory* is to remain philosophical. Having succinctly cautioned the reader, Maimonides outlines first the two particular reasons that lead to perplexity and hence necessitated the composition of the treatise, refines his previous definitions of the audience, and defines the nature of their perplexity. Second, he exemplifies the types of difficulties encountered in parables simultaneously as he carefully uses the parables themselves for their explication. Third, he enumerates the seven causes of contradictory statements found in books. In addition to reiterating the principles of study outlined in the Preface, the Introduction is essentially a justification for the seemingly disordered nature of the *Guide*. Given the ambiguous nature of language in general and of prophetic speech in particular and given the necessarily parabolic form of prophecy, the pious, philosophically apt person initially perceives a contradiction between the teachings of philosophy and the teachings of the Torah taken in their literal sense, a contradiction that casts doubt upon the truth of both. Lacking proper guidance, the potentially perfect person is forced to abandon the teachings of either discipline, to become skeptical, and thereby, forsake the possibility of actual perfection or understanding. According to Maimonides, aiding even one such human being in times of spiritual decay is an act performed for the sake of Heaven.

Since the perplexity in question occurs only to the potentially wise, the resolution of apparent difficulties must proceed in a manner proportionate to their intellectual capacity. However, since the vulgar may chance upon the book, it is necessary to proceed with greater caution than had the instruction taken place in private; faced with 'strange' notions, their inability to withstand ambiguities as well as to recognize their ignorance may be detrimental to *them*.[91] Simultaneously however, when caution is exercised, when great care is taken with language, the vulgar too will benefit from the composition.[92] Moreover, since the perplexity arises out of the nature of biblical speech and since biblical speech does not proceed *more geometrico*, the *Guide* will resolve difficulties best by proceeding in a similar manner. This "method" is pedagogically most expedient both because it follows biblical prudence, which counsels great caution in disclosing divine matters, and because it follows philosophical prudence, which teaches by developing the capacity for the pursuit in the student, rather than indoctrinating true opinion.

Having outlined first the extent of the difficulties, and having explained that much of the truth contained in prophecy cannot be expressed clearly by recourse to the language and methods of the natural sciences, Maimonides next mentions the limitations of human reason for apprehending divine science. At the same time, he assures the reader that, not only are divine and natural science consonant, but also true knowledge of the former is subsequent to and consequent upon knowledge of the latter. Thus, although by means of revelation the believer may possess true opinions about divine subjects, nevertheless he or she can understand them only after gaining knowledge of natural science. That is why God decreed that the Bible commence with the Account of the Beginning, and the philosophers begin their study with physics.

In the last section of the Introduction Maimonides enumerates seven causes for contradictions (and/or apparent contradictions) found in all books, briefly explains their causes, and classifies them according to their literary loci

1. Numerous differing opinions are cited without explicit mention of their varied sources. This type of contradiction occurs in the Mishnah, the Baraithoth, and the Talmud.
2. The author cites two of his own opinions despite the fact that the latter opinion has superseded the former. This type of contradiction occurs in the Talmud.
3. Statements that should be understood in their internal sense are taken literally. This type of contradiction occurs in the prophetic books.
4. A stipulation has not been stated explicitly in its logically appropriate place out of some *necessity*. This type of contradiction also occurs in the prophetic books and, consequently, together with the third cause it constitutes the stated purpose of the Introduction.
5. Given that understanding proceeds from sensible apprehension to the intelligible, pedagogical *necessity* dictates that subjects should be taught in an ordered manner, each stage requiring a distinct mode of discourse and distinct language. This type of contradiction occurs in the books of the philosophers or, rather, those who know the truth.
6. Carelessness of the writer. This type of contradiction is the most frequent, it is found in most texts and commentaries excluding the ones mentioned previously, but including some of the Midrashim and the Haggadah.
7. In speaking about very obscure matters it is *necessary* to conceal some parts and disclose others. Sometimes in the case of certain dicta this *necessity* requires that the discussion proceed on the basis of a certain premise, whereas in another place *necessity* requires that the discussion proceed on the basis of another premise contradicting the first one. In such cases the vulgar must in no way be aware of the contradiction; the author accordingly uses some device to conceal it by all means.[93] This type of contradiction also occurs in the Midrashim and the Haggadah.

Whereas the Sages, according to Maimonides, sought to resolve contradictions found among commandments and prohibitions that concern only conduct, Maimonides' purpose is to identify verses that seem to be in conflict with commonly held opinions and beliefs. Whereas the Sages examined univocal proscriptions, Maimonides examines ambiguous teachings. Moreover, whereas the Sages were concerned with moral conduct that, as will become evident, does not pertain directly to the final human end—intellectual perfection—Maimonides is concerned with true or false opinions and beliefs about speculative subjects or subject that pertain to final perfection and belong to the "mysteries of the Torah."[94]

The order in which Maimonides posits the deliberate causes of contradictions exhibits both a close relationship between them and a progressive development from simple general statements to more specifically complex ones. Properly speaking, these causes do not constitute four distinct causes of contradictions as such, but rather indicate different aspects of two causes that lead to two types of contradictions underlying perplexity.

The third cause simply draws attention to the general nature of biblical discourse that, excluding the strictly legal and historical books, uses metaphor, similitude, and parable; its purpose is to express a simple general statement of fact, namely, that prophetic discourse is comprised of several layers of ambiguous meaning. These may constitute either real contradictions or contrarieties.

The explanation of non-univocal discourse begins with the enumeration of the fourth cause where it is stated that implicit speech and suppressed premises are the result of some yet to be unspecified necessity.[95] Only with the fifth and seventh causes does Maimonides identify the nature of the necessities to be both pedagogical and epistemic. With respect to the fifth cause, it is important to note that, although Maimonides does not identify it explicitly or implicitly as a cause of contradictions present in the Bible and despite its obvious Aristotelian origin,[96] his statement that it occurs in the books of "those who know the truth" as well as the pedagogical and epistemic import of the necessity pertaining to the fifth cause, justify the conclusion that it can be found in prophetic discourse. For prophecy, in Maimonides' view, is the paradigmatic mode of knowing, a knowledge that is subsequent and superior to the philosophical. Whereas the fifth cause points to the pedagogical necessity that pertains to a single audience, the seventh, which presupposes all the previous reasons for contradictory statements, directly addresses the necessity for deliberate concealment from the vulgar. Thus, the two types of closely related necessities that emerge from Maimonides' enumeration are (1) an internal one that is consequent upon the obscure nature of the subject and (2) an external one that is the result of the intellectual capacity of the audience. Likewise, there emerge two types of contradictions, one real and the other apparent, that do not correspond directly to the necessities but rather result from both simultaneously, only in different degrees.

Real contradictions occur when the subject matter is so obscure that it not only exceeds demonstrative reasoning, but also does not permit consistent accounts among the different orders of discourse about that subject nor in some cases any coherent account even within a single order. The most glaring examples of real contradictions directly addressed in the *Guide* are found in Maimonides' investigations of questions such as (a) the origin of the universe, (b) prime matter, and (c) divine attributes, all of which will be discussed in subsequent chapters.

Real contradictions are the ones outlined in the seventh cause, where the subject matter is described as *very* obscure. Although apparent contradictions, too, result from the obscurity of the subject matter, they can be resolved with progressive understanding. Unlike real contradictions, however, the resolution of apparent contradictions is possible only because the conclusions of one order of discourse serve as the primary premises for the following one.[97] Examples of apparent contradictions can be found in different discussions[98] about distinct faculties of the composite human soul, such as the material and the actual intellect, and are abundant in all discussions of principles that can serve as both physical and metaphysical premises. These contradictions are addressed in the third, fourth, and fifth causes.

Prior to addressing the question whether the seventh cause of contradiction occurs in the prophetic books, and Maimonides' reluctance to attribute it to them, it is important to underline the fact that Maimonides' theory of biblical language is a consequence of his theory of cognition, a theory that presupposes a distinction so great between the intellectual capacities of the vulgar and those of the elite as to require something akin to an ontological difference. He also states explicitly that the *Guide* was written exclusively for the elite although it was written in such a way as to preclude the possibility of vulgar understanding of the mysteries of the Torah, one of which, as pointed out above, is the contradictory nature of some prophetic parables. It is for the latter reason that the *Guide* includes contradictions of the seventh type, those deliberately intended to conceal.[99]

In the concluding section of the Introduction, where he identifies the correspondence between contradictions and the books in which they are to be found, Maimonides seems to contradict an assertion made in a preceding section about prophetic parables. Whereas in the former he states: "Whether contradictions due to the seventh cause are to be found in the books of the prophets is a matter for speculative study and investigation. Statements about this should not be a matter of conjecture,"[100] in the latter he distinguishes between two types of prophetic parables:

In some of these parables each word has a meaning, while in others the parable as a whole indicates the whole of the intended meaning. In such a parable very many words are to be found, not every one of which adds something to the intended meaning. They serve rather to embellish the parable and to render it more coherent or to conceal further the intended meaning; hence the speech proceeds in such a way as to accord with everything required by the parable's external meaning.[101]

The second type of parable seems to satisfy the conditions specified in the seventh cause; the parable is expressed in such a manner as to simultaneously provide a coherent exoteric account, and thus communicate a true opinion about the subject, and to conceal the esoteric meaning "by all means." In both instances, Maimonides does not suggest that there is no real conflict either between the esoteric and exoteric account or between one parable and another. However, as will become evident, this contradiction, too, may be only apparent. Above all, in both statements, by drawing attention to the great difficulty inherent in understanding biblical parables, Maimonides cautions against hasty interpretations and conjectural classification.

Since the enumeration of the deliberate contradictions clearly indicates that the purpose of many of them is not concealment, two related questions arise: (1) whether or not all deliberate acts of concealment are intended to hide real contradictions, be they biblical or philosophical, and (2) whether real contradictions reflect two conflicting accounts of reality so that the true philosophical one ought not be revealed. The latter question is especially significant to Maimonides' "negative theology" since biblical discourse not only employs positive attributes in general, but also predicates corporeal and anthropomorphic attributes of God. Consequently, Maimonides' choice of a radical *via negativa* is either consequent upon philosophical reflection upon the biblical narrative itself or its outright rejection. From some of my previous comments, it should be evident that I do not think that this is the case. It seems to me that Maimonides suggests that neither do all instances of concealment hide real contradictions nor do real contradictions primarily reflect the notorious conflict between philosophy and revelation. Rather, the instances of real conflicts between philosophy and revelation, all of which are reducible to the difference between understanding of the "ultimate form"[102] of the universe as the Creator God and as the Aristotelian first cause, are reflections of the limitations of natural human reason to apprehend certain metaphysical truths. On the other hand, the real contradictions occurring within the Bible and the *Guide* are manifestations of both the limits of natural reason and the limitations of language to adequately account for the prophetic apprehension of these truths as well as for differences between degrees of prophetic perfection.[103] It should be noted here that some philosophical discourses, especially Neoplatonic ones, should probably be included within the category of the prophetic. In other words, at least with respect to metaphysical discourses that directly address the divinity, the real contradictions between philosophy and revelation are found in the books of the Philosopher par excellence, whom, I think, Maimonides considered to manifest the perfection of natural reason, but no more. Aristotle's status as the paradigm of natural perfection only is significant not only with respect to his *Metaphysics*, but also in relation to his *Physics* since, according to Maimonides, the impossibility of providing a clear exposition extends even to the principles of natural science, of which the true reality cannot be deduced from their composite physical modes of existence.[104]

The major principle of interpretation to be derived from the Preface and the Introduction, and repeated throughout the *Guide*, also exhibits Maimonides' debt to Aristotle. Following Aristotle's *dictum* that "it is the mark of an educated man to look for precision in each class of things just so far as the nature of the subject admits,"[105] Maimonides does not seek demonstrative proofs where these are inappropriate; namely, in divine science and in subjects the principles of which are derived therefrom. In a manner of speaking, Maimonides interprets Aristotle's *dictum* to signify that philosophical interpretation begins where demonstration ends. He states that, excluding ignoramuses, no one disagrees about truths known through demonstration. Rather, the less the subject admits of demonstration, the greater the disagreement. "The things about which there is this perplexity are very numerous in divine matters, few in matters pertaining to natural science, and non-existent in matters pertaining to mathematics."[106] Throughout the *Guide*, when he attempts to interpret subjects that cannot be explained by means of demonstration, Maimonides appeals to two different criteria of knowledge. First, that contrary opinions should be posited as hypotheses to be accepted or rejected by recourse to the type of doubts attached to them.[107] Second, with respect to opinions contrary to the foundations of the Torah, the authority of revelation, especially the prophecy of Moses and Abraham, ought to be accepted.[108] In a context where oppositions occur between the philosophic and the revealed understanding of creation, Maimonides refers to Aristotle as "prince of the philosophers," whereas the prophets are depicted as "the pillars of the well being of the human species."[109] However, the criteria for judging whether an account is true are set neither by authority nor by the number of doubts attaching to an opinion, but rather by the degree of its congruence with what exists. Consequently, it seems that Maimonides is evaluating the degree of knowledge ensuing from non-demonstrative explanations, prophetic or philosophic, according as they conform to what exists, that is, to knowledge gained from the study of natural science, a knowledge that includes a recognition of its limits.[110] These criteria for establishing truth posit not so much the superiority of revealed knowledge to philosophic knowledge or vice versa, as their respective spheres.[111] More significant for us, it sets up a real relation between them as two modes of cognition that can be evaluated without revelation and thus resolve the tensions, and of course false perplexity, between them. Consequently, it can be maintained that revealed knowledge, like the Torah, "although it is not natural, enters into what is natural."[112]

Maimonides never abandons the "principles" outlined in the Preface and Introduction. However, it cannot be overemphasized that these are general guidelines only; they do not constitute a method but rather manifest the virtue of interpretation and, hence, are adapted in a fitting way to the text and the context.

If Maimonides' style of writing is very complex, at times too complex, ambiguous and inelegant, and if inadvertently it can promote perplexity, rather than resolve or explain it, Aquinas' style is 'deceptively' simple and consequently may lead the reader to interpreting his thought with less rigor than it requires. A clearer exposition of difficult texts, such as *De Hebdomadibus* and *De Divinis Nominibus*, is hard to conceive. At the same time, however, it is as difficult to understand how Aquinas was able to extract from the text the coherent interpretation that he puts forth. In the light of *De Divinis Nominibus*, Chenu's conclusion that Aquinas, in fact, appropriates as his own the texts upon which he comments is far more plausible than O'Reilly's.[113] Moreover, Aquinas' Prefaces, both to individual works and to each topic, in themselves, do not suffice for deriving his methodological principles since, apart from general guidelines, he derives the appropriate principles from the specific text and context. Consequently, the tendency evident in Thomistic scholarship to divide the works, and the overconcentration on the *Summa Theologiae*, can result in erroneous, because partial, interpretations of Aquinas' thought. Notwithstanding, given the sheer volume and diverse nature of Aquinas' writings, the *Summa* provides the best starting point for determining the nature of Aquinas' interpretation, both because it is a mature work and because it attempts to address methodologically most of the problems encountered in earlier works. As such, the *Summa* can outline diverse positions on given disputed questions, draw upon conclusions reached in previous comprehensive discussions of these questions and thereby, refer the readers to these contexts. Beginning with the principles derived from the *Summa*, supplementing them with a number of Prefaces from diverse works, and briefly analyzing their application in distinct contexts, we can provide a coherent account of Aquinas' approach to interpretation.

The Prologue to the *Summa*, like the Preface to the *Guide*, is Aquinas' *apologia* wherein he outlines his justification for composing the work. In the first paragraph, Aquinas designates forthwith the audience of the work and its purpose. He states that, since the text is composed for instructing beginners in orthodox truth, it will teach them those things that belong to the Christian religion in a manner fitting for the instruction of beginners.[114] Aquinas adds that these beginners are impeded in their study by the diversity of texts written on the subject. These texts have hindered study rather than facilitated it, first, since they utilize a multiplicity of unnecessary questions and arguments; second, because they either pursue the topic in accordance with the expository requirements of books or treat it as an occasion for disputation, rather than proceed in the order appropriate for teaching the subject; and third, through frequent repetition they produce both distaste and confusion in their audience.

At first glance, Aquinas' designation of the audience and purpose of the *Summa*, seems to offer no occasion for disagreement. A reflective pause, however, brings into relief a question about the identity of the *incipientes* that continues to occupy Thomists without agreement among some of the most notable ones.[115] Although the Preface does not provide sufficient information about the intellectual preparation of the audience and although it is only a posteriori that one can reach a judgment about it, nevertheless, it seems to me that the Preface does provide *some* clues about the audience, when it is read in its historical context.

Since the purpose of the *Summa*, according to Aquinas, is to rectify a condition occasioned by the multiplicity of writings and the careless methods used for instruction in Christian truth and since Aquinas' use of the imperfect tense indicates that he is depicting a specific existing condition rather than a perennial one, it seems to me that he is describing the general state of mind, *fastidium et confusionem*, already present in the would-be student of the *Summa*. That is, irrespective of whether Aquinas is criticizing the methods of teaching in the classroom or the methods of writing, the students to whom he is addressing the *Summa* are assumed to have studied some things about the subject prior to reading this text.[116] Moreover, after reading the I^a Pars with its constant references to Aristotle, it seems clear that Aquinas' audience, at least in the I^a Pars and the I^a-II^{ae}, are beginners in theology, rather than in learning.[117]

If my conclusion is correct, then the audience of the *Summa* are the Christian equivalent of the audience of the *Guide*; they are expected to have studied the Bible and the tradition, on the one hand, some logic, physics, and metaphysics, on the other. Like Maimonides' students they are confused or perplexed because of their inadequate previous instruction. Moreover, these students are the few, handpicked intellectual 'elite' of Christendom who have been deemed worthy of such a lofty pursuit.[118] Only to an informed, but confused student can Aquinas speak about sacred doctrine "briefly and clearly,"[119] thus clarifying problematic questions simultaneously as he demonstrates the proper approach to interpretation through the very activity of interpretation.

Although Aquinas does not designate it as such, question one is the general introduction to the entire *Summa*, since it is the attempt to determine the nature and the proper questions of sacred doctrine, as well as to delimit its scope. Article one reinforces the conclusion reached above about the nature of the audience, first, since only to a learned audience can Aquinas quote both Scripture and Aristotle's *Metaphysics* in the same context (especially when discussing *sacra doctrina*) without hesitation. Likewise, only a well-prepared student would gain from, rather than become confused by, the generic distinction posited by Aquinas between philosophical theology and the theology of sacred doctrine.[120] This distinction presupposes sufficient knowledge of philosophy, which assumes both an understanding of its composite parts and an understanding of the objects constituting its distinct orders of discourse. Moreover, the distinction between philosophical theology and sacred theology according to genus, which also sets up a relation between them as species of knowledge, presupposes an understanding of genus, species, relations, and difference, since as species of knowledge they cannot be related as contraries.[121] The generic difference between philosophical theology and the theology of sacred doctrine is rooted in the difference between the respective media through which they are known, the light of natural reason and the light of divine revelation. Although sacred doctrine receives its primary principles from revelation, being first and foremost a speculative species of knowledge, it also requires both the principles and the methods of philosophy and addresses some of its questions. Theology, like every other branch of knowledge, does not discard prior true principles, but rather supplements them with its own. Like metaphysics, divine science can argue convincingly about its principles only with one who concedes some of them. However, since first principles are not subject to demonstration, if none of the first principles are admitted, divine science (and metaphysics) can prove its principles only by refuting the opposing view.[122] In addition to receiving its primary principles by means of revelation, divine science can be distinguished from philosophical science through the greater unity of its object since its certainty about the final end of human life unifies both speculative and practical knowledge. Rather than conflicting with the truth of philosophy, divine science is the wisdom that completes it; being free from error, it gives philosophy the certitude it lacks and succeeds in overcoming philosophy's unresolved difficulties.

As Maimonides explains in the Introduction to the *Guide*, so Aquinas, throughout the introductory question to the *Summa*, repeatedly emphasizes that the limitations of natural human reason make revelation necessary owing to the supranatural final human end, to which all other ends of human life are subordinate and by which they are ordered. The understanding of the correlative nature of all human ends to the final end overturns the Philosopher's apparently sharp separation between moral and intellectual virtue, practical and theoretical reason. However, these limitations can be understood only once natural human reason has been actualized fully. The way of philosophy is not only expedient, but also necessary for the theologian. Insufficient or inadequate preparation for theology results in inadequate books and methods for teaching sacred doctrine.

By first outlining the nature and general scope of theology, Aquinas habituates the student in the attitude necessary for its pursuit. Subsequently, he can turn his attention to its fundamental text, Sacred Scripture, in order to formulate the principles specific to biblical interpretation. First, he outlines two principle causes for the metaphorical language evident in Scripture; second, he explains the nature of the relations between its four senses.

Since the inherent order of human cognition requires that knowledge proceed from sensible perception to intelligible apprehension, it was fitting for biblical language to reflect this order, teaching spiritual and divine truths by means of corporeal similitude. Moreover, since Scripture addresses all of humankind, it was necessary that it express divine truths in a manner that would benefit both the wise and the ignorant and, simultaneously, be proportionate to the intellectual capacity of each group. In response to an objection, Aquinas respectively distinguishes poetic metaphors from biblical metaphors as metaphors aimed at pleasure and metaphors that are both necessary and useful. "The poet uses metaphors for the sake of representation; for representation is naturally pleasing to man. But sacred doctrine uses metaphors on account of necessity and usefulness."[123] In response to two other objections to the use of metaphors, Aquinas adds a further justification for their utility; namely, they are a convenient means for hiding the mysteries of divine teachings both from the unworthy and from the mockery of the impious.

Article ten of the introductory question to the *Summa* explains the nature of, need for, and relations between the layers of meaning in Scripture. Unlike human signification, which can adapt only words to the desired signified object, God, the author of Scripture, also can adapt the very objects. Consequently, when divine science designates objects, it simultaneously points beyond the signified object to something else. Whereas the object signified is always the historical or literal sense, the words also point to three additional, spiritual senses. The Old Testament contains the historical facts that are signs of due deeds. When the Old Law points to the New, the sense signified is allegorical. When Scripture points to the deeds of Christ, or other due acts, the sense signified is moral. But, when the signifiers point to eternal glory, the sense signified is anagogical. Although there are four layers of meaning in Scripture, Aquinas maintains that the literal sense is both the one upon which all the other senses are founded and the one posited by the author, since God, as author of Scripture, "comprehends all things in his intellect simultaneously."[124] Aquinas adds, in response to an objection, that the manifold senses of Scripture lead neither to equivocation[125] nor to any multiplicity, since biblical terms signify objects that in turn can be signs of other objects. Consequently, the first object signified is indispensable for understanding any other object to which it points.

In the Preface to the *Summa*, Aquinas outlines the nature of the obstacles confronting students in sacred doctrine and adds that the work will attempt to teach the subject in the manner appropriate to it. Although no principles of interpretation are articulated explicitly, the critique of the methods of teaching and the stress placed upon the *ordo disciplinae* clearly suggest that no methodological principles can be applied to a discipline prior to engagement in it. It is the nature of the discipline itself, its particular objects and language, that must dictate the procedure of interpretation. That is, rather than being a skill, a know-how, to be universally applied, interpretation is practical philosophy in the classical sense of the term.[126] Consequently, in the first question, Aquinas defines the nature of the discipline, its unique objects, and the vocabulary particular to it. This vocabulary is defined by the unique nature of prophetic language, and hence, it requires the correct understanding of the intimate correlation between its layers of meaning. Whereas the explanation of the specific nature of biblical language informs Aquinas' biblical commentaries and theological works, philosophical topics and commentaries require explanations concerning their linguistic distinctions. Precisely because these general principles apply to every discipline, no particular ones can be specified out of context. Hence, apart from the general understanding of the multifaceted nature of language taught by question one, each distinct question or subject within the *Summa* begins with a brief Preface explaining its relation to the previous topic and outlining its scope.

In accordance with the procedure for interpretation outlined above, all of Aquinas' works open with a preliminary definition of the nature of the problem and/or scope of the subject. Thus, the prologue to the *De Divinis Nominibus* explains the extraneous difficulties that hinder the comprehension of concepts articulated in the "archaic" language of the Platonists, prior to addressing the nature of the subject and its intrinsic difficulties. On the other hand, the preliminary statements to commentaries on Aristotle, such as the *De Interpretatione*[127] and the *In Meta.*, begin directly with explanations on the nature of the subject, its scope, and its inherent problems. In both texts, Aquinas first establishes to which part of philosophy these subjects belong and then defines the scope and objects of their respective inquiries.

Having determined that *De Interpretatione* belongs to logic in the Preface, in *lectio* one, Aquinas elaborates in great detail the nature of verbal expressions.[128] In contradistinction to the *Summa*, the explanation does not deal with layers of meaning, but rather with the nature of the language required for demonstration. When they are examined within the order of logic, names and words can be distinguished according as their signification is used absolutely, according as they are composite parts of an expression, and according as they determine the syllogistic order. The *De Interpretatione*, according to Aquinas, is addressed to interpretation of significations of names, words, affirmation, and negation as parts of non-syllogistic, complex expressions. Although the entire text as well as other commentaries on the books constituting Aristotle's logical works are of primary importance to an inquiry into the nature of language, signification, and interpretation, here I shall limit myself to a brief examination of the distinction between names and definitions, a distinction essential for understanding the difference between philosophical and biblical modes of predication.

In the *De Interpretatione*, Aquinas defines a name as a conventional vocal sign, independent of time, and signifying only as a whole. Since the signification functions like (*quasi*) the form of the name, the integrity of names extends to compound names equally as they do to simple ones. In themselves, single names reflect single intellectual concepts rather than an essential quality of some thing; hence, *per se* they are neither true nor false, although, as signifying, positive names presuppose either a determinate nature or a determinate person. While negative names, too, are neither true nor false *per se*, they signify only by negating determinations and, hence, are related to reality indifferently. *Per se*, any type of name is significant only to a hearer who already possesses some like concept or knowledge. Thus, names can communicate knowledge only as statements, explicitly or implicitly placing the name in relation to some thing. Unlike names, definitions are essential or follow upon the essence of a thing and are the *ratio* for their significative role. Thus, of that whose essence we can have no cognition, we can have no definition.[129]

Since names do not communicate anything *per se*, the context in which names are employed decides their meaning. Whereas the name *god* means "*nous*" or "first mover" in Aristotelian metaphysics, the name *God* means provident creator in the context of the Book of Job. The preceding brief outline of the status of names and definitions in the *De Interpretatione* makes evident the necessity for diverse interpretations; discipline, or context, determines the language and specific methods most fitting for application and for evaluating its consistency. Above all, names and definitions are not only distinct but also, unless they are clearly distinguished, may easily lead to error.

The Preface to *In Meta.* is of significance to understanding Aquinas' approach to interpretation insofar as it illustrates the application of the same general principles outlined in the *Summa* to a generically distinct discipline that, nevertheless, belongs to the same species of knowledge and possesses the same objects, namely, the intelligibles. Although Aquinas begins with a statement similar to that found in the *Summa*—that all knowledge is ordered to one end, the perfection which is *beatitude*—in contradistinction to the preliminary remarks in both the *Summa* and the *De Interpretatione*, which are adapted to the requirements of theology and logic respectively, the Preface to *In Meta.* proceeds *more prima philosophia*, using vocabulary and concepts that are most adequate to that discipline. It is striking that, in the context of a philosophical discussion of metaphysics, Aquinas does not draw a distinction between philosophical metaphysics and divine science, rather he insists that what appears as composition within it is not intrinsic to the discipline. The apparent composition originates in the three modes of understanding the single subject: the study of first causes, that of universal being, and that of separate substances. The three modes of understanding give rise to three designations of metaphysics that together form its single perfection. "For it is called *divine science* or *theology*, in so far as it examines the aforementioned substances [separate and separable]. *Metaphysics*, in so far as it examines being and the things proceeding from it. . . . Moreover, it is called *first philosophy*, in so far as it examines the first causes of things."[130] The identification of theology with metaphysics here need not be read as contradictory to the generic distinction between philosophical and sacred theology, since their subject is the same absolutely speaking, but is modally distinct. In fact, given that the distinction between the two disciplines is derived from their respective media, natural human reason and the divine light, and given that their object is one, *In Meta.* reinforces the conclusion reached above about the identity of the *truth* sought by both disciplines. Divine science lends certainty to philosophical theology where metaphysics fails; it supplements, at times even modifies its conclusions with additional knowledge about its subject in ways (*media*) exceeding the scope of natural human reason. Thus, both in the *Summa* and *In Meta.*, both in the context of "theology" and in that of "philosophy," Aquinas underlines the primary *aporia*: How can theology and metaphysics be distinct in genus while "sharing" the same species (*eidos*), namely, *ta noeta*?

Both Maimonides and Aquinas do not hesitate to use insights gained from one discipline to inform another nor do they refrain from criticizing their coreligionists' methods of interpretation. However, since they are keenly aware of the complex nature of language, they use great care in its application to specific texts and contexts. It is striking that the single type of restraint in combining traditions that can be found in the works of either thinker is shared by both and can be explained by the context of the discussion and by Maimonides' and Aquinas' general "method." In those works addressed to the less learned within their respective communities, direct references to the pagan philosophers and to other thinkers who are not members of their specific religious communities are rare, since both Maimonides and Aquinas held that the study of the Bible, at least in its first phase, should precede divine science and the study of physics, that of metaphysics.[131] Moreover, since those ignorant of philosophy could despise it out of ignorance, proper procedure was requisite for eradicating prejudice. The procedure that counsels the proper division of the sciences reflects the pedagogical prudence common to both philosophy and the revealed tradition(s).[132]

As interpreters, Maimonides and Aquinas seem quite modern insofar as they satisfy the demands of some of the most attentive contemporary approaches to hermeneutics.[133] Both avoid the control of method over the subject matter, and thereby are able to question the method's fittingness and define its limitations;[134] both maintain a balance between the historicity of the narration and its claim to universal truth;[135] and by understanding the dialectical nature of discourse, both make manifest the overlap between explanation and understanding.[136] That is, as interpreters, both Maimonides and Aquinas undertake to actualize a shared sphere of meaning by unfolding the multiplicity of intermediate, indeterminate terms between understanding and explanation, the historically specific and the universally true. The recognition that the Torah, as well as philosophy, speak human language manifests the necessity both for unfolding the range of meaning of the terms in which the search for universal or, more precisely, essential truths were expressed and for translating them into contemporary idiom, without diminishing the value of the letter. Upholding the essential unity of truth, both Maimonides and Aquinas strive to re-present it through all the intermediate, indeterminate transformations and disciplinary differences of its expression.[137]

2

THE BOOK OF JOB

Early Approaches to the Book of Job

As already noted, modern approaches to biblical hermeneutics fail to recognize or to take cognizance of the essential role played by the Bible in the historical development of Western and Westernized society. In fact, to the extent that a 'Western community' exists, it is constituted by the one, presumably common, text of the Old Testament. In addition to its obvious role in establishing moral norms and regulating human interaction, until the twentieth century the Bible has been the principal vehicle for the transmission and general dissemination of literacy. Sedimental as the origins of most contemporary concepts may be, the foundations for a substantial part of the Western conceptual vocabulary can be found in the Bible. Moreover, the linear concept of time upon which all Modern[138] Western thought is based, originates with an interpretation of the word(s) *bereshit, en arche, in the beginning*, and so forth, a beginning that is understood to connote a progressive development toward a final moment of fulfillment, both immanent and transcendent.[139] Despite their transformations, the meaning of biblical terms received a binding force from the belief that the Bible was the word of God, and hence, its language and concepts were both indisputable and the archetypes for the things signified by them. Unlike their modern successors, medieval scholars sought to 'strip' the words of Scripture of all their accidental meanings in order to approach their essential meaning, God's message to humankind. The possible Aramaic, or Ugaritic, origins of terms and concepts in Job were accidental to the true meaning conveyed by the concepts; their relative significance merely reflected the socio-geographical location of their utterance,[140] necessary for human perfection rather than intrinsic to divine teachings.

Given the Neoplatonic nature of pre-Maimonidean Jewish thought, given the Kalam's influence upon it, and given the broad use of allegory evident in biblical interpretation, the absence of allegorical or philosophical exegesis on the book of Job is both striking and curious.[141] Despite this absence, Maimonides' relation to the tradition with respect to providence can be evaluated through an examination of the question of reward and punishment, and especially the suffering of the righteous, which is central to Jewish thought in general, and to the book of Job in particular.[142]

The most thorough speculative discussion of reward and punishment can be found in the writings of Sa'adia Gaon, whose opinions are generally compatible with the tradition and manifest the strong influence of the Kalam upon his thought.[143] Sa'adia enumerates three common explanations for the suffering of the just: punishment, trial (testing), and moral education. Punishment in this life is essentially a cleansing from sin and, hence, the suffering experienced by the just must be understood primarily as mercy. In trial the just suffer for the sake of *certain* reward in the world to come and hence, trial too is essentially mercy. Suffering for the sake of acquiring moral virtue and knowledge also manifests an act of mercy decreed by God for the sake of human perfection. In interpreting Job's opinion as a belief in a divine will free from the constraint of justice, Sa'adia identifies it with the Ash'arite doctrine of providence. On the other hand, Sa'adia designates Elihu's opinion as true, explaining that it affirms a threefold doctrine of justification by means of atonement, acquired rewards, and above all, suffering for the sake of trial. As Efros points out, Sa'adia's endorsement of suffering as trial manifests his acceptance of the Mu'tazilite doctrine of providence, which is not incongruent with several books of Scripture.[144] As will become evident below, Maimonides vehemently denies not only the validity but even the exoteric utility of any teachings endorsing trial as suffering out of love, since, *inter alia*, it undermines the foundations of moral education by dissolving the unity between human actions and their consequences. Even though Sa'adia's position is in greater accord with the letter of Scripture and the tradition, it also contains an intrinsic contradiction. Since, according to Maimonides, the Torah is the vehicle to knowledge of God and since such knowledge is a prerequisite to the love of God enjoined by the Torah, it is inconceivable that undeserved suffering, a suffering that is not consequent upon a willed act, or rather, choice, will result in love, rather than in fear. In fact, in contradistinction to Sa'adia, Maimonides characterizes the true understanding of providence, which is manifest as a passionate love of God, by absence of suffering.[145]

The most prominent and influential commentator on Job in the pre-thirteenth century Christian tradition is undoubtedly St. Gregory the Great. His *Moralia in Iob*,[146] not only established the moral level of interpretation of the text as the most significant approach to Job, but it also initiated a tradition that overlooked the literal-historical level of this scriptural book almost entirely. Despite the fact that the Preface affirms the importance of the literal sense as the historical foundation upon which the explanatory edifice is built, St. Gregory rarely heeded his own counsel. In fact, in a letter dedicated to the bishop of Seville, he clearly explains why he often neglected the literal sense: "But sometimes we have neglected to explain the plain words of the historical [sense], lest we arrive at the obscure [sense] too late; sometimes, however, they could not be understood according to the letter, since, on the surface, the plain [sense] produces no instruction whatsoever for the readers, but rather error."[147] Rather than following the letter and having accepted quite literally Augustine's dictum that the Bible contains all *useful* knowledge, Gregory uses the text to meet every daily need of his monastic community. Consequently, his exposition is composed of long digressions strung together for the express purpose of moral and doctrinal instruction. Beryl Smalley notes that "To us, this is a most annoying system. Everything in St. Gregory's teaching is attached, however loosely, to the thread of the text, which precludes any attempt at coherence or logical arrangement. . . . Exegesis is teaching and preaching. Teaching and preaching is exegesis. This was the strongest impression left by St. Gregory on medieval Bible study."[148]

The importance of the letter of Job was recovered fully in the thirteenth century by Albert the Great, Aquinas, and others who were influenced by them.[149] The immediate assumption about Aquinas' debt to Albert with respect to Job, an assumption verifiable in relation to numerous other works, has been seriously challenged by the Leonine editors of Aquinas' *Expositio*, on the bases of both the disputed date of composition of Aquinas' text and some inconclusive textual comparisons.[150] Consequently, given that the anteriority or posteriority of Albert's commentary on Job has not been established and given the absence of a comparative study of the two commentaries, I shall refrain from assuming Albert's magisterial influence upon Aquinas and shall note only significant points worthy of further comparison between Albert's commentary and those either of Maimonides or Aquinas.[151]

The most significant conclusion about Aquinas' relation to the Christian tradition preceding him is his radical departure from it.[152] After acknowledging his great contribution to the topological interpretation of the text, Aquinas, in fact, overlooks Gregory's teachings entirely. However, Aquinas' designation of his exposition in the Preface as literal does not indicate an intention to refrain from articulating senses other than the literal, but rather serves to distinguish his undertaking from Gregory's and to emphasize the primary importance of the letter.

The Nature of the Inquiry

Before I turn to the textual analyses of Maimonides' and Aquinas' respective explanations of the questions central to understanding the nature of Job's calamities, it is important to outline what I consider to be the major obstacles to such an inquiry as they are manifest in the scholarship on the question. At the outset, I also wish to point out that this chapter does not aim at providing comprehensive analyses of Maimonides' and Aquinas' understanding of the book of Job. Rather, my textual analyses aim at outlining what Maimonides and Aquinas considered the comprehensive inquiry into the question of providence to consist in. Since, by emphasizing Job's piety in the opening statement, the text challenges either the actual existence, or the possibility of understanding, divine justice and providence, it provides the opportunity for a radical critique of two of the most fundamental principles of the revealed tradition(s), an opportunity which neither Maimonides nor Aquinas can overlook.

Whereas the Old Testament Book of Job is central to Maimonides' discussions of providence and, hence, Maimonidean scholarly investigations of providence cannot ignore it, most Thomistic scholars do not treat Aquinas' commentary on Job as an essential part of his explanation of providence. In fact, as a glance at Thomistic bibliographies makes evident, only Martin Yaffe and Marcos Manzanedo address this commentary specifically, and only the former also attempts to compare Maimonides' exposition to Aquinas'.[153] Moreover, both David Burrell and Norbert Samuelson,[154] two exemplary scholars among the few who compare Maimonides' and Aquinas' views on providence, address the subject indirectly. That is, rather than asking what providence may be or how it can be understood, they question the possibility of affirming the freedom of the human will in the light of divine (fore)knowledge.[155] But, even from the perspective of strictly natural human knowledge, precisely insofar as providence is a question, that is, insofar as the definition (as distinct from the name) of providence is not known, the question of divine knowledge cannot be assumed to be identical with that of divine providence. Although, if it is assumed that the divinity is the source of universal order, so that there must be some relation between divine knowledge, providence, and human, free choice, such a relation is far from self-evident or else it would not be in question.[156]

Given the one-sided inclination of Thomistic scholarship in general and of comparative works in particular, I base my inquiry strictly upon Maimonides' and Aquinas' commentaries on Job since the question that they consider most fundamental to the text is the very possibility of attaining human knowledge of providence and the relation between knowledge and freedom of choice, rather than the affirmation of such freedom in the light of divine knowledge. That is, for both Maimonides and Aquinas, understanding God as *providens* is prior to understanding the very problematic notion of *praevidens*. My focus is chosen not only in order to balance the scales somewhat, but especially because it seems to me that understanding the ontological and noetic aspects constituting the human relations to providence is a prerequisite to understanding the relation between the human will or choice[157] and divine knowledge. First, since choice is that moment when the "will" (appetite or desire) is informed by the intellect, the nature of human choice must be determined prior to the examination of its function in human actualization. Second, since the nature of divine knowledge can be understood, if at all, only by means of a remote analogy with human knowledge, the role of human knowledge in the providential order must be investigated prior to an inquiry into the relation between divine knowledge and human choice.

At first glance, there seems to be no basis for comparing Maimonides' and Aquinas' expositions on Job.[158] Properly speaking, Maimonides never wrote an exposition on Job nor on any other biblical text. Rather, the text is explained in two of the chapters comprising the general discussion of providence,[159] and it is said to be a parable, possessing no historical reality. On the other hand, Aquinas comments on the text verse by verse, *ad litteram*, and insists on the historical veracity of the story. Notwithstanding these disparities and numerous other dissimilarities between their respective accounts,[160] in my opinion, the conclusions reached by both Maimonides and Aquinas are strikingly similar, both with respect to the nature of Job's transgression and with respect to the relation between divine providence and human action. It should be emphasized, however, that I limit my assertion concerning the similarity between their respective interpretations to providence as it pertains to rational creatures, rather than to its relation to the entire sublunar realm.[161]

The only other study comparing Maimonides' and Aquinas' expositions on Job, Yaffe's "Providence in Medieval Aristotelianism: Moses Maimonides and Thomas Aquinas on The Book of Job," concludes quite differently that, despite their shared Aristotelian philosophy and biblical tradition of interpretation, Maimonides and Aquinas take radically opposed positions on Job because they use the text to address specifically different and urgent concerns within their respective communities. Regarding the shared traditions, the philosophic is seen by Yaffe as a strength due to its proper procedure of scientific inquiry, whereas the biblical is seen as a certain hermeneutic encumbrance imposed upon the unity and coherence of the book by rabbinic and ecclesiastical doctrines. Since I have already discussed the nature of their relation to their respective traditions, I will forgo repeating my conclusions. It is interesting to note in passing that Yaffe's view is the mirror image of Chenu's, which emphasizes the integrity of the scholastic method of biblical exegesis, and of the Leonine editors of the *Expositio*, who applaud the outstanding clarity and coherence of the commentary.[162]

By insisting upon the protreptic intention and propaedeutic nature of their procedure and in stressing that the full scope of Aristotelian science includes metaphysics, Yaffe demonstrates both Maimonides' and Aquinas' debt to Aristotle. However, his designation of either thinker as Aristotelian can be maintained only if Aristotle is understood to be the first Neoplatonist,[163] an understanding that I endorse but that does not seem to accord with Yaffe's analysis. This disagreement is not purely semantic. Rather, the designation of

Maimonides and Aquinas as Aristotelian provides Yaffe with the opportunity to offer "an 'Averroistic' account of their meaning,"[164] which is based upon the radical separation between reason and revelation, physics and metaphysics, and in this context, leads to a radical juxtaposition of Maimonides' and Aquinas' accounts.

The difference postulated by Yaffe between Maimonides' and Aquinas' interpretations of Job can be summarized as follows: Whereas Maimonides understands Job to be perfectly just but unwise, Aquinas understands him to be perfectly wise but unjust. Consequently, Maimonides is seen to use the text for teaching the rabbinic student that wisdom ought to be the object of his temporal quest since his reader is religiously intolerant of philosophic wisdom. Aquinas, on the other hand, perceiving his reader's shortcoming to stem from an overemphasis on speculative reason, is understood to use Job as the example of the generic teacher's failure to communicate his wisdom to those untrained in the subtleties of philosophy. Despite its compact symmetry and its attempt at contextual grounding, this interpretation cannot be textually supported both because it is based upon an a priori assumption that reason and revelation are irreconcilable and because it identifies the readers of both Maimonides and Aquinas incorrectly. These two elements are not independent of one another, but rather one reinforces the other. That is, the assumption that reason and revelation necessarily conflict leads to the separation between speculative and practical reason to such an extent that these acts seem to belong to two different faculties of the soul. Consequently, it can be assumed that either wisdom or justice can be possessed perfectly independently of one another.

With respect to the audience of the *Guide*, Maimonides' Introduction seems unambiguous in its designation. Rather than the rabbinic student who is dogmatically complacent in his knowledge, the text is addressed to one who has progressed beyond the tradition to philosophy and is perplexed because unable to harmonize their teachings.[165] Neither the perplexed nor Job could be understood to possess either wisdom or justice perfectly; few, if any, do. In a like manner, Yaffe mistakenly identifies the audience of Aquinas' biblical commentary. For even if we assume that the *Exposition on Job* was addressed to students advanced in biblical studies, it is far from evident that they were perfectly wise. On the contrary, given Aquinas' judgment, in the Prologue to I^a Pars of the *Summa*, concerning the impediments to knowledge in the path of its readers, it is doubtful that he would have considered the reader of the exposition wise.[166]

Although Maimonides identifies the opinions of Eliphaz, Bildad, and Zophar with the opinion of the Torah, the Mu'tazila, and the Ash'ariyya doctrines, respectively, and Aquinas does not, both clearly differentiate their views from Elihu's and Job's. What characterizes the three opinions in both expositions is their assertion of so radical a disproportionality between natural human knowledge and either revealed truth or divine knowledge that it can lead either to blind pietism or despair, not dissimilar to Burrell's shipwrecks, mentioned in the Introduction. In fact, both Maimonides and Aquinas seem to divide the five opinions into either those based upon rational assent or those originating in non-rational, blind obedience. Moreover, although both are rather contemptuous of blind obedience, both also view a narrowly rational understanding of providence as erroneous and dangerous. The narrow domain of unaided natural reason is the symbolic realm of Satan and (unfortunately) of Aristotle,[167] where speculative and practical reason are radically separated, as is divine knowledge, will, and justice.

In contradistinction to Yaffe, it seems to me that their accounts of Job exemplify Maimonides' and Aquinas' view that wisdom and justice are fully interrelated. In fact, I consider the view that the designations *wisdom* and *justice* respectively, as corresponding to speculative and practical reason erroneous, since the term *wisdom* (*sophia* or *sapientia*) subsumes both theoretical and practical reason (*episteme* and *phronesis*).[168]

Since both Maimonides and Aquinas emphasize the fact that Satan is denied dominion over Job's soul and since both explain the term *soul* as immortality,[169] it seems to me that neither considered Job *perfectly* just or wise, given that his status in the world to come is still in question. Rather Job is their occasion for elaborating a coherent noetics of wisdom as the ultimate perfection possible in this life that overcomes the Aristotelian[170] separation between theoretical and practical reason on the basis of principles known through revelation. Overcoming this separation is a prerequisite for the soul's permanence. Although these principles are not attainable by natural reason and, hence, are not possessed by the philosopher, qua natural scientist, they are, nevertheless, held with greater certainty and function in the same way as, and in cooperation with, the primary principles of theoretical reason.[171]

Since I disagree with the existing scholarship on Maimonides' and Aquinas' interpretations of Job, the remainder of this chapter will be an exegetical analysis of the questions considered by both thinkers to be central and essential to the biblical text, which in turn will establish the topics of the following chapters of this study.

Maimonides' Account of Job

Maimonides opens his explanation of Job with the assertion that the topic belongs to the class of subjects that do not lend themselves to demonstration; hence, their investigation should proceed in a different manner.[172] The opening statement is clarified by adding that the story is a parable that outlines the varied *opinions* held by people concerning providence. From these brief statements Maimonides expects the careful reader to recall both his discussion of the interpretation of parables and his exposition concerning the indemonstrability of divine matters with the perplexity consequent upon it.[173] Indeed, the first disagreement (due to perplexity) mentioned by Maimonides concerns the nature of the story itself; it is believed by some to represent an account of a historical fact, whereas others, Maimonides included, believe it to be a parable. It is precisely the reader's inability to distinguish between an historical and a parabolic biblical narrative to which Maimonides attributes the origins of perplexity in the introduction to the *Guide*.[174] Moreover, Maimonides' insistence on the parabolic nature of Job is independent of the question concerning the historical facticity of the events recounted.[175] Rather, the significance of the story is independent of its facticity since situations like those depicted in the text *always occur*.

The divergent opinions about the nature of the narrative do not *originate* in its essential teachings, according to Maimonides, since no individual endowed with an intellect can doubt that the discourse between God and Satan is a parable.[176] However, unlike many other biblical parables, Job is "one to which extraordinary notions and *things that are the mystery of the universe* are attached. Through it great enigmas are solved, and truths than which none is higher become clear."[177]

In accordance with the general principles outlined by Maimonides with respect to parables explaining the mysteries of the Torah, Maimonides' exposition proceeds with great caution so as not to transgress the counsel of the Torah (and of philosophy) by clearly revealing the essential meaning of the parable to those entirely incapable of understanding it.[178] Since in such a parable many words are superfluous to its real meaning,[179] Maimonides will draw attention only to significant words and topics, expecting the attentive, capable reader to understand the whole on the basis of these with the aid of the hermeneutic principles repeatedly outlined previously and recalled here. In fact, Maimonides maintains that the opening sentence of the biblical text offers the same counsel he has given by using the word '*Uṣ*', an equivocal term meaning counsel, to refer to Job's land, but intended to be read as an imperative issued to the reader to reflect and meditate.[180]

Having prepared the reader to adopt the appropriate disposition towards the text, Maimonides turns to the first important question appearing in Job, the figure of Satan. It is noteworthy that the discussion of the meaning of *Satan* occupies almost half of the explication of Job. In fact, Maimonides maintains that the interpretation of the problem 'Satan' encompasses all the essential questions raised in Job, apart from those contained in the conclusion.

According to Maimonides, at the outset, the text draws a clear distinction between Satan and the sons of God. Since Satan is not included in the collective verbs of the sentence, the syntax indicates that Satan, unlike the sons of God, came uninvited. The relation of non-identity between Satan and the sons of God is reinforced by the depiction of Satan as one who roams the earth, which, we are told, signifies his exclusion from the supralunar realm. Satan's delegation to the sublunar realm and Job's delivery into his hands clearly designate Satan, rather than God, as the cause of all Job's calamities and, hence, all human misfortunes.

In accordance with his assertion that the parable of Job reveals some mysteries of the universe explained by the Torah, in *Guide*, 3. 22, Maimonides draws attention to two of these; namely, the omission of wisdom from the virtues ascribed to Job, and the denial to Satan of dominion over Job's soul. With respect to the first Maimonides states: "The most marvelous and extraordinary thing about this story is the fact that knowledge is not attributed in it to *Job*. He is not said to be a *wise* or a *comprehending* or an *intelligent man*. Only moral virtue and righteousness in action are ascribed to him."[181] Directly following this assertion, Maimonides' adds that, had Job been wise, he would have understood his situation clearly. As will become evident below, this statement would be modified at the end of the explication to read that had Job been truly wise, he would have experienced his misfortunes minimally and would not have questioned providence in the sublunar realm.[182]

The two chapters comprising Maimonides' exegesis on Job never address directly the question begged by Maimonides' assertion that the refraining from attributing wisdom to Job is an extraordinary mystery of the Torah, namely, the possibility of affirming divine justice in light of the suffering experienced by the righteous. Consequently, if we wish to maintain that Maimonides believed in the infallibility of divine justice, we must seek some clue to what will become evident upon reading the entire *Guide*, that is, the just ground for Job's suffering. The explanation given at the end of *Guide*, 3. 23, seems to suggest merely that divine justice is beyond human comprehension. Whereas this explanation may be sufficient for satisfying some theological schools, not only does it not constitute a philosophical explanation (not even by the weakest dialectical methods) since it circumvents the question, but it is also a solution which Maimonides himself considers invalid, even repugnant, given his harsh criticisms of the Kalam.[183] Moreover, such facile and trivial solution undermines the significance of Maimonides' assertion that had Job been wise, he would have understood his situation, as well as the principle of human moral responsibility that underlies Maimonides' entire ethical teachings. That is, the very notion of justice requires that real suffering be punishment for a willed act; the human being can be held responsible only for those actions chosen freely or rationally.[184] The absolute transcendence of divine justice and its total lack of accessibility and intelligibility also nullifies the possibility of affirming divine providence over individual human beings and thus leaves them subject to blind fate. Ultimately, despite its adoption by some theological schools, the unknowability of divine providence destroys the foundations of the Torah and all religious belief that presuppose that revelation is the best means for attaining moral perfection. Although human beings still may obey the commandments out of fear, moral actions ensuing from fear cannot transform fearful ignorant practice into voluntary action out of love.

The only clue Maimonides offers to the resolution of the seeming contradiction consists in the emphasis he places upon a proper understanding of the moral virtue attributed to Job. Attaching the greatest significance to the predication of Job's righteousness, Maimonides argues that the predication limits Job's moral virtue to his actions. This assumption is supported by an outline of the varied types of misfortune befalling different people that, initially, seems to constitute a disruption of the logical order, or an unreasonable digression, in Maimonides' interpretation of the mystery of 'Satan'.[185] However, the purpose of the seeming interruption becomes manifest in Maimonides' conclusion that however patiently most people *seem* to endure their suffering, "none of them supports patiently the pain of the body without complaining and repining either with the tongue or in the heart."[186] With this brief outline Maimonides draws attention to the tension between action and intention, appearance and 'true reality', or the limits set to human knowledge by sensible existence.[187]

The greater part of *Guide*, 3. 22, is devoted to bringing into relief the functions assigned to the metaphoric figure of Satan in the providential order. Resuming the interpretation of the Satan parable, Maimonides adds nuances to his previous conclusion by means of a comparison between Satan's first and second appearances before God. In contradistinction to his first appearance, in the second, Satan is said to have presented himself before God and, consequently, to "exist as subject to His order in what he wills."[188] The very fact that the text presents two distinct accounts of Satan's appearance before God is understood by Maimonides to constitute an extraordinary method for revealing the secret of Satan.[189] Whereas the first account radically distinguishes between the status of the sons of God and that of Satan, the former being "more permanent and lasting," the second account reveals that Satan "also has a certain portion below them in what exists."[190] Moreover, God's injunction against Satan's dominion over Job's soul reveals that his dominion extends to terrestrial things only, rather than to anything lasting or permanent. The equivocal term *soul*, Maimonides recalls, applies, here, only "to the thing that remains of man after death."[191]

Having summarized his own understanding of 'Satan', Maimonides buttresses his interpretation with numerous dicta of the Sages and with other biblical accounts. He asserts rather strongly that the saying of Rabbi Simon ben Laqish, "*Satan, the evil inclination, and the angel of death are one and the same,*"[192] reveals most of the mysteries of the Torah to those endowed with an intellect by identifying Satan, simultaneously, with the evil inclination and the angel of death, thus uniting them into a single concept. The same notion is expressed in other rabbinic sayings and certain biblical accounts related as prophetic visions, as well as in the nominal derivation of the word *Satan* from the verb *satah*, which means "to turn away." The Sages who recognize the "nature" of the biblical Satan are, according to Maimonides, sage not so much in virtue of their authority as in virtue of their true wisdom that is made manifest both by deed and speech inasmuch as their explanations succeed simultaneously to reveal and conceal the mysteries of the Torah.[193] Satan is the evil inclination turning human beings away from truth to error and hence death. Satan stands for or embodies the negation of the good inclination which "is only found in man when his intellect is perfected."[194] The numerous quotations from the Torah and the tradition that he chooses thus not only lend support to Maimonides' previous conclusion, but especially supplement the conclusion with the notion that the perfection of human justice (good inclination) is concomitant with the perfection of the intellect. Error is the source of death because the human intellect is the only part of the soul that is potentially immortal.

Maimonides' claim that he understood the meaning of Job through something akin to prophetic revelation and the attention he draws to the fact that many biblical accounts addressing the same concept are said to have been transmitted "in a vision of prophecy" are reinforced in the final interpretation of Satan, as well as of good inclination, as angels who accompany every human being. Maimonides maintains that this rabbinical saying reveals many mysteries and abolishes false opinions; it is simultaneously true and useful.

Even though Maimonides refrains from interpreting the angelic status of Satan, Maimonides' account is neither esoteric nor deliberately mystifying, in the sense of falsifying. He does not consider it necessary to interpret the mystery since he has addressed the subject of angels twice and at some length, both in Book 2 (3-12), in the context of the Account of Creation and in Book 3 (1-7), in the context of the Account of the Chariot, the greatest mysteries of the Torah. Consequently, the reader is expected to interpret the mysteries of Job in the light of these discussions. The discussion indicates clearly that the correct understanding of the suffering of the righteous, evil inclination, and the limitations of human knowledge can be acquired only after one possesses the correct understanding of metaphysics, ontology, psychology, and noetics.[195]

In *Guide*, 3. 23, Maimonides first summarizes the various opinions outlined in the text and then draws distinctions between them. He points out that there was a general agreement between the five friends on numerous points. All agreed that God was the cause of Job's sufferings, that God was just, and excluding Job, they also affirmed reward and punishment. The purpose of the account, however, according to Maimonides, is to bring into relief the differences between the respective interpretations presented, rather than to affirm reward and punishment. Job's interpretation is in keeping with Aristotle's, and amounts to a denial of individual divine providence and the assertion of God's indifference toward the universe He has created.[196] Eliphaz, echoing the opinion of "our Law,"[197] maintained that, whereas all punishment is recompense for deficiencies, "the deficiencies for which we deserve punishment and the way in which we deserve to be punished because of them are hidden from our perception."[198] This interpretation amounts to a denial of the possibility of attaining righteousness. Bildad's opinion reflects the Mu'tazilite doctrine that interprets suffering to be an acquisition of future rewards, or punishment as trial.[199] Zophar's opinion reflects the Ash'arite doctrine emphasizing the absolute opacity of anything related to the divine to the extent that no question can be raised concerning the divine plan. In contradistinction to the others, Elihu is said to possess knowledge, in fact to be "the most perfect among them in knowledge."[200] His intellectual superiority is manifest from his immediate rebuke of Job's ignorance, his characterization of the others' opinions as senile drivel, and the enigmatic nature of his speeches. The significance of the latter qualification consists of its deliberate intention to conceal from the multitude the notion added by Elihu to those propounded by the other friends. The additional notion simply mentions the intercession of an angel.[201]

It is noteworthy that Elihu's practice of revealing and concealing mirrors not only the truly wise Sages but also the practice of the divinely informed author of Job. That is, concealment is practiced deliberately a least three times, on two levels, but with a single aim in mind; namely, to hide the divergences among possible interpretations of providence from the masses. Although the twofold concealment reflects a difference in kind between the hidden 'objects' of knowledge, with respect to the masses the end is not distinguished by the objects, precisely because any knowledge that distinctions may exist among pious opinions about providence constitutes a danger to those incapable of sustaining the *aporiae*, let alone apprehending the hidden nature of truth, on the one hand, and the limitations of human knowledge and discourse, on the other. Consequently, in reproducing the prudence exercised by the biblical author, Elihu practices what was depicted previously as philosophical hermeneutics.[202] Moreover, Elihu's philosophical hermeneutics reflects biblical and rabbinic teachings by adopting the parable as the most appropriate means for conveying a metaphysical truth. Elihu's parabolic account of an intercession of an angel is no more likely to confuse those incapable of understanding the true meaning of the concept 'angel' than any other biblical narrative about angels.

Elihu's notion is comprised of three essential interrelated features represented, respectively, by an angel, prophetic revelation, and Job's ignorance. Elihu's wisdom is manifest both by the recognition of the elements essential for understanding the events and by the order of their presentation, which reflects the nature of their relation. Maimonides presents Elihu's rebuke of Job's ignorance twice, each instance manifesting a distinct deficiency in Job's knowledge, the first moral, the second theoretical. First, Job's opinion is reproved by Elihu for its ignorance "because of his having manifested his self-esteem. . . . For he had expatiated at length on the goodness of his actions."[203] As in the preliminary interpretation of Job, so in *Guide*, 3. 23, Maimonides draws attention to Job's good actions. In fact, Elihu's rebuke does not deny Job's virtuous deeds, but rather indicates that Job's pride is somehow related to his inability to understand that his good deeds in themselves do not constitute perfect moral virtue. In some manner, human pride is a barrier to knowledge, that is, to human perfection. Conversely, perfect moral virtue is impossible without intellectual virtue, and only their concurrence constitutes human perfection.

A second element distinguishing Elihu's rebuke from those of the others, in addition to presenting an understanding superior to Job's, is his realization that human well-being requires angelic succor. Elihu's enigmatic parable, which describes the intercession of an angel on behalf of a sick man, so that he is "saved and restored to the best of states,"[204] receives no clarification. As in the preceding chapter, so here, Maimonides is guiding the reader toward the solution without providing it since he has already explained the meaning of *angels* in the contexts most fitting for such a discussion and hence need only hint at it.[205] Likewise, without further elaboration, he praises Elihu's reference to prophecy and his allusion to its quiddity in relation to providence. Elihu's immediate transition from speech about prophecy to speech about natural phenomena makes evident that there is an essential relation between providence, prophetic knowledge, and the correct understanding of the content of prophecy. According to Maimonides, both Elihu's explanation of providence and Job's subsequent prophetic revelation do not go beyond explanation of natural matters, "for our intellects do not reach the point of apprehending *how* these natural things that exist in the world of generation and corruption are produced in time and conceiving *how* the existence of the natural force within them has originated them."[206] Given the weakness of the human intellect with respect to natural subjects and especially their principles, Maimonides points out that it is presumptuous to wish to explain divine providence and government as similar to human institutions.[207]

The correct understanding of the radical dissimilarity between human beings and God is the guarantee that misfortunes will be borne lightly by human beings, will not lead to doubt about God, and above all will increase love. The story of Job, irrespective of its historical veracity, is the biblical warning not only to the pious but also to the philosophers about a perpetual need for safeguards against intellectual hubris. As Maimonides points out both in the interpretation of Job and in the previous discussion of providence in 3. 17, neither unexamined belief nor demonstrative reasoning suffice for understanding divine providence. Hence, he maintains that although he has not reached his conclusions about providence by means of demonstration, nevertheless, his opinion "is less disgraceful than the preceding opinions and *nearer than theirs to intellectual reasoning.*"[208]

Maimonides' interpretation of Job does not constitute a full explanation of providence. Rather the indication that the account should be read as a parable and the emphasis placed by Maimonides upon its key concepts guide the reader toward the appropriate contexts within which a comprehensive investigation of providence should take place. A proper understanding of the origin of the world, its nature, the human place in it, and the extent of human knowledge of it are prerequisites to an understanding of providence.

` Aquinas' Exposition on Job

Like Maimonides, Aquinas considers it necessary to inquire into the nature of the Book of Job. Following the Christian tradition, he maintains that the story of Job is the account of an historical event. Since this opinion is stated twice, since Aquinas attempts to establish the historical veracity of the events at some length, and since he is clearly juxtaposing his opinion to that of others,[209] his explanation calls for a closer examination. Aquinas uses two distinct terms to differentiate the events of Job from a fabricated parable. The terminology Aquinas uses in Chapter 1, *res gesta* as opposed to a *parabola*, does not lead to any ambiguity. On the other hand, the Prologue sets up a different distinction, one between *aliquid in rerum natura* and *parabola confecta*. I agree with the conclusion of the Leonine editors of the *Expositio* that Aquinas' attempt to establish Job as "something in the nature of things" seems also to be an attempt to refute Maimonides' claim that it is a parable. In this light, it is significant that Aquinas' refutation uses no traditional Christian arguments for this purpose, but rather is based entirely upon scriptural quotations.[210] However, the distinction between a fabricated parable and something in the nature of things is especially curious given that the text in question is a biblical one. Since the significant source of any biblical parable is God, the distinction cannot imply in any way that the 'fiction' is an untruth.[211] Moreover, Maimonides' argument does not require that the account of the events in Job conflict with "something in the nature of things." On the contrary, it is precisely because the events recounted manifest a perennial condition that Maimonides concludes that their historical veracity is irrelevant. Like Maimonides, Aquinas dismisses as irrelevant to his investigation the questions concerning the authorship of the book, the precise historical period of occurrence, the parentage of Job, and so forth.[212] He also states that the historical veracity of Job is of minor importance to the central purpose of the text, that is, to the explanation of providence as it operates in human affairs.[213] Consequently, unless we conclude that Aquinas failed to understand the thrust of Maimonides' argument, it seems to me that the disagreement with Maimonides' was not Aquinas' main concern.

Rather, as pointed out in Chapter 1, Aquinas' emphasis upon the importance of the letter of Scripture is a radical break with and criticism of the Gregorian tradition.[214] Hence, since the text compares Job to Noah and Daniel,[215] two truly historical figures, Job, too, must have been a historical figure. Moreover, as the following discussion would make clear, Aquinas' emphasis on the *rerum natura* (as juxtaposed to *res gesta*) in the Prologue is based upon his understanding of the ultimate purpose of the Book of Job.

At the outset of the *Expositio*, in the Prologue, Aquinas sets up most of the questions essential to Job—the human place in the universe, the nature and limitations of human knowledge, the role of revelation, and the nature of divine providence. First, Aquinas states the general cause for difficulties in understanding the nature of certain subjects. Just as natural perfection is an end of a process progressing slowly from the imperfect to the perfect, so also human knowledge of truth is a gradual process toward perfection. In the beginning of the process of intellectual perfection, on account of imperfect cognition, many subjects are misunderstood. The comparison between human knowledge and things generated immediately establishes not only the nature of human knowledge, but also places human knowledge, and thus human beings, in the order of things generated.

Having outlined the general problem, Aquinas summarizes the common opinions concerning providence in the historical order of their origins, and thereby establishes the relations between these opinions as a progressive development from the less to the more perfect. The earliest accounts of providence denied divine providence outright, attributing all things to chance. Next came opinions that attributed most things to chance. Later philosophers, according to Aquinas, exhibited a keener understanding, recognizing that the order evident in nature indicates that things are ordered by an intellect. However, whereas they admitted divine providence over strictly natural things, they doubted that it played a role in human affairs. In fact, since they could not perceive a due order in human affairs, they concluded that divine providence is indifferent to humanity, having left human affairs to human government and to chance.[216]

Aquinas does not attribute the latter opinion to any particular individual philosopher or philosophical school.[217] He maintains, however, that it is the most harmful among all the preceding opinions since by destroying divine providence it destroys the foundations of reverence or fear of God and, consequently, the basis for moral education. According to Aquinas, the principal cause for prophetic revelation is the need to combat this harmful opinion.[218] "Whence the first and foremost urgent task of those who have received the wisdom of the divine spirit for the teaching of others was to remove this opinion from the hearts of men."[219] The whole purpose of the Book of Job, like that of all other books transmitted by the holy spirit, is human education concerning providence, "so that by *probable reasons* it can show that human affairs are governed by divine providence."[220] Aquinas adds that the book presents the afflictions that befell Job "as a kind of theme"[221] by means of which the question of the suffering of the just, the central obstacle to the belief in divine providence, can be explored.

In pointing out the fact that the principal reason for prophecy was the refutation of opinions denying its efficacy in human affairs and in stating that the teachings in Job proceed by probable reasoning, Aquinas is also underlining the limitations of demonstration, on the one hand, and of natural human reason, on the other, for understanding certain truths. Not only is demonstrable certainty impossible concerning providence, but also, with respect to metaphysics, natural human reason cannot attain the primary principles for probable reasoning without aid.[222] Moreover, the assertion that the book presents the events in Job as a theme for the purpose of education seems to indicate that Aquinas' juxtaposition of *parabola ficta* and *aliquid in rerum natura* is intended primarily for reinforcing the truth of the teachings. That is, whereas a divinely inspired, "fabricated" parable always refers to the universal truth of the proposition (or to the mystical sense), but may not refer to any specific instance of actualization, it establishes the proposition only as a rational truth. On the other hand, the particular occurrence establishes the proposition as a natural truth as well or as one that is empirically verifiable.[223]

Given the great stylistic difference between Aquinas' and Maimonides' commentaries on Job and given that my concern is with their conceptual relation, the remaining inquiry will focus upon the central subjects of the two texts: the angels, the figure of Satan, the human soul, the nature and limitations of human knowledge, and the nature of Job's transgression.[224]

Precisely because Aquinas' commentary, unlike Maimonides', consists of a detailed *ad litteram* explication and owing to the distinct requirements of its audience, it is more accessible to immediate interpretation. Not only is Aquinas ready to offer detailed explications of pertinent topics and to draw explicit attention to their implications, but also he is able to "depart" from the text in order to place the discussion in its appropriate broader context.[225] After a detailed description of Job's virtue, Aquinas briefly outlines the multifaceted and interrelated nature of biblical language. This condensed outline serves as a preface to an explication of the nature of divine government, which in fact constitutes a departure from the text but, nevertheless, is essential to what follows.[226]

Since the event directly following upon the general description of Job's condition is the appearance of the sons of God and of Satan before God, Aquinas considers it necessary to explain these figures and their function in the order of the universe. He explains that divine providence functions in such a manner that the lower creatures are ordered through the higher; the corruptible lower bodies are subject to the motion of the heavenly bodies; the lower spirits, the rational souls, are governed by higher spirits since human souls are united to mortal bodies.[227] Aquinas recalls here that the Christian tradition holds that some of the incorporeal spirits are good, others evil.[228] The good spirits are the angels who are called both messengers and sons of God; the former designation refers to their relation to human beings whom they in-form; the latter designation refers to their participation in the divine glory. The evil spirits are not evil by their nature, having been created by God, but rather through their own sin or *actus essendi*.[229] The first among them is the devil or Satan the adversary. The purpose of the brief metaphysical explanation is the conclusion that both good and evil spirits have a function in divine government and do not act independently of the divine ordered plan. Only after he establishes that all created beings are subject to God and have a specific place in the universal order can Aquinas return to the biblical text and explain the appearance of the angels and Satan, especially, Satan's role in the events befalling Job.

Aquinas' exposition utilizes the equivocity of the Latin word *assistere* to unfold the status and position of the angels, Satan, and human beings. He first explains that whereas all creatures are present before God and hence, can be scrutinized by Him, only the good angels can enjoy the sight of God. That is, whereas absence characterizes most creatures relation to God, some kind of presence characterizes that of the good angels. Or, whereas an unknowing pertains to creatures who are only *scrutinized* by God, some knowing (vision) belongs to the good angels.[230] Second, he explains that both the good angels and Satan, under God's scrutiny, assist in divine government. Aquinas draws an additional distinction between the sons of God and Satan that, despite its greater detail, recalls Maimonides' discussion.[231] He explains that the sons of God and Satan are related to God's justice in different modes; the former measure all their actions in relation to God, the latter does not wish to act according to the divine plan. Since angelic assistance in divine government is described in the language of scrutiny rather than vision, actual angelic knowledge, willed or proper agency, does not seem to be necessary for it. The equivocity of the word *assistere* allows Aquinas to allude to the concurrence and disjunction between first and second order causality.[232] Hence, the biblical text presents simultaneously the natural similarity and willful dissimilarity between the angels and Satan, stating that Satan came among them, but that the good angels alone presented themselves (or recognized their presence to God). However, even though Satan's intention is always evil, his actions are never independent of the divine will; rather, what he wills as an evil, God has intended as a good, namely, the punishment of the unjust and the active habituation of the just. Like Maimonides, Aquinas also emphasizes the facts that Satan's activity is limited to the sublunar realm and that he is the cause of evil on earth. As will become evident below, Aquinas' discussion of Satan and his emphasis upon Satan's role in human ills is resumed at great length in the final chapters of the commentary.

The final chapters of the commentary also substantiate my claim that, despite significant differences between Aquinas' and Maimonides' methods of exposition, respective audiences, and numerous specific details, their conclusions are strikingly similar. Chapters 32-37, the chapters comprising Elihu's speech, are devoted to a comprehensive analysis of the limitations of natural reason to arrive at many principles of natural science, as well as to emphasizing the mediating role of the heavenly bodies (or the angels) in human knowledge. And Chapters 38-41, the section comprising God's response, consist of lengthy explanations about the insufficiency of the natural power of reason for *understanding*[233] divine providence and about the relation between human ills and pride, the figurative symbol of which is Satan.

All the essential questions raised by Maimonides with respect to the text of Job are brought into full relief by Aquinas and receive detailed consideration in the context of Elihu's speech and of God's teachings. Like Maimonides, Aquinas distinguishes between Elihu and the three other friends. He, too, points out that Elihu's youth has no bearing upon his wisdom, which is superior to that of the others. However, he does not consider Elihu's understanding to be superior to Job's, but rather maintains that its inferiority is made manifest by means of his misinterpretation of Job's lament as blasphemous. Still, despite their different interpretations of Elihu's and Job's speeches, and irrespective of the possible grounds for the disagreement between them, a fundamental agreement between Maimonides and Aquinas concerning the nature of providence can be established.[234] In other words, the essential agreement between the two thinkers on providence appears to be independent of textual and doctrinal constraints. Their philosophical understanding of providence precedes their explication of the text and informs it, not because they overlook the letter of Scripture, but because the subject of providence belongs to divine science, of which the correct *understanding* is posterior to the study of natural science and philosophical metaphysics.

Aquinas' explications of God's and Elihu's speeches constitute exemplary manifestations of the medieval teaching method. The first instance of explaining the letter of the text is used by him as the occasion to teach the elements of natural science upon which he later constructs the fuller explanation not only of the text *qua* biblical teachings but also *qua* introduction to philosophy. In a manner fitting for the instruction of beginners in philosophical exegesis, Aquinas proceeds through progressive stages, each unfolding various layers of meaning. In the context of Elihu's speech several layers of meaning, which will be repeated and explained with greater subtlety in the context of God's speech, are articulated progressively.

For Aquinas, Elihu's speech is the occasion to demonstrate the imperfect understanding of one knowledgeable in natural science and in many things pertaining to metaphysics, who, nevertheless, is imperfect in interpretation.

Elihu's understanding of Job is partial and hence, it is also partially erroneous. On the one hand, his understanding of philosophical subjects and some aspects of providence is correct and consonant both with revelation and with Job's understanding. On the other hand, his failure to comprehend the full significance of providence leads him to the conclude that "all adversities in the present life occur in proportion to sins"[235] and, hence, that Job must be guilty of some wrong. At the same time, however, Aquinas does not attribute Elihu's misunderstanding of Job solely to his own intellectual imperfection, but rather explains that the erroneous apprehensions of all the friends are caused by Job, who, having spoken "lightly" *seemed* to blaspheme against divine justice and providence.[236]

In addition to limiting Elihu's responsibility for failing to understand Job's lament, Aquinas explains that Elihu's reference to divine instruction during sleep can be understood to refer to prophetic revelation, and he supports this possible interpretation with a quotation from Numbers.[237] Prophetic instruction, which is carried out through the mediation of the angels, since human beings cannot accede to God by themselves, is given "for instruction in those things which present to man [what is] to be done or to be shunned, not for knowledge of the speculative sciences, which are not customarily revealed in sleep."[238] Although revealed instruction does not add to speculative knowledge, nevertheless, the latter is in-formed by it in a different way, since revealed instruction is the safeguard against pride. That is, since Aquinas maintains that "pride is the root of sins wherefore God's precepts are despised"[239] and since one of the punishments consequent upon pride is the corruption of the soul "through the disruption of the powers of the soul,"[240] pride must affect all parts of human knowledge.

Aquinas explanation of the need for prophecy thus not only elucidates the cause of both Elihu's and Job's shortcomings, but also alludes to a general problem facing the religious philosopher, namely, the moral deficiency of one perfect in the sciences. Since the *Expositio* is not addressed to philosophers, however, Aquinas does not deal with the problem either comprehensively or philosophically. Notwithstanding, by emphasizing both the need for prophecy and the limitations of natural human reason to arrive at the metaphysical and ontological principles underlying the natural science, Aquinas delineates the contexts within which further inquiry can take place. In particular he places the ethical question in its proper context.[241] Initially, Aquinas' interpretation of God's response to Job seems to limit God's rebuke of Job to a criticism of Job's improper manner of expressing a correct understanding. A closer study of the opening statement, however, discloses that Aquinas is drawing a nuanced distinction between comprehension and unexamined acceptance of an opinion (which may be true) upon which the remaining discussion is based. He states:

But since human wisdom does not suffice for *comprehending* the truth of divine providence, it was necessary that the aforementioned disputation be determined by divine authority. But since Job has *perceived* correctly concerning divine providence, but has transgressed in the mode of speaking to the extent that thereby an offence arose in the hearts of the others so long as they thought that he was not displaying due reverence to God; therefore the Lord, as an arbitrator of the question, reproved both Job's friends concerning what they have perceived incorrectly, and Job concerning the disordered mode of speaking, and Elihu concerning the unfitting conclusion.[242]

And, according to Aquinas, disordered speech is a manifestation of a defect in reason that may lead to a disruption of the whole soul and, hence, may have moral consequences for both the individual and the community.[243]

God's response, according to Aquinas, can be interpreted metaphorically as an interior divine inspiration to Job, that is, as prophetic revelation. In addition, Aquinas maintains that in this life, because of "a certain obscuring of sensible similitude,"[244] we cannot perceive divine inspiration clearly. The interrogative form of God's response and especially the focus on the sensible world is aimed at demonstrating to human beings the extent of their ignorance, rather than at teaching them directly. Consequently, although Job held a correct opinion about divine providence, his disordered speech reflects not only the limitations of human reason, but also a lack of understanding and acknowledgment of such a limitation. Job's opinion may have been correct, but it was an unexamined opinion and therefore neither was it assented to rationally nor could it result from the recognition of the limitations of human reason.[245]

Prior to explaining Job's restoration to well-being, Aquinas summarizes Job as follows:

it ought to be considered that God began to manifest his operation which he employs against evil men in relation to the proud and ends the narration with the proud, in order to show that Job should have feared this especially, lest the devil who had sought to tempt him, would attempt to lead him especially to pride, so that thus he could be transferred to his own realm, and therefore he should have guarded against the disposition and the words which may savour of pride.[246]

Satan, the root of all human ills, begins and ends Aquinas *Expositio*, since it is the correct interpretation of human ills that the text aims at teaching. In the final chapters of the inquiry, Aquinas outlines the extent of Satan's domain and his powers in order to conclude that the opposition to Satan ought to be a constant and active concern of all human beings throughout life. Not only the ignorant and imperfect are susceptible to Satan's temptation, pride, but even the wise and morally upright. Job may have resisted Satan's power longer and better than others may have been able to but still he failed to "guard against the disposition and the words which may savour of pride." Both at the beginning and at the end of the *Expositio* the discussion of Satan is complemented by a discussion of the good angels, their sameness and difference simultaneously explain their respective roles in divine providence and government. In relation to human beings, Satan's and the angels' roles are exercised at the noetic level, the former symbolizing the pride that impedes knowledge, the latter the recognition of the limit that makes possible further understanding.[247] According to both Maimonides and Aquinas,[248] it is knowledge that guards against intellectual pride, a wisdom (*sapientia*) possessed by those who acknowledge the natural limitations of human reason (*scientia*) and manifests proper human understanding of providence and the possible modes of participating in the divine order.

Maimonides' and Aquinas' commentaries seem to suggest that it is highly doubtful that provident wisdom ever can be attained without revelation. At the same time, however, they seem to indicate that revelation without intellectual knowledge does not suffice for ultimate human perfection. Thus, although the biblical text of Job raises questions concerning the relations between reason and revelation, between moral and speculative perfection, and between the temporal and final human ends, and although it suggests that these questions are closely related to providence, it does not provide the occasion either for their resolution or for inquiring into the nature of the relation between them and providence. Notwithstanding this, the commentaries do delineate the orders of discourse within which further investigation should proceed, namely, metaphysics, ontology, epistemic psychology, noetics, and ethics. Since this study deals with religious thinkers, these subjects will be pursued in the contexts within which these questions are raised traditionally, namely, creation and God's relation to the world, matter and evil, the nature of human knowledge, ethics, divine law and providence. Finally, each of the following chapters will investigate Maimonides' and Aquinas' philosophical reflections on these subjects, simultaneously as they will address their respective attempts to harmonize the teachings of the philosophers and revelation.

3

THE ACCOUNT OF THE BEGINNING
OR CREATION

Introduction

The question of the origin of the universe is discussed, primarily, as a confrontation between philosophy and religion; secondarily, a distinction is drawn between Aristotle's doctrine that is in conflict with the revealed tradition and the teachings of philosophical schools following the Platonic or Neoplatonic tradition that are perceived as more congruent with revelation. The traditional expression of the question asks whether the world is eternal or created, with the latter position comprising two distinct aspects, often presented as two alternatives: creation in time (*ḥuduth* or *de novo*), and creation out of nothing (*min 'adam*[249] or *ex nihilo*). Whereas these aspects become the respective foci of many subsequent debates in the Christian and Jewish traditions, in their medieval garb, neither the Platonic nor the Aristotelian formulation is presented as ambiguous.[250] According to the medieval Plato, the world is created out of an eternal matter simultaneously with time, the possible dissolution of the former necessarily implying the dissolution of the latter.[251] According to Aristotle, both the universe and time are eternal.

Although many contemporary scholars studying Aquinas, whether in conjunction with Maimonides or not, have focused upon the question of time,[252] this question is not the primary concern of either Maimonides or Aquinas. Rather, for both thinkers, what is at issue is whether the universe is eternal or created and, if created, whether it was created out of something or out of nothing.[253] In addition, the question of *ex nihilo* occupies not only a priority in importance, but also a priority in the order of inquiry. Despite a difference in their formulations concerning the relation of the origin of the universe to time,[254] both thinkers do not accord it priority and both are concerned not only with establishing creation as a possibility, but also with the determination of the place of matter in creation. The question, therefore, is not simply one of creation as opposed to eternity, but also one concerned with the very nature of creation and, thus, of the created, or creature. Consequently, I prefer to phrase the problem more ambiguously, as an attempt to think and give a reasonable account of the origin of the universe, rather than as a clear-cut choice between the creation and the eternity of the world.

This is not a pedantic, semantic question. Rather, in the present chapter, I hope to demonstrate that 'the debate with Plato' has significant philosophical consequences, metaphysical, ontological, and ethical, equal in weight to those ensuing from 'the debate with Aristotle'. In fact, I shall argue that Maimonides' explicit assertion that the Platonists "believe in eternity"[255] results from his recognition that, from a philosophical perspective, the position of the Platonists has similar, if not identical, consequences to the Aristotelian, despite the fact that, unlike the Aristotelian position, it does not undermine the foundations of the Torah. Although Aquinas is not as explicit as Maimonides on this point, his various arguments for the created nature of matter seem to arise out of considerations similar to Maimonides'. In addition, in all his articulations of the history of the question, Aquinas groups Plato and Aristotle together in order to distinguish their teachings from the opinions of earlier philosophers. If my assertion is correct, then the refutation of Aristotle is not only logically prior to that of Plato, but also, as a consequence, the degree of philosophical clarity we can attain in attempting to refute Plato will be determined by the possible refutation of Aristotle.

As is evident in every question that cannot be resolved by means of demonstration, Maimonidean scholarship manifests greater and more radicalized differences in interpretation than its Thomistic counterpart.[256] Whereas no scholar ever has doubted Aquinas' acceptance of the scriptural teachings on creation, until recently, Maimonidean scholars held one of two diametrically opposed views. They maintained either that Maimonides rejected the Torah in favor of Aristotle or that he followed the Torah uncritically. In recent years, the question has been reawakened and numerous, more nuanced, interpretations have been suggested. Rather than survey the burgeoning scholarship, particular, diverse interpretations will be outlined and examined in the context of articulating the distinct aspects upon which Maimonides focuses when discussing the origin of the universe. Likewise, Thomistic scholarship will be discussed according as it bears upon the general problem under consideration. It should be noted, however, that the three main themes constituting the focal points of Maimonidean scholarship—Maimonides' esotericism, necessity and possibility, and prime matter[257]—do not correspond to the focal points of Thomistic scholarship, *ex nihilo*, and *de novo*. In order to avoid misappropriations and conflation of their respective teachings, my analysis will follow the order or the logic of Maimonides' and Aquinas' arguments, rather than attempt to organize the explanations of one thinker in conformity with those of the other. Thus, whereas the examination of Maimonides' thought will address the question of possibility at some length, that of Aquinas will pay greater attention to prime matter.

The question of the origin of the universe has direct and fundamental implications for the nature of providence, since it determines the possible relations between God and beings other than God. For, after the philosopher demonstrates the existence of the First and Final Cause following Aristotle, it still remains to be determined whether Aristotle's understanding of the deity reflects the limits of possible human knowledge of God. In addition, the religious philosopher will attempt to determine whether it is possible to demonstrate philosophically that the Aristotelian indifferent deity, the self-thinking Thought, (*Meta.*, 12. 7. 1072b14) can be reconciled with the good, provident, governing God of revelation, and if and when these respective understandings are incompatible, whether Aristotle's position can be disproved by means of demonstration.

Prior to examining Maimonides' and Aquinas' respective treatments of the question of the origin of the universe, it is important to emphasize again that the Platonic and Aristotelian positions outlined below will follow Maimonides' and Aquinas' articulations rather than present my own understanding of Plato's and Aristotle's teachings on the subject.[258] My primary concern here, then, is to reexamine Maimonides' and Aquinas' respective, teachings and speculations upon the origin of the universe, to determine the degree of conceptual agreement between them, and to draw out the central implications of each position, especially those which have important consequences for the nature of providence in relation to human beings.

Maimonides' Arguments for Creation

Discussions directly addressing the question of the origin of the universe are found throughout the *Guide*. In the Introduction to Book I, Maimonides, first, identifies the Account of the Beginning with natural science and then immediately *seems* to contradict himself, stating that "with regard to natural matters as well, it is impossible to give a clear exposition when teaching some of their principles as they are."[259] That is, at the very least, Maimonides seems to claim that the limited scope of demonstrative reasoning is evident not only in divine science, but also in natural science so that we cannot possess demonstrative knowledge of natural science. However, as Klein-Braslavy has pointed out,[260] whenever Maimonides discusses the Account of Creation as one of the secrets of the Torah, he is concerned with 'the principles' of natural science, rather than with the demonstrative science of which they are the foundation. Moreover, rather than discussing the initial intuitive (*epagogic*) possession of the first principles underlying natural science that are held by all human beings, Maimonides is underlining the understanding of these principles 'as they are'. As such, these principles do not belong to the domain of physics, but rather to that of metaphysics;[261] they derive from the encounter with the question of

Being as such, or as the origin of all possible modes of existence. Consequently, the true reality[262] of some of them cannot be discovered by means of demonstration and is reached either by dialectical reasoning, or by means of revelation. But, apart from, and exceeding difficulties pertaining to understanding or coming to some mode of knowing of some first principles, especially those "known" through revelation, are the difficulties pertaining to explanation. The immediacy of some modes of knowing cannot be translated into discursive, mediated speech without ambiguity, even obscurity.[263]

Following the lexicographical chapters of Book 1, Maimonides returns to the question of the origin of the universe in the context of his critique of the methods of the Mutakallimun.[264] Although, initially, it may seem to be a curious (or an intentionally misleading) digression preceding the proofs for God's existence, the critique is pedagogically necessary given the audience and expressed purpose of the *Guide*. Maimonides neither disagrees with all the premises set down by the Mutakallimun nor considers Kalam a practice to be eradicated. On the contrary, since the science of Kalam seeks to defend religious beliefs, principal among which is the belief in creation, and to refute opinions detrimental to the foundations of such beliefs, Maimonides considers it both necessary and useful in principle. In a manner of speaking, and as has often been claimed,[265] Maimonides' *Guide* can be understood as Kalam. Consequently, it is impossible to conclude that Maimonides judged the science of Kalam to be necessarily antithetical to philosophy. Rather, the very language used in *Guide* 1, seems to indicate that, following al-Farabi's distinctions between religious communities according to the temporal priority of the development of either philosophy or religion in them,[266] Maimonides is criticizing a certain kind of Kalam; namely, Kalam ignorant of or inept in proper philosophical procedure, because it is uninformed by philosophy. Although the core of Maimonides' criticism of the Mutakallimun seems to be methodological only, in fact it is based upon a primary epistemic principle; namely, that understanding requires that there be some kind of relation between actual, phenomenal existence, being, and explanation, let alone, justification (Kalam). If Kalam is to be not only didactic but also propaedeutic and if it is to constitute an effective defence of revelation, then it must be based upon an appropriate (*conveniens*) relation between the orders of knowing and the order(s) of being and becoming.

Maimonides' critique is twofold. First, he criticizes the early Mutakallimun for neglecting to account for sensible experience adequately since they inverted the order of knowledge; beginning their inquiry with metaphysics rather than with physics, they "did not conform in their premises to the appearance of that which exists, but considered how being ought to be in order that it should furnish a proof for the correctness of a particular opinion, or at least not refute it."[267] Notwithstanding, Maimonides designates these Mutakallimun "men of intellect"[268] since they recognized the nature of the question and attempted to discover demonstrative means for investigating it. These men were neither entirely ignorant nor inept. Their successors, on the other hand, fall short of every requirement belonging to men of intellect, since they neither understood the nature of the problem nor the nature of their predecessors' endeavors. Being ignorant, the latter Mutakallimun can be dismissed entirely from the philosophical discussion. However, despite the superiority of the early Mutakallimun and despite his fundamental sympathy with their intention to defend the principles of religious belief by means of demonstration, or precisely because of it, Maimonides considers it necessary to demonstrate their error and to establish firmly that "that which exists does not conform to the various opinions, but rather the correct opinions conform to that which exists."[269] The danger in following the methods of the Kalam may result not simply from error concerning the nature and extent of demonstration, or from ignorance concerning the order of knowledge; rather, these 'methodological' errors ultimately render the order of being contingent upon the order of becoming since they destroy the reciprocal hierarchy constituting the order of the sciences. For these methods entail that the demonstration of the creation of the world precede, and serve as the basis for, the demonstration of the existence of God. Consequently, it may lead to the absurd conclusion that the existence of the world is a necessary requirement for God, rather than the result of his freely willed act that depends upon Him.[270] The impossibility of arriving at a demonstrative proof for the origin of the universe would, at the very least, entail the indemonstrability of God's existence. The errors of the early Mutakallimun originate, quite simply, in their attempt to do philosophy. Rather than acquiesce to the conclusions of the philosophers and accept them as the foundations for their arguments or remain silent on subjects wherein the philosophers had failed to reach demonstrative proofs, they overreached the boundaries of Kalam, thus, harming both philosophy and the faith.[271]

In contradistinction to the Mutakallimun, Maimonides disengages the two discussions and shows the necessity for reversing their order, beginning with proofs of God's existence as prerequisite for establishing the possibility of Creation. The very existence of the world, motion, and time requires that one thing be permanent, uncaused, and unchanging, which must be understood, at the very least, as its necessary cause. If demonstration begins with the nature of existence, proofs for the existence of God must be not only independent of demonstrations of the origin of the universe, but also valid irrespective of them. Therefore, the demonstration of God's existence is necessary and valid both for those professing an eternal universe and for those who believe in a created universe, either *ex nihilo*, or *de novo*, or both.

Maimonides' critique of the early Mutakallimun is also an implicit defence of philosophy, of its necessary, and necessarily independent, role in the order of knowledge. Properly obtained philosophical conclusions may, and should, be used in defending religious beliefs, if and only if they have been arrived at independently or unhindered by dogmatic constraints. Conversely, the use of philosophy merely as a tool will lead to error about philosophy and, more significantly for the critique of Kalam, can undermine the very principles of the religious belief they attempt to defend.[272] In fact, after juxtaposing Kalam arguments to those of Aristotle, Maimonides emphasizes that, apart from the doctrine affirming the eternity of the world and irrespective of it, on most subjects wherein the Mutakallimun attempted to defend religious beliefs, Aristotle's teachings are not only fully congruent with revelation, but as a consequence also serve as a superior defence of revelation.

After he demonstrates the existence of God and descriptively outlines the nature of the supralunar realm and the role of the angels in existence, all of which hold true whether one follows Aristotle or revelation (keeping in mind, of course, that [1] *angels* is an equivocal term[273] and [2] truth is measured neither by certainty nor by the form or clarity of its account), Maimonides focuses his attention upon the question of the origin of the universe. He enumerates and examines the three opinions possible with respect to the question, that of the adherents of the Torah, that of Plato, and that of Aristotle. The first opinion affirms creation out of absolute non-being through a freely willed act of God; the second, although affirming the generation and corruption of the heavens, also affirms creation out of an eternal matter based upon the assumption that it is inconceivable that existence originate from absolute non-existence; the third, affirms God as the cause of the coeternal world that He causes out of the necessity of His nature.

Herbert Davidson argues that each position can be examined from two distinct, and to some extent independent, aspects, a theological one and a philosophical one, each presenting distinct, perhaps contradictory, logical requirements.[274] He claims that "Maimonides' presentation of the possible positions on creation and eternity . . . contain a contradiction"[275] that, although it is concealed, can be gleaned from the fact that he "lumps together" the Platonic and Aristotelian positions despite their lack of identity and, more significantly, despite fundamental differences between their theological implications. The alleged contradiction leads Davidson to the equivocal conclusion that either Maimonides secretly held the Platonic view that matter was coeternal with God or that he was "less immune to error and carelessness than he and his readers through the centuries have imagined."[276] In the light of either of Davidson's suggestions, it is necessary to reevaluate Maimonides' own statements since the clearer the determination of the position held by Maimonides concerning the origin of the universe will be, the clearer will be the understanding of its consequences for the relations between the supra- and sublunar realms and, hence, what can be said about providence.

In light of my earlier conclusion that Maimonides' critique of the early Mutakallimun is based upon the assumption that the defence of religion is successful only when it is informed by philosophy and is philosophically consistent, either alternative suggested by Davidson's claim can be established definitively only if Maimonides' presentation is demonstrated to be philosophically inconsistent. The only difference between the two possibilities would be whether the contradiction is deliberate or not.[277] Consequently, first, I shall examine the distinctions made by Davidson, purportedly following Maimonides, between the theological and philosophical domains, delineating both the theological and the philosophical implications of the respective opinions concerning the origin of the universe. Thereafter, I shall inquire into the implications of the Platonic position for each domain. For the sake of convenience, when outlining the argument, Davidson's, rather than Maimonides', order of exposition will be followed.

According to Davidson, the main theological implication of the biblical doctrine is that "[c]reation *ex nihilo* goes hand in hand with God's possessing free will."[278] In my opinion, the biblical doctrine (at least in its Maimonidean garb) comprises two major philosophical implications: (1) God's will is *absolutely* free, and (2) for Maimonides, the affirmation of creation *de novo* is the logical consequence of the affirmation of creation *ex nihilo* since time is an accident inhering in motion, itself an accident in that which is moved and hence requires a substratum that precedes it.[279] According to Maimonides, strictly speaking, the term *creation de novo* (understood as in time) is an affirmation of eternity because the assertion of a temporal beginning requires that time exist prior to the world or as the substratum of motion. The theological and philosophical implications of the Aristotelian position are identical. They consist of the affirmation of the eternity of the world and of a conception of a deity devoid of free will, because bound by necessity.[280] With respect to the Platonic position, Davidson correctly emphasizes that "the theological implications of the Platonic position are by no means identical with the theological implications of the Aristotelian position."[281] However, he concludes that the dissimilarity consists in the fact that creation, even from pre-existent matter, not only does not deny God's possession of a will, but in fact, that its meaning is identical with His being unbound by necessity.[282] Hence, Davidson further concludes that the only theological difference between the Platonic and biblical doctrines is the former's rejection of one specific miracle, namely, the creation of matter out of nothing. Davidson's primary emphasis upon the theological distinctions between the Platonic and Aristotelian positions results in an oversight of important philosophical similarities between the two positions. The similarities, which are not directly evident, represent logical consequences of the Platonic position incongruent with the biblical doctrine. In fact, I shall attempt to show later that this oversight leads him to the imprecise conclusion that affirming a divine will is identical with affirming that God is unbound by necessity.

The major contradiction discovered by Davidson in Maimonides' discussion of origin is between the assertion in *Guide*, 2. 13, that there is no difference between the Aristotelian and Platonic positions, and that in *Guide*, 2. 25, where Maimonides acknowledges that the theological implications of the Platonic doctrine are in harmony with biblical teachings. However, when a distinction is drawn between theological and philosophical implications and both kinds of implications are evaluated within their disciplinary context, this seeming contradiction can be eliminated or, at least, mitigated. After all, nowhere in the discussion of the three positions does Maimonides himself use either the term *theological* or the term *philosophical*.[283] Rather, he draws a distinction between the biblical position and a specific philosophical one—the Aristotelian—maintaining that the Platonic position should be included in the latter category.[284] Within both disciplines, Maimonides' grounds for verification are (1) that the arguments would not violate an understanding of God that affirms His unity, incorporeality, and absolute freedom of the will (with the term *will* understood as pure equivocation) and (2) that the explanation would conflict neither with the nature of what exists nor with principles of the Torah.

Maimonides outlines the difference between the Platonic position and the biblical one as follows: Whereas the Platonists assert that creation *ex nihilo* is an impossibility for God, the Torah does not. Notwithstanding, according to the philosophers, this impossibility does not constitute a limitation upon the divine will since it belongs to the class of rational impossibilities, which have a firmly established nature, are unchanged and unchanging, and require no act of an agent for their existence.[285]

Since eternal prime matter is a philosophical rather than a biblical category, its relation to biblical doctrine and the determination whether or not its affirmation places a limitation upon the divine will belong neither to biblical nor to theological discourse but rather to the philosophical since theological discourse, according to Maimonides, following the Islamic tradition, is dialectical rather than demonstrative and, hence, aims at producing immediate assent. The believing philosopher will investigate the claim of the philosophers (rather than assent to it) and ask the following question: If prime matter is coeternal with God and if it is a condition necessary for creation, then is it also a condition limiting the divine will? That is, does the affirmation of eternal prime matter constitute an empirical or a logical condition, a natural or rational one? Could it not be argued, despite the philosophers' claim that, with respect to creation, the rational impossibility posited by them has metaphysical, ontological, and ethical implications? In fact, is it not the case that coeternal prime matter, since it is the material principle of existence, constitutes a natural condition restricting divine operations in this world to a set of necessary, unchanging, natural laws that preclude not only all miracles but also divine providence and, consequently, render them a natural impossibility? Moreover, since it is the principle of change, and thus of corruption, would prime matter's relative independence of the divine will, however limited it might be, not render human matter, to some extent, independent of human form—the image of God and His likeness—granted to human beings by God so that form would subjugate matter and bring it to the best possible state?[286] Ultimately, the philosophical consequences of the affirmation of a coeternal prime matter may be more far-reaching than those of the Aristotelian position, although, extrinsically, the Platonic position does not conflict with the letter of the Bible. It seems to me that Maimonides could not have held secretly the Platonic position for both theological and philosophical reasons precisely because he held that theology, or Kalam *qua* science, must be informed by philosophy. Affirming the Platonic position, clearly, has no consequences for the vulgar. It has, however, important consequences for the philosopher, which will effect his apprehension of God. But, most important in the context of the *Guide*, it is its reader, the perplexed, for whom the Platonic position can undermine the foundations of the faith.

When we recall that what has been termed *theology* is the teachings of the Torah, then no contradiction is involved in Maimonides' two assertions. On the one hand, since neither the status of prime matter nor the distinction between rational and natural possibilities is mentioned in the Torah, Maimonides can maintain that the Platonic position does not undermine the foundations of the faith. On the other hand, upon philosophical examination, the Platonic position leads to the logical affirmation of eternity, although the Platonists were unaware of it. This lack of awareness manifests the philosophical flaws of Plato's method,[287] criticized by Maimonides in the letter to Samuel Ibn Tibbon, stating: "The writings of Aristotle's teacher Plato are in parables and hard to understand. One can dispense with them, for the writings of Aristotle suffice, and we need not occupy [our attention] with the writings of earlier [philosophers]."[288] Given that Plato wrote parables, properly speaking, he was not a philosopher in the strict sense in which Maimonides employs it.[289] However, the non-philosophical nature of Plato's writings neither indicates a judgment regarding their validity nor signifies anything about their content.

Consequently, Maimonides does not ignore what he understands to be the Platonic position, but rather addresses it when focusing upon generation and corruption. Nor is it surprising given his exact justification for the conjoined investigation of the Platonic and Aristotelian positions. He states: "[I]t is useless for us to wish to prove as true the assertion of the people holding the second opinion, I mean that according to which the heaven is subject to generation and passing away. For they believe in eternity; and there is, in our opinion, no difference between those who believe that the heaven must *of necessity* be generated *from a thing* and pass away *into a thing* or the belief of Aristotle who believed that it is not subject to generation and corruption."[290] If we examine Maimonides' presentation of the Platonic position carefully, two elements of it seem to be of significance to our inquiry, namely, the affirmation of necessity and the designation of eternal prime matter as a thing or 'creature'. Each of these aspects constitutes an essential part of Maimonides' disagreement with the philosophic tradition.

Before he discusses the nature of necessity and possibility, Maimonides points out repeatedly, and at length, that none of the questions pertaining to the origin of the universe can be resolved by means of demonstration. He also emphasizes that, unlike many lesser philosophers, Aristotle did not confuse the nature of his arguments with demonstrative reasoning and was fully aware of the disciplinary domains to which it was applicable.[291] Whereas arguments for necessity and possibility can be inferred about all things belonging to the realm of generation and corruption, they cannot be extended to a state preceding generation and corruption. The mistake of many philosophers and the Mutakallimun had been to infer what is possible about creation from the nature of what exists *in its formed and stable state*. The former have inferred necessity and eternity from the stability of what is, once it had been actualized and had become stable, whereas the latter have inferred the possibility of creation and hence, the fact of creation from it.[292] Maimonides denies the validity of both inferences precisely because "a being's state of perfection and completion furnishes no indication of the state of that being preceding its perfection."[293] Moreover, he maintains that, if one begins with the nature of what is, then Aristotle is correct in claiming that prime matter is subject to neither generation nor corruption. However, whereas for Aristotle the non-generated state of prime matter signifies eternity and necessity, for Maimonides it designates the possibility of bringing something into existence out of absolute non-existence, a possibility preceding generation and corruption and rendering it possible. He argues that his conclusion about the nature of inference can be derived from sensible experience, insofar as even in the realm of generation and corruption the perfected, or actualized, state of a thing does not provide the data required for inferring that thing's purely potential or privative state (of non-existence or *steresis*). He provides a lengthy example of a man who has reached a fully grown state who, for various reasons, had been brought up in isolation and had never observed the natural process from conception to full growth. He argues that when such a person is presented with an explanation of natural human generation, he finds it ludicrous or false.[294]

Thus, Maimonides is suggesting that, in natural science, the domain of demonstrative reason, the order of knowledge corresponds to the order of existence but is inverse to the order of being, or metaphysics. He is also suggesting that the less evident or familiar something is, the less it lends itself to discursive reason. The laws constituting the logic of possibility are an abstraction from the repetitive regularity in the order of existence, of which they are not the cause. That is, Maimonides is pointing out that human knowledge of the natural universe not only originates in sensible experience, but also is never independent of the imagination, and hence, the observed actualized event or existent does not furnish sufficient grounds for demonstration.[295] That is, since demonstration is based upon abstract universal concepts that are a product of reason and since the imagination is never independent of the particular impression together with its inherent accidents, true knowledge of a unique particular past event cannot be obtained either from its present actualized consequence or by means of the "laws"[296] derived from it.

Thus far, Maimonides' arguments do not seem to be incongruent with the Aristotelian tradition. Indeed, precisely because he follows Aristotle can Maimonides maintain simultaneously that Aristotle was fully aware of the non-demonstrative nature of his arguments and disagree with him on method-ological grounds, since arguments concerning the origin of the universe that begin with the present (temporal) order of existence are not verifiable.[297] Having cast doubt on the admissibility of Aristotle's use of inference, and thus suffi-ciently undermined his arguments, Maimonides turns to three arguments advanced by Aristotle's successors, who attempted to demonstrate the eter-nity of the universe "not by starting from the nature of being, but by starting from the judgments of the intellect with regard to the deity."[298] The three argu-ments are based upon a particular understanding of agency and conclude that the concept 'act of creation' conflicts with conclusions known about God. They maintain that (1) an agent must be an agent in potency before he is an agent in act and, hence, requires a prior cause; (2) an agent refrains from acting only when hindered, and acts are consequent upon changes in the will; and (3) a prior absence of the object for the sake of which an act is performed sig-nifies a lack of perfection in the agent. Maimonides' response to all three argu-ments can be reduced to one: They are all based upon an inadmissible analogy between the 'laws' governing the natural universe and 'laws' that can be inferred regarding divine acts.

Still, it is significant that Maimonides both accepts the basic premise of these arguments, that no conclusion is valid if it violates the proper under-standing of the deity, and maintains that the most adequate, perhaps the only, method to investigate the problem is by appeal to intellectual judgments about God, in particular, judgments about God as maker of the heaven. In addition, it is important to emphasize that he does not argue that God can act contrary to logical possibility. Maimonides' acceptance of these premises is not surprising given (1) that he held that knowledge about God is demon-strative, (2) that the divine act is entirely unlike other acts,[299] and (3) that, by *heaven*, he is referring to the separate intellects and like beings, all of which are not subject to generation and corruption. Consequently, Maimonides will attempt to argue for the possibility of creation on the basis of premises inde-pendent of sensible experience.[300]

To maintain that Maimonides extends the notion of possibility and admissibility beyond the range of human experience, in fact that he holds that experience does not constitute the grounds for acts of judgment concerning possibility does not entail a concomitant claim that he was a mystic.[301] Rather, this reading of Maimonides emphasizes that he was less an Aristotelian and more a Neoplatonist with respect to metaphysical knowledge, a fact clearly evident from his repeated dual claim that, whereas Aristotle's teachings are the most excellent with respect to all things below the sphere of the moon, human matters are incomparable to divine matters, the true reality of which is almost, if not entirely, beyond human knowledge.

As Fackenheim points out, Maimonides was able to discern an essential weakness in the philosophical arguments; namely, that the rational 'laws' of possibility deriving from the nature of existing things upon which the philosophers base their arguments "already presuppose the *absolute* metaphysical validity of the laws by which these things are governed."[302] Consequently, if philosophical validity must be based upon the actually existing universe, then "'*absolute* validity', 'necessary emanation', and 'free creation', are questions exceeding the grasp of philosophical proof."[303] Moreover, since the philosophers do not deny the metaphysical priority of God, the later Aristotelians in fact postulating it as the ultimate criterion for validation, and since the philosophers postulate that God is the origin of all actual existence, inasmuch as all admit that they derive the 'laws' or rules of logic from the present state of the actually existing universe, they can neither prove the validity of their arguments nor disprove those of Maimonides.

Even though Maimonides seems to equivocate, or even contradict himself (some would argue intentionally) in the various chapters dealing with possibility, I do not think that he is doing either when stating simultaneously that God cannot act contrary to the rules of logical possibility and that he can bring something into existence out of absolute non-existence; nor is he falling into the errors of the Mutakallimun. Rather, he is maintaining that, in the light of the nature of what now exists, provided that God does not alter it, he cannot act contrary to the rules of logic pertaining to it. Likewise, prior to creation and to the fully developed actualized state of the universe, the rules of logical possibility did not exist. Whether God be the prime mover of the philosophers or the Creator, He is the Cause of changes from potentiality to actuality; He is also the Cause of possibility and, hence, 'the possible' could not have determined His 'actions' in any sense. Basing his opposition to the philosophers upon philosophical grounds, Maimonides can posit biblical teachings on creation as an alternative postulate to be investigated.

Thus far, Maimonides' argument constitutes a response to the position professed by Aristotle and his followers. However, it does not constitute an adequate, or sufficient, response to the Platonists, especially since their position does not seem to deny creation nor, according to Davidson, does their position deny that God possesses a will and, hence, does not preclude all possibilities other than creation out of absolute non-being. In fact, as already alluded to, creation out of absolute non-being is, in my opinion, a central issue both in Maimonides' discussion of the origin of the universe and in some Maimonidean scholarship. It can be argued that, in addition to the seeming harmony between the Platonic doctrine and the letter of the Torah, accepting the existence of eternal prime matter would resolve the major philosophical difficulty of positing God as the cause of corporeal existence. Nevertheless, in my opinion Maimonides could not have accepted the eternal existence of any principle other than God because it would have violated one of his intellectual judgments about God—the most fundamental principle of validation posited by him—namely, the *absolute* freedom of God's will or act.

Recently, Ivry has proposed an interesting and novel interpretation of the old problem of creation *ex nihilo* on the basis of both philosophical and philological arguments. After he emphasizes the important distinction between absolute and relative privation,[304] the latter state designating the instant *after* the appearance of prime matter and form and thus the possibility of all substantial existence, and after he points out that Maimonides' various discussions of creation and emanation emphasize the second instant of creation rather than the first, Ivry attempts to demonstrate that absolute privation "possesses a certain ontic meaning, and serves as the passive cause for that which subsequently emerges as matter, in all its stages."[305]

Although Ivry admits that we must exercise great caution in attempting to describe this concept, he insists that Maimonides understood it to be something actual rather than absolute nothing; or that "he designates an actual, subsistent situation of non-existence . . . an actual space."[306] Ivry believes that this interpretation serves as a solution to the logical impossibility of bringing something into existence out of absolute non-existence. Although the suggestion is tempting, because philosophically respectable insofar as the claim initially seems to affirm only the pre-existence *a parte ante* of *steresis*, the insistence that *nihil* is a certain "ontic," "subsistent" "actuality" still conflicts with Maimonides' "*absolute* privation." I do not believe that either Maimonides or the interpreter must replace one incomprehensible concept, creation out of nothing, with another, the intelligibility of a certain ontic subsistent actuality of nothing—in a sense other than relative privation—to resolve the philosophical difficulty. Nor do I consider Ivry's solution compelling, despite its philosophical ingenuity.[307] Whether or not we draw a distinction between 'after privation' and 'from non-existence' does not alter the fact that Maimonides is attempting to explain a unique event for which no given term is either adequate or precise. More precisely, *after privation* is philosophically inaccurate since privation is always relative. Given that the preposition *after* (*ba'd*) does not refer to time, but rather to order, given that the preposition *from* is equally imprecise, and given that both expressions clearly designate an ontological change, one that makes possible any kind of ontic actuality, the distinction between them does not seem to render the event more intelligible. Rather, it seems to me that by *absolute privation* Maimonides designates the single, simple, and unique existence of God alone.

Maimonides first mentions the creation of prime matter in *Guide*, 1. 28, when he explains the true meaning of biblical terms referring to divine limbs appearing in the account of the apprehension of Moses, Aaron, and the elders of Israel. He states,

> For what they apprehended was the true reality of prime matter, which derives from Him, may He be exalted, He being the cause of its existence. . . .
>
> Accordingly their apprehension had as its object the [prime] matter and the relation of the latter to God, inasmuch as it is the first among the things He has created that necessitates generation and corruption; and God is its creator ex nihilo.[308]

Although these statements do not constitute an explanation of prime matter, nevertheless, Maimonides' assumptions are quite clear and can help elucidate additional discussions of prime matter elsewhere in the *Guide*. The postulates affirmed in this context are (1) prime matter derives from God, who is the cause of its existence; and (2) it is the first created thing in the order of generation and corruption. In conjunction with latter statements maintaining that prime matter itself is neither generated nor corrupted, it is clear that it is one of the essential conditions for generation and corruption, *steresis, dunamis,* or natural possibility and impossibility, and thus, also, it is a condition for our derivation of the logical laws of possibility.[309] Thus, given that Maimonides' affirmation of the created nature of prime matter seems to be beyond dispute, his denial of the validity of what he takes to be the Platonic position seems to be established. In addition, the statement claiming that prime matter is *derived* from God seems to undermine the possibility of interpreting the nature of the condition obtaining prior to its creation as one either requiring or necessitating the affirmation of real, subsistent "nothing" or "ontic actuality," except for the prior reality of God.[310] In fact, in my opinion, Maimonides denies such a possibility for reasons similar to his denial of the validity of both the Platonic and the Aristotelian positions: (1) that no valid inference can be made about the unique and singular originary state from the many possibilities to which it gave rise[311] and (2) that the affirmation of the eternal pre-existence of anything whatsoever, be it understood as an ontic state, "real subsistence" or a thing, circumscribes the divine will to some extent.

Since Maimonides' specific linguistic formulations about any single topic are inconsistent and have given rise to diametrically opposed interpretations, it does not seem to be possible, nor productive, to base arguments upon them. Consequently, I shall attempt to set forth an alternative, tentative solution to the problem that is consistent with one of the hermeneutic principles outlined in Chapter 1; namely, that unless the reader is willing to grant that the author—in this case, the *teacher*—not only wished to communicate something true, but also wished that this knowledge be accessible to those who truly desire it, he would neither be able to understand the text nor to withhold judgment based upon principles entirely extrinsic to the arguments.

If we grant that Maimonides' affirmations reflect his true belief, we have to accept the related intelligibility of the following: (1) prime matter derives from God alone, (2) creation is a unique act that is entirely dissimilar to any other activity, such as, making or producing, (3) prime matter is not subject to generation and corruption and, hence, it is primarily a metaphysical and ontological principle and only secondarily a physical one.

In *Guide*, 2. 17, Maimonides repeatedly affirms that prime matter had been brought into existence out of nothing in a unique manner, rendering it entirely dissimilar to any entity in the realm of generation and corruption. Once created and stabilized, it is one of the permanent conditions for composition, potentiality, actuality, in fact for the existence of all composite entities. Like time and motion, prime matter is everlasting, the single possibility for its destruction being divine choice. Despite his repetitive references to it, Maimonides says little else about prime matter, except that "it does not exist devoid of form."[312] No doubt, it is both difficult to conceptualize anything that is simultaneously everlasting and non-existent. Notwithstanding, I think that Maimonides is attempting to formulate a distinction between non-being proper and non-existence entirely different from that found in any unactualized formed matter in the first instant of its composition. The difference consists in the fact that, in its first instant of existence, formed matter, or natural substance, is in a state of non-existence that is already determined toward something. That is, whereas formed matter is a privation of existence with respect to its individual form and accidents proper to it—a *dunamis* of some form or kind—prime matter is not a privation of any specific thing, precisely because it is undetermined. Whereas privation is with respect to something, prime matter is not. Properly speaking, neither prime matter nor form are existents, but rather each has an essence proper to it that in their conjunction renders existence possible. The difficulty in understanding and speaking of prime matter arises from the impossibility of predicating anything, even 'thingness', of any unformed 'thing', since it is not a thing. In the final analysis, apart from the arbitrary, hence tautological, term *prime matter*, all that can be said about prime matter is by way of negating every predication. In my opinion, it is prime matter to which we could apply Ivry's attempt to explain that state prior to creation to which he refers as a certain real condition.

I wish to point out that I doubt whether I would have been able to reach all the preceding conclusions about this elusive (and philosophically paradoxical) condition without insights from reading Aquinas, as will become evident in the following section. Yet, I consider the explanation neither implausible nor a violation of Maimonides' account. On the contrary, in my opinion, in order to read the *Guide* not only as a coherent text but also as a cohesive one, it is necessary that no principle be posited as coeternal with God, since it would limit the divine will and the nature of design, thus introducing external (i.e., logical or natural) necessity into the divine will. In addition, given that privation inheres in natural substance on account of matter, and given that in the sublunar realm matter is understood as cause for, at the very least, the possibility of evil, the coeternity of prime matter would undermine the possibility of human perfection, especially moral perfection, rendering divine revelation, and hence divine action, vain.

Aquinas' Arguments for Creation

As noted earlier, there are substantial dissimilarities between Maimonides' and Aquinas' procedures and focal points in their respective treatments of the question of the origin of the universe that have shaped the nature of the scholarship about their thought. The difficulties facing Aquinas' student result from the multiplicity of very distinct texts, each written for a specific purpose and a distinct audience, thus giving rise to differences that simultaneously complement understanding and complicate it.[313] Moreover, since some of Aquinas' commentaries on Aristotle touch upon issues central to the question, a decision has to be made whether or not to take them into consideration. Despite the centrality of the commentaries on Aristotle, however, the following analysis will not use them, since on the question of the origin of the universe, as on other controverted issues, to avoid doing violence to his text, Aquinas refrained from importing into his exposition certain aspects central to his own understanding, but foreign to Aristotle's. Consequently, the positions presented below as Plato's and Aristotle's will outline only those formulated by Aquinas where he did not consider criticism of a given argument to conflict with the *intentio auctoris*.

As in the case of most questions, one of the clearest and most succinct formulations of the question of the origin of the universe can be found in the *Summa* and, hence, it can serve as the springboard for analysis. In the *Summa*, Aquinas devotes three questions, Iᵃ Pars, Qs. 44-47, to the question of creation. The first, treats the procession of creatures from God;[314] the second, their emanation *or* creation; the third, their principle of duration. First, Aquinas asks whether it is necessary that all beings should be created by God and answers that it is, basing his argument upon the known distinction between essence and existence. He argues that, since all beings other than God are not self-subsisting, it is necessary that they receive their substantial existence through participation in the divine essence, their diversity manifesting the degree of their participation in it. The response also traces the origins of this argument back to both Plato and Aristotle, the former positing unity as the necessary ontological antecedent to multiplicity, the latter arguing that every categorical predication requires a supreme (ontological) standard as its cause. Based upon the five ways proving the existence of God demonstrated in a previous question (Q. 2), Aquinas repeats briefly that God is both the exemplar and the final cause of all created things. He argues further that, since the perfection of the universe requires individuation, it is necessary that prime matter be created by God because, together with form, it is a determining principle of certain modes of existence and, hence, is prior to these modes.[315]

Although the three articles constituting question 44 are rather brief, they are highly informative, especially since they indicate both the unique nature of Aquinas' 'Neoplatonic' metaphysics and his departure from both Plato and Aristotle. As Pegis has argued, Aquinas was able to criticize and defend Plato and Aristotle simultaneously, accepting principles from their doctrines, the full import of which, in his view, they were unaware. Aquinas was able to appreciate that "[t]o have made God one and the measure of reality was to have laid the foundation for discovering His universal causality."[316] That is, Aquinas was able to appreciate Plato's and Aristotle's contribution to his own philosophical development of a doctrine differing from theirs in some essential aspects. Thus, when affirming that prime matter was created by God he also maintains that Plato and Aristotle were able to perceive the necessity to postulate universal causality as an explanation of change.

Even though, throughout question 44, Aquinas seems to use the verbs *to create* and *to cause* indiscriminately, by positing God simultaneously as the exemplary determining cause of every being and as their final cause, the good toward which all strive, he succeeds in establishing a relation between the universe and God that is entirely unlike the necessary relation between cause and effect. Unlike effects, the consequent existence of which is independent of their causes, created causes—creatures—depend upon and are related to their cause in every aspect of their existence.

When he turns his attention to the question of *ex nihilo* in the following question, Aquinas also turns from considerations of the nature of causality to an examination of the manner in which things proceed from God as their first principle. The change in focus is not surprising if we recall that the *Summa*, like the *Guide*, embodies a pedagogy. Consequently, a consideration of particulars must precede the examination of the universal. Creation *ex nihilo*, according to Aquinas, is nothing other than the emanation of the whole of being from the universal cause. Unlike the emanation of particular beings, which can proceed into a particular, determinate state of being only from a prior state of determinate and particular non-being, the emanation of the whole of universal being from a first principle could not possibly require a prior particularized being, since the creative emanation is the first instant of particularization from the essence of the first universal principle. The difference between particular generation and emanation is exemplified simply "just as the generation of man is from a non-being which is a non-man, so creation, which is the emanation of the whole of being, is from non-being which is nothing."[317] Moreover, creation provides the possibility for subsequent acts of further determinations both from principles of substantial existence and from already determined entities. The designation of acts that produce a change from one particularized state into another as acts of creation manifests the scope of the linguistic analogies employed. Only the divine act of creation brought the universe forth out of nothing, with the concomitant term *out of nothing* (*ex nihilo*) meaning precisely no being (*nullum ens*) as a contradictory rather than a contrary.

The understanding of Aquinas' affirmation of *ex nihilo* poses fewer difficulties than does that of Maimonides' since his explication in the *Summa* is both clear and brief. The objection to the possibility of bringing something into existence out of nothing is meaningful only in the realm of generation and corruption, where a substratum is required for a change from one form into another, or between contraries. On the other hand, since creation is the emanation of the whole of being from God and since there can be nothing in being that is not from God, only God is necessary for creation. *Ex nihilo*, thus, signifies precisely God alone and nothing but God.[318]

Most of Aquinas' arguments for creation *ex nihilo* embody either an implicit or an explicit criticism of most objections brought forth against the biblical position; namely, that they are based upon an inadequate analogy between sensible acts and a unique singular act. Although his arguments are posited in response to known objections and although his methods are distinctly different, Aquinas' criticisms are essentially identical to Maimonides' arguments against inferences drawn from the observed state of the actually existing world to the unique act that made it possible. Thus, Aquinas argues that a change of state (*mutatio*) does not pertain to the act of creation but is only a distinction required for understanding, since a change of this kind presupposes particularized substance, time, and motion, all of which are a consequence of creation. Creation, on the other hand, is an act initiating a unique relation between God and creatures that does not signify any change in God because it is motionless, but rather relates the creature to the principle of its existence. As a unique act that neither requires nor produces change, properly speaking, it belongs to God alone and thus, no other being can be said to create. Again, the unique act of creation differs from every other act insofar as it produces not only existence, but also the principles of subsistent existence; that is, it produces the forms, the matter, and hence, the possibility, for all the accidents required for subsistence and actualization. In the context of establishing the scope of creation, Aquinas draws an important distinction between creation and con-creation, the former designating the origin of subsistent being, the latter, the origin of its principles that are co-existents, rather than beings.[319] The importance of this distinction will emerge in the consideration of prime matter.

Prior to an exposition of Aquinas' response to those who affirm the eternity of the world, it is important to raise the question whether Aquinas maintained that creation *ex nihilo* can be demonstrated since it has been maintained often that he had.[320] Presumably, one reason why this conclusion had been reached is Aquinas' 'silence' about the logical status of his arguments in questions 44-45. However, in question 46 he states clearly that neither the eternity nor the temporal beginning of the world is demonstrable. Moreover, whereas in questions 44-45 Aquinas either refrains from addressing the status of an opposing argument or simply claims that it is false, in question 46, he repeats Maimonides' assertion that Aristotle's arguments were not demonstrative. Consequently, since Aquinas never claims that creation *ex nihilo* is demonstrable and since he argues for the uniqueness of the act of creation, I think that the claim for the demonstrability of creation *ex nihilo* remains untenable.

The attempt to argue that the analogy between the act of creation and that of artistic production qualifies as demonstration not only ignores Aquinas' emphasis upon the unique nature of creation but also overlooks the great dissimilarity between physical and metaphysical substrata—let alone the state where substrata are absent. But, even if we restrict our objection to the distinction between physical and metaphysical principles, it is evident that whereas the former are known only as subsistent and subject to change, irrespective of secondary agents, the latter are neither subsistent nor subject to change. Moreover, as Jordan argues,[321] even in a discourse about physics, it is an error either to conflate the modes of knowing with the modes of being or to assume that any, or all, given significations both encompass and exhaust knowledge of an object. A proper understanding of the nature of discourse in philosophical physics ultimately leads beyond discourse and hence, beyond demonstration in physics. It is important to note, however, that this does not indicate a necessary limitation of the science of physics, but rather delineates its boundaries and emphasizes the interrelatedness of the sciences. If Jordan is correct about the nature of Aquinas' method, which I think he is, then no demonstration can be had of metaphysical principles that are distinctly different from the physical, precisely because they are their principles and, thus, also the principles both of human existence and of intelligibility.[322]

After he enumerates ten positions affirming the eternity of the world, Aquinas argues that, irrespective of them, it is possible to posit a beginning to the world.[323] His argument, like Maimonides', is based upon the nature of possibility and necessity. Necessity, he maintains, can be affirmed in one of two ways, namely, from the nature of the cause or from the existence of the effect. The first is absolute, the second relative. From an absolute perspective, only if the effect can be demonstrated as a necessary consequence of the cause would the effect be necessary. Thus, since it is not necessary that God will anything other than Himself, the existence of the world is not necessary. From a relative perspective, however, it can be said that since God is eternal and since he has willed the existence of the world, the world is eternal as a consequence. Aristotle's arguments, he explains, were *secundum quid*, as responses to the mistaken reasonings of Anaxagoras, Empedocles, Plato, and others whose methods are similar to theirs. Not only was Aristotle's concern limited to establishing the probable, rather than demonstrative, nature of earlier methods, but also, according to Aquinas, in the *Topics* 1,[324] Aristotle explained that the only method possible for inquiry concerning the question is dialectical. Having established the non-demonstrative nature of the question, Aquinas openly admits that the creation of the world, just like the mystery of the Trinity, is an article of faith rather than a principle of reason.[325]

In response to the objections raised against the possibility of creation, Aquinas either uses Aristotle's previous arguments against similar objections or insists that they are based upon the misapplied inference from the state of an already existing world to a previous, entirely different state. Reason can proceed only from a given principle or fact, "it abstracts from the here and now; wherefore, it is said that "universals are everywhere and always.""[326] Conversely, it is not possible to demonstrate that any existing thing is *not* eternal. Just as it is not possible to argue for or against creation from the 'here and now', so it is not possible for reason to inquire into the divine will, except with respect to absolutely necessary things, unrelated to any created being.[327] Aquinas' argument for the indemonstrability of the origin of the universe, in fact, goes beyond Maimonides'. Whereas Maimonides restricts his arguments to demonstrative reason, Aquinas states that, although it is *believable* that the world had a beginning, it is neither demonstrable, nor *knowable*.[328] Thus, unlike Maimonides, he either does not consider his arguments more compelling than Aristotle's or does not grant dialectical arguments any cognitive status, at least in the context of the debate with Aristotle.

The recognition of the indemonstrable nature of the question is important for Aquinas not simply for pedagogical purposes; more significantly, it is essential for the defence of the faith. He warns that the presumptuous attempt by believers to find demonstrations for creation can provide only grounds for ridicule by unbelievers, so that discussions and arguments of more competent religious philosophers who understand the nature of demonstration will be ignored.[329] Only after he has examined the scope of the question and has established the difference between an article of faith and a principle of demonstration, does Aquinas affirm creation by reference both to Scripture and to the tradition, stating that the term *beginning* does not signify a previous time in Genesis. Rather, according to Aquinas, in the beginning of the order of the universe, God created four things simultaneously, "namely, the empyrean heaven, corporeal matter, which is what is understood by the term earth, time, and the angelic nature."[330]

If the presentation in the *Summa* is characterized by its brevity, the *De Potentia*[331] carefully examines every possible detail of, and objection to, the question of "beginning," irrespective of its importance. But, precisely for this reason, it can supplement the discussion in the *Summa*. Although the text brings no new issues into the discussion,[332] certain elements, such as, time, unity, and multiplicity, are developed in greater detail. In fact, the centrality of the one universal principle of the existence of multiplicity for Aquinas' thought emerges very clearly from question 3 of the text.

One of the most striking elements of Aquinas' examination of the diverse aspects comprising the question of the origin of the universe is his repeated emphasis upon the difference between secondary and natural causality, on the one hand, and divine causality, on the other. Not only is the discussion reminiscent of Maimonides', to whom he refers a number of times, it also constitutes both an implicit and an explicit critique of most of the preceding philosophical attempts to address the question. In a number of articles, Aquinas emphasizes that secondary causality is meaningful or efficacious only insofar as it is influenced by divine causality. Secondary causes can be said to produce existence only to that extent to which they participate in the divine power. The beings that are in act and have no potency in them are not pure act and, hence, they cannot determine the modes of being of those things to which they give existence.[333] Paradoxically, it is precisely because the universal cause produces the whole of subsistent being in one unique act, that creatures are existentially related to God through participation and cannot possess knowledge of the nature of the very act that relates them to it by means of the natural powers given to them through this act. Therefore, they cannot understand the nature of the emanation of multiplicity out of unity.

Unlike many philosophers, who concluded from the natural order that unity cannot give rise to multiplicity and hence posited a necessary progressive procession of beings from the one through the mediation of inferior beings, having established that the natural order does not provide any cognitive data with respect to the question of origin, Aquinas can both conclude that it fails to provide "adequate" knowledge pertaining to the relation between the one and the many and posit a contrary hypothesis that "Things proceed from God through the mode of knowledge and intellect, according to which <mode> nothing prohibits that multiplicity issue from the one, first, and simple God immediately, according as his wisdom contains all things."[334] According to Aquinas, both Plato and Aristotle recognized that there must be one universal cause of all things. With respect to the relation between God and the universe, the *De Potentia* does not add to the *Summa*'s account of Aristotle. It does add an important dimension to the account of the Platonic doctrine of unity, attributing to Plato a great appreciation of the existential role of unity. According to Aquinas, in attempting to account for the existence of common properties in diverse things, Plato concluded that in addition to numerical unity, there must also be actual unity preceding multiplicity, since multiplicity itself cannot account for what is common. Thus, although Aquinas' Plato may not have appreciated the full implications of the immanent aspect of seeking out unity in things themselves, he comes quite close to establishing a real relation between God and the world that extends to the whole of being.[335]

When he examines what can be either demonstrated or affirmed as a possibility or an impossibility about creation in *De Potentia*, Aquinas juxtaposes the Catholic and philosophical tradition in a more radical manner than is evident in other questions. The argument is highly reminiscent of the discussion of possibility in the *Summa*. Whereas elsewhere he undermines the assertions of the philosophers on the basis of logical arguments, here he does not *seem* to extend the applicability of these arguments to the nature of possibility. Quoting Aristotle's *Metaphysics*, he states that something can be understood as possible either in relation to a potency, be it passive or active, metaphorically, or absolutely. Passive potency and metaphorical signification are the equivalents of arguments from effects, whereas active potency and absolute designation equal arguments from causes. Thus, the former arguments belong to the class of natural possibilities, the later, to rational possibilities.[336] Given that knowledge that God exists, at least as the first cause, is a philosophical or rational conclusion and that this knowledge determines that there can be no deficiency in the active power of God, it is a rational possibility for God to have created another essence—thus diversity— from eternity. Consequently, the denial of such a possibility is an article of faith, according to Aquinas, and cannot refer to the active power or pure actuality (*esse tantum*) of God; rather, it is a statement about the passive potency of created things (*esse commune*). The argument put forth in support of this statement by religious thinkers maintains that anything for which existence is at some time possible and at some time impossible is not possible of permanent existence. On the other hand, Aquinas argues that no rational impossibility is involved in affirming that God has produced a diversity of distinct essences from eternity. The eternal production of diversity, which can be rationally affirmed, must be restricted, however, to beings not subject to change since the mutable cannot be eternal or lack the permanent actuality that precedes genesis.

Despite the seeming equivocation involved in affirming temporal creation simultaneously with the denial that eternal 'creation' is impossible, Aquinas is not thereby setting up an opposition between philosophy and revelation. On the contrary, his critique of both the philosophers and some religious thinkers, like that of Maimonides, is based upon the principle restricting the applicability of the rules of reason. Argument from the effects apply only to the created universe as it is, since these arguments are based upon laws derived from the effects themselves and, thus, from the already existing universe. As argued earlier in the context of Maimonides' critique of both the Mutakallimun and the philosophers, those inferring the origin of the universe from its present state fail to recognize that, by basing their arguments upon the laws of possibility that derive from the nature of these effects, they implicitly grant the absolute metaphysical validity of these laws. In other words, all arguments from the effects entail the priority and primacy of their cause(s) but are incapable of saying anything essential about the nature of the cause(s). Thus, both the philosophers and the Mutakallimun implicitly place the question of absolute metaphysical validity beyond the domain of rational demonstration so that they can neither prove the validity of their principles nor disprove or buttress the doctrinal position. Like Maimonides, Aquinas will not only grant but also insist that, once the world has been created, its Creator cannot act contrary to the rules of possibility (natural or rational), provided that He would not choose to change the nature of what exists. This stipulation, however, neither affects the divine will nor limits the possibility of miracles since God had willed that it be so.[337]

Having limited radically the boundaries of logic, Aquinas, following Maimonides and quoting him, turns to the question of the eternity of the world. Once the philosophical weakness of positions denying creation has been exposed, Aquinas changes the entire tone of its affirmation. Whereas in earlier arguments he maintained only that demonstration cannot prove either position, here he states that "it ought to be held firmly that the world had not always existed, just as the catholic faith teaches. Nor can this be repudiated effectively by any demonstration from physics."[338] The entire response is based upon the previous claim that no argument based upon sublunar causality can address the question properly since the production of the whole of being is entirely unlike the production of particular beings. The same argument is brought forth against the Aristotelian position and against later Peripatetics.[339] Moreover, no reason can be given concerning the first determinations of the universe, except to state that the divine will and wisdom had determined that it be so. Aquinas adds that the dependence of the entire universe upon the divine will and providence is the reason why Maimonides pointed out that Scripture directs us to contemplation of the heavens.

Apart from stating that at the first instant of creation four things were created—namely, the heavens, the earth, time, and motion—and explaining that time could not have existed prior to creation, even if the imagination can conceive the existence of an eternal common time, Aquinas does not elaborate upon the meaning of these created 'things' in question 3 of the *De potentia*. Likewise, the text does not provide any explanation of the statement in the *Summa* that matter and form are co-existent principles, rather than entities, apart from repeating the affirmation that God is the sole eternal being and the only principle of all that exists, evil being merely a privation of existence. Consequently, in order to understand the significance of these metaphysical principles and their implications for sublunar existence we must look else-where. Two texts where Aquinas discusses matter and form *qua* metaphysical and ontological principles are his commentary on Dionysius' *De Divinis Nominibus* and *De Principiis Naturae.*[340] In the former text, Aquinas exam-ines prime matter as one of the principles pertinent to understanding God as the good, which is the common principle of all creation, whereas, in the latter, he discusses it as one of the principles requisite for generation and corruption.

In *De Divinis Nominibus* Aquinas is attempting to dissociate the material principle of existence from evil and to relate it to the good since it is one of the principles necessary for, *inter alia*, the actualization of rational souls. In fact, he maintains that, in order to understand the procession of creatures from God as the good, we must begin with matter. Although Aquinas is in general agreement with some principles of Platonic (*Platonici*) metaphysics, he criticizes the understanding of matter as privation and non-being. Nevertheless, although criticizing the Platonic position, he also underlines its strength, upon which he constructs his own metaphysics. He argues:

> The causality of being does not extend except to beings. Thus therefore, according to them, the causality of being did not extend to prime matter to which, nevertheless, the causality of the good extends. The indica-tion of this is that it desires the good above all. Moreover it is character-istic of an effect that it be turned towards its cause through desire. Thus therefore, the good is a more universal and higher cause than being, since its causality extends to more things.[341]

Upon reading *De Divinis Nominibus*, Aquinas approbation of Plato's under-standing of the origin of the universe becomes clear since the recognition that the good is a more universal cause than being makes it possible to encompass within it all the principles of existence. Moreover, as the exemplar and final cause of the universe, it is both the end sought by all things and the perfection that can render them similar to itself. Consequently, it is necessary that God be the cause of prime matter since it is "the first subject among the effects" and, hence, "should be the effect of the first cause alone, which is good, while the causality of secondary causes does not reach as far as this."[342] That is, the entire chain of sublunar, secondary, or natural causality depends upon prime matter, the principle of its operations, for its actualization.

De Divinis Nominibus provides the best example of Aquinas' synthesis of (Neo)Platonic and Aristotelian principles, essential elements of which are brought together to form his own metaphysics. He rejects the Platonic interpretation of matter as "non-being because joined to privation"[343] in favor of an Aristotelian explanation, distinguishing matter from privation, and posits the latter as joined to matter *per accidens*. He then adds that, like all caused things that are turned to their cause through desire, prime matter's desire for the good as its cause "seems to be nothing other than privation and its ordering to actuality."[344] In Aquinas' unique metaphysics the act of creation must be understood, first and foremost, as the manifestation of the good since God, as the good, is inseparable from His act, the effects of which can be nothing other than good. Consequently, not only must prime matter be distinct from privation, but also it must have a positive, or real, function in the order of being, rather than merely a logical one. The distinction drawn between prime matter as *non est* (or the contrary of actuality) and *non ens* (or the contradictory of actuality) both recalls Aquinas discussion of principles as co-existents and explains the shortcomings not only of Plato's, but also of Aristotle's metaphysics. For if the good is the primary and more common principle of all creation and if its extension is greater than that of being, then an Aristotelian metaphysics of being cannot account fully for the whole of being.[345]

A clear distinction between matter and privation remains to be given. At the outset of *De Principiis Naturae*, Aquinas outlines a difference between prime matter and the subject in which privation inheres, designating the former as "that which is in potency to substantial existence," the latter as "that which is in potency to accidental existence."[346] The basic distinction is developed further in the subsequent explanation of the principles of generation and nature. According to Aquinas, generation denotes the change from that specific state of nonbeing which is a being in potency rather than an absolute absence of being. Generation is a process requiring three principles, "namely, being in potency, which is matter; and nonexistence in act, which is privation; and that through which it comes to be in act, which is form. . . . Therefore, there are three principles of nature, namely matter and form and privation; one of which, namely form, is that for which generation exists; the other two exist from that quality of it according to which it is generation. Whence matter and privation are the same in the subject, but differ in reason."[347]

Although privation is an accidental principle, nevertheless, it is a necessary one, given the receptive nature of matter. Rather than manifesting the negation of form, it denotes its absence where it should or could be present. Since it is by means of matter that both form and privation are known, the latter manifesting the absence of a due form in a subsisting subject, matter differs, in reason, from both privation and form. In fact, the three concepts can be understood as distinct principles precisely and only because they differ in reason. Matter, like form and unlike privation, is absolutely and always necessary for existence, whereas privation is a necessary accident for the particular existence of this or that thing; matter and form endure in generation and corruption, privation does not.[348]

Since, according to Aquinas, matter endures in generation, but privation does not, he also maintains that whereas matter and form are principles both in existence (*in esse*) and in becoming (*in fieri*), privation is a principle only in becoming. The matter that endures despite all changes is prime matter, the form is a universal. Prime matter and form are the universal, intrinsic causes of natural substances in which particular privations can inhere as extrinsic causes through accidents; the former are principles, or causes, *per se*, the latter are principle, or causes, *per accidens*. The Good is the unmediated, efficient cause of both prime matter and form, the composition of which is natural being (*ens*) and which, in turn, in composition with privation make existence (*esse*) in act possible. Properly speaking, neither matter nor form is being (*ens*); rather, they have being. Following their composition into a determinate substantial being, privation can inhere in the subject. Thus understood, prime matter's desire for the good is one of the necessary conditions for the perfection of the natural universe, and as a principle, it is distinct from that principle which can inhibit it in the particular case; that is, privation.

Whereas for Aristotle the desire for the good has a very limited function in the universal order,[349] for both the Platonists and Aquinas the desire for God, primarily as the good, is the *ratio* of universal order. For Aquinas, this desire is for the unifying principle into which all things return to the extent that they desire Him as an active principle, a conserving one, and an end. Departing from both Aristotle and Plato, Aquinas maintains that, rather than designating non-being, the seeming privation associated with prime matter is its desire for perfect being or for its own actualization. In addition, Aquinas disengages prime matter from its association with evil, on the one hand, and, on the other, attributes to it a real function in the order of existence, beyond the epistemological. For Aquinas, prime matter is one of the necessary causes for the actual perfection of all created beings; privation is the cause that hinders or may hinder this perfection.

Notwithstanding the differences between the formal aspects or procedures of their respective explanations, Maimonides and Aquinas are agreed upon the most essential aspects of the question of the origin of the universe, as well as the upon the consequences of the different positions outlined above. The main differences between them seem to be the relative weight they give to each of the subjects examined. Maimonides pays greater attention to undermining the arguments of both the Mutakallimun and the philosophers, whereas Aquinas is more concerned to develop a consistent metaphysics of the good. Although some of these differences can be explained by the different intellectual milieux in which they lived and wrote, others may be evidence of conceptual incongruities. As will become evident in the following chapters, I believe that there are some essential differences between Maimonides and Aquinas, especially with respect to the universality of moral perfection.

4

MATTER, PRIVATION, AND EVIL

Introduction

It is a commonplace for scholarship on ancient and medieval thought to mention a certain, but varied, degree of immanent tension between the material and immaterial aspects or ends of human existence and also to characterize the medieval philosophical tradition as homogeneously affirming a direct relation between matter and evil. Material human existence, thus, is the source of the tension. Yet, very few studies examine the alleged relation between matter and evil in detail, and fewer still attempt to explain either the attribution of a qualification originating in practical reason, namely, evil, to an ontological principle or the relation between evil as an ontological principle and as a moral principle. To my knowledge, no study views this relation as paradoxical in the context of an Aristotelian noetics or epistemic psychology that is concurrent with revealed cosmogony.

For both Maimonides and Aquinas, however, the attempt to establish a harmony between reason and revelation necessarily entails a thorough examination of the relation between the material and immaterial dimensions of human existence and of problems consequent upon positing an essential relation between matter and evil, on the one hand, and asserting, on the other, that God is the creator of matter. In addition to the imminent danger of (mis)understanding the perfect God to be the ultimate cause of evil, the affirmation of a necessary relation between matter and evil raises problems not only regarding the possible attainment of human perfection, but also regarding the nature, even the intelligibility, of sublunar existence, let alone providence. For the religious philosopher wishing to harmonize the God of revelation with the God of the philosophers must explain philosophically not only how the perfect incorporeal first cause can be the cause of the material principle of existence, but also how that God can be understood as personally provident over the sublunar realm of generation and corruption and, thus, the cause of the lack of perfection in it.

The least ambiguous or most direct cosmological doctrine conjoining ontological and ethical principles originates with Plotinus, for whom, as Rist points out, the "scale of existence" and the "scale of value . . . are different ways of looking at the same metaphysical facts, for metaphysics in the *Enneads* is, strictly speaking, an *indivisible* synthesis of ontology and ethics."[350] For Plotinus, the radical indeterminacy and "impotent potency" of prime matter render it a real source of evil. Thus, by endowing matter with a real ontological status, even though negative, and by seemingly overcoming the Aristotelian dichotomy between ontology and ethics,[351] Plotinus introduces an independent principle of evil into the realm of corporeal existence.

In light of the general 'Neoplatonic' nature of earlier medieval cosmology and of the impossibility[352] of reconciling Aristotelian cosmology with revelation, Maimonides and Aquinas have inherited a problem they could have resolved in one of two ways: Either they had to break away entirely from the Neoplatonic tradition and offer an alternative cosmological theory or they had to modify Neoplatonism with the aid of Aristotle so that the necessary relation between matter and evil could be denied, if they were to avoid inconsistency, even incoherence. As will become evident in the following analysis, in my opinion, Aquinas was more successful, or more Aristotelian, in resolving the problem than Maimonides. By drawing a radical distinction between natural material corruption and evil and by simultaneously affirming the reality of prime matter and denying the natural reality of evil, Aquinas is implicitly denying the validity of the synthesis between evil as a moral category and as a natural material one. On the other hand, Maimonides, despite his affirmation of the created nature of prime matter and despite (perhaps, even because of) his denial of the rational status of evil, posits matter as the source of evil and thus, undermines the possibility of endowing it with a real positive role in substantial existence.[353]

Maimonides's Ambivalence Toward Matter

Maimonides' numerous discussions of matter manifest a strong antagonistic tension that may best approached initially through an examination of his concomitant acceptance of two distinct ontologies, an Aristotelian one and a Neoplatonic one, without being able to bring them into a coherent relation. Thus, in his critique of the Mutakallimun he provides an account of matter that emphasizes the distinction between matter and the privation of form, whereas in all other discussions of matter a strong emphasis is placed upon the close relation between matter and evil. Although the distinct contexts, aims, and foci of the diverse (and dispersed) accounts of matter in the *Guide* may account for some of the difficulties, I do not think that they suffficiently account for the tension.

The conflicting interpretations evident in all Maimonidean scholarship and, especially, the perennial problem of Maimonides' esotericism could be explained, to some extent, by Maimonides' equivocal accounts of matter. However, to emphasize a tension in Maimonides' thought does not necessarily entail a concomitant affirmation of a deliberate intent at concealment. Rather, in my opinion, we need to reexamine the general consensus that Maimonides is predominantly a pure Aristotelian in all branches of philosophy apart from ethics and politics. Conversely, a reexamination of the general consensus may help shed new light on the tension or discontinuity between Maimonides 'Aristotelian' theoretical and 'Platonic' practical philosophy. Moreover, although, in his account of creation, Maimonides (pace Aristotle) repeatedly affirms the created nature of prime matter, this affirmation does not give rise to an ontology that assigns to material existence a positive or active role in human perfection. As will become evident, for Maimonides (following Aristotle), the composite nature of human existence requires a simultaneous resignation to the necessity of this composition, a noetic rather than pietistic resignation, and a consequent striving to overcome the limitations of the material element to the extent that it is possible.

Maimonides' ambivalence toward material existence is evident whenever he discusses the realm of generation and corruption. Even in the lexicographical chapters of the *Guide*, the aforementioned distinct ontologies are evident. In Chapters 6, 7, and 14 of *Guide* 1, a strictly Neoplatonic negative attitude toward material existence is exhibited, whereas in Chapter 17, Maimonides presents a more Aristotelian 'scientific' account of the nature of generation and corruption.

The explication of the equivocal nature of terms originating in, and associated with, the generative principles, male and man (*ish* and *adam*), female (*ishah*), and child bearing (*yalod*) initially, does not seems to present an occasion for any discussion beyond semantics. However, although the explanation of terms in *Guide*, 1. 6, the first chapter addressed to these terms, does not seem to assign a moral value to the distinction between the two generating principles but, rather, to clarify the equivocity of some Hebrew terms designating gender; nevertheless, this chapter serves as a philological foundation for subsequent moral designations or significations consequent upon ethical or moral judgments.

In Chapter 7, after he explains that the term *yalod* is used figuratively to signify the production of knowledge in another, Maimonides draws a qualitative distinction between the respective effects of the literal and figurative productive activities. In arguing that "none of the children of [Adam] born before [Seth] had been endowed with true human form,"[354] whereas Seth was produced truly in the image of Adam and thus in God's image, and that Seth has attained this image only after he had been instructed by Adam, Maimonides is also maintaining, quite explicitly, that a human form in potency is not *the* determining factor in human composition. Thus, Maimonides is also insinuating both that until the intellect is fully actualized, human beings have no share in immaterial existence[355] and that, until such a time, the human form plays a less potent role in attaining, or failing to attain, human perfection than does the material principle of existence. Moreover, he argues that a human shape in which the intellect has not been actualized yet is utterly evil, or a devil.[356] But, unlike other sublunar composite beings who, devoid of the intellective faculty, cannot produce harm, or evil, an ignorant person "has a faculty to cause various kinds of harm and to produce evils that is not possible by the other animals. For he applies the capacities for thought and perception, which were to prepare him to achieve a perfection that he has not achieved to all kinds of machinations entailing evils and occasioning and *engendering* all kinds of harm."[357]

And, according to Maimonides, human beings who are ignorant in such a manner as to deliberately cause harm are worthy only of extinction. The short paragraph, which is Chapter 14, reinforces the radical separation established by Maimonides between the material and immaterial elements of human existence. Explaining that the term *adam* is derived from *adamah* (earth), that it signifies the elements most common to the human species, and that it is used to designate the multitude rather than the elite and drawing attention to the distinction between 'sons of Elohim' and 'daughters of man', Maimonides is arguing, again, that members of the human species are indistinct from the other members of the genus 'animal' until they have perfected their intellect, in fact, that they are worse. A less favorable judgment concerning the nature of material existence is hard to imagine. Indeed, it is striking that Maimonides does not consider it possible that one whose intellect has not been actualized refrain from evil activity. In fact, it seems to me that Maimonides' implicit denial of such a possibility is itself a witness to his attitude toward matter, as well as to his judgment about the overwhelming potency of matter over form. In this light, Maimonides' view, as it is expressed here, far exceeds Plotinus' view of matter as "impotent potency."

In Chapter 17 of Book 1, Maimonides refers to the principles of generation and corruption in a less negatively critical fashion. In fact, no moral categories enter into the account. He explains that three principles are required for generation and corruption—matter, form, and 'particularized privation'—and that precisely because privation is always conjoined with matter, the latter can receive form. According to Maimonides, the difficulties inherent in understanding the distinction between these principles of natural science are the cause for the injunction against non-figurative speech about the Account of the Beginning since, exceeding the apprehension of the multitude, they are potentially dangerous.[358]

Although Maimonides' uses Aristotelian physics in the account of matter and privation in Book 3 and in fact quotes Aristotle's *Physics*, his repeated designation of matter as the source of evil and the immediate succession of the discussion of generation and corruption by an explanation of evil sets it far apart from Aristotle. Despite the fact that matter is necessary for substantial existence, it is never presented by Maimonides as an essential principle in the actualization of the human form; that is, human composition is not integrated. Rather than present matter as pure potentiality and, hence, as the possibility for human actualization, Maimonides underscores its role in corruption. Again, he likens matter to the feminine principle, in fact, to a married harlot, who, never satisfied with her husband, seeks others continuously. ". . . notwithstanding her being *a married woman*, she never ceases to seek for another man to substitute for her husband, and she deceives and draws him on in every way until he obtains from her what her husband used to obtain. This is the state of matter. For whatever form is found in it, does but prepare it to receive another form."[359] The figurative account presents form as impotent before the corruptive power of matter. Rather than emphasize the power of form over matter as the governing principle in a composite being, Maimonides presents composition primarily as the subjugation of potential form to matter to such an extent that not only physical ills, but also all spiritual ills and sins, are understood to result from corruptible and corruptive matter. The language used by Maimonides to describe the nature of material existence is highly poetic rather than 'scientific' and, if we are to avoid psychologizing, must be understood as a device used to bring about immediate assent to the premise that asserts that all material needs are shameful and repulsive by definition.[360] Depicting matter as turbid and dark, Maimonides repeatedly interweaves descriptions of material needs, such as eating, drinking, and copulating, with unpleasant images both physical and mental: vomit and male subjugation to women. Concomitant with Maimonides' repulsion by matter is a great admiration towards all asceticism, including physical humiliation, since it is a practice that embodies the rejection of material existence for the sake of intellectual perfection.[361]

Yet, unlike the discussions of generation and corruption in Book 1, the explanation presented in Book 3, despite its strong language, does not limit the range of possibilities constituting human existence to the two diametrically opposed choices between bestiality and perfection. Drawing a distinction between 'suitable' and 'unsuitable' matter, Maimonides not only designates suitable matter metaphorically as "a woman of virtue," but also calls it "a divine gift"[362] because it is easy to control. Unsuitable matter, on the other hand, is said to be "not impossible" to subdue by means of exhortations and the commandment and prohibitions of the Torah. Thus, in a manner of speaking, Maimonides' poetic account constitutes model exhortations habituating human beings to shun material pleasures and satisfy material needs only to the extent that they are necessary rather than in pursuit of pleasure.[363]

There can be no doubt that Maimonides' exhortations do not aim at promoting moderation with respect to material needs but rather strive to produce an immoderate denial of any reality to their benefits. This attitude is especially striking in view of the fact that Maimonides claims that "the commandments and prohibitions of the Law are *only* intended to quell all the impulses of matter."[364] Consequently, Maimonides is either denying that most conventional laws and at least some of the commandments of the Torah aim at the development of practical reason, or he is departing entirely from the Aristotelian understanding of practical reason.[365] The distinction he draws between the acts of disobedience consequent upon matter and those consequent upon form could be interpreted to reinforce both possibilities, each applicable to a different class of individuals distinguished through the nature of their matter. Since it is clear that Maimonides divides the human species into very distinct classes, the question is whether or not any or some of these divisions are *essential*. This question will be at the background of much of the remaining inquiry. At present, in order to continue the present discussion, suffice it to say that unless we were to conclude that the 'elite' are endowed with unchanging matter similar to the supralunar, they, too, cannot be said to exercise full rational control over matter since Maimonides' account minimizes the relation between matter and form or the potency of reason to control matter.

In arguing that all acts of disobedience are reducible to bestiality, "but thought is one of the properties of a human being that are consequent upon his form [and that c]onsequently, if [man] gives his thought a free scope in respect to disobedience, he commits an act of disobedience through the nobler of his two parts,"[366] Maimonides is also arguing that there is a class of acts consisting of acts of disobedience that is entirely independent of thought. Not only is it unclear how acts that cannot be said to involve choice constitute acts of disobedience, but also Maimonides' pessimistic view of human nature raises doubts about the validity and utility of conventional laws originating with human beings. If some acts of disobedience are independent of thought, reason can neither 'discover' (*invenio*) laws to restrain them nor choose to obey them; they will be useful only to the extent that their enforcement will instill fear. Since very few human beings can be said to possess the uniquely excellent incorruptible matter and since this matter is described by Maimonides as a divine gift, it seems that no human being can reach true perfection without divine intervention.[367]

Maimonides' view of matter as evil clearly manifests a judgment that could not possibly be derived from the conclusions of natural science since, as the domain of theoretical reason, it is concerned strictly with the true and the false, rather than with good and evil. For the same reason, however, Maimonides seems to be violating his own 'epistemological'[368] principles when he translates ontological considerations into moral conclusions. Notwithstanding the seeming lack of consistency, it is clear that the elements giving rise to this judgment are theoretical as well as practical: the limitations of natural reason to arrive at metaphysical knowledge irrespective of the degree of the human desire for it and the tragic dilemma of the philosopher who cannot escape life in the polis, be he or she Er of the *Republic* (in the generic sense of every human being) or the philosopher of the *Ethics* X (provided that one remembers that the 'Ethics' is the first part of the *Politics*). It is evident that rather than understand material existence as the possibility for human perfection, Maimonides chose to emphasize primarily the limitations for human participation in Being consequent upon material composition and constituting a barrier to all apprehension of the true reality of being and beings. This view is especially striking when we consider that, when he asserts that matter constitutes a barrier to perfection, that is, to knowledge of God, he does not limit the judgment to sublunar beings but maintains that "[i]t does this even if it is the noblest and purest matter, I mean to say even if it is the matter of the heavenly spheres. All the more is this true for the dark and turbid matter that is ours."[369] The judgment that matter is a veil to apprehension, according to Maimonides, manifests not only a philosophical conclusion but also a biblical one. This judgment, which is the primary aim of the prophetic books, is consequent upon a true understanding of matter brought about by means of the repeated depictions of all epiphanies metaphorically as visions surrounded by a cloud or some other enveloping dark substance. Images of darkness, Maimonides maintains, give rise to notions emphasizing the material limitations of composite beings to apprehend the pure divine light. Not only the unique Sinaitic epiphany, the obscurity of which could be explained by the presence of the entire community, whose members were clearly diverse, but also all prophetic epiphanies are dimmed, with the possible exception of a few instances of Mosaic prophecy.[370]

The first 'scientific' discussion of the distinction between matter and privation, the meaning of privation, and the latter's relation to evil is presented as a critique of the Mutakallimun's understanding of privation. According to Maimonides, their account of privation is based upon two major errors: (1) a notion of privation, or non-being, that recognizes only absolute non-being, and yet (contradicting their first premise), (2) an understanding of privation as an existent thing. That is, although the Mutakallimun did not distinguish between absolute and relative privation, although they limited privation to contrariety, and although, as a consequence, they maintained that it did not require the act of an agent, nevertheless, they understood absolute non-being to correspond to an actual existing state, thus endowing it with an independent ontological status.

All the errors of the Mutakallimun can be reduced to an ignorance concerning the nature of existence.[371] Having failed to comprehend the distinction between essential and accidental qualities of subsistent existence, they concluded that accidents were in no way related to the act of an agent and, consequently, they were unable to account for them. Composite existence, on the other hand, requires both essential and accidental qualities, the former representing the real effect of the act of an agent, whereas the latter are related to that act as an accidental effect. Moreover, only God, in the unique act of creation, brings something into existence out of *absolute* privation, or non-being; all other agents produce a change from relative privations that are absences of due perfections and relative with respect to these perfections.

Maimonides' critique of the Mutakallimun brings into sharp focus one of the major difficulties inherent in understanding privation in the Arabic-language tradition. This difficulty is made manifest here both through the errors attributed by Maimonides to the Mutakallimun and through the perennial difficulties encountered by scholars attempting to understand Maimonides. Since the Arabic term *al-'adam* signifies both privation and non-being, any significant distinction between these concepts either has to be read into the text or the relevant predication has to be added to the term so as to signify either an absolute or a relative state of absence. When limited in English by the respective predications *absolute* and *relative*, it is clear that the former signifies a state prior to subsistent existence, or the composition of matter and form, whereas the latter designates the absence of a specific form in a subsistent being. Nonetheless, it should be noted (1) that the only predication used by Maimonides is 'absolute', and (2) that it can and has been argued that Maimonides may be inconsistent in his use of, or failure to use, this predicate.[372] In contradistinction to the Mutakallimun, Maimonides insists that all evils are relative privations (*'adam*). The failure to comprehend this proposition (evident in the teachings of the Mutakallimun) occurs only in "one who does not distinguish between privation (*al-'adam*) and *habitus* (*malaka*) and between two contraries or one who does not know the nature of all things."[373]

Since no agent can be said to produce privation, or evil, essentially,[374] it is ludicrous to assume that evil is something existing, let alone that God's unique act brought about the evils evident in the world. Given that God alone produces *only* being and given that being is good by definition, all His acts produce absolute good. Consequently, all things understood as evil in this world including matter are essentially good and can be understood as evil only accidentally. In fact, understood in terms of their essence, all things existing in the universe without exception, are, exist for, and promote being. "Even the existence of this inferior matter, whose manner of being it is to be a concomitant of privation entailing death and all evils, all this is also *good* in view of the perpetuity of generation and the permanence of being through succession."[375] Thus, the distinction drawn by Maimonides between absolute and relative privation in his refutation of the teachings of the Mutakallimun leads to the conclusion that, properly speaking, nothing is essentially evil, evil being merely a category imposed upon the object by human convention or understanding. And as Maimonides repeatedly points out throughout the *Guide*, "the Torah speaks in human language," or in the language of Adam's descendents, and language is merely conventional rather than natural.[376]

The differences between Maimonides' accounts of matter, as a metaphysical category underlying change only or as both a metaphysical category and an ethical category to which all evils can be reduced are rather pronounced. Whereas earlier accounts are poetic and collapse moral and ontological categories into one, the critique of the Mutakallimun not only distinguishes between them but, more significantly, circumscribes their respective meaning and applicability, and reduces the attributions of moral categories to ontological entities back to the limitations of human understanding and language. One of three possible explanations can be offered for the seemingly blatant contradictions:

1. Maimonides was unaware of irreconcilable tensions between his diverse explanations.[377]
2. Maimonides intentionally provides two accounts, an esoteric one representing his true but concealed opinions and a revealed exoteric one.[378]
3. Maimonides was aware of these tensions, but either did not consider them irreconcilable, or considered the contradiction(s) they manifest necessary.[379]

Since Maimonides' distinct accounts are expressed clearly rather than in an oblique fashion and in view of my conclusions in Chapters 1 and 2 that he regarded layers of meaning as closely interrelated rather than opposed, the second possibility is either inapplicable to his interpretations of matter or needs to be refined considerably. On the other hand, in view of the tension that exists between Maimonides' distinct accounts of matter, it seems to me that no decisive judgment can be reached with respect to the other possibilities. Nonetheless, since, in addition to being condescending, perhaps even anachronistic, the first option questions the intelligibility and validity of the text a priori, it also undermines the possibility of providing a coherent account of Maimonides' arguments. If Maimonides' *apologia* is to be taken seriously, that is, if his emphasis upon the great care he has taken in writing the *Guide* (which includes an explicit outline of contradictions and their *necessity*) is not to be dismissed, then the dual ontology presented must be consistent in some way with his philosophy as a whole, and consequently, the third option is the only one that justifies reading the text at all. Moreover, as will become evident in the following chapters, Maimonides' understanding of the human soul, of human knowledge, and of human perfection as well as his demand that revealed law play an epistemic role in human perfection become more consistent when he is understood to have embraced a dual ontology consciously.

Since evil, according to Maimonides, is a category imposed by human beings upon things, rather than something existing in them, the remaining discussion of evil in the *Guide* is addressed to the classes of things interpreted by human beings as evil. The two main premises upon which the discussion is based are (1), properly speaking, all evils are the result of ignorance or "privation of knowledge,"[380] both in the sense that ignorance is evil and that (therefore) it is the cause of evil, and (2) teleological accounts that posit a final end of all existing things are erroneous since a final end, *qua* end, implies privation of a perfection in that which is posited as the end and hence is applicable and meaningful only in the realm of generation and corruption.

The proliferation of the mistaken opinion that more evils than goods exist in the temporal world is attributed by Maimonides to ignorance concerning the nature of evil that is exhibited not only by the multitude but also by some the learned, all of whom follow their imagination rather than reason. This mistake, which violates the concept of God, implying that He is the cause of evil, results from the absurd assumption that all creation exists for the sake of human beings. Once the nature of existence is understood, however, and the very limited human portion in it becomes evident, it follows necessarily that all existence is a good consequent upon the divine will or wisdom. Moreover, argues Maimonides, human existence is a very great good, in fact, it is a divine gift, since of all creatures subject to generation and corruption human beings alone were given the capacity to perfect themselves so that they could overcome the necessary and natural limitations of sublunar existence. Consequently, evil is either a good that in our ignorance (itself an evil) we misconceive or "we suffer because of evils that we have produced ourselves of our free will; but we attribute them to God, may he be exalted above this."[381]

Having asserted the general proposition that the only things which can be understood as essentially evil are the result of human ignorance and pertain to human beings alone, Maimonides examines the three species of things designated by human beings as evils. Since the first species of evils examined by Maimonides is consequent upon human matter and affects the body alone, it is not surprising that he dismisses it as irrelevant. He argues not only that this species of evils is necessary and that it befalls very few individuals, but most importantly, that it is precisely because of their material composition that human beings are subject to impressions, that is, that they can know anything, or attain their proper good.

It is curious that despite his emphasis upon the sensible origin of human knowledge, Maimonides is willing to grant at all the fittingness of the designation *evil* to this class of events rather than dismiss the validity of the attribution outright as an ignorant misunderstanding. Moreover, unlike the other two species of evils examined by Maimonides, which are the direct effect of human ignorance, the first species does not result from human agency; rather, the explanation here seems to suggest not only that these events are the necessary consequence of human nature but also that the same necessity out of which these 'evils' arise is the cause of human knowledge. That is, properly speaking, the first species of events can be designated as evil only if material existence is understood as evil or as a real limit to human perfectibility. Since, on the one hand, Maimonides singles out events such as death and ill health to exemplify these evils and, on the other, emphasizes that material individuation is the prerequisite for knowledge, he is either accepting the term *evil* provisionally, following the understanding of the vulgar while implicitly denying the fittingness of the designation, or else he is suggesting that although these events are real evils, nevertheless, the greater good—knowledge—consequent upon composition that is procured by some individuals makes naught of the evils visited upon others.

In my opinion, Maimonides is accepting both premises as correct, each pertaining to a different class of individuals. On the one hand, and in concert with other accounts, he posits an essential dichotomy between human matter and form that in most individuals translates into an inability of form to exercise effective control over matter. Consequently, for these individuals natural corruption constitutes a real evil, perhaps because natural perfection is the only one they can attain. On the other hand, for those individuals endowed with quasi-divine, tame matter, these events are insignificant because they do not experience them as evils. Notwithstanding, apart from ill health and death, which are inevitable, even the latter class of individuals are not free from the potential danger constituted by the corruptive power of matter over form and, hence, must guard against it and strive to overcome its limitation to whatever extent is possible. Consequently, all classes of human beings must resign themselves to their conditions; the less fortunate must be habituated to a passive resignation, whereas the elite must struggle actively, lest their form be corrupted by matter.

The second species of evils is constituted of acts human beings inflict upon one another in their struggle for power. Since the victims of these acts are powerless against them, this species, like the first, is necessary and requires resignation. Given that the perfection of the universal order requires the existence of distinct classes of human beings, it could be argued that these evils too are a condition that pertains to human beings by nature and cannot be overcome, not even by perfect laws, although they can be minimized by them. "The evils of the third [species] are those which are inflicted upon any individual among us by his own action; this is what happens in the majority of cases, and these evils are much more numerous than those of the second kind. All men lament over evils of this kind; and it is only seldom that you find one who is not guilty of having brought them upon himself. He who is reached by them *deserves truly to be blamed.*"[382] Maimonides maintains that these evils result from the vices—identified here with physical pleasures—and are the cause of both physical and spiritual ills, the latter affecting the soul in a twofold manner. First, since the soul is a corporeal faculty, any change affecting the body affects the soul necessarily, corrupting its moral virtues. Second, once it is affected by vain pleasures, the soul becomes habituated in these vices and desires things that are not necessary for the preservation either of the individual or the species, a desire that, by definition, is in(de)finite because *unnecessary*.

As in previous accounts of matter, so in the explanation of the third species of evils, Maimonides' argument is a poetic exhortation for ascetic frugality. He presents all activities that are not directed to the true human end—apprehension[383]—as superfluous and conducive to evil, including political activity.[384] Had human beings attended only to their true end and had they satisfied their needs only to such an extent as was necessary, activities directed to any purpose other than apprehension would require little effort on their part. Unlike the animals whose acts conform to their true nature (or conform to necessity) and are all directed to fulfilling their role in the perfect order of the universe, human beings do not act strictly in conformity with their true nature since they strive to satisfy vain or unnecessary desires for false ends. Not only does Maimonides fail to acknowledge any end other than apprehension as a true or a relative good,[385] but also he does not provide an explanation of the relation between the will and the intellect that could account for false desires, apart from rooting them in matter.[386] Nor does Maimonides account for the nature of the relation between the human governing faculty and other human faculties when he argues that "His bringing us into existence is absolutely the great good . . . and the creation of the governing faculty in the living beings is an indication of His mercifulness with regard to them.[387]

Moreover, in the context of the discussion of evils, by dismissing all human activities unrelated to intellection as superfluous, rather than relating them in an ordered hierarchy of ends, and by presenting the possibility of conformity to the necessity that *is* one's nature as strictly consequent upon the apprehension of the true reality of the universe, Maimonides in fact renders the shunning of evil and the actualization of human perfection an almost natural impossibility without divine intervention, or revelation. Since he does not explain the nature of the relation between the will and reason, Maimonides seems to suggest that the will is merely a natural inclination that follows the imagination as long as the human being lacks the full apprehension of the true reality of all existence. Consequently, Maimonides seems to argue, in what may appear to be a circular manner, that the perfection of practical reason is consequent upon and subsequent to the development of theoretical reason, of which the perfection, paradoxically, requires the possession of the moral virtues. In addition, since the imaginative faculty depends upon material impressions, and matter constitutes a veil to the apprehension of the true reality of being, human beings can never arrive at this knowledge by their natural powers.[388] Para-*doxically*, then, the necessity of human nature renders impossible the perfection of its single necessary (true) end. The relation between

human potency and act is presented by Maimonides as if they were contradictories rather than contraries or else cannot be accounted for by Aristotelian
physics and modern logic.

Maimonides' failure to account for matter as an essential part of human
existence amounts to establishing a radical dichotomy not only between the sub-
and supralunar realms, but also between the rational faculty and all other faculties.
Moreover, since human beings are the only creatures who belong to both realms
by nature, they are also the only creatures whose existence and essence neither are
in natural harmony nor can be harmonized naturally. Consequently, Maimonides'
inability or (more likely) reluctance to develop a coherent synthesis between a
Neoplatonic metaphysics and an Aristotelian physics, each requiring a different
understanding of human cognition and *epistemai*, results in a tension between
human existence and human perfection that could not be reconciled without revelation. However, since Maimonides, following the tradition, repeatedly emphasizes that 'the Torah possesses seventy faces'—that is, it may be interpreted in a
multiplicity of ways—the understanding of which requires intellectual perfection,
the question of the perfection of the multitude and their natural inability to avoid
evils consequent upon their ignorance cannot be overlooked. For, the possibility
of the perfection of the vulgar is ultimately a question concerning the nature of
divine providence. Consequently, to the extent that *good* and *evil* are useful
terms, either those things experienced by the vulgar as evil have to be affirmed as
good, or the vulgar must be able to attain some of the essential perfection proper
to the human species, or the category of "species" is problematic in relation to
human beings.[389] Conversely, since categories are imposed upon things by natural reason, the "problematic" status of the human species may itself disclose the
limits of reason.

Since Maimonides insists that the created universe is perfect, since no
divine act could be interpreted as vain or superfluous, and since the differences between individuals are consequent upon their matter, the existence of a
right proportion of each class of individuals necessary for the preservation of
the universal order, in itself, must be evidence of divine munificence. As he
points out, the repeated qualification *good* used in the Torah to describe the various beings created by God is an expression used by human beings to refer to an
object's conformity to its purpose, and hence, it is intended to instruct us that all
that exists conforms to the particular purpose intended for it by the divine will,
a purpose of which we neither have nor can have knowledge. At the same time
as he affirms the goodness of creation, however, Maimonides also and always
underscores the distance between human beings, the creatures who are most
perfect in the sublunar realm and all other beings not subject to change, even as
he explains that *good* is a term used by humans to describe that which is beyond
language, even the language of the Torah, namely, conformity to the divine will
or wisdom (neither of which are proper divine names).

If we are not to conclude that the *Guide* is merely an exoteric text and hence, that it is philosophically insignificant, we must accept that for Maimonides the first and foremost principle of intelligibility is God, the meaning and importance of all other beings deriving from Him. In light of his Neoplatonic view of matter, on the one hand, and his Aristotelian understanding of perfection, on the other, it seems to me that Maimonides indeed judged any degree of human perfection, beyond the natural perpetuation of the species, as evidence of divine providence or as a divine gift. Consequently, the very fact that human beings possesses reason, let alone the event of revelation, were manifestations of divine providence over the entire universe. The Torah was given to human beings so that through it, if they so choose, they may gain real knowledge and be able to participate in divine providence and avoid "evil." Since, by definition, that is, literally as guidance, the Torah must play an essential cognitive role in human perfection, failure to be instructed by it manifests the freely willed human rejection of the divine gift or, conversely, the human choice of evil.

Aquinas' Understanding of Matter, Privation, and Evil

Since one of Aquinas' most integrated discussion of the relation between matter, privation, and evil, occurs in the *De Divinis Nominibus*, I shall use this commentary as the springboard for my discussion. This text is the best witness for the claim made in the previous chapter that in his metaphysics and ontology Aquinas synthesizes the Platonic and Aristotelian doctrines into his own unique and coherent system of 'Neoplatonism'. This text also demonstrates the manner in which Aquinas was able to develop an ethical theory on the basis of metaphysical and ontological conclusions without collapsing moral and ontological principles into an untenable unity. In fact, in my opinion, Aquinas' ethics would be incoherent to the modern philosopher without a prior understanding of his metaphysics and ontology, especially in view of the Christian doctrine of original sin.

It is in his teachings about matter in general and about the material substratum of human existence in particular that Aquinas' philosophical doctrine differs most clearly from Maimonides'. For, if Maimonides' ontology can be characterized as one that emphasizes the radical difference between corporeal and incorporeal existence, focusing upon the corruptive role of matter, Aquinas' ontology underlines the unity of all existing things in virtue of their first and final cause—the good, irrespective of composition. By focusing upon matter's relation to the good and arguing for matter's essential role in actualization, rather than in corruption, Aquinas establishes a continuity between sub- and supralunar existence that overcomes the Neoplatonic problematic of the relative independence of evil from the divine order. In fact in the *De Divinis Nominibus*

Aquinas argues that the understanding of the good as the *ratio causae* of the universal order is subsequent to and consequent upon the correct understanding of matter.[390]

Rather than view the indefinite potency that is prime matter as evil, because it is impotent, Aquinas presents its role in existence as a manifestation of the good. Based upon the clear distinction outlined in the previous chapter that he draws between *non ens* and *non est*, Aquinas argues that the potency manifesting a privation of a particular form (*non est*), which seems to be an evil, is in fact a manifestation of matter's natural inclination, or desire, for the good. Since the good is the final cause of all existing things—to be the final cause is to be the good—and since no being can be said to desire non-existence *per se*, neither can privation be said to be essentially evil nor can anything (whether it exists *in se* or *in alio*) be understood as utterly evil. In fact, it is precisely because no being can desire evil, that evil neither can be caused nor be the cause of anything *per se* and, hence, rather than subsisting *per se*, it must be caused by the good *per accidens*. Consequently, Aquinas argues not only that nothing is essentially evil, but also that what is understood as evil can be only an absence of a good that ought and can be possessed, a goodness that properly belongs to the nature of the thing as the effect of the good cause.[391]

One of the most striking features of Aquinas' exposition of the *De Divinis Nominibus* is his ability to dissociate matter entirely from any evil designation in a commentary on a Neoplatonic text that exhibits all the tensions inherent in the Plotinian understanding of matter. He repeatedly argues that change in the natural universe, the principle of which is matter, may in no way be understood as a defect or an evil. Natural corruption is the source of further generation and therefore is necessary for the perfection of the universe; a perfection that must comprise all grades of existence. Consequently, given Aquinas' distinctions between *non ens* and *non est* and between matter and privation, it would be more accurate to explain his understanding of natural corruption as a decay into particular non-existence that makes further existence possible, rather than into non-being, where the latter is understood as an absolute non-state, the former as a constitutive element in the process of becoming.

Diversity of effects, the material cause of evil, cannot be attributed necessarily to a natural agent that does one thing only, but rather, to a rational willing agent. In fact, the distinction between good and evil can be found only in the will the proper object of which is the good, "since it is characteristic of that which is contrary to virtue to be evil, and it is not found in any other genus that certain species be distinguished through a difference between good and evil, except in the virtuous and wicked *habitus* of the soul."[392]

Moreover, if the natural universe is perfect, then evil cannot be attributed to a natural inclination or appetite so long as these conform to the natural order. Consequently, only an intellectual being can choose evil; that is, only an active principle of the natural universe can choose to act contrary to nature. But, when acting in opposition to the natural order, human beings desire non-existence *per accidens*, insofar as they act against the principle of their self-preservation, opposing their first good and the first principle of natural law, which is defined in the *Summa Theologiae* as "the imprint of the divine light in us. Whence it is clear that natural law is nothing other than the participation of the eternal law in rational creatures."[393]

In all intellectual beings, the desire for the good, or perfection, is a desire for knowledge of God, which in distinctly rational beings—that is, humans—is cognitive.[394] The divine light, naturally imprinted in human beings, expels all culpable ignorance and error from souls, the former being a withdrawing from truth, whereas the latter is a cleaving to falsehood. And, as will become apparent, with respect to evil, culpable ignorance (*nescientia*) alone, rather than error, is properly termed a fault. Whereas error is attributed only to human beings, ignorance is applicable to both human beings and the angels. However, since angelic ignorance is of a kind different from human[395] and since it does not effect my discussion directly, I shall limit the inquiry to culpable human ignorance.[396]

Ignorance plays a major role in determining a moral evil, because it is that unknowing applicable to those who ought to know by nature and who are ordered to knowledge of God to the extent that they are able to attain it. The natural desire for perfection, understood as a desire for knowledge of God, is self-perpetuating and is augmented by increased knowledge, both as a desire for additional knowledge and as its unifying principle. Ignorance negates, but does not deny absolutely, the unifying principle—truth. Ignorance is not truth's contrary. Error, on the other hand, denies the validity of truth inasmuch as it affirms the opposite or contrary of truth. Since truth is one and error multiple, error is the cause of division and disunity. Consequently, error is never freely, that is rationally, chosen by human beings, but is adhered to as a seeming truth, or good. In a manner of speaking, both ignorance and error are modes of disregarding or forgetting truth; but, whereas the former is a turning away from what can be known, what is accessible without external mediation, the latter manifests a lack of access to truth that cannot be overcome without external mediation.[397]

Love for the good and the beautiful, as the object of desire, is the root of all appetitive operations. This condition is a relation of the appetite to the object loved as its good, desiring to make present something absent of which one knows oneself to be deprived. The degree of knowledge of the object of desire, which is identical to the degree of awareness of its privation, determines the aptitude for and order of its receptivity. It is especially striking that Aquinas exemplifies the nature of the relations binding the appetite to its object by drawing an analogy between the appetite's desire and matter's receptivity to form. It could be argued that, insofar as Aquinas departs from Dionysius' text by using this analogy, he alludes to the material substratum of all cognition, a premise originating in an understanding of human cognition distinctly different from Dionysius' Neoplatonic one. In so doing, Aquinas also succeeds in overcoming the difficulty inherent in the Neoplatonic understanding of matter as a hindrance to knowledge of God.

The most lofty appetite for the object of desire is the one consequent upon understanding and, therefore, it is designated as free choice, that appetite which moves itself because it recognizes what ought to be loved.[398] Consequently, a desire for anything other than the highest object of love is love *per accidens*, which can be demonstrated always to be caused by an object's similitude or seeming fittingness to that which is loved *per se*. In virtue of the human ontological status, that superior appetite designated as free choice is the cause of real evil in the universal order.

The problem of evil raises two questions that are central to any philosophical inquiry pursued within a tradition of revelation and that are closely related; namely, how can a rational creature whose will is informed by reason desire its own destruction, even *per accidens*, and how is this possible under divine providence? Since Aquinas' response to these questions occurs in the context of a commentary on a Neoplatonic text and since his disagreement with some of Dionysius' principles brings into a sharp focus some important instances manifesting the differences between Aquinas' and Maimonides' respective ontologies, I shall postpone the discussion of these questions briefly in order to outline Aquinas' critique of Dionysius' position. Subsequently, I shall draw out the essential elements of the critique that also constitute Aquinas' disagreements with Maimonides.[399]

Although he concurs with Dionysius' assertion that evil is found in particular rather than universal nature, Aquinas rejects the premise that universal nature is something separate, arguing that forms exist in matter as principles of action and, consequently, have to be understood as "the active force of a first body which is first in a genus of natural causes."[400] Natural universal principles, such as prime matter and form, according to Aquinas, do not have existence *in se*, but only *in alio*; they can be said to exist only as particulars subsisting in composite natures. Natural powers, *qua* natural, depend upon the natural order for their actualization, are never independent of it, and hence, cannot act entirely against it. Natural powers, *qua* natural, exhibit their own necessity. Consequently, evil is a particular act *praeter* rather than *secundum naturam* or *necessitatem*. Aquinas adds that, since Dionysius himself excludes the possibility of positing the body as the cause of the corruption of the soul, the particular act manifest as actual sin makes evident that the evil of the soul originates in free choice that uses corporeal things. For, if matter, *qua* natural potency, was posited as the cause of the corruption of the soul (form), not only would it follow that it is independent of it in some essential way, but more significantly, the corruption of the human soul would occur *necessarily*. "For an effect follows upon a posited cause out of necessity unless something should impede it. But, we see that this is false; for many souls look to the good, which could not happen if matter were to draw them entirely to evil. Whence it is manifest that evil in souls does not originate in matter, but in a disordered impulse of free choice, which is sin itself."[401]

In emphasizing the essential relation between natural universal principles and natural particulars and in arguing that forms constitute the active principles in subsistent existents, Aquinas is also arguing against the understanding of any particular matter as a hindrance to the perfection of the particular being composed of it.[402] Consequently, neither can any instance of natural corruption, such as ill health, be understood as evil, except *per accidens*, nor can it inhibit the true perfection of any natural being. Moreover, *qua* natural power, matter can only act *secundum naturam*, and hence, it can never be argued that a corrupt matter exists nor that any matter whatsoever constitutes an obstacle to the perfection of the soul. As Aquinas points out, were it the case that any matter corrupts its form or is independent of it in any way, the corruption of that form would follow necessarily.

Based upon this critique, Aquinas responds to the two main problems ensuing from the analysis of evil. In answer to the first question, how any existent can desire its own demise, he concludes that, although no one desires evil except as a good, nevertheless, no one can be excused on account of ignorance, since not to know in the particular what one knows in the universal is a result of a disorder in the will rather than in the understanding. To pursue this question further would require a development of the distinction between will and intellect and a subsequent investigation of the reasons why disorders occur in the will. Although Aquinas briefly mentions original sin as the cause of that stain of the body that has disrupted the unity of the human soul,[403] in order to shed some light on the question why disorders occur in the will, he does not pursue it in this context, since it does not belong properly within the context of the discussion. Consequently, the explanation of evil will have to be supplemented with discussions in other texts in order to present a more comprehensive account of Aquinas' understanding of evil.

In answer to the second question, Aquinas responds that precisely because divine providence is conserving rather than corruptive of nature, it does not impede evil. To interfere with the possibility of an evil choice would constitute a corruption of the nature of those things that are self-moving, in this case, human beings, the rational creatures whose nature is corruptible, because perfectible, through a freedom of choice that can fail. Since it is characteristic of divine providence to provide for each created thing in proportion to the good proper to it, no particular being can receive goodness in the same proportion as it belongs to the universal concept 'being', nor can any being occupying a lower status within a species receive what is proper to a higher one. Rather, the particular perfection of each being is determined by its assigned status in the universal order. Consequently, to desire a perfection greater than the appropriate one is hubris, to desire a lesser perfection amounts to willed annihilation, both of which constitute evils.[404]

The manner in which divine providence assists and conserves natural things is explained in the concluding chapters of the book.[405] With respect to human actions, it directs and inclines human beings to the correct government of things, their proper natural end, the rule of which is law and the primary principles of which are inscribed on the hearts of rational creatures. As in his brief mention of original sin, so in his swift reference to law, rather than develop an explanation the scope of which reaches beyond the text, Aquinas only draws the reader's attention to the proper context for continued investigation. Despite its brevity, however, the allusion underlines the epistemic function and voluntary aspect of law that together establish the practical grounds for human perfection or for participation as a practical activity.

Whereas the discussion of Aquinas' exposition on *De Divinis Nominibus* establishes certain metaphysical and ontological principles pertaining to human existence, it also raises questions about their practical consequences that Aquinas does not attempt to answer in the context of a metaphysical inquiry. Nevertheless, by establishing the former and alluding to the latter, Aquinas defines the principles informing and the boundaries circumscribing his moral philosophy. It seems to me that the most significant aspect of Aquinas' interpretation of Dionysius' metaphysics for moral philosophy is the outright rejection of a necessary relation between matter and evil. This denial not only endows all the creatures comprising the sublunar realm with varied degrees of nobility through participation in divine goodness, but more importantly, it bestows upon human beings a dignity transcending the merely natural one and, consequently, a responsibility corresponding to it. The essentially intellectual human participation in divine goodness, because it establishes that human beings are potentially in *imago Dei*, renders them free to bring their proper perfection into actuality. Consequently, the failure of human beings to realize their due perfection is a moral evil originating in a refusal to partake of the divine gift through which they may fulfill their end.[406] By refusing to realize their essential nature, human beings freely elect to place themselves in the rank of strictly material existents. Thus understood, moral evil is both a sin against oneself and a sin against God that manifests the voluntary human violation of the perfectly ordered universe.

Since the causes of actual sin or actual evil are not addressed in the exposition on *De Divinis Nominibus*, they must be explored in Aquinas' other writings in order to complement the theoretical discussion of evil with its practical consequences, especially in view of the Christian doctrine of original sin. In the *De Malo*,[407] Aquinas both affirms the metaphysical principles established in the *De Divinis Nominibus* and elaborates further on some of these. After stating that evil is something only *per accidens*, that it is an absence of due perfection, that it belongs to the class of voluntary things, and that the good has a fuller extension than that of being, Aquinas inquires into the moral implications of these propositions.[408] By first establishing that a good is something that conforms to a rule and a measure and that evil is the absence of conformity to any rule or measure, Aquinas repeats the conclusion reached in *De Divinis Nominibus*. This definition, however, is refined immediately in relation to particular acts. He concludes that the fault of the will designated as moral evil does not consist in ignoring the rule of reason or that of divine law, "since the soul does not possess nor can it attend to such a rule always in actuality."[409] Rather, the fault stems from the fact that the will proceeds to choose when lacking a rational rule or measure of either kind. That is, since it belongs to the will to choose according to a rule of reason or of divine law, failure to do so is a defect. In addition, every moral evil, even that of omission, is said to require an act of the will as its cause. Consequently, although some moral acts can be indifferent when they are considered according to species, in the particular case, no act is morally neutral. Evil can be distinguished only according as it is found in acts of rational willing agents; *culpa* (fault or blame) pertains to an act that follows the will, whereas *poena* (penalty) is applicable to an act that is opposed to it.[410] That is, both *culpa* and *poena* pertain to the will as privation and actuality; penalty is the contrary of fault.

When he investigates the nature and consequences of original sin in the *De Malo*, Aquinas maintains that although sin is primarily a withdrawing of original justice that affects all human beings insofar as they are descendants of Adam, nevertheless, considered in the particular case, it does not render any individual culpable, since culpability requires actual sin, which is an act of the will.[411] In fact, the assumption that original sin necessarily entails actual sin not only conflicts with the teachings of philosophy and undermines the possibility of moral philosophy, but also is contrary to the faith. Moreover, all moral concepts, such as evil and vice, would be devoid of meaning if human beings were not free to choose otherwise; that is, if original sin were an actuality. Whereas the form or principle of action of strictly natural beings is a natural appetite, the form inclining the human will toward an act is intellectual. The difference consists in the fact that "the form of a natural thing is a form individuated through matter; whence also the inclination consequent upon it is determined to one thing, but a form intellected is a universal one under which many things can be comprehended; wherefore, since acts consist of singulars, in which there is nothing proportionate to the power of the universal, the inclination of the will remains indeterminately disposing itself to many things."[412]

Hence, if original sin necessarily entailed actual sin, human beings could neither be said to be intellectual beings nor could they be held responsible for their actions.

In denying the essential causal determination of original sin, Aquinas' conclusion to the specific investigation of evil in the *De Malo* is fully compatible with his metaphysical investigation in *De Divinis Nominibus*, even when it refines it; namely, that evil is the result of the ontological human status as intellectual beings.

Whereas Maimonides does not establish a relation between the will and reason such that the will can be understood as an essential part of the intellectual soul that plays an important role in the functioning of both practical and theoretical reason, Aquinas' explanation of evil assumes an essential relation between the will and the intellect that determines each human activity, whether it is theoretical or practical. The qualification of a given end as good or evil and the hierarchical ordering of ends are consequent upon the conclusion that this relation obtains.

In the *De Veritate*[413] Aquinas develops a detailed explanation of this relation, which is repeated in all his subsequent writings. After he outlines a distinction between the will and the intellect as two separate powers of the soul, Aquinas further qualifies the distinction adding that, not only are they diverse powers, but also "they refer to diverse genera of powers."[414] This distinction is based upon the diverse kinds of relations existing between the soul and its object. When the soul is related to its object according to its own mode of existence, that is spiritually, the power whence this relation originates is cognitive. On the other hand, when the soul inclines to an object according to the object's mode of existence, the power whence the inclination originates is appetitive. However, although they are distinct powers in the soul, the will and the intellect belong to the same part of the soul and are not independent of one another either in desiring or in acquiring the object. Rather, the intellect moves the will as a final cause, whereas the will moves the intellect as an efficient cause. Consequently, as a superior appetitive power the will is simultaneously sensitive and rational and so can be moved only by a rational apprehension of an object toward which it moves itself as an end and as a good.[415]

Since good and evil are distinctions pertaining to the modes of particular objects extrinsic to the mind, the mind's objects being universal and hence either true or false, and since human beings can realize their perfection only through those actions resulting in things that they cause and hence of which they are the measure, rather than being measured by them, it is the will *qua* efficient cause to which good and evil can be directly attributed. According to Aquinas, properly speaking, the will and free choice are the same natural faculty considered *aliqualiter* (in some way) rather than *simpliciter* (absolutely).[416] Whereas the designation *will* is a broad reference to the willing potency or to the cause of rationally willed actions, the designation *free choice* is a more nuanced definition of the same faculty considered in the order of existence. That is, the designation of a choice as free emphasizes simultaneously the will as a principle of action belonging to human nature and the will as a potency that must be actualized through its own particular acts.

Since nothing is evil *secundum se*, since, properly speaking, the object of the will is the good, and since the human will is a rational faculty that is moved by the intellect as a final end, Aquinas' account seems to require the conclusion that failure of the will to desire the good would be extremely rare. In fact, only after we understand the significance of original sin and its effects can we recognize that Aquinas posits two distinct modes of existence, pre-and post-lapsarian, within which the actualization of practical cognitive principles are distinct and consequently, require different ethical orders and *epistemai*. It is important to note that in the context of strictly metaphysical and ontological discussions, Aquinas does not address the question of original sin and its consequences, whereas in his ethical discussions original sin is a primary consideration.

The most succinct account of original sin and its effects can be found in the *Summa Theologiae*. And it is not without significance that the discussion of sin precedes the long explication of law. According to Aquinas, in the state of innocence, human beings possessed as much knowledge as was required for the perfection appropriate to their metaphysical and ontological status, a perfection that was not inhibited by the sensible appetites since all the inferior human virtues were subject to, or ordered by, reason. In addition to the perfect ordering of the powers of the soul, human beings possessed all the virtues, including charity and justice, some only as inclinations, but others *in actu*. However, as a result of original sin (the actual, culpable ignorance that makes possible not only subsequent ignorance but also error), all human beings have been deprived (as a penalty) of the natural inclination to original justice, and consequently, they are deprived of the capacity to choose the good exclusively and lack all actual grace and actual virtue. The major practical consequence of original sin, which is applicable to all humans, is the possession of a corrupt *habitus* resulting from the dissolution of the harmonious order of original justice and consisting in the *lex fomitis*, an obstacle raised between the natural inclination to virtue and its end.[417] In fact, original sin is 'the natural law' that necessitated the promulgation of the divine law insofar as an obstacle was placed between the principles of natural law (the rule of reason) and the end toward which they incline, so that they cannot be applied immediately. That is, the immediate hierarchically ordered relation between reason and the will was severed and their interaction impaired in a manner such that reason no longer can determine immediately the fittingness of a particular end desired by the will to the ultimate end. The actual virtue/knowledge that is justice can no longer determine or cause acts of the will. Consequently, the human will may be attracted by a seeming good that is contrary not only to the final human perfection, but also to the corporeal one, or the principle of self-preservation, the first precept of natural law. For, insofar as all perfections are determined by the final end (actuality), and insofar as, by nature, human beings are self-moving, they are not preserved in the natural order out of necessity, but rather belong to it by choice. Consequently the choice for an apparent good is a choice contrary to human nature.

Although, initially, post-lapsarian human beings appear to have been deprived of all dignity, including that belonging to the natural order,[418] nevertheless, Aquinas maintains that they had not been deprived of the principles comprising their nature, principles that, by definition, incline them to virtue and among which free choice is numbered. Having lost the internal principle of original justice, human beings were given law and grace as external principles of action so that they may restore the perfect order among the powers of their souls. Consequently, although they no longer possess the praeternatural gifts human beings are now open to modes of participation in a supranatural state. They can internalize these aids through the power of reason that, as a consequence, can discern and choose its appropriate end. Thus understood, the role of divine law in human perfection is, first and foremost, cognitive and only secondarily moral. Being comprised of the first principles of both theoretical and practical reason, the strange *poena* that is divine law establishes the essential relation between them, sets the rule and measure for the interaction between the will and the intellect, and functions as a mediating vehicle through which human beings may freely, that is, rationally, choose to participate in the divine order and thereby recover the actual dignity commensurate with their ontological status.

Only upon supplementing Aquinas' philosophical accounts of the relation between the will and the intellect with principles acquired through revelation can we recognize that, despite some substantial differences between Maimonides' and Aquinas' philosophical positions, their respective theories about the nature of human existence after the fall are rather similar. Although Aquinas does not collapse ontological and moral concepts, never attributing evil to matter, as Maimonides (sometimes) does, nevertheless, the dissolution of the ordered relation between the will and reason consequent upon original sin amounts to an inordinate inclination of the appetites to sensible, that is, material, goods. Consequently, since the good, *qua* final end—that is, *qua* intellectual principle—is occluded to the will, matter can be said to exert a greater power over human beings than their form, a disorder that cannot be overcome by means of the natural powers of reason alone.

Nevertheless, since Aquinas' metaphysics is, first and foremost, a metaphysics of the good and is one of act only as a consequence, not only does it succeed in dissociating matter from evil, destroying its reality by positing the all-encompassing goodness of creation, but also it overcomes the tension between sub- and supralunar existence. In contradistinction to Maimonides who, by minimizing the active role of matter in perfection, renders partial ends superfluous and perfection beyond the reach of most individuals, by 'translating' the seeming privation inhering in matter to signify its desire for the good, Aquinas provides a consistent account of the relation between partial ends and the final end and, in this way, renders the possibility of attaining perfection universal.

5

NATURAL HUMAN PERFECTION
AND ITS LIMITS

Introduction

Since both Maimonides and Aquinas conclude that Adam's primordial act of disobedience originated a significant modification of human nature such that true human perfection could no longer be attained without extra-natural intervention or divine law, prior to discussing the epistemic role of divine law in the following chapter, the present chapter will examine the scope and limits of natural human possibilities. For, irrespective whether or not the transformation occasioned by the primordial act amounts to a radical ontological change, it certainly indicates a full existential one: The human being is the only natural being unable to attain its true or full natural perfection by its own powers.

For both Maimonides and Aquinas, following the medieval Aristotelian philosophic tradition, natural perfection consists in the actualization of the form of the body or in the possession of the soul in act; the specifically human perfection consists in the actualization of the intellect, that part of the human soul on account of which the human being can be said to have been created in *imago Dei*. However, although the entire medieval philosophical tradition exhibits a semantic agreement that postulates that human perfection consists in *imitatio Dei*, this agreement does not constitute a general consensus about the precise meaning of perfection, nor about the means to its acquisition. Clearly, however, since the human form is intellectual, the means for acquiring intellectual perfection are the various branches of knowledge; and since the intellect is a power of the soul, its perfection must be related to the perfection of other powers of the soul. Moreover, although both Maimonides and Aquinas consider knowledge to constitute the essence of human perfection, neither thinker can be said to have developed an explicit theory of cognition,[419] but rather, what is generally called their *epistemology* is a consequence of their psychology. Hence, in order to examine what either thinker understood the nature of human perfection to be, we must first investigate their respective discussions of the nature of the soul.

Two substantial differences between Maimonides' and Aquinas' respective explanations of the nature of the soul will emerge from the following analysis. As will become evident, these differences, in turn, condition their understanding of knowledge and, hence, of human perfection. The first difference concerns the very nature of the composition of the soul, or of the status of and relations among the distinct components of the human soul. Since this difference between Maimonides and Aquinas consists of the different degrees of relative autonomy or heteronomy, or both, that they attribute to each power and especially to the will, it has significant consequences for their understanding of the nature of human choice. The second difference concerns the nature and status of practical reason as an essential part of the distinctly human intellect, especially, the nature of its relation to speculative reason. It is the latter difference that determines their understanding of the nature of human perfection, with respect to the possibility of its acquisition, with respect to the relative significance of each aspect of reason, and finally, with respect to what constitutes actualized human perfection. Thus, since the two major differences between Maimonides' and Aquinas' psychologies concern those parts of the human soul that directly affect human action in the moral realm, these differences necessarily will determine their explanations of the epistemic status of ethical precepts, the relative significance of moral perfection for final perfection, and hence, the role of divine law in human perfection. Moreover, as will become evident in the following analyses, the differences between Maimonides' and Aquinas' psychologies have fewer and less significant consequences for their theories of sublunar existence than they do for their understanding of final perfection.

As a convenient starting point, the differences between Maimonides and Aquinas can be reduced to two distinct traditions of philosophical psychology and practical philosophy, namely, the Islamicate and the Western Christian. In Islamicate philosophy the perfection of practical reason is viewed as possible only subsequent to the perfection of speculative reason,[420] and no real distinction is drawn between will and appetite until the latter is fully informed by the intellect.[421] Christian philosophy, on the other hand, develops a comprehensive theory of the will as a distinct faculty of the human soul, the proper activity of which constitutes free choice, and also elaborates a theory of the relative and partially autonomous perfection of reason. Consequently, whereas Maimonides' ethics restricts the possibility of attaining true perfection to a very limited number of an intellectual elite, Aquinas' ethics extends the possibility of perfection to the morally perfect 'vulgar' as well as to the intellectual elite. If we are to seek a philosophical underpinning for the disagreement between them, without recourse to theological explanations, it may well be argued that Maimonides' ambivalent attitude toward matter, at least in part, can account for his pessimism concerning the possibility of attaining moral perfection. Aquinas, on the other hand, having emphasized the possibility inherent in matter, rather than its role in corruption, does not understand matter to constitute a barrier to human perfection.[422]

The Nature of the Human Soul According to Maimonides

The most thorough discussion of the soul in Maimonides' writings occurs in the "Eight Chapters," the introduction to his commentary on Avot, a mishnaic tractate devoted to ethical questions. In his prefatory remarks, Maimonides points out that his introduction presents no new thoughts concerning ethics or true perfection, but rather, is a collection gathered from numerous writings of the Sages "as well as from the discourse of both the ancient and modern philosophers, and from the compositions of many men. *"Hear the truth from whoever says it."*[423] But, he adds that, although he may repeat whole discussions that occur in some well-known text, he will refrain from identifying their author(s) since, on the one hand, such a practice would place an unnecessary encumbrance upon the discussion, and on the other, it may prejudice the reader against accepting the extra-traditional teachings, notwithstanding their importance.[424] Thus, clearly, Maimonides not only considers the discussion of the soul and its perfections to be preliminary to ethical teachings, but also believes that, precisely in this context, he should alert the readers and habituate them to accept the relevance and importance of philosophy for attaining perfection.[425]

Thus, already in the beginning of the "Eight Chapters," Maimonides is (1) establishing a necessary relation between philosophical and rabbinic teachings, and (2) alluding to the fact that philosophical perfection, or the perfection of natural reason, is a prerequisite for moral perfection, premises that will form the conclusions of his introduction to the mishnaic text known as 'The Ethics of the Fathers'. Whatever the nature of the relations between philosophical/natural and rabbinic/moral teachings may be, then, whatever tensions there may be between them, they cannot be irreconcilable, else Maimonides would have refrained from indicating them in the context of a traditional text.

Maimonides begins his discussion by emphasizing the fact that the soul is a singular composite unity within which the distinctions into diverse powers merely reflect its capacity to perform different acts. He argues that since all beings possess a soul that is their form, the term *soul* is clearly equivocal. Thus, although the human soul shares two of its five parts with the souls of other material beings, namely, the nutritive and the sensitive, the similarity between the activities performed by these parts and signified by identical terms is one in name only when the names designate the activities of different species: nutritive activity manifesting the form proper to the soul of plants, sensitive activity manifesting the form proper to animals, and rational activity manifesting the form proper to human beings. Consequently, when members of different species are said to perform a given activity identified by the same name, this activity does not originate in the same faculty: A palm is nurtured by the palm's nutritive soul, a human being, by the human nutritive soul. According to Maimonides, the equivocity of names, commonly signifying the different parts of the souls of distinct species, has been a stumbling block to many philosophizers, (*al-Mitfalasfin*) and has led to many erroneous psychologies.

The powers[426] that are uniquely human are the imaginative, appetitive, and rational faculties, the latter being that through which the human being has substantial existence. The imaginative faculty is the place where sensible impressions are stored after the sensations have departed. The appetitive faculty is the locus of all desires and affects of the soul, whose tools are the varied powers of all parts of the body. The rational faculty is the locus of intellection, in virtue of which the human being both acquires knowledge of the sciences and distinguishes good actions from base ones, both speculative and practical.[427] Whereas speculative activity is unified, its objects being the universal and unchanging things, the knowledge of which is an end in itself, practical activity is divided into a reflective part and a productive part, neither of which is an end in itself. By means of the latter, the human being acquires skills in the arts; by means of the former, he or she deliberates whether or not a particular activity is possible, and if it is, how it ought to be performed.[428] The singular soul in all its powers, Maimonides states, "is like matter, and the intellect is its form. If it does not attain its form, the existence of its capacity to receive this form is for naught, and is, as it were, futile."[429] That is, the human soul without the knowledge that is in potency in its intellectual form is no soul at all or constitutes a privation and an evil.

Even though the rational faculty exhibits perplexities, being able to hold false opinions as true, and hence can be said to be obedient and disobedient, rectitude and transgression cannot be attributed to it since its activities cannot be made subject to commandments and prohibitions.[430] Nor are the nutritive and the imaginative faculties responsible for transgressions since neither faculty acts nor refrains from action proceeding from opinion and terminating in choice. The sensitive and appetitive faculties alone are responsible for obedience and disobedience, the former serving merely as the tool of the latter. Properly speaking, then, the appetitive is the only power at which ethical prescription is aimed. But, since there exists no direct relation between reason and appetition, since appetitive objects are either immediate sensibles or imaginative sensibles, and since immediate sensibles *qua* sensibles in themselves can be neither false nor bad, transgression must originate elsewhere, namely, in the intimate relation between appetite and imagination.

Precisely because the imaginative faculty does not act in accordance with any knowledge whatsoever, but is merely a storehouse of sensible impressions that it combines indiscriminately, it is the source of all error, distinguishing and uniting diverse perceptions into composite imaginative entities that have no basis in reality, without consideration for what is possible and impossible of actual existence.[431] For the same reason, however, even though the imagination is the cause of error, neither virtue nor vice can be attributed to the imaginative faculty or to its handmaiden, the nutritive faculty. "Rather, one says that they flow properly or improperly."[432]

Insofar as he argues that, properly speaking, no commandments and prohibitions can be placed upon the rational faculty, be it upon either its speculative part or its practical part, Maimonides attributes no moral virtue or vice to it, but only rational virtues and vices. He divides these into two general categories, namely, knowledge (al-ḥikmah)[433] of the remote and proximate causes of the defined object of inquiry, and intellect (al-'aql), which comprises three types of qualities, the speculative intellect, (al-'aql al-nazari) that signifies the natural human possession of first intelligibles, the acquired intellect (al-'aql al-mustafad), and qualities such as clear understanding and quick judgment. When he defines what constitutes the rational faculty, Maimonides states that he will not discuss the nature of the acquired intellect, nor its virtues, further in this context and proceeds to address the moral virtues. He attributes the moral virtues and vices only to the appetitive faculty and, following Aristotle, characterizes the moral virtues by moderation.

Maimonides' explicit reticence to discuss the nature of the acquired intellect and its virtues is neither surprising nor an indication of esotericism.[434] Rather, I would like to suggest that such a reticence exhibits prudent interpretative practice or pedagogy, a suggestion supported by the following discussions where the question of pedagogy constitutes the unifying thread of the various examinations of habituation into moral virtue. Since the text upon which he is about to comment is an ethical one and since he has concluded that neither the intellect nor reason possess moral qualities, or actions, and having defined what the distinct parts of the soul are, Maimonides can turn his attention to those parts of the soul that, in his judgment, directly involve moral virtues and vices. This judgment, however, also indicates what I consider a major difficulty in Maimonides' account of human perfection, both intellectual and moral, namely, the disjunction between the appetitive faculty and the rational one. Appetitive activities, according to Maimonides, are relatively (if not entirely) autonomous from rational choice, until the rational part of the soul has acquired its final perfection fully and can exercise its dominion over the other faculties as the form of the soul in act. That is, until the intellect becomes the source or form of all the soul's activities, most of its "activities" are sensitive and appetitive, originating in or informed by the "animal" soul. Properly speaking, these are activities in name only since their source is external to the soul. Both the sensitive and the appetitive faculties are passive or acted upon rather than being self-moving or active. The problem, however, is that, to the extent that reason possesses its own activity, to the extent that its activity originates in the first intelligibles, so it is radically separated from the sensitive and appetitive powers. Although reason, *qua* reason, cannot be moved by an external principle of action and hence cannot be subject to commandments and prohibitions, it also cannot command the "lower" powers of the soul since it is not its proper form, according to Maimonides; rather, the intellect is. But, since the appetite can follow imaginative representations without reflection and since the imagination is the source of error, unless the perfection of the intellect also implies the possibility of possessing knowledge entirely freed from the imagination to an extent such that the imagination, *qua* autonomous power, is rendered impotent or unless, by nature, the imagination "flows properly," the overcoming of error, or vice, does not seem possible in this life.[435] Consequently, unless the desire for true perfection is posited as a first intelligible, *qua* human natural desire that is distinct from the natural inclination to perpetuate the species, it can be fulfilled, if and only if a proper natural order preexists in the soul that renders the imaginative and the appetitive faculties entirely subservient to reason or intellect. Conversely, in the absence of such a subjugation, it is necessary that there should exist some a-natural impetus, such as divine law, for establishing right order. Moreover, as should be evident by now, Maimonides' commentary on Job (Chapter 2), as well as his remarks about Joseph's unruly desire for knowledge (Chapter 1), indicate that even the potentially perfect do not possess perfect natural dispositions or the natural desire for true perfection as a *natural inclination*.

In the light of Maimonides' insistence upon the unity of the soul, on the one hand, and, on the other, the disjunction between the deliberation and choice he attributes to the practical intellect and moral virtue, not only does it appear as if moral virtue is a-rational (if not irrational) but also it seems to follow that the commandments and prohibitions are a-rational. As will become evident in the following discussions, however, reason cannot yield the measure of perfection, precisely because reason is not the highest intellectual-human perfection. Rather, it is the highest natural virtue. For Maimonides, then, reason and nature are co-extensive. But, if this is, in fact, the case, and if natural perfection is not to be the contradictory of final perfection, there would have to exist some relation between reason and moral virtue, even if indirect, since moral virtues and vices are exhibited as actions in the realm of natural human existence.[436]

"What, then, are the moral virtues, how are they acquired and why are they necessary for final perfection?" In the "Eight Chapters," where the only sustained discussion of moral virtues and vices is undertaken, Maimonides argues that moral virtues and vices are habits of the soul acquired as a result of long repeated practice reflecting familial and social conventions, rather than natural, or rational, dispositions of the soul. Since the acquired habits in fact may be vices, rather than virtues, and since moral virtues manifest the mean between excess and defect, extreme measures contrary to acquired vices would have to be practiced repeatedly in order to achieve moderation. And, according to Maimonides, people *often* err about the mean, confusing one of two extremes with virtue. However, since no rational reflection was involved in acquiring moral habits, none is entailed directly in the remedy, although, clearly, a *knowing* 'physician' must prescribe the cure and, hence, reason is related indirectly to the acquisition of moral virtues. That is, reason is extrinsically related to moral virtue insofar as it is an active principle of the physician/teacher/agent, a passive one for the patient.[437] In addition, since Maimonides argues that no human being is inclined to all the moral virtues and vices by nature, natural reason cannot arrive at the mean *per se* and requires some a-natural source in order to establish the principles of moral virtues.[438]

The relation between physician and patient is the relation between agency and passion, act and potency, above all, reason and appetite. But, whereas with respect to all strictly natural things actuality and potency are internally related so that, even when the potency is understood as privation and as the contrary of actuality/perfection, natural motion is the progressive movement or internal inclination towards actuality, in the case of human moral virtue the relation between potency and act seems to be strictly external. Although Maimonides claims that "by nature man does not possess either virtue or vice at the beginning of his life,"[439] he insists that unless obedience becomes an intrinsic principle as choice, "the commandments and prohibitions of the Law would be nullified and they would all be absolutely in vain."[440]

The "Eight Chapters" does not provide an explanation of the transformation of the relation between reason and appetite except for stating that divine law is necessary for such a transformation. It does, however, briefly indicate what the hindrance to perfection, both moral and rational is, namely, the imagination. Those who do not possess moral virtues desire "bad" things as "good" following imaginative representations.[441] Since moral perfection is not natural, since the proper object of the appetite is material, and since imaginative objects are material in origin, the appetite by nature follows imagination rather than reason in the absence of a greater attraction or cause for repulsion. The perfection of the appetite, then, would depend upon the prior perfection of the imagination, and imagination is directly related to reason. As will become evident in the following chapters, it is the latter relation that simultaneously constitutes the most problematic question for Maimonides and can resolve some, if not all, the tensions in Maimonides' account of the soul, in particular through the distinction between reason and intellect.

Although in the "Eight Chapters" Maimonides does not address the nature of the ordered relation between the a-rational appetite and reason, and although he explicitly refrains from discussing the intellect, the text does provide ample indication that Maimonides considered divine law to be absolutely necessary for both appetitive and rational perfection. When he argues that, whatever their proximate ends may be, all human actions should be directed, and subordinated, to the knowledge of God and that such knowledge exceeds natural reason, he also indicates that the subordination to knowledge requires another mode of knowing. Moreover, since he does not believe that the human being, by definition, possesses a natural inclination to the good, he implicitly denies the possibility that what is naturally pleasing is a consequence of the recognition of a goodness inherent in the desired object.[442] In arguing that one who desires perfection needs to acquire the sciences, an acquisition to which all physical perfections and all activities should be subordinate, Maimonides states not only that utility, rather than pleasure, ought to be the measure of all non-intellectual activities, but also that if an activity "happens to be pleasant, so be it; and if it happens to be repugnant, so be it."[443] Consequently, it seems that Maimonides does not consider the human appetite, *qua* natural inclination, to be naturally inclined to the well-being of the human species, natural or supra-natural; and in fact, he characterizes all non-intellectual activities as proper to beasts rather than human beings.

The necessity of divine law for perfection is made evident again in Maimonides' discussion of the seeming incongruity between the mishnaic praise of the continent person as superior to the one virtuous by nature, in contradistinction to the philosophers' praise of natural virtue as superior to all others.[444] He explains that those things that the philosophers designated as evils "are the things generally accepted by all the people as bad, such as murder, theft, robbery . . . and things like these."[445] The desire for this class of actions exists only in souls that are defective by nature; conversely, the soul characterized by the philosophers as virtuous is but the healthy one, whose owner does not desire these things nor refrains from them as a result of continence. Thus understood, the conventional accord characterized by Maimonides as a manifestation of "natural virtue" is nothing other than the natural appetitive disposition or desire to preserve in being and the repulsion from its opposite. On the other hand, the actions designated by the Sages as the manifestation of continence are ones proscribed by the Torah; and notwithstanding their origin, Maimonides maintains that "if it were not for the Law, they would not be bad at all."[446]

Why then does the Torah proscribe actions that may not be bad at all? What constitutes the nobility or baseness of an action? Does reason not legislate the giving, or the withholding, of assent either to conventional practice or to divine commandments? Although Maimonides criticizes 'some Jewish Mutakallimun'[447] for interpreting the class of actions commonly abhorred by human beings to represent rational commandments, in this context he does not offer an alternative explanation for the origin of any type of conventional

accord among people, an accord that he clearly considers a given consequence of human nature (or of creation) and upon which he elaborates in the *Guide*; nor does he explain the extra-rational/natural legislative power of the Law.[448]
When we read the "Eight Chapters" it becomes evident that, strictly speaking, the text is meant to be primarily a didactic text and secondarily, perhaps, a propaedeutic one, rather than a philosophical text. Apart from outlining the nature and composition of the soul and detailing its virtues, apart from drawing distinctions between the theoretical and moral virtues and among the moral virtues the ones possessed through conventional accord and those possessed through the Torah, all of which, he asserts, are necessary for acquiring final perfection, Maimonides does not provide an explanation of the relation obtaining among the different faculties of the soul nor does he explain the nature of the relations (if any[449]) between the rational and moral virtues. Although he explains that the perfection of the moral virtues consists in moderation and insists that the true and final end of moderation is intellectual perfection and that the perfection of the moral virtues requires extrinsic guides, whether they are teachers or laws, he does not explain the nature of the relation between the two perfections, nor does he explain how knowledge can gain dominion over the irrational inclinations of the appetite.

The greatest gap in the account, however, seems to me to originate in two unreconciled assertions, namely, that practical reason deliberates about actions and distinguishes between good acts and base ones and that moral virtues and vices pertain to the appetite rather than to reason.[450] For how can the human being be held accountable for transgressions of extra-rational principles if, on the one hand, the theoretical perfection of practical reason precedes moral perfection and, on the other, moral perfection is a prerequisite for final perfection but is not grounded in reason? Nevertheless, Maimonides does allude to the resolution of this question when he draws the distinction between speculative and final perfection, stating that, whereas speculative perfection does not require moral perfection, final perfection is proportionate to the perfection of the moral virtues. Although no comprehensive account is put forth by Maimonides, either in the "Eight Chapters" or in the *Guide*, explaining the nature of the transition from speculative to moral perfection and the nature of the subsequent transformation of both perfections into the synthesis manifesting full intellectual perfection, when the two texts are read as complementary, they offer sufficient detail from which to understand Maimonides' teachings on the nature of, and internal relations within, human perfection.[451]

In contrast to the discussion of perfection in the "Eight Chapters," the *Guide* provides no account devoted strictly to the nature of the soul and its perfections, but rather, apart from the four final chapters of the book, it presents scattered discussions of human perfection in two distinct contexts, namely, discussions of intellectual perfections and discussions of the commandments and prohibitions of the Torah. Moreover, the *Guide* makes explicit what Maimonides understood the meaning of the corporeal human soul to be.[452] The claim that the material intellect is radically other than the acquired one requires that a distinction be drawn between that part of the soul that is immortal and the potential powers constituting the human soul with which the human being is endowed at birth, a distinction that allows Maimonides to resolves the conflict between the corruptibility of matter and the incorruptibility, or immortality, of the soul.[453]

In addition to the distinction between the generated soul and the immortal soul, Maimonides outlines a difference between the rational faculty, which he identifies with the material (hylic) intellect,[454] which he judges to be merely the potentiality to receive form, and the acquired intellect, which is the immortal soul.[455] The distinction between the "two" intellects, which is explicitly drawn in the *Guide*, is reminiscent of the ones outlined in the "Eight Chapters" between the rational soul and the intellect and between the theoretical and the acquired intellects. The *Guide* also recalls the claim in the "Eight Chapters" that the term *soul* is equivocal and, hence, "should be interpreted in every passage according to what is indicated in the context."[456] Consequently, it seems that substantial existence in potency, or the fact of the particular composition of matter and form constituting the human being, in no way guarantees and, perhaps, does not even safeguard the acquisition for any human being of the true human form in act. Rather, the possession of a human soul guarantees merely the perpetuation of the species, or of those parts of the human soul that are not controlled fully by the human form and that are analogous to those possessed by other strictly natural beings.[457]

In order to understand Maimonides' twofold assertion that, on the one hand, the human soul is a corporeal entity or a mere undetermined potentiality for human existence and, on the other, that the human soul is immortal, we must undertake a careful examination of the different accounts he puts forth about the nature of the intellect. Prior to providing an exegetical analysis of the various and varied accounts, it should be noted, once again, that not only does Maimonides refrain from presenting an account of the soul in the *Guide*, but also he does not provide a comprehensive account of the nature of the human intellect. Nor does he address the human intellect as a distinct subject independent of other considerations, either of the limitations of human knowledge, or of its place in the hierarchy of intellects, or of the perfection of the universal order in general.

Notwithstanding the absence of a sustained single account, Maimonides both begins and ends the *Guide* with considerations of the nature of true human perfection, or the perfection of the intellect, commencing with an explication of terms commonly used in the Bible to designate the intellect, and closing with the existential manifestations of acquired intellectual perfection in specific activities. When he explicates the statement that the human being had been created in the image and likeness of God, Maimonides states that these two attributes are notions used generally to refer to a being's natural form by means of which it possesses substantial existence. "It is the true reality (*ḥaqiqa*) of the thing insofar as the latter is that particular being. In man that notion is that from which human apprehension (*al-'idrak al-ansani*) derives. It is on account of this intellectual apprehension (*al-'idrak al-ᶜaqli*) that it is said of man: 'In the image of God created He him'"⁴⁵⁸ (Gen. 1:27).

Intellectual apprehension, the act that constitutes the human being as human, distinguishes the human being from all other sublunar existents and is entirely independent of the human senses or of material composition, consisting in the conjunction with the agent intellect.⁴⁵⁹ The perfect state of the human intellect, the one possessed in actuality by Adam before his act of disobedience, is one in which the human being knows truth from falsity concerning intelligible or unchanging things. Maimonides insists that, in its perfect state, the human intellect did not possess knowledge of good and evil since these notions belong to the category of generally accepted things.⁴⁶⁰ The possession of a faculty able to distinguish good from evil is the punishment imposed upon Adam or human beings as a consequence of disobedience, a punishment reducing human beings to a status closer to beasts and further from intellects.⁴⁶¹ Although he states that Adam's sin consisted in following an imaginative desire,⁴⁶² he does not explain how it was possible for Adam in the state of intellectual perfection, the state in which the intellect is in act and thus governs all other psychic faculties, to follow such a desire either in the opening chapters or elsewhere in the *Guide*. What is especially puzzling about this 'strange' assertion is the presence of an imaginative faculty in a being whose intellect does not seem to require sensible objects for its knowledge, since it cognizes only the intelligible species. Clearly, Maimonides does not wish to maintain that the primordial human intellect was immaterial nor even that the human soul, at some actual historical time, was devoid of an imaginative faculty because, among other things, the possession of the imaginative faculty can account for the act of disobedience that ensued from Adam's perfectly ordered *intellective* soul.⁴⁶³ However, since Maimonides argues simultaneously that the intellectual apprehension constituting the actualized, or perfect, human intellect has no need of the senses and that Adam's intellect was the archetypical instance of the ultimate perfection of the human intellect, and since he does not provide an explanation to account for the necessary role of the imagination in Adam's perfect, or acquired, intellect, it seems to me that the assertion cannot be supported philosophically. Nonetheless, the brief explanation of the fall does seem to indicate that there exists an important relation between the imagination and the capacity to acquire conventional knowledge. Consequently, apart from its punitive role, the practical intellect would have to play a remedial role in acquiring perfection, exercising prudential judgments over the particular representations of the imagination, at the very least, whether they are necessary or possible of existence. For even as intellectual entities, actualities can be judged as necessary, possible or impossible.

Irrespective of the status of Adam's transgression, since the human intellect occupies the lowest rank in the hierarchy of intellects, its capacities to apprehend certain things is limited by its very nature. These limits, which are manifest in varied degrees of human knowledge of the beings, also manifest the hierarchically inverse relation between certainty in human knowledge and the order of being. Paradoxically, these limits also exhibit the progressive distanciation between certainty and actual existence so that the demand for certainty as the measure of knowing emerges as a barrier to knowledge.[464] *Per se*, the human intellect can apprehend some existents perfectly, some only partially, through manifestations of some of their modes of existence, and some not at all. In addition to the intellectual limitations belonging to the human species, a great divergence exists among the individuals of the species—differences that are clearly manifest regarding all their physical capacities and that extend equally to their intellectual capabilities. Given the natural limitations of the human intellect in general and of individual intellects in particular, Maimonides argues that precisely because of these natural limits, the human soul does not desire to apprehend those objects beyond its natural capacity.[465]

> Moreover, every perfect man—after his intellect has attained the cognition of whatever in its nature can be grasped—when longing for another apprehension beyond that which he has achieved, cannot but have his faculty of apprehension deceived or destroyed— . . . —unless divine help attends him.[466]

Consequently, if we are not to assume that Maimonides is contradicting himself intentionally, or inadvertently, the longing of the perfect human being must be not simply disproportionate to the natural human capacity, but also must exhibit a disorder in the soul manifest in its desire for the impossible and, hence, for non-being. As in the case of Joseph, the exemplary perplexed reader of the *Guide*, such a longing also indicates that he has not yet attained full knowledge of that which is within his natural capacity. For if the object of knowledge is beyond natural human grasp, then the longing must be a desire for an object of the imagination rather than for something true[467] and thus must exhibit an improper relation between the intellect, the imagination, and the appetitive power. That is, the desire for an imaginative object, in itself, makes manifest the absence of full natural perfection since perfection is the actuality that precludes passion (longing) and thus presupposes the prior recognition of limit,[468] and since what is in act cannot be destroyed or undergo change.

Among the objects that are within the intellect's natural scope of cognition, those accessible by means of demonstration are rarely subject to disagreement, except among the ignorant. Conversely, the less a subject admits of demonstration the greater the disagreement and confusion concerning its nature. Defining the sciences according to the scope of their knowability, Maimonides states, "[t]he things about which there is this great perplexity are very numerous in divine matters, few in matters pertaining to natural science, and nonexistent in matters pertaining to mathematics."[469] That is, the greater the significance a subject has for the perfection of the intellect, the greater is the difficulty in attaining it and the lesser is the degree of certainty about it.[470] Consequently, Maimonides' repeated emphasis upon the inverse nature of the relation between the order of being and the order of knowing must be based upon the conclusion that the order of the acquisition of the sciences determines the foundation of right order between the faculties of the soul. If proper order and due speed are observed in acquiring the sciences, then proper order can be established in the soul, and the limitations of knowledge within each subject will be observed, whereas without due caution, the imagination will overpower and weaken the intellect. It is important to note, however, that when Maimonides cautions the acceptance of limitations and the observation of a due rate of progress, he is not counseling acquiescence to ignorance. Rather, he argues that undue haste will lead to error in a manner such that it will both prevent the acquisition of possible knowledge and, through hasty judgment, lead to a pursuit of what the imagination rather than reason, deems possible. Ultimately, improper procedure can produce a corrupt *habitus* in one capable of perfection so that the potentiality of which the material intellect consists will be no more than privation and lead only to destruction.

Maimonides discusses the perfection of the intellect in two contexts, namely, its mode of cognition, and the nature of prophetic knowledge.[471] Apart from the possession of first principles that form the natural intellectual faculty and that all human beings possess, the perfection of the intellect, or its acquisition of knowledge, proceeds in three stages, namely, abstraction, the formation of concepts, and apprehension.[472] In the first two stages, the intellect divides and distinguishes composite things into diverse notions, discerning their true reality and their causes. Distinguishing between the essential predicates of objects and their accidents, the intellect derives the universal from the individuals, "and no demonstration is true except by means of universals."[473] Apprehension "is the very being and true reality of intellect."[474] In apprehension, the intellect becomes identical with its subject and object; that is, the potentially knowing intellect, the potentially knowing subject, and the potentially known object, become one, or *are* the actualized intellect. Because apprehension is the essential act of the intellect, it refers equally to the knowledge acquired at the culmination of abstractive activity and that acquired through the conjunction with the agent intellect, since the knowledge possessed is now immediate to the intellect.[475]

Since the two psychological hindrances to intellectual perfection are the appetitive faculty and the imaginative faculty and since neither faculty acts in accordance with knowledge, it remains to be determined how order in the soul can be established so that perfection be acquired. Maimonides' most succinct formulation of the specific perfection of each faculty of the soul is found in *Guide*, 2. 36, in the context of the discussion of the nature of prophecy. He states that the perfection of the rational faculty consists in study, that of the imaginative faculty consists in a natural disposition, and that of the appetitive faculty, or the perfection of the moral habits,[476] consists in "the turning away of thought from all bodily pleasures and the putting an end to the desire for the various kinds of ignorant and evil glorification."[477] Since human beings have neither choice about nor control over the original natural disposition of their souls which is determined by the celestial bodies, and especially by the agent intellect[478] and since Maimonides does not consider it possible to prescribe a remedial measure for improving an imagination corrupt by nature, he is arguing, in fact, that ultimate human perfection will be determined to a great extent by the original natural disposition of the imagination. Moreover, although he does not discuss the nature of the relation between the perfection of the intellect and that of the imagination in the same context, apart from affirming its existence and importance, and although he states that rational perfection consists in the acquisition of the sciences, it is clear that the imaginative faculty must be well—although not necessarily perfectly—disposed in order to achieve rational, let alone ultimate, perfection since reason depends upon imaginative representation for the acquisition of its concepts. And yet, Maimonides argues that "the act of the imagination is not an act of the intellect but rather its contrary."[479] Whereas the actual apprehension of the intellect manifests its freedom, even potential separability, from the body, the imagination is strictly a corporeal faculty that is affected by all bodily changes. Consequently, the control of the appetites by law, at least in part, must precede the perfection of reason since their moderation will make possible the stability of the imagination.[480] Ironically, as will become evident in the following chapter, prophetic perfection is simultaneously a perfection of the intellect and of the imagination, and the promulgation of divine law by the prophet is mediated twice, first through the imagination and then through language.

Aquinas and the Harmony of the Soul

Distinct examinations of the nature of the soul in general and of the human soul in particular are abundant throughout Aquinas' works, both in the form of commentaries, and in the context of his own philosophical and theological inquiries.[481] The centrality of psychological inquiries in Aquinas' works is not surprising when we acknowledge (1) the central role of psychology in Aquinas' discussions of human knowledge and ethics, (2) its location in the ordering of the sciences as the transitional discourse from physics to metaphysics,[482] and most important, (3) the ontological grounds of the continuous unity in the hierarchical universal order or in the community of being, despite the evident multiplicity of diverse existents.[483]

Whereas in the discussion of creation I have argued that Aquinas' ontology requires that the possibility of specific human existence, first and foremost, should be understood in terms of the infinite extension or diffusion of the good, the discussion of the soul and its proper acts requires that actual, particular human existence should be understood in terms of the extension of being and the act of being or becoming. When existence in general, human existence in particular, is understood as the simultaneous unfolding of a twofold ontology,[484] Aquinas psychology emerges as the discourse that locates and articulates the relation between the good and being as the internal motion of the soul. The perfection of the human soul, especially the actualization of the human intellect, amounts to the progressive apprehension of the unity of the good and the true as essential acts of being manifest in the very activity of the soul. The greater extension of the good than that of being makes it possible for Aquinas to extend the desire for being to all powers of the soul, including the ones whose activities are strictly material. Aquinas' twofold ontology, which is indebted to both Aristotle and Neoplatonism but adheres to neither authoritatively, also makes it possible to understand how he could simultaneously praise and criticize Aristotle in a single commentary, such as the one on the *Nicomachean Ethics*,[485] using another Aristotelian text, the *De Anima*, as his basis. As will become evident, with respect to the human intellect, Aquinas' departure from Aristotle also constitutes his most significant divergence from Maimonides, from the Aristotelian commentators, from the medieval Islamicate philosophers, and in my opinion, should be understood in the context of the dispute with the "Averroists" concerning the unity of the intellect.[486]

Before I turn to a close textual analysis of Aquinas' teachings on the soul, it is important to point out, again, that Aquinas—like other medieval thinkers in both traditions—did not develop an epistemology since, for him, the question of human knowledge is an essential constituent of psychology and since he held that the being of the soul is both inseparable from and manifest in its proper act. And, as will become evident, the full discussion of the soul must also encompass ethics since the human being is simultaneously a knower and an agent.

In light of the multiplicity of texts addressing the nature of the soul, the following analysis will use the explanation in the *Summa Theologiae* as its focus, both because the comprehensive account is placed structurally in its proper ontological context and because the text does not present the additional difficulties inherent in commentaries[487] and, finally, for the sake of ease. The discussion of the human soul and its operations is situated after the discussion of creation and the angels or separate substances and before the discussion of the fallen human state. Thus, the human soul as the form of human existence or the grounds of actual human existence manifests the proper human place in the ontological order and serves as the basis for demonstrating the continuity between the physical and the metaphysical orders.

After he defines the soul as the principle of life evident in the acts proper to the body of each species, rather than as a body (in Q. 75, a. 1), Aquinas, immediately, opens up the discussion of the human soul in the *Summa Theologiae* with the assertion that the human soul is something immaterial and self-subsistent since (1) it can know all corporeal things, which would not be the case had it been a body, and (2) it is the principle of its own intellectual operations. The general discussion of the soul, its powers, and non-intellectual operations is here postponed to a later question (Q. 77), following the discussions of the essence of the soul and its union with the body (Q. 76). Thus, the metaphysical order, or actuality, the order of descent originating in *esse tantum* and whose articulation is in terms of *esse commune* rather than the physical or existential order(s) of ascent or the orders articulated in terms of *actus essendi*, the motion of which is from potency to act, orders the discussion of the soul in the *Summa* from the very beginning, reversing, as it does, the Aristotelian order of inquiry not only in the *De Anima* but also in the *Ethics* and even in the *Metaphysics*. Thus understood, by definition (i.e., essentially), the intellect or intellective soul[488] must be immaterial in order to know sensible objects and must have some inherent actuality if it is to act *per se*. "For to act belongs to nothing other than a being in act; whence to the extent that something acts, so it is."[489]

When Aquinas discusses the soul in the order of self-subsistent beings, or as an intellect, he argues that it is immaterial and, insofar as it has immaterial actuality, it is incorruptible. Although later on in the discussion it would become important for Aquinas to argue for the soul's necessary union with the body, viewed from the perspective of its ontological and noetic status, he first emphasizes its immateriality in order to safeguard its capacity for knowledge. Were the soul intrinsically dependent upon its union with the body, were its operations governed by corporeal powers, it would not be able to know corporeal things. Beginning from the premise that it is evident that the intellectual principle that is called the *human soul* can know the *nature* of all corporeal things, Aquinas concludes that it can have no part of their *nature* in it.

> If, therefore, the intellectual principle should have in it the *nature* of something corporeal, it would not be able to know all corporeal things.

Moreover, every body has some determinate *nature*. Therefore, it is impossible that the intellectual principal be a body.—And, likewise, it is impossible that it should understand through a bodily organ, since if it were [so to understand], the determinate *nature* of that bodily organ would prohibit the knowledge of all corporeal things.[490]

That is, since every natural determination, *qua* actual, according to Aquinas, is a limitation of the essential possibility to become in act what some thing is in potency, natural *necessity* precludes the possibility of an essential change. Human being is essentially or by nature a knower, hence "it" cannot become identical with a being whose operations are governed by any other determinate principle (form), such as sensation. Indeed, sensation is indispensable to human knowledge, but unlike the animals the form of whose soul is sensitive, human sensation is governed by the human *telos*; namely, knowledge. Hence, both *qua* sensation and *qua* one source of human knowing, the form of human sensing is radically/originally and causally different than animal sensing. Whatever we will be able to understand then by the "identity" of knower and known, be it sensible or intelligible, in the act of understanding, it could not be the assimilation of the known as it exists sensibly to the knower; rather, as known, natural things will be transformed into the mode of the knower.[491] Thus, although Aquinas quotes Augustine's *De Trinitate* in the *sed contra* preceding the response to the question "whether [or not] the human soul is self-subsistent" and although his conclusion, like Augustine's, is that it is, for him, the consequences of this conclusion are diametrically opposed to those of Augustine. That is, whereas, for Augustine, the self-subsistence of the human soul guarantees understanding without or independent of sensation, for Aquinas, it guarantees the noetic stability of sensation.[492] Ironically, Aquinas' insistence upon the immaterial status of the soul renders possible the fuller participation of all its faculties, in particular, sense perception and imagination, in knowledge.

The intellective soul is common to all the individuals comprising the human species and, hence, defines it as a distinct species. It is only in the next question (Iª Pars, Q. 76) that Aquinas fully elaborates upon the nature of the essential union of body and soul, an essential union that precludes the "Platonic" view of the soul as using a body.[493] In fact, only after he insists that the soul is immaterial and self-subsistent does it become significant to explain why the soul's immateriality in no way entails a denial that the human soul by its very nature must be united with a body of which it is the natural form. For, were such a union denied, it would entail the consequence that the human species, like each angelic species, would be comprised of a single individual.[494]

In contradistinction to angelic species, it is in virtue of the soul's union with the body that a distinction within the human species into unique individuals is realized. Because of its necessary conjunction with matter, the human soul occupies the lowest rank in the order of intellectual beings, requiring sense organs for its operations. Properly speaking, the soul does not unite with matter, but rather, it is the absolute form of a natural body of which it is the active principle and hence, it is distributed throughout all its parts and constitutes its unity. It cannot be overemphasized that, for Aquinas, the unity of body and soul is substantial and hence, properly speaking, neither the soul nor the body is the principle of individuation, rather the very union is. Were the body or matter the principle of individuation, Aquinas would be unable to defend individual immortality against the "Averroist" claim; were the intellect alone the principle of individuation, there will be as many species of human beings as there are individuals who share in name by a *pros hen* analogy rather than by definition or essentially.

Because of its intermediate status between the sub- and supralunar realms, the soul consists of the diverse powers belonging to the creatures of both realms. The faculties (powers) of the soul are distinguished, first and foremost, by the end toward which they are ordered, and secondarily, they are distinguished by their object; where the former distinction manifests an active potency, the latter manifests a passive one.[495]

Before proceeding, it is important to note here that the twofold aspect of psychic powers not only reflects the twofold ontology of the act of being and the good—the former being the active, the latter the passive aspect of each power—but also that this twofold ontology makes possible the elimination of a real distinction between the active and passive intellect(s), a distinction vehemently rejected by Aquinas. Thus, by introducing a Neoplatonic element— the causality of the good—into Aristotle's psychology, Aquinas is able to overcome the tension between the two human ends as well as safeguard individual immortality.[496]

After he determines that the faculties of the soul are diverse, Aquinas explains that they are interrelated in accordance with three distinct orders, namely, the order of being, the order of generation and corruption, and the natural order of their respective objects. The first two orders are intrinsic to these powers, *qua* faculties or determinate possibilities, respectively signifying their perfection and changeability, their active and passive aspects. The third order is extrinsic to the soul, depending upon the natural order of existence. The first two orders thus reflect the intrinsic teleology of the soul or its formal and efficient causality, whereas the latter reflects the natural teleology of all created things or the soul's relation to them *qua* moving causes.

The faculties that originate in the soul alone independently of its union with the body, such as the intellective and the volitional powers, are those that remain in the separated soul as its actuality. On the other hand, all the powers that arise from the soul's union with the body, such as the sensitive and the nutritive powers, are destroyed with the body.[497] That is, since, in contradistinction to Maimonides, Aquinas argues that the intellective soul is immaterial and possesses some measure of self-subsistence independent of its union with a material body, all human beings, by definition and irrespective of their particular natures, belong to the realm of intellects and have a share in immortality.

Following Aristotle, Aquinas distinguishes five faculties of the soul: vegetative, sensitive, appetitive, locomotive, and intellective;[498] and each faculty is distinguished further into its component powers according to the bodily organs that serve as their instruments and according to their objects and specific ends. For the sake of brevity, we shall limit our outline to those faculties and their internal distinctions that are directly relevant to the limitation of natural reason.

Apart from external motions, the human sensitive faculty, according to Aquinas, also possesses internal motions; these are the locus of intrinsic intentions received through the external senses, but representing the form of sensibles or their unchanging aspect. Following Avicenna, Aquinas distinguishes four internal senses: the *sensus communis*, the imagination, the estimative power, and memory.[499] The *sensus communis* receives the forms of sensibles, the imagination stores them, the estimative power perceives[500] their purpose, and memory retains and recalls them. Aquinas maintains that the human estimative power is cognitive rather than sensible since it collates impressions according to their purpose; it can therefore be designated as particular reason since it assigns particular determinations to individual things in a manner similar to universal reason that assigns them to universals.[501] Unlike the animal estimative faculty, which is an immediate natural instinct, the human estimative faculty is discursive or intermediate insofar as it collates discovered intentions, which are not sensible or present to immediate perception. As a consequence, human memory, too, is discursive and investigates past memories, which are general, in relation to individual or particular intentions. In designating the estimative process of collation "cogitative" and that of memory "quasi syllogistic," Aquinas is paving the way for bridging the gap between sensation, imagination, and reasoning, particular and universal judgment, practical and speculative reason. Initially, Aquinas' attribution of internal motions to faculties shared by human and other natural beings seems to recall Maimonides' explanation of the equivocity of common terms; the form of the soul of each species is that which constitutes it as a unique species. But, unlike Maimonides (whose disdain for matter renders almost impossible[502] a real relation between the material and immaterial), Aquinas establishes an analogical relation between the souls of different species that underlines the continuity rather than disjunction in being.[503] Where Maimonides underscores the radical or essential difference among species belonging to the same genus, Aquinas emphasizes their essential same-

ness. This is not surprising, of course, in the light of the fact that genetic sameness refers to the matter, a matter to which, for Aquinas, the good extends,
whereas specific difference refers to form.

In a similar manner Aquinas argues that the human appetitive faculty
must be distinguished into a sensitive appetite that is merely a passive natural
inclination and an intellective appetite that is an active power that moves itself
to apprehended goods and thus can be said to constitute the form of the human
appetite. The argument for an intellective appetite, in my opinion, constitutes
one of the two most significant differences between Maimonides' and Aquinas'
psychologies; for, by positing a real relation between the appetite and knowledge, Aquinas greatly extends the possibility of establishing order in the soul.

Aquinas draws a distinction within the human intellective faculty into that
part which is potential, namely, the possible intellect, and that which is always
in act, namely, the agent intellect. He argues for the existence of a multiplicity
of agent intellects proportionate in number to the created human souls "since it
cannot happen that one and the same power belong to diverse subjects"[504] and
since "the separate intellect, according to the teachings of our faith, is God
himself, who is the creator of the soul."[505] In positing the distinction between the
possible and agent intellect Aquinas is careful to avoid the understanding of the
possible intellect either as external or as strictly passive, a caution motivated,
first and foremost, by a doctrinal rather than a philosophical concern, namely,
individual immortality. Thus, in response to an objection that relies upon the
opposition between the *passive* and agent intellect*s* in order to conclude that,
were the agent intellect, in addition to the passive intellect, "something belonging to the soul," human beings would be able to understand at will, which is
manifestly false (Q. 79, a. 4, 3m), Aquinas immediately replaces the term *passive intellect* with the term *possible intellect*. The response, whose background
is clearly the Averroist controversy, also bears out my previous claim that
Aquinas' primary concern here is doctrinal. For Aquinas acknowledges the
fact that philosophically, with respect to human knowledge, "it makes no difference whether the agent intellect is something belonging to the soul or something separate,"[506] for the motion from potency to act can be brought about
either by an external or an internal principle of actuality. Since, however,
Aquinas denies emanation (recognizing that *philosophically* it may compromise
divine power, deny divine volition, etc.) and insists on creation and since he
argues that the separate intellect is God, he also insists that the relation between
intellectual potency and actuality is internal to the soul; the possible intellect
possesses the principles of its own actuality by participation or as a real power
(*virtus*) and thus as a principle of action.[507]

Aquinas further points out that the response to the question "whether or
not the agent intellect is one" depends upon the premises. The different
premises reflect the difference between principles of emanation and of cre-

ation. For the former, there are separate intermediate intellects between the divine and the human, for the latter, especially as presented by Aquinas, the separate intellect is a creator God. It thus becomes clear that the question concerning the status of the universe, whether it is eternal or created, a question that, for Aquinas, is coextensive with the question whether the universe is emanated or created, governs his psychology. This is not surprising given that the discussion of psychology is based upon ontological principles of which creation, a principle believed by faith but not known, is the first. And, as in the question of creation, so in the debate with Averroes and the Averroists concerning the status of the agent intellect, the question cannot be settled by demonstration but can be investigated only dialectically. Ironically, although he follows Maimonides quite closely in the discussion of creation and although he draws heavily upon Aristotle's *De Anima* in discussions of the human soul and its knowledge, with respect to psychology and noetics, Aquinas' argument for the multiplicity of agent intellects constitutes not only the most significant difference between him and Maimonides but also a radical departure from Aristotle.

Since first principles are indemonstrable, Aquinas can, indeed, posit a different first principle as a basis for his ontology and psychology without, thereby, violating the philosophical status of his subsequent discussions. As will become evident, by positing an individual agent intellect Aquinas is able not only to unify human cognition as well as cognition and action to a greater extent than Maimonides and Aristotle have done, but also to safeguard human knowledge against imaginative error to a greater degree. Thus, whereas for Maimonides the initial disposition of, and possibility of ordering the imagination present the greatest epistemic and moral difficulties, for Aquinas the only faculties whose initial dispositions cannot be fully safeguarded by the possession of the actuality that is the agent intellect are the sensitive.[508] That the latter difficulty is minimized by the belief in the perfect creator and providence, which safeguards the species against all but accidental causes, should be amply clear.

After he clearly establishes the ontological status of the human intellect, Aquinas turn to its diverse modes of knowing. The intellect can be understood in one of four ways: illumination. receptivity, practical activity, and speculative activity. The agent intellect, which is that immaterial, self-subsistent part of the soul in act from its coming into being, is the abstractive power of the soul. The others are capacities of the possible intellect to become an intellect in act. These capacities are its three distinct potencies—namely, memory (receptivity) of which the distinctly human aspect is intellective rather than sensitive,[509] the practical intellect, and the speculative intellect—all of which have to be actualized by means of distinct activities requiring the other faculties of the soul.

Although Aquinas follows the traditional Aristotelian distinction between the practical and the speculative intellect, respectively designating that part of the intellect ordered to act and that which is ordered to knowledge of truth as an end in itself, he argues not only that each part possesses its own inherent primary principles, but also that the perfection of both functions of the single intellect are closely related and together constitute acquired human perfection or that perfection proper to the prefallen human being. Thus, unlike Aristotle and especially Maimonides,[510] Aquinas regards the possession of the practical intellect neither as a 'penalty' nor as the unfortunate consequence of corporeal existence which is manifest as a tension between the two human perfections. Rather, irrespective of the human existential status, human knowledge, by definition, is primarily abstractive; intuition, or apprehension of intelligible essences, is the *natural* culmination of the ratiocinative process. Whereas the term *intellect* refers to the state of rest that denotes the initial possession of the primary principles and the final acquired perfection of the form, the designation *reason* refers to the state of motion that investigates these principles discursively, distinguishing and uniting cognitional objects until the intellect apprehends the universal forms and the intelligibles.[511]

After the intellect has performed its primary activity, abstracting the species from the particular sensible objects present in the imagination, it neither possesses the objects immediately as intellectual objects nor does it cease to require the objects of the imagination for its subsequent activities.[512] Rather, by means of ratiocination or discursive reasoning, the intellect unites, separates, and distinguishes the properties, accidents, and relations between objects, until it knows them in their simplicity, as universal forms, or as intelligibles.[513] Whereas the intellect through the agent intellect acquires direct knowledge of universal forms and intelligibles,[514] *qua* intellect, it knows singulars only indirectly through the mediation of the imagination.[515] Irrespective of its mode of acquisition, all knowledge acquired through the mediation of the senses is indirect and cannot be reflected upon without intermediate phantasms.[516]

In agreement with Maimonides, Aquinas locates the source of intellectual error in the imagination and the other powers of the soul that originate in its composition with the body. First, the imagination is impeded, when the body is injured; second, fatigue impedes memory and recollection even of knowledge acquired previously; third, when an attempt is made to understand, or make another understand, an object that had never been perceived, imaginary objects replace true ones and are treated by reason as real. In contradistinction to Maimonides, however, who emphasizes the discontinuity between the imagination and the intellect, minimizing its role in intellection and emphasizing its role in error, Aquinas establishes a continuity between them as faculties of the unitary soul. "For the intellect and the imagination are both powers of one and the same substance, and therefore, they can together perform one (composite) operation."[517] That is, Aquinas emphasizes the fact that, since the perfection of the human intellect is acquired through sensation and discursive reasoning, human knowledge would be entirely impossible without the imaginative faculty, including knowledge of the universal forms, "[a]nd therefore, in order that the intellect may understand its own proper object, it is necessary that it would turn itself to the phantasms, so that it could observe the universal nature existing in the particular."[518] In addition, since the intellect knows itself through its intellective activity and since this activity proceeds by abstraction from phantasms, the imagination is essential for its self-knowledge.[519] For, when the human intellect understands itself as knowing, according to Aquinas, it understands its knowledge as a knowing of this or that sensible object that, again, requires the imagination.[520]

Aquinas' deliberate use of *cognoscere*, instead of *intelligere*, to discuss the intellect's self-knowledge clearly indicates that the quintessential mode of human knowing, including self-knowledge, is always discursive. Although it is the case that the intellect, *qua* agent intellect, understands first principles immediately, it should be noted that, properly speaking, first principles *are* the agent intellect rather than *are known* by the intellect. That is, first principles refer to the ontological status of the intellect as the condition for and termination of any knowledge, whereas its knowledge and self-knowledge refer to its existential status. As the intrinsic condition of self-knowing, however, Aquinas' agent intellect, unlike Maimonides' acquired intellect, which is actualized by the extrinsic agent intellect, safeguards human knowledge against assent to most unreal imaginative objects. *Qua* actual, the agent intellect knows the necessary as necessary and, hence, is far less likely to give assent to the impossible, that is, to non-being.

Since knowledge *qua* knowledge is acquired through a series of mediations, sensible, imaginative, and ratiocinative, the question arises whether and how the intellect can know singulars.[521] Yet, knowledge of the singular is constitutive of every stage of ratiocination and of paramount significance when we consider practical reason, since in order to act the intellect must know the singular *qua* singular. That is, the practical intellect has to judge an object's relation to first principles in terms of the object's composite mode of existence with all its accidental qualities and in its relations to other objects and their accidents, rather than in accordance with its simple intellectual mode of existence as a universal cognitional object. Although practical activity is about the possible and the particular rather than the necessary and so never entirely free from the possibility of error, practical reason can still judge the best means to an end since it recognizes that necessary relations obtain in the contingent circumstances pertaining to a particular object.[522] One cannot overemphasize that, for Aquinas, the practical and speculative intellect are but one power; their distinction arises from the order of the object rather than from the nature of the activity, an activity through which the intellect knows itself and that originates, first and foremost, in external objects. Ironically, owing to the nature of the distinction between the objects of speculative and practical activities, Maimonides not only denies their identity but does not name practical activity as properly intellectual. Since, for Maimonides, the agent intellect is not a power of the soul, from an ontological perspective, if the intellect is its knowledge then either there can be no practical intellect or, at least, its manifestation in practice would be accidental to its intellectual status.

Whereas for Maimonides the appetitive faculty has no direct relation to cognition and hence must be compelled to act in accordance with right order, Aquinas not only argues that there is an intellective appetite distinct from the natural appetitive inclination toward an object, but also, in maintaining that this power is the volitional faculty, he is maintaining in fact that it originates in the soul itself independently of its composition with the body.[523] "[T]he act of the will is nothing other than a certain inclination consequent upon an intellectual form, just as the natural appetite is an inclination consequent upon a natural form. . . . Whence the natural inclination is naturally in a natural thing; and moreover, the inclination which is the sensible appetite, is sensibly in the sentient being; and likewise, the intelligible inclination, which is the act of the will, is intelligibly in the intelligent being."[524]

Since the volitional faculty is a power of the soul, independent of matter, and since it properly belongs to human being *qua* intelligent being, Aquinas argues that the will must have a portion in self-subsistence and immortality.[525] Moreover, since, as I have pointed out in the previous chapter, the proper object of the will is the good, Aquinas maintains that "[i]ndeed, it is necessary that, just as the intellect necessarily inheres in first principles, so the will necessarily inheres in the final end, which is *beatitude*; for the end functions in operations as principles [function] in speculation."[526]

Aquinas' conclusion that the will is ordered to its proper end as to a first principle of intellection determines that the will participates in the process of deliberation rather than that it is compelled to act by its end.[527] When it considers particular objects, the will chooses or refrains from choosing them following judgment about their commensurability with its ultimate good—beatitude. That is, just as many intelligibles do not have a direct self-evident relation to primary principles of intellection, so also many particular goods do not have a necessary relation to beatitude and so require deliberation and judgment.

Throughout the discussion of the will, Aquinas establishes a twofold relation between the will and the intellect that is not merely analogical. In addition to the analogical relation between the will and the intellect, Aquinas posits a direct causal relation between them; the intellect moves the will as a final cause, whereas the will moves the intellect as an efficient cause.[528] The will is related to free choice as intellect is related to reason, that is, as its proper activity, since free choice is nothing other than deliberative, discursive judgment about an end as a good. Thus, like the intellect and reason, the will and free choice are the same faculty viewed *aliqualiter* from the perspectives of rest and motion;[529] will is the principle of action in which the good inheres as a primary principle, free choice is the intermediate discursive activity that judges an object's proportionality both to the first principle possessed as the good and to the final principle intellectually known as good because it is judged to be true.[530] By positing will and choice as moments in intellective appetition, and by positing the good as an intrinsic *cognitive* principle of the will, Aquinas overcomes the difficulty faced by Maimonides of reconciling the natural inclination of an appetite toward an external object that has no cognitive, let alone ethical, content (as internal, "it" is a different object) and the freedom to choose an object through an act of judgment that deliberates about it from first principles of which the first is the good. The good, for Aquinas, is a proper object of practical intellection precisely because, through the act of creation, it inheres in things that participate in it proportionately. Since the human soul is created *directly* by God, it participates in divine goodness in an intellectual manner through an innate possession of the good as a first principle and as the true final end. Aquinas' twofold ontology, thus, makes it possible for him to overcome the difficulty faced by Maimonides between the will/appetite as a power of the soul whose perfection is necessary for intellectual human perfection and the will as moved by external objects, which have no cognitive status, and so is a hindrance to intellectual perfection.

So long as Aquinas discusses the human soul, the intellect, and their operations as part of the original ontological order obtaining before the fall, the dominion of reason over all parts of the soul and especially the intellectual status of the will guarantee the perfection of all parts and habits of the soul and, hence, the acquired perfection of the human intellect. However, the disruption of the original order of justice in the soul consequent upon the fall modified the internal relations within the soul to an extent such that the perfection of the intellect, both in its practical and in its speculative operations, cannot be achieved without divine aid since the internal relation between the will and the intellect had been disrupted as well. Since, as will become evident, the disorder in the soul consists, primarily, in a barrier between the will and its final end and since the will is the human sovereign appetite, the intellect can no longer fully provide the rule and measure for the human appetites in its function as a final cause. Moreover, since the will, as an efficient cause, moves the intellect to consider its objects as good, it cannot evaluate their proportionality to the end; consequently, it can present 'base' objects as good to the intellect since now the proximate causality of objects may be (mis)understood as final causality.[531] The disruption of the original order of justice, thus, introduces a distinction and a tension between will and intellect of a kind that may bring about an opposition between the good of the intellect (the final cause), which is identical with its perfected being and the (efficient) "goods" of the will. Ultimately, without extra-natural aid, the human being will be able to neither know nor reach proper perfection or beatitude. Like Maimonides, Aquinas concludes that this extra-natural aid must take the form of instruction through divine legislation as well as the aid of grace.

Conclusion

In the brief statement introducing my analysis of Aquinas' theory of the soul and its activities, I have alluded to a connection between the order of being and the hierarchy of the sciences, or the order of knowing, a connection outlined in the first chapter and referred to numerous times throughout this study. This connection, which is no less evident in Maimonides' thought than it is in Aquinas', is also the locus of the differences between the them.

Since for Maimonides determinate matter is the source of discontinuity between the sub- and supralunar realms, the only act of being that can be designated "good" properly is that act which is least related to matter, namely, speculative intellection. Conversely, strictly material objects, qua seeming goods, have no inherent goodness in themselves, apart from their "utility"[532] for the true good. Consequently, so long as the true reality of material objects is not intellectually apprehended, they constitute "evils" since they affect the powers of the soul in a manner such that it is drawn away from its proper order and its true perfection. On the other hand, by arguing that the causality of the good extends further than the causality of being, Aquinas overcomes the disjunction between the sub- and supralunar realms[533] and, thus, endows matter not only with pure potentiality, but also with an inherent goodness, regardless of whether it is prime matter or particular material objects (determined matter). Consequently, since all material objects possess both being and goodness, intellectual apprehension of their true reality consists of knowing them as both good and true.

The internal constitution of the order of being is translated into the internal relations between the powers and activities of the soul in both Maimonides' and Aquinas' teachings. However, whereas Maimonides concludes that the human soul cannot be self-subsistent since it is the form of the body, and that there is but *one* agent intellect, Aquinas argues that there is a *multiplicity* of agent intellects proportionate to the number of created human souls in virtue of which human souls are constituted as the self-subsistent principles of their proper intellectual acts. Consequently, in contradistinction to Maimonides, Aquinas can conclude that, by definition, all human beings can achieve some degree of final perfection, both proximate and remote. Maimonides' argument, which limits the proper object of the intellect solely to the true, leads him to conclude that the practical intellect in its role of formulating and assenting to commonly accepted opinions concerning "good" and "evil", is a 'penalty' consequent upon Adam's transgression. Consequently, a desire for a perceived good that precedes the apprehension of the true reality of the object, its truth, is a desire for an imaginary object and, thus, it is merely the inclination of an irrational appetite manifesting the disorder, rather than the perfection of the soul. On the other hand, the self-subsistent nature of the intellective soul permits Aquinas to posit the intellectual possession of the good as a primary principle of practical reason as well as an intellectual will that desires being, first, as its proper good and, then, as its true end. Consequently, despite the errors attributed to the imagination, as the efficient cause, the will can move the intellect to deliberate about the degree of proportionality between a seeming good and the true good or end.

However, notwithstanding the substantial differences between Maimonides' and Aquinas' understanding of the nature of intellectual perfection prior to Adam's transgression, the similarity between their conclusions about the human intellectual capacity of Adam's descendants to achieve the final perfection is rather striking. Despite his assertion that the will is an intellectual appetite, Aquinas concurs with Maimonides that the historical human being has lost the capacity to perceive his or her true end without divine aid.

Insofar as the present chapter discussed the possibilities and limitations of natural human knowledge and the consequent necessity for revelation, it set out to establish primarily the propaedeutic role of divine law in human perfection. In the following chapter, I will, first, examine the implications of the limitations of natural human knowledge as they are manifest in a strictly philosophical/Aristotelian ethics and, second, I will examine how the law perfects philosophical ethics in a manner such that it renders possible proper, intellectual human perfection in excess of natural/rational perfection.

6

DIVINE LAW AS A PERFECTION
OF PHILOSOPHICAL ETHICS

Introduction

Insofar as the previous two chapters sought to clarify the ontological aspects underlying the natural limitations of human knowledge and to exhibit the ontological bases of the tension between the two human ends, the discussion of ethics was onesided since, to a large measure, it bracketed the question of habituation, the distinction between the natural powers of the soul and virtuous habits and the a-natural status of moral virtue. But, no philosophical discussion of legal obligation, let alone a discussion of thinkers who seek to establish the necessity for divine law as both a complement and a supplement to Aristotelian ethics, can ignore the distinction between nature and habit. Consequently, prior to a discussion of the epistemic status of divine law, the present chapter will, first, address the tension between nature and habit.

Both Maimonides and Aquinas concur with Aristotle (*De An.* II) that (1) virtues are human habits acquired through repeated practice rather than being natural powers of the soul and (2) virtue is a habit determined by the rule of right reason. Thus, although virtue is not a natural habit, its determination by reason immediately exhibits its relation to its natural origin since reason is, indeed, a natural power of the soul. Moreover, since, *qua* power, reason, too, is acquired through instruction, that is, habituation to knowledge, actual *episteme* and actual *doxa* are ontologically prior to power and habit. In addition, as the discussion in the previous chapter made evident, with respect to the nature of the soul both Maimonides and Aquinas follow Aristotle quite closely in viewing the human soul as a single unity, although their understanding of this unity differs substantially and although existentially the unity of the soul is neither simple nor simply actualized. Consequently, however subtle, ambiguous, or obscure the relation may be between moral virtue and knowledge, and whatever the relation may be between practical and speculative reason, in the order of time and in individual human beings the acquisition of a virtuous habit and that of reason must be related. It is not surprising, therefore, that both Maimonides and Aquinas insist that a deficiency in moral virtue will necessarily affect the possibility of intellectual perfection.[534] Likewise, it is not at all surprising that the *Nicomachean Ethics* is as much a psychology and a pedagogy as it is an "ethics" and a politics. The tensions in the text, then, are the tensions between ontology (natural power *qua* natural) and ethics (habituation) and will be reflected in any discussion informed by the *Nicomachean Ethics*.[535]

The Limits of Philosophical Ethics According to Maimonides

As has been repeated numerous times in this study, the question of pedagogy, both moral and intellectual, is preeminent in all of Maimonides' writings. Not only are the "Eight Chapters" and *Guide* exemplary and very deliberately pedagogical discourses, discourses attuned to differences between audiences and orders of discourse, but also from the Preface of the *Guide* to its conclusion, Maimonides' explicit purpose is to identify as well as rectify errors and perplexities arising out of improper habituation. As early as the Preface, Maimonides identifies undue haste, or unruly desire for knowledge, and improper instruction as the causes of the perplexity of Joseph, the exemplary reader of the book, causes that are later said to have hindered the nobles of Israel in Sinai from proper apprehension, thereby damning them to extinction, that is, mortality.[536] Thus, from the Preface onward Maimonides both underlines the relation between moral and intellectual perfection, which is manifest by the claim that there can exist an unruly *desire* for *knowledge*, and indicates that improper instruction is a hindrance to perfection. Properly understood, then, proportionate pedagogy is a question of ethics.

The internal psychic tension between reason and appetite, rational and moral perfection, which is manifest in the disordered desire for knowledge, also makes manifest the fact that the tension between theory and practice is not reducible to the problematic relation between intrinsic knowledge and external application, on the contrary. The unruly desire for knowledge is a paradoxical manifestation of the limits of reason or its incapacity to apprehend the mean, its failure or immoderate refusal to recognize its own limits. That is, the paradox named by Maimonides an *unruly desire for knowledge* consists of the limits of reason made manifest in reason's inability or refusal to recognize its own limitations. How, then, can reason, which cannot be made *subject* to external commandments, recognize its limits or refrain from *hubris* and how can one distinguish between ruly and unruly desires for knowledge?

As he continues to outline measured procedure as distinct from undue haste in the first chapters of the *Guide*, Maimonides paraphrases Aristotle's statement in the *De Caelo*: "There are two difficulties (*aporian*) which might naturally be felt, and we must do our best to give the most plausible solution, looking upon a readiness to do so as evidence of *modesty* rather than of rashness, if the seeker out of thirst for philosophy, rests content with but a little resolution (*euporias*) in matters where we are surrounded by such great difficulties (*megistas aporias*)."[537] Although Maimonides' paraphrase omits explicit mention of modesty or lack of *hubris*, its tone clearly emphasizes the fact that Aristotle's "endeavor to acquire and achieve true belief to the extent which this is in the power of man" was properly ordered. Maimonides' judicious use of terms such as *true belief* (*i'tiqadat ṣaḥiḥa*) and extent of human power simultaneously highlight the non-demonstrative nature of metaphysical inquiries and Aristotle's procedure as an exemplary manifestation of the "ethics" of philosophy.[538] That is, speculative reason must exhibit moderation rather than "effrontery," "temerity," and "excess of haste."

Maimonides further underscores the concurrence between speculative and moral perfection when he contrasts Aristotle's moderation with the overdue haste that condemned the nobles of Israel to mortality, claiming that their intellectual incapacity was manifest in their *actions* inasmuch as improper apprehension inclines its possessor to things of the body so that one's attention is drawn away from the true human good. That is, the unruly desire for knowledge, which already exhibits a disorder in the soul, in turn, leads to further disruption of the soul's order. Only proper preliminary instruction, one combining training in the sciences with moral habituation, one guided by an *actually* knowing physician as opposed to a pseudo-philosopher (Mutakallim) can safeguard the soul from corruption. Conversely, so long as *actual* ordered knowledge is an extrinsic principle of training and habituation, the desire for knowledge may, in fact, be a desire originating in the imagination and, thus, inadvertently a desire for the impossible, for non-being or the destruction of the soul.

That same relation between reason (nature) and habit is later exhibited in Maimonides enumeration of causes of philosophical disagreement when he discusses the nature and limits of human knowledge. Whereas the discussion in *Guide*, 1, 5, emphasizes the salutary aspect of habituation, here, in *Guide* 1, 31, Maimonides specifically identifies convention as a hindrance to perfection. Ironically, despite, or precisely because of his insistence upon the a-natural and a-rational nature of moral categories, in this context, Maimonides either refuses or fails to distinguish between moral habituation and intellectual instruction. For, as he claims in the "Eight Chapters," until the soul attains its final intellectual perfection, not only does reason not suffice for establishing order in the soul but it is also hindered from attaining its own perfection.

The intimate relation between all aspects of human perfection, between moral habituation and intellectual instruction and, thus, between natural inclination or possibility and existential actualization is constitutive of the enumeration of causes of disagreement that are impediments to proper instruction and understanding. The first three impediments listed repeat Alexander of

Aphrodisias list to which Maimonides adds a fourth that recalls Aristotle's discussion of custom in the *Metaphysics*.[539] These are (1) love of strife and domination, which are said to be impediments to the apprehension of truth; (2) the subtlety and obscurity of the object of apprehension, that is, the natural limits of human understanding of the highest human good, in themselves constitute barriers to apprehension; (3) impediments constituted by ignorance of that which is within the natural human power to know; and (4) the impediments constituted by habit and upbringing. "For man has in his nature a love of, and an inclination for, that to which he is habituated. . . . Man has love for, and a wish to defend, opinions to which he is habituated and in which he had been brought up and has a feeling of repulsion for opinions other than those. For this reason also man is blind to the apprehension of the true realities" (*Guide* 1, 31, 67). Love and hate, attraction and repulsion are the *natural* conditions underlying both habit and knowledge. Thus, viewed from the perspective of the temporal (existential) order, the affects or natural appetites determine the motion of the intellect, for until knowledge is acquired, until it is in act, the intellect, like the affects, is passive or moved. This is also the reason why, even though Maimonides, following Aristotle and the Islamicate philosophers, denies that good and bad are proper objects of the intellect and identifies them with the beautiful and ugly (attractive and repulsive) as well as considers the will as a strictly appetitive faculty, he considers love of God/truth as the source of psychic order. For love of God/truth is the single intellectual commandment given to Adam and the only source of psychic order and human perfection. The discussions of prophetic revelation, its degrees as well as hindrances both in the *Guide* and in the "Eight Chapters," substantiate my claim and further exhibit how intimately related the two perfection are, if, in fact, there are two. Love of God or the desire for truth is the cardinal intellectual virtue. That is, love of God/truth is either a habit or is acquired in a manner similar to habit rather than being a natural inclination.[540]

For Maimonides then the ambiguity of moral virtue reflects the tension between the two orders of human existence. That is why so long as the human intellect is not fully in act, so long as it is embodied, the natural or appetitive order necessarily affects existential possibilities to such an extent that even Moses could not exercise full control over the affects; for, like the intellectual virtues, the moral virtues are not natural. Thus, when Maimonides enumerates the five causes that hinder the study of divine science, causes that Aquinas repeats as rendering revelation necessary, two of the causes, the fourth and fifth, explicitly concern moral virtue and (at the very least) one other, the third, concerns the ethics of preliminary studies.[541] In this light the entire first book of the *Guide*, indeed, "is not a treatise on language,"[542] but the moral training propaedeutic to the study of philosophical metaphysics[543] and, especially, divine science. That is why in the concluding statements of *Guide*, 1, 76, Maimonides provides an ethical admonition to the reader:

Consider, therefore, you who are engaged in speculation, if you give the preference to the quest for the truth and cast aside passion, blind following of authority, and obeisance to what you are accustomed to hold great. Your soul should not be led into error by the circumstances of these men engaged in speculation, neither by what has happened to them nor by what has come from them. For they are like one who flees from torrid heat into fire. For they have abolished the nature of being . . . (230)

Irrespective of their authority, irrespective of the esteem with which they may be held, the authority of the Mutakallimun is not only undeserved but also dangerous.[544] Unexamined opinion, including opinion about the law, leads only to the corruption of the soul. In this light, Maimonides is indeed sincere when he claims that the recognition of the limits of the human intellect is not "a statement made in order to conform to law (*shari'yya*). For it is something that has already been said and truly grasped by the philosophers without their having concern for a particular doctrine or opinion."[545]

It is ironic that, despite his Aristotelian ethics, Maimonides' highly Platonic view of matter predominantly as the principle of the change that is corruptive, rather than as that potentiality to become actually perfect, leads to the conclusion that the unity of the corporeal human soul is of a kind that precludes the separation of the two perfections. Moreover, even at the natural level, even if we bracket the question of conjunction, for Maimonides, the tension between natural inclination, on the one hand, moral habituation and rational instruction, on the other, is much greater than it is for Aristotle. Thus, even though perfection is presented as the *internal* motion from potency to actuality when he discusses the second cause that prevents instruction in divine science, Maimonides claims that the obstacles to this internal motion are "very many, and the objects that distract from it abound."[546] The third cause identifies some of these obstacles as natural, that is, internal to the soul, others as habitual, that is, external to the soul.

Upon reading the discussion of the third cause we finally discover how there can be an unruly desire for knowledge. What is most striking about the discussion is the claim that, *qua* natural, the desire for knowledge is *ipso facto* unruly since, *qua* end, knowledge is sought as if it were (1) an external sensible object and (2) attainable without preliminary studies. But, if the preliminary preparations are seen as superfluous to knowledge, then, clearly, the natural desire for "knowledge" is a desire for something other than, in fact, contradictory to, knowledge. The unruly desire for "knowledge" is a desire for mimetic appropriation of some external, imaginative or appetitive object.

Insofar as the origins of natural knowledge are sensible objects, insofar as preliminary rational instruction requires sensible and imaginative objects, and insofar as the hylic intellect depends upon representations, its desire for knowledge is intimately related to the appetite. Ironically, since reason cannot be subject to commandments and since practical reason deliberates about external, that is, appetitive, ends, unless appetitive habituation is concurrent with rational instruction, reason cannot even attain its natural end. That is why the "commandment" to love God was given to Adam on account of his perfect/acquired intellect rather than his reason, for the rational desire to know is appetitively bound and, hence, cannot possibly be a desire to know God or to attain the true human end. Maimonides's understanding of the nature of psychic unity clarifies the reason for this striking conclusion. For as he claims in the "Eight Chapters," if the soul does not attain its highest form, the acquired intellect, "its capacity to receive this form is for naught, and is, as it were, futile" (1, 64). But, since the acquired intellect is not a natural power of the soul, since its act is received from the agent intellect, unless and until conjunction occurs, only another extra-natural impetus, such as divine law, which is the result of conjunction, can enact right order in the soul. The perfect habit, then, would be acquired only by means of divine law.

Divine Sanction as Universal Imperative[547]

When Maimonides discusses the 'law' (*al Shari'yya*) as the most excellent means to acquiring perfection, by *law* he designates *all* the teachings of the Torah, both written and oral, of which only a portion comprises the commandments and prohibitions. All the teachings of the Torah were communicated to Moses, who promulgated some of them in the form of commandments and prohibition. Whereas Moses attained the highest degree of human understanding of the entire Torah, the other prophets and Sages attained some knowledge of the Torah according to their varied degrees of intellectual perfection, all of which were considerably inferior to Moses. Whereas the *Guide* does not discuss the entire body of instruction transmitted by any person other than Moses, the content of Mosaic prophecy is analyzed as a whole since it is both the foundation and the full perfection of all subsequent prophetic-biblical, rabbinical, and Maimonidean teaching.[548]

Since, prior to Adam's transgression, the content of Mosaic prophecy required no promulgation, the understanding of the entire content of the Torah, or its intellectual possession in act, is the prerequisite for the human restoration to Adam's originating ontological status or for possessing an acquired intellect, at least as an intrinsic power of the soul. It cannot be overemphasized, however, that even in his original state, Adam was given a 'law', or a single commandment "that was imposed upon him on account of his intellect."[549] That is, in contradistinction to the commandments and prohibitions that, first and foremost, are imposed upon the appetitive faculty, and second, *qua* knowledge, are directed to the power receptive to conventional knowledge or to practical reason, the commandment given to Adam was an intellectual one. However, since

Maimonides argues in the "Eight Chapters" that commandments do not pertain to reason, whose perfection is the intellect, it remains to be determined how this intellectual commandment can become the intrinsic act of the soul.

Prior to discussing the Law, Maimonides considers and refutes two closely related, problematic positions held by the Mutakallimun, namely, the denial that divine "actions" have a purpose and that the Law has a cause or causes. The latter denial clearly entails the denial of a "rational" status of the Law. Based upon an inference from human actions, some Mutakallimun (the Asharaites[550]) draw conclusions concerning all actions, including divine "acts." Since the Law is the external manifestation of divine "action" or actuality, since human actions aim at some end, and since, as external, the ends of actions exhibit a privation in the agent, in order to "safeguard" divine perfection and freedom the Mutakallimun claimed that divine actions are consequent upon the arbitrary will rather than the wisdom of God.[551] In addition, as Maimonides presents the collective Asharite position, their inability to discern a purpose for the world as a whole led them to deny not only a purpose for the world, but also for all particular entities in it. It is important for Maimonides to take up this question at this point, even though he has already devoted a lengthy discussion to the futility of the attempt to discover an end for the world as a whole and pointed out that causal language is appropriate and disclosive only in natural science,[552] because the Asharite position entails the denial of the purpose, cause, or end of divine Law. For, if divine Law is a consequence of an arbitrary will rather than perfect wisdom, not only is a real distinction introduced into the divinity (a problem discussed in the first book), but also the commandments are futile. If divine Law has no end, then either it cannot be enacted, for human beings act for the sake of an end, or it will be enacted for the wrong end, namely, fear of punishment or desire for reward.[553]

Since no analogy can be drawn between human and divine knowledge[554] and since divine "action," be it in the form of revealed Law or of the existence of the world as it is, is nothing but the manifestation of divine wisdom and entirely unlike human action, any inference about the true reality of divine acts derived from human experience will result in a false conclusion concerning divine "action" as it is. More precisely, the categories most appropriate for understanding the natural universe as it is, categories such as cause and effect, actuality and potency, are least fitting for understanding God. Thus, what is perfect and free from the perspective of divine action is either necessary or possible from the perspective of human action. That is why Maimonides insists that the love of God that is the ultimate end of all the commandments is possible only after the apprehension of the whole of being to the extent possible for human beings, that is, as it is manifest in nature.[555]

As in the case of the status of the "act" of creation and of prime matter, so in the case of the divine "act" manifest as prophetic revelation, Maimonides emphasizes the radical difference between God as originating cause or principle and all subsequent causality, God as the unique metaphysical actuality and the acts made possible by it. Divine Law as a manifestation of a singular perfect wisdom is the actuality that renders all possibility, including possible inference concerning human action according to understanding. The more one understands what divine wisdom renders necessary with respect to the perfect arrangement of the whole order of nature, the more one is capable of inferring what is and is not possible and acting accordingly.

Whereas necessity refers to the perfectly arranged, entire natural order of which the contradictory is impossibility, possibility refers to the natural internal motion (*dunamis*) of particular entities. Divine Law is the communication to the prophet, in accordance with his or her *particular* capacity of an aspect (or portion) of the perfect natural arrangement as it pertains to human beings. Since, as will become evident in the following chapter, what is properly named *prophetic* revelation, in contradistinction to perfect understanding *simpliciter*, signifies an excess that *must* be communicated further, the Law is the linguistic mediated communication of what has been immediately apprehended according to the particular circumstances. Consequently, Maimonides concludes, the attempt to discover a cause for *particular* commandments, such as a commandment to sacrifice a lamb rather than a ram, is as absurd as the claim that the "generalities of a *commandment* are not designed with a view to some real utility."[556] In a language highly reminiscent of Aristotle's *De Interpretatione*, Maimonides points out that the choice involved in some particular commandments "resembles the nature of the possible, for it is certain that one of two possibilities will come to pass.[557] But, in order to understand the possible, one must clearly first understand the necessary or apprehend the order of nature as it is.[558] What the perfect prophet, Moses, apprehended is the universal, necessary, *real* utility of a sacrifice, an apprehension originating in necessary divine wisdom, what he communicated in prophecy is the result of a choice between equally possible particulars. The epistemic neutrality of such a choice, however, is circumscribed, on the one hand, by the priority of ontological necessity to epistemic and logical possibility and, on the other, by the historical/existential circumstances.[559] Given the ontological status of the final end of the law, however, it follows that historical/existential considerations are ontologically circumscribed as well. As Maimonides states explicitly in the discussion of providence, with the exception of the human species, God does not know particulars or does not choose between equally neutral possibilities.[560]

Since human beings act for the sake of an end, however, and since human choice concerns particulars, Maimonides first divides the commandments into two general categories *ḥuqqim* (statutes) and *mishpatim* (judgments) and, second, divides the commandments into general classes, in order to show the reason (cause/end) for most of the particular commandments. He claims that the *mishpatim* do not present particular difficulties since "their utility is clear to the multitude," whereas the *huqqim* do, because their "utility is not clear to the multitude."[561] In the light of Maimonides' distinction in the "Eight Chapter" between virtues and their corresponding laws concerning which there is no disagreement between the philosophers and the Sages, laws that manifest generally accepted opinions arising out of natural human repulsion and whose observance does not reflect continence, and laws that classify some actions as "bad" only because they are prohibited by the Law, Stern's thesis that the explanation of the *huqqim* "serves as a model for his conception of *ta'ame hamitzvot*, the project of giving reasons for . . . the commandments"[562] is most perspicuous. Whereas the *mishpatim* that belong to the class of generally accepted opinions and, thus, clearly aim at moral perfection do not present particular difficulties beyond those involved in dialectical reasoning,[563] the *huqqim* must represent the exemplary form of those commandments to which the disobedience would not be bad at all if it were not for the Law. Obedience to the *huqqim*, then, is an exemplary mode of obedience to divine law precisely because they (1) do not belong to the class of generally accepted opinions and (2) cannot be derived by that aspect of practical reason that distinguishes between "base" and "noble" actions. But, since moral categories are not the proper objects of the speculative intellect and since Maimonides insists that all the commandments have reasons that exceed their historical particularity, namely, the eradication of idolatry, the true end of the *huqqim* must be final perfection.

Given the "compromised" rational status of the *huqqim*, it is clear that not only the vulgar but also the elite must be habituated in them prior to acquiring the ability to discern their utility. Although initially it may appear that the major difficulty of obeying the *huqqim* pertains only to the vulgar and that the *mishpatim* present no difficulty either to the vulgar or the elite, I believe that to each group there pertains a distinct difficulty: to the vulgar, the difficulty of obedience to all the commandments for the wrong reasons; to the elite, the difficulty of disobedience. Ironically, precisely because the vulgar can be easily habituated to obey the *mishpatim* strictly for their extrinsic utility, they cannot be easily habituated to obey the *huqqim* that have no evident extrinsic utility nor can they ever obey them for the right reasons. With respect to the elite, on the other hand, a perennial difficulty of antinomianism exists at both levels so long as final perfection is not fully acquired. Ironically, as will become evident, if final perfection is attained, it is the *mishpatim* rather than the *huqqim*, that present a difficulty for the elite.

The *single* end of divine Law, according to Maimonides, is the acquisition of the *two* human perfections, namely, "the welfare of the soul and the welfare of the body,"[564] the acquisition of the latter is a prerequisite for the acquisition of the former and is possible only in a well ordered or law abiding society. However the first perfection is understood, insofar as it is a prerequisite for final perfection and insofar as it is ordered to that end, properly speaking, there exists only one perfection consisting of two aspects. Paradoxically, however, since the single perfection of the human species requires that the greatest diversity exist among its members at all times, divine wisdom rendered necessary that this species be ordered in a way such that among its members there be rulers capable of legislating "actions and moral habits that all of them must always practice in the *same* way, so that the natural diversity is hidden through the multiple points of conventional accord and so that the community becomes well ordered."[565]

The class of legislative rulers outlined by Maimonides can be divided into three broad categories: rulers who promulgate *nomoi* without laying claim to having received revelation, rulers who received divine revelation on the basis of which they promulgate *nomoi*, and rulers who promulgate laws borrowed from revealed Law to which they lay personal claim.

True divine Law is contradistinguished from *nomos* inasmuch as the former aims at the perfections of both body and soul, whereas the latter aims only at the perfection of the body; the promulgator of the latter possesses a perfect imaginative faculty, that of the former possesses a perfect intellect. The perfect *nomos* cannot, in principle, be a perfect law since its end is imaginative rather than real, it is generic rather than specific.[566] Since the class of rulers who promulgate *nomoi* does not lay claim to revelation and since, in the light of the single *human* end, true Law is revealed Law, Maimonides dismisses laws promulgated by them as irrelevant to the discussion whose concern is the status of divine Law. But, since Maimonides states that all rulers belonging to the two non-prophetic classes adopt the prophetic *nomos*, two questions need be asked: (1) How does divine Law differ from non-prophetic *nomoi*? and (2) How does one distinguish between the two non-prophetic *nomoi*?

Qua adopted or received from the prophet, all *nomoi* belong to the class of generally accepted opinions that Maimonides divides in *The Treatise on [the Art of] Logic* into conventions and traditions.[567] Conventions, according to Maimonides, originate in human appetitive attraction and repulsion and, thus, are natural or originate in human nature. Since they are "universally" accepted, they require no further justification. Traditions, on the other hand, require some general "proof for the trustworthiness of the transmitter"[568] in order to be accepted. In addition, the greater the number of communities sharing a tradition is, the more "universal" it is, the less the tradition requires justification. Given the appetitive origin of *nomoi*, despite the distinction between *physis* and *nomos*, the necessity for *nomoi* arises out of human nature.

In the light of their distinct ends, when Maimonides designates divine Law as *nomos*, the term is used equivocally rather than univocally or analogically, since conventional laws that do not aim at intellectual perfection do not subordinate the perfection of the body to that of the soul. That is, since, according to Maimonides, the perfection of the body is not the perfection proper to a human being, laws that do not aim, first and foremost, at the final end cannot be understood as laws proper to human beings. In this light, however, since the material intellect is perishable, divine Law is both extra-rational, for reason is a natural power of the material intellect, and a-natural. Nonetheless, there is, at the very least, an apparent similarity between divine Law and *nomos* and an ambiguity in Maimonides' discussion of the distinction between them insofar as both are said to aim at "hiding" the great diversity within the human species, a diversity manifest in the moral habits whose origin belongs not only to the matter but also to the form. "The cause of this is the difference of the mixtures, owing to which the various kinds of matter differ, and also the accidents consequent to the form in question. For every *natural* form has certain accidents proper and consequent to it, those accidents being other than those that are consequent to matter."[569] Unless we conclude that Maimonides is deliberately glossing a serious problem concerning the authority and permanence of Mosaic Law, divine Law and *nomoi* must hide the diversity among members of the human species differently.

I believe that the two interrelated keys to understanding the distinction between the two "laws" is to be found (1) in the distinction between the modes in which they are first known and (2) in Maimonides insistence upon considering the end of the Law as a *whole*, as distinct from *particulars* of the Law. Whereas divine Law is *known* immediately through the single actuality of the agent intellect, *nomoi* are "known" *seriatim* through the mediation of the imagination and of language. Whereas Moses *understood* the end or cause of the Law as a whole and thus, was able to promulgate *particular* commandments that fully accorded with such end according to the circumstances, non-prophets do not *understand* the prior actuality of the end to the particular commandments and, hence, cannot determine the possibilities proportionate to it. Rather, since the relation between the actual or real end of the Law and their habituation into it is inverse—the first perfection temporally precedes the second—their knowledge of the Law originates in the corporeal imagination. But, since the "good" and the "base" are not proper objects of reason, reason, too, cannot determine the proportionate measure between the two perfections.

Since the natural diversity implied by the distinction between the two perfections is consequent upon both the matter and the form, since moral perfection is simultaneously material and formal, those who lack a true understanding of the priority of the actuality of the final end or form cannot, in principle, legislate moral precepts proportionate to the true end. Consequently, the diversities among individuals that all *nomoi*, including the "best" *nomoi*, hide is either strictly that consequent upon the matter or, at best, also those consequent upon the form of the body, that is, the material intellect. In contrast, divine Law hides the material and formal diversity among individuals in proportionate accord with the form of the soul or the acquired intellect. Since all commandments, conventional as well as divine, aim at the appetites and, since, as became clear in the last chapter, reason cannot command the appetite, which nonetheless affects the "flow" of the imagination, *nomoi* can only follow rather than determine the "flow" of nature.[570] In this light, divine Law "enters into what is natural,"[571] at a more radical, active level than any *nomos* and can, at least in principle, bridge the gap between the two human perfections.

The distinction between plagiarized law and *nomos* poses no difficulties. First, its promulgator lays a claim to prophecy and, second, as plagiarized, some of its precepts must *appear* to aim at the true end. It should be added that, although Maimonides attributes imaginative perfection only to the pretender rather than to all promulgators of *nomoi*, this does not preclude the possibility that such perfection is not to be found in the promulgator of *nomos simpliciter* nor does it preclude some rational perfection in both classes.

In the light of both its stated prophetic status and its formal *resemblance* to divine Law, how is plagiarism distinguishable from it? At first glance, Maimonides' response to this question seems quite simple, "The way of putting this to the test is to consider the perfection of that individual, carefully to examine his actions and to study his way of life."[572] That is, an individual's stated perfection can be truly known through his or her actions. But, given that *careful* examination is required, given that such an examination requires some understanding of the true human end, given that Maimonides' choice of exemplary pretenders are of individuals known as pretenders through traditional sources rather than through careful examination and his choice of exemplary actions as truly excessive sexual conduct, repulsive conduct that would be forbidden by all rationally ordered *nomoi*, such as fornication with a friend's wife, it is far from clear how a distinction is to be drawn in the temporal present. In the light of Maimonides' claims that (1) no individual possesses perfect moral virtue, (2) even Moses after prophecy was unable to rule all his passions, and (3) many prophets inferior to Moses could be judged as morally wanting, e.g., David, it seems to me that such a distinction is possible only if we possess knowledge of the entire course of life, a knowledge that is highly improbable without the mediation of authority.[573] Moreover, were Maimonides' claims for the superiority of Mosaic prophecy over all others and for its absolutely unchangeable status based upon this explanation, they would remain unconvincing. Whatever the purpose may be of the discussion of pretenders it cannot be meant to be sufficient. For, Maimonides' explanation can be convincing only if he can show that *all* prophecy posterior to Moses *originates* in Mosaic prophecy and, thus, depends upon it for justification. What the discussion of and distinction between "laws" makes clear is the necessity for prophecy of which Mosaic prophecy is the *arche*.

Paradoxically, the limitations of human reason consequent upon Adam's transgression serve as the explanation for the natural human inability to know the true reality of final/proper human perfection and hence, for the inability to legislate the means to attain it without divine aid. The commandments are a reminder to reason to recognize its own limits. Moreover, since reason does not possess legislative power over any law, let alone divine Law, obedience to it cannot be consequent upon rational assent; rather, rational assent must follow upon habitual obedience or upon the understanding of the limitations of human reason. Consequently, obedience to divine commandments is also the necessary condition for understanding the inherent "rationality" of the Law to the greatest possible extent, an understanding that renders possible the "perfect" arrangement of the city. For, only in the city perfectly ordered by divine Law can the diversity among individuals be "hidden" in a manner such that will simultaneously render possible the proportionate perfection of each of its members in accordance with her or his capacity.

Given the necessity of divine Law for human perfection, it is not surprising that the various discussions pertaining to establishing the inherent "rationality" of the Law as a whole constitute the largest portion of the *Guide*. Nor is it surprising, in the light of the radical distinction between divine and human knowledge and action, that Maimonides insists that the rationality of the Law *as a whole* becomes manifest only after we understand some of the reasons for distinct classes of commandments. "Intellectual commandments" communicate the end for which they aim, albeit succinctly;[574] conventional commandments communicate necessary rules for acquiring moral perfection that guarantee stable political organization.[575] He maintains not only that the intellectual commandments communicate "correct opinions concerning the whole of being—opinions that constitute the numerous kinds of all the theoretical sciences through which the opinions forming the ultimate end are validated,"[576] but also that the acquisition of the theoretical sciences, as the only means to ultimate perfection, is alluded to succinctly in the Torah when it calls upon human beings to love God.[577] Thus, the distinction drawn by Maimonides between intellectual and conventional commandments touches the very core of the tension between the two perfections if the first perfection is not ordered by and apprehended under the final end, since the perfection of the body is motivated by fear of punishment or by the desire for reward as its proper end, whereas the perfection of the intellect is motivated by love as its only end. But, although it can be argued that fear of punishment can be prescribed—in a manner of speaking—surely love, an internal motion of the soul, cannot.[578] In order to possess legislative power, love requires a true understanding of the desired as its only end. Maimonides is not unaware of the difficulty to which he alludes when stating: "We have already explained in the *Mishneh Torah* that this love becomes valid only through the apprehension of the whole of being as it is and through the consideration of His wisdom as it is manifest in it."[579]

It is precisely the tension between the human two ends that may lead to dangerous perplexity in the potentially perfect person. Just as the epistemic status of generally accepted opinions may be understood in one of two ways, so also that of the conventional commandments, except that the perplexity generated by the latter poses a greater danger to the potentially perfect precisely insofar as they are said to originate from perfect divine understanding. Paradoxically, although the commandments cannot be derived by rational demonstration, the utility of some conventional commandments becomes evident after they have been inculcated and become habitual through fear. However, as soon as reason perceives the rational foundation for some commandments—that is, as soon as fear is replaced by reason as the operative principle of obedience—doubt may arise with respect to other commandments of which the external meaning does not manifest their utility. The possibility of rational dissent pertains only to the elite; the multitude, whose rational faculty is most defective, do not seek the causes of things and always obey all the commandments out of fear. Divine Law inculcates moral behavior in them that, nevertheless, does not become an intrinsic principle of action. They neither seek nor acquire ultimate perfection, but possess only the corporeal perfection desired by them. The possible disobedience that may be consequent upon dangerous doubt pertains only to those capable of desiring and attaining true perfection. Once fear is overcome and reason gains autonomy, these human beings are devoid of a principle of obedience to the seemingly irrational commandments, since reason cannot apprehend the cause of these, and love cannot become an intrinsic principle so long as human beings are devoid of the apprehension of the whole of being. Unless and until these intellectual adolescents recognize the limitations of natural reason that becomes evident through proper guidance in divine science, they cannot become as morally perfect as is possible for them (individually, of course) so that they may subordinate all the faculties of the soul to the apprehension of the whole of Being; that is, so that they may love God "with all their heart and all their might and all their being." In my opinion, this single commandment is the translation of the commandment given to Adam.

The strictly intermediate role played by reason between fear and love necessitates the conclusion that positive law can be only the interpretation and adaptation of the divine Law, the *whole* of which can never be superseded or abrogated, both because the abrogation of a single commandment will undermine the Law as a *whole* and because the entire law is the intrinsic principle of action manifesting the apprehension of the *whole* of Being. Through the explication of divine Law, Maimonides succeeds in establishing the elusive order in the human soul and safeguards the integrity of the Law. Thus, it seems to me that when Maimonides argues that true law aims at *hiding* the diversity between members of the human species, he refers to all its members still *in via*, since ultimately this aim overcomes, to whatever extent is possible, the consequences of Adam's transgression that befall all human beings, the vulgar and the potentially perfect, since all suffer in varied degrees from similar disorders of the soul that originate in the appetites.

The Limits of Legislative Reason

Although the *question* of pedagogy is not identified explicitly by Aquinas as the major impetus to all his writings as it is by Maimonides, I do not believe that I need to belabor the point that it underlies all of the Angelic Doctor's endeavors. As has been discussed in the first chapter, Aquinas opening statements of the *Summa Theologiae* identify the current improper methods of teachings leading to boredom and confusion in the student as the reason for composing the work. But, while Aquinas shares Maimonides' concern for both speculative and moral instruction and while he, too, identifies improper instruction as the cause of perplexity (confusion), owing to his radically different understanding of the nature of the human soul, Aquinas does not nor, initially, seems to countenance a possibility of an unruly desire for knowledge. In other words, for Aquinas, the desire for knowledge as an end is *ipso facto* an intellectual one and, hence, in principle, cannot be unruly.[580] Nonetheless, since the proper order of acquiring the sciences is emphasized by Aquinas, even were it not for the fall and the disruption of the natural order of justice, given the unity of the soul, it is clear that any improper pursuit of knowledge will result in a disruption of the order of the soul. In addition, since he clearly chastises those more concerned with argument and eloquence than with teaching in the Preface to the *Summa*, he, too, regards proper pedagogy as a question of ethics. Aquinas' *Commentary on the Nicomachean Ethics*[581] clearly identifies the pursuit of truth as the highest human good. Commenting on Aristotle's reluctance to criticize Plato's opinion concerning the Good and extending Aristotle's explanation or justification, Aquinas states: "Although we should have friendship for both truth and human beings, we ought to love truth more than human beings since we should love human being especially on account of truth and virtue. . . . Moreover, truth is a divine thing, for it is found first and principally in God."[582] Aquinas also indicates that it was from Plato that Aristotle learned to love truth above friendship or honor a friend in the pursuit of truth. For, by criticizing his beloved teacher, Socrates, Plato exemplified in act the priority of truth to friendship or the fact that truth is the measure of friendship. And here Aquinas refer to a statement he attributes to Plato, a statement that was later attributed to Aristotle and that served as the basis for arguing for the essential harmony between Plato and Aristotle; namely, *"Amicus quidem Socrates, sed magis amica Veritas."*[583]

What is most remarkable about this statement is, first, the intimate relation established by Aquinas between friendship, truth, and the Good; second, the claim that there exists an essential identity between Aristotle's and Plato's respective endeavors in virtue of their *telos*, an end unified in the identity between God and Truth; and third, the implication that genuinely philosophical pedagogy is essentially ethical. For Plato's critique of his teacher Socrates, whose entire life was given to ethics, is exemplary of the ethics of pedagogy. By identifying truth with the virtue of the Socratic *daimon* and with the God of revelation, Aquinas not only exceeds the Aristotelian text—an excess made possible by the language of the text—but also indicates that the intimate relation obtaining between moral and intellectual perfection exists in virtue of their divine origin.

Aquinas' preliminary observations preceding his *Commentary on the Nicomachean Ethics* effect a subtle but significant transformation of Aristotle's text. These observations also lend greater credence to the sense in which, from a strictly philosophical perspective, an unruly desire for knowledge is impossible for him. After he clearly distinguishes between natural science whose order reason beholds but *does not establish* and sciences whose order reason establishes (e.g., logic and ethics), when he comments upon the fact that moral philosophy is concerned with action, Aquinas claims that there are two principles of human *action*, reason and appetite. Being fully aware of the fact that many appetitive motions are not actions (hence, not truly voluntary), a fact he discusses numerous times later, Aquinas adds,

> [i]n the intellect or reason the speculative and the practical are considered, in *the rational appetite*, however, choice and execution are considered. Moreover, all these are ordered to some good as to their end, for the true is the end of speculation. Therefore, with respect to the speculative intellect he posits teaching by which knowledge is transferred from the teacher to the student; but, with respect to the practical intellect he posits art, which is right reason of things to be made . . . ; but, with respect to the act of the *appetitive intellect* he posits choice; and with respect to execution he posits act.[584]

This modification of Aristotelian epistemic psychology is striking not so much because the introduction of an intellectual appetite into Aristotle's ethics radically changes the status of the good as the *telos* of human actions[585] but rather because, as in the *Summa*[586] so here, the appetitive intellect is posited as the efficient cause (*actus*) of the intellect *simpliciter*. Moreover, the efficient causality of the appetitive intellect, whose act pertains to the speculative as well as the practical intellect, is simply a manifestation of the agent intellect, whose actuality establishes the unity between the potential and actual intellect.[587] This unity, in turn, reflects the originating identity between the true and the Good in God.[588] In this light, teaching is to speculation what deliberation and choice are to making, namely, the external enactment of understanding, for teaching is a making or founding (*transfundo*) of knowledge in another. Both making and making understand depend upon the prior actuality (read, agent intellect) that acts upon something in determinate potency.[589]

Whereas what is named Being is the unifying *telos* of understanding, deliberation and choice, what is named *Good* is the unifying *telos* of teaching and making. That Aristotle's ethics is to be transformed *ab initio* as a consequence of a Neoplatonic ontology (itself modified) is made clear by the remarks immediately following the positing of the intellective appetite. Considering the Good as *telos* further, Aquinas, first, recalls the *Platonici* enumeration of the Good among the primary entities and their claim that it is prior to Being,[590] but then corrects them, saying that "according to the truth of the *res*, good is convertible with being."[591]

Whereas Aristotle's claim for the similarity between good and being in the *Nicomachean Ethics*, 1, 4, (1096a24-30), is limited to the many ways in which they can be said and whereas he clearly distinguishes between the true and the good, both in the sense that the good cannot be known as a universal and insofar as the *teloi* of distinct entities are distinct, Aquinas insists upon their originating identity. Consequently, unlike Maimonides, who follows Aristotle quite closely, Aquinas also posits a greater harmony and continuity between the two human ends and, thus, between the two kinds of human virtues. Aquinas' critique of Aristotle's distinction between the agent and the possible intellect should be read in this light, for it is not simply a disagreement about the status of the agent intellect but one about the possibility of knowing contingent things and of acting accordingly. Where Aristotle (and Maimonides) argues that there exists a *generic* difference between the necessary and the contingent and that such a difference entails that they are known by *different* powers of the soul, where, for Aristotle, the difference between moral virtue (character) and theoretical virtue is generic, Aquinas counters that "necessary truth and contingent truth seem to be related in the genus of truth as perfect and imperfect; moreover, we know the perfect and imperfect in the same genus by the same power of the soul.[592] Necessity and contingency, for Aquinas, vary according to the particular order of the object, an order known through the mediation of the senses.

Despite his disagreement with Aristotle about the order of the intellect, Aquinas follows Aristotle more closely than does Maimonides about the possibility of moral virtue or the temporal order of habituation. Where, for Maimonides, appetition is contrary to reason, for Aquinas, the appetitive powers, the powers of attraction and repulsion, are naturally disposed to obey reason. Rather than moving reason, the natural appetitive powers can, indeed, be moved by reason.[593] Since the moral habits are neither natural nor contrary to nature and since the appetites are naturally disposed to obey reason, it follows that, for Aquinas, the habituation into moral virtue would be relatively unhindered, for it would not require the performing of activities that are repulsive by nature. Rather than interfere with nature, the moral habit perfects it. Rather than deprive an already existing power of its capacity to act, moral habits are the empowerment, the *providing* of a power to act, to that which is otherwise passive or acted upon. It is in this sense that the more we are habituated to act in accordance with reason, "the more often we act according to reason, the form of reason is *impressed* upon the appetitive power, which impression is nothing other than moral virtue."[594] Appetite impressed or in-formed by reason is the rational appetite.

However, even though, for Aquinas, the possibility of moral perfection is intrinsic to the soul, even though the good and the true are convertible, not only does convention or custom determine the first order in which moral habits are acquired but also particular natural powers vary to an extent sufficiently significant to render some individuals well-disposed, other ill-disposed to obedience. Since, moreover, in the temporal order the acquisition of the customary moral habits precedes rational instruction, unless a society is well-ordered by a good legislator, bad moral habits will both impede the acquisition of knowledge and require coercion as remedy. Conversely, since no human being possess power over the original composition, given that the original composition may be of a kind such that an individual will possess a well-disposed rational capacity together with an ill-disposed appetitive power or with an originally ill-accustomed one, unless familial and social customs as well as laws are properly ordered, they will hinder both moral and intellectual perfection. As for Aristotle and Maimonides so for Aquinas, incontinent and intemperate persons are exemplary of human beings who are not deficient in reason but are corrupt by habit; in the former the original disposition is not completely perverted, whereas in the latter it is. Where the incontinent person may be persuaded, the intemperate requires coercion. In addition, Aquinas agrees with Maimonides that the continent person is superior to the one *morally* virtuous by nature.

Although Aquinas' discussion of the distinction between natural and acquired virtue does not directly address the question of continence, the discussion entails the conclusion that acquired continence is superior to natural moral virtue.[595] The reasons given for the superiority of acquired moral virtues can be succinctly summarized as follows: (1) natural inclinations are devoid of reason and are found in children and beasts whose actions do not pursue the good as a principle; (2) without intellectual discernment, natural virtue may be harmful since natural inclinations without discretion can be, and often are, immoderate; but (3) moral virtue consists of moderation, which is nothing other than an inclination (desire) according to right reason, hence; (4) "if an inclination of such a kind is received with understanding in operation, namely, so that it operates with discretion, then it will greatly differ in the excellence of goodness, and the habit which will be similar to such an operation done with discretion, will be virtue properly and perfectly, which is moral."[596]

Moral virtue is perfect virtue precisely because it is a manifestation of the necessary concurrence and reciprocity between all the moral virtues and prudence. Since, *qua* perfect, moral virtues are not natural; since, *qua* habit, continence is a subordination of natural desire to right reason without fail; since natural desire is immoral or a-moral (excessive or defective) only from the perspective of the ethical mean provided by right reason, it follows that, *qua* ethical, habitual continence is superior to natural virtue. Moreover, since the ethical and legal mean pertain to the common rather than individual good,[597] the continent person is an exemplary model of perfect obedience since his or her adherence to right reason is an intrinsic principle of action insofar as he or she habitually and without fail masters natural desires to which the majority are enslaved and can overcome only by extrinsic means. The superiority of continence over natural virtue is the manifestation of "the impression of the form of reason upon the appetites," which are neither good nor bad in themselves but may be harmful from the perspective of reason. Thus understood, continence is the active manifestation of the uniquely human, intellective appetite.

Although the subordination of natural virtue to habitual moral virtue may seems to be required only for the common good, I would like to suggest that, for Aquinas, the intellective appetite unifies the individual and the common good. Given the natural diversity among human beings, given that such a diversity is consequent precisely upon the composition,[598] the intellective appetite is the unifying principle that renders possible the concurrence of common and individual perfection. Since no individual possesses moral perfection by nature and since in the temporal order natural, intellectual potencies can be actualized only in conjunction with moral virtues, a well-governed society is a necessary condition for individual perfection. But, since legislation concerning good laws and moral actions require both knowledge and experience, unless one already lives in a well-ordered society, the acquisition of good moral habits is diminished to a significant extent.

Whereas the *Commentary on the Nicomachean Ethics* discusses the need for and effects of habituation or custom (*consuetudo*) and law in the acquisition of virtue, it does not dwell upon the impediments to knowledge brought about by habituation. Ironically, in fact, the commentary may give the opposite impression insofar as precisely where it underlines the superiority of a-natural habitual virtue over natural virtue, it implies that all customary habits, moral as well as intellectual, are readily changeable.[599] In contradistinction, in the *Commentary on the Metaphysics*[600] (995a1-20) Aquinas explicitly identifies habituation as an impediment to teaching and learning. Both commentaries are concerned with the distinction between nature and habit simultaneously as they seek to show the ways in which habit affects human nature in such a manner as to enhance as well as impede it. After he recognizes the effects of custom on the capacity of the hearer to understand a lecture, the general preference for the familiar that engenders a resistance to the unfamiliar and an inclination to reject the strange as false, Aquinas explains that the reason for such comportment is "because custom is turned into nature, whence also habit comes into being which inclines in the manner of nature"[601] Thus, irrespective of the proper distinction between natural inclination and a-natural *habitus*, in the order of existence and time the relation between natural reason and the habit of virtue is so intimate as to render the distinction strictly a distinction of reason. In fact, in the order of acquisition the relation between nature and habit are reversed.

When he attempts to account for the resistance (repulsion) to truth on account of its tension with the familiar or customary, Aquinas points out that, even though *by nature* all human beings possess innate first principles, in the temporal order insofar as acquired habits are actual principles of action, they are better known than first principles. Thus understood, conventional habits become barriers to the actualization of the knowledge to be derived from first principles. As for Maimonides then so for Aquinas, conventional moral habits are principles of attraction and repulsion that can, and often do, disrupt the relation between the true and the good. In this context Aquinas also identifies the power of custom with the origin of assent to human law, a power that he maintains is greater than that of knowledge of truth so that, irrespective of their moral or rational status, human beings approve of (are attracted by) the traditional laws "which they have heard from childhood more than of knowledge of truth."[602] Departing from Aristotle's text, Aquinas adds that in contrast to human laws which are imperfect, "divinely given law orders human beings to true happiness to which every falsity is opposed. Wherefore, no falsity is contained in divine law."[603]

The Displacement of Legislative Reason by Divine Law

It is not unexpected that Aquinas' lengthiest discussion of law in general, and divine Law in particular, occurs in the *Summa Theologiae* directly after his discussion of original sin and its consequences, a fact which conditions the discussion, explains its length, and is recalled in the paragraph introducing the subject: "Consequently, the external principles of action ought to be considered. On the one hand, the external principle inclining to evil is the devil, whose temptation was discussed in the first [part]. On the other hand, the external principle moving to the good is God, who both instructs us through law and helps [us] through grace."[604] Nor is it surprising, when we survey the numerous and seemingly conflicting definitions of law given by Aquinas, that, at the outset, he explains that the term *law* is not used univocally.[605] Since the distinction between the definitions is essential to the following discussion, I shall enumerate them and provide a brief synopsis of their content prior to the discussion.

The constitutive characteristics of law, according to Aquinas are

1. Law is the rule and measure of action, the principle of which in human beings is reason (Q. 90, a. 1).
2. Law is the first principle of practical reason with respect to action that subordinates private goods to the common good as an ultimate end (Q. 90, a. 2).
3. The proper definition of law is nothing other than a certain ordering of reason promulgated by a ruler for the sake of the common good (Q. 90, aa. 3-4).
4. It belongs to the proper definition of law that it be obligatory (Q. 90, a. 4).

Law is subsequently divided into five categories: eternal, natural, human-positive, divine, and *lex fomitis*; and divine law is distinguished further into the old law and the new law; the former being the law of fear, the latter, the law of love. Given that obligation belongs to the proper definition of law, it must extend in some manner to all categories of law.

Eternal law is defined by Aquinas as the plan of universal government in God's "mind," the human participation in which is natural law. Thus, eternal law and natural law are the formal determination of the respective relations between God and human beings in the order of being. With respect to obligation, given the unchangeable necessary actuality of the divinity, the eternal law is the active unchanging and thus "obligatory" order of all determinations entailed by it. The determination that renders human agency possible is natural law. Positive law is the positive, rational extrinsic determination of the eternal law by the ruler that is promulgated in order to establish or actualize a rational order within the community. Its binding character can take either the force of external coercion or internal conviction. Thus, positive law is the attempt to imitate divine government insofar as it strives to establish a hierarchical relation among the individuals comprising the community, the unity of which is determined by the final end—the common good. The *lex fomitis* is defined as the corrupt *habitus* in the human soul that is the divinely imposed penalty consequent upon the fall. Both as divinely imposed and as a habit, the *lex fomitis* is binding in the same manner as is natural law; it inclines in the manner of nature.

As should be evident from the preceding, Aquinas' definition of law is equivocal rather than analogical and encompasses within one category definitions that are either conflicting or, at the very least, seem to render others superfluous. To single out but one problem inherent in the inclusive definition of law: Whereas law is said to require promulgation, only positive law and the old law are explicitly promulgated, all other laws are said to be inscribed on the human heart. The equivocity of the term *law* presents a difficulty that is not merely semantic but also epistemic since, as will become evident, some of these laws, such as the natural and the *lex fomitis*, are either contraries or contradictories; they belong to different orders of existence, consist of different first principles of knowledge and action, and belong to different orders of discourse. In addition, and precisely because of the *lex fomitis*, the derivation of positive law from natural law is rather problematic.[606]

The rational participation in the eternal law, which is natural law, is both passive and active. Passively, it is the imprint upon the human "heart" of first indemonstrable principles by divine illumination. Actively, it is the rational use of these principles for the purpose of acting in accordance with divine providence, and thus, it constitutes the determinate possibility of participating in it.[607] Human law, which is the efficacious participation in the natural law deriving the particular determinations from its general indemonstrable principles, is the actualization of natural law, and thus, it is one manifestation of the activity proper to the provident human being.

Notwithstanding the possibilities inherent in both natural and human law, natural law must be supplemented by a promulgated divine law, according to Aquinas, for four reasons. First, natural human reason is disproportionate to the final end. Second, despite the agent intellect and precisely insofar as true knowledge of particulars requires the understanding of the universal, necessary unchanging order, human judgment is most fallible with respect to the determinate possibilities pertaining to contingent particular cases. Third, human judgment cannot be applied to interior actions that, nonetheless, are necessary for the perfection of human virtues. Fourth, human law cannot forbid all evils without simultaneously destroying many goods required for the common good.[608] In agreement with the *Commentary on the Metaphysics*, the enumeration of the reasons for promulgating divine law make amply evident that human law cannot achieve its end—worldly perfection—*per se* because of the limitations of natural human reason.

In contrast to Maimonides, for whom, by definition, there can be only one perfect divine law that aims at both perfections, Aquinas argues that there are two divine laws, which can be distinguished not only by their different final ends but also by their efficient ends. The old law, which aims strictly at natural human perfection, maintains its efficacy and obligatory force by means of fear, whereas the new law, which aims at supranatural human perfection, is rendered obligatory by the love instilled in the human heart through the grace of Christ.

Although an analysis of the scope of, and relation between, the two divine laws is beyond the limits of my discussion, two major problems ensuing from Aquinas' exposition should be spelled out. First, how can there be an imperfect divine law? Second, if the two human ends under each divine law are subject to two distinct legislations, and if these ends present conflicting demands, what authority has the power of arbitration and on what grounds is the decision rendered? Conflict between the obligatory "commandments" of the two laws are more than a remote possibility within this schema, especially since the demands of the new law often seem to enjoin the transgression of the other's precepts (e.g., the observance of the Sabbath and circumcision).

Because of its blatant and "embarrassing" incongruity with post-Enlightenment thought, it is not surprising that the last category among the laws enumerated by Aquinas, the *lex fomitis*, is also the least heeded by contemporary scholars, despite its significance to the argument and, especially, to the concept and extension of natural law. At best, the modern moral philosopher deems concepts such as original sin and divine penalty metaphorical. Paradoxically, in fact, the *lex fomitis* provides an insight into the obligatory status of law insofar as its binding force is consequent upon determinate natural possibilities.

Questioning whether there is a *lex fomitis*, Aquinas explains that it can be considered a law in a derivative sense insofar as it is an inclination.[609] The *lex fomitis* is an inclination to sensuality that departs from the order of reason, the order proper not only to the human being *simpliciter*, but also to human being as creature. Thus, when Aquinas argues that the *lex fomitis* "can be called a law not essentially, but as if in a participative way,"[610] he is indicating the fact that the quasi-natural habit named by this law is the manifestation of the human participation in a natural order other than its proper one. This is also the order where the meaning of *law* is transformed from a natural principle to a conventional prescription. Aquinas' repetition of the Pauline saying "I see another law in my members warring against the law of my mind"[611] is more than conformity to tradition. It is the explanation why two conflicting inclinations are constitutive elements in the human soul, manifesting a real conflict within it that necessitates the legislation of external principles of action. Consequently, it also explains the limits of natural ethics.

As laws, inclinations manifest the rule of subjects by a lawgiver directly, when he or she orders them to specific and diverse ends, and indirectly, when he or she deprives them of their proper dignity, placing them under another participative order, as if subject to another law and measure. All creatures can be said to be under divine legislation insofar as they possess distinct inclinations that are proper to them alone; the proper human law inclining to action in accordance with right reason ruled Adam. When he turned away from God, Adam and all his progeny fell under the influence of, or inclination to, sensuality and, hence, the more human beings fail to follow reason, the more they come under the influence of its opposite, placing themselves in a lower order of existence wherein they resembles the beasts. However, whereas animal sensuality is a natural law, in human beings such a sensuality is the perversion of the rational law punished by divine decree that deprives them of their proper dignity, namely, original justice and the *force* of reason.

Since law is defined as an ordinance of reason and since the *lex fomitis* is a deviation from it, it is a law in a very special sense. However, it should be emphasized that, notwithstanding the difficulty that may arise from subsuming a natural inclination under the category of law, Aquinas' definition is based upon the principle that all natural inclinations, including the *lex fomitis*, are manifestations of right reason/measure and, hence, of the perfect measure that is eternal law—reason's unchanging exemplar. Unlike the other laws, no further specific question is devoted to the *lex fomitis*. Still *lex fomitis* is one of the major reasons for the necessity of grace in addition, or as an aid, to all law, including the new law. Aquinas does not deem further discussion of the *lex fomitis* necessary in the *Summa* since (1) its facticity is not doubted by his audience, (2) he has addressed it in scriptural commentaries, and (3) the discussion of sin preceding the one on law has explained it in great detail.

In the commentary on Romans, the *lex fomitis* is said to have produced two effects in human beings: it opposes reason, identified here as the law of the mind, Mosaic law, and natural law, and it leads to human servitude on account of which the human being "cannot be freed by his own powers from either bodily or spiritual corruption, even though he may accord with reason against sin, but only through the grace of Christ."[612]

Thus understood to have its origins in divine law, the *lex fomitis* can be superseded only by a second divine dispensation. Although the *lex fomitis*, as the effect of original sin, manifests the human privation of actual virtue and actual grace, Aquinas maintains that, nevertheless, it has not deprived human beings of all good since, by definition or as a species, they cannot be deprived of all the principles constituting their essential nature. Rather, the *lex fomitis* is an obstacle raised between the natural inclination to virtue and its end that renders the promulgation of divine law necessary. In the light of the *lex fomitis*, the category natural law, in fact, is applicable only to innocent Adam; consequently, the assessment of the capacity of natural reason to determine secondary precepts from primary ones must take full account of the existential change consequent upon original sin. One of the most significant consequences of the "barrier" that is the *lex fomitis* is the disruption of the immediate relation between the possible and agent intellect, a disruption that undermines rational appetitive choice considerably.

After he draws a careful distinction between the intellectual *habitus* itself and the actions consequent upon it, Aquinas asks whether the natural law is composed of a single principle or of many. The distinction between the *habitus* itself and the act of *habitus* is essential for Aquinas' argument that the definition *natural law* requires that one of two conditions be true, namely, either that there be one natural law composed of a single precept or that there be several natural laws, each possessing its single corresponding primary principle. He further argues that natural law precepts are to practical reason what the primary precepts of demonstration are to speculative reason; namely, the principles *per se notae* that inform all actions. As in the discussion of the speculative intellect, so in this context, Aquinas states that without primary principles no action is possible.

Following Aristotle,[613] Aquinas distinguishes two modes of self-evident knowledge. The first distinction explains the mode of the object and refers to knowledge of a *propositio per se notae* of which the predicates are contained within the definition; knowledge of such propositions both includes knowledge of the predicates and depends upon them. Such a proposition is known *per se* only if the definition is *known*. The second distinction explains the intellectual mode of the proposition, the mode of the knower,[614] and refers to both principles possessed by all human beings in common and principles known only to the wise[615] (*solis sapientibus*). Properly speaking, then, the latter principles cannot belong to that natural law inscribed on the hearts of all human beings.

The cognitive order of first principles follows the metaphysical hierarchy so that being is the foundation of all else. To apprehend is to apprehend being, which is also the immediate assent to the principle of non-contradiction. This apprehension precedes all operations and from it follow the primary precepts of reason. With respect to practical reason, the first apprehension is that of the good, which entails the immediate assent to the principle "good is what all desire." Consequently, the first proposition of natural law is "good ought to be done and pursued and evil ought to be shunned." Although the total number of first principles is three, they constitute a single natural law, since they are the essential predicates contained within the first proposition. From the first follow the other principles of natural law, which are nothing other than the order in which practical reason apprehends the fundamental human goods: self-preservation, conservation of the species, and life in accord with reason. However, since *habitus* here signifies the passive possession of principles only,[616] the will and reason are required for transforming them into both cognized principles and ends of actions. Moreover, since original sin has disrupted the causal relations between the will and reason, the apprehension of the final, proper human good—beatitude—as the true human end and the determination of the proportionality of specific goods to the end cannot be achieved by ratiocination alone. Human laws commensurate with it cannot be legislated without aid.

Aquinas' investigation of the scope and durability of natural law repeats many of the arguments presented in the previous discussion of the intellect. He explains the causes of failure of the intellect in general, and of the practical intellect in particular, to reach true conclusions and emphasizes the contingency of particular objects especially, all of which disclose additional obstacles to the derivation of secondary precepts. Error concerning conclusions is attributed by Aquinas to two types of causes, which can be designated *natural* and *human*, the mode of the object and the mode of the knower. The former is attributed to the corruptible nature of things, whereas the latter is attributed specifically to the fallibility of human reason whereby "some men possess reason perverted by passion, or by an evil custom, or by an evil disposition of nature."[617]

When discussing either the mutability of natural law or the possibility of its obliteration from the human heart, Aquinas does not address the specific methods appropriate for deriving secondary precepts from primary precepts of natural law, apart from stating that, *qua* principles of natural law, they must be proximate to the primary ones.[618] Moreover, Aquinas explains that natural law can be changed either by addition or deletion that can originate both in divine and in human laws. However, since changes affect only secondary principles and since they can also arise from acquired corrupt habits, the derived principles cannot, properly speaking, constitute natural law without rendering the distinctions among the various laws insignificant. Likewise, the obliteration of natural law from the heart, which is consequent upon an inclination to evil, can be understood either as a divine punishment or as a new law or both—as happens in *lex fomitis*—which will significantly change the original definition of the natural law. Since human laws are further removed from the primary principles than secondary natural law precepts and since even the latter cannot be derived without error after the fall, the discussion of human law is extraneous to my inquiry, apart from pointing out that it should be evident by now that conventional laws cannot aim at the true, final human end.[619]

The fallibility of human reason and the necessary diversity in the states of human perfection render the promulgation of divine law necessary in order to overcome the human inability to attain not only the proper final perfection, but also the proper temporal one. Hence, the old law aims, first and foremost, at promulgating natural law precepts, and second, it aims at preparing human beings for the reception of the new law. Consequently, only the moral commandments that are but natural law precepts were binding on all human beings, the remaining precepts were binding only on the Jews and only for a limited purpose and time. Since the old law was given to imperfect human beings who had yet to be habituated in virtue in accordance with right reason, inducement to obedience was accomplished through fear of punishment and promise of temporal rewards. The new law, the law of love, renders most of the old law superfluous since it is its actualization; its reward is supranatural.[620]

Aquinas designates the new law an inner law, consisting in "the grace of the Holy Spirit which is given through faith in Christ,"[621] and distinguishes it from natural law precepts as a gift super-added to, rather than grounded in, human nature, which not only legislates what ought to be done, but also assists in its actualization.[622] Although this explanation seems to indicate that the qualification can be extended to differentiate between the old and new law, Aquinas rejects an understanding of the old law as strictly and explicitly legislating right action by adding that faith in Christ, through which grace is granted, can be either implicit or explicit. In virtue of such faith, whether implicit or explicit, one belongs to the new covenant. Since Aquinas argues that some human beings are saved by the old law, it cannot represent the natural law alone. Moreover, Aquinas explains that the new law is not altogether devoid of external elements that further dispose human beings toward the grace of Christ and pertain to its exercise. However, although the predominant quality of the new law, as grace, is the aid sufficient to avoid sin, it does not confirm human beings in the good so that they are unable to avoid sin and, hence, the new law too can kill.[623]

Aquinas presents revealed law as a successive process of perfection that is determined by the varied relations toward the law in which human beings are found and that are consequent upon their varied states. Accordingly, the diversity of places, times, and persons determines the diversity in the legislative extension of the law, be it old or new. This diversity is the necessary consequence of temporal existence since the perfection of the universe requires a manifold diversity in degree within each species and class of things. The a-temporal, a-historical, relation between the two divine laws is repeated, emphatically, several times in I^a-II^{ae}, Qs. 106-8, and is expressed most strikingly by the statement that "the gospel has not been preached yet throughout the world, but once this has happened, the consummation of the world will come."[624]

In emphasizing the a-temporal aspect of the divine law, Aquinas safeguards the claim of the Christian message from an historicist interpretation or rather, distinguishes between an historical one and an historicist one. In so doing, he also, at least implicitly, rejects an altogether historicist interpretation of the old law and establishes its claim to universal truth. For if the truth of the new law is not to be usurped by yet a more perfect truth, *ad infinitum*, then the old and new law must be understood as a single universal truth. Since ultimate perfection does not occur *in* time and since its universal actualization will happen only at the consummation of the world, law, as an external principle of action, can be abolished only at the end of historical time. Conversely, law, as an internal principle of action, whether based upon nature, grace, or both, is not subject to time. It may announce time, but it is not *in* time. Consequently, the inherent permanent stability of divine government and providence guarantee that, within historical time or the order of things *in* time, all grades of human perfection fitting to that particular time must exist. For Aquinas then, as for Maimonides, the law conceals the necessary natural diversity required for the perfection of the species.

Since the internal human disposition toward the law is the factor deter-mining whether human beings will reach worldly or spiritual perfection, or no perfection at all, and since implicit faith can suffice for spiritual perfection, Aquinas' exposition seems to indicate that, at all times, in some way, there exist individuals who are under one of three laws, namely, the *lex fomitis*, the old law, and the new law, and that potentially, although not actually, all human beings can choose to proceed progressively from sin, through fear, to love. Thus, when Aquinas argues that if at the age of discretion individuals choose to order their life to the proper end, they would receive pardon from original sin through grace,[625] such individuals must represent all human beings, at any time, in whom a remnant of grace remains. This remnant of grace must be the actu-ality that is the agent intellect in virtue of which the original order of justice or right reason can be recovered. Moreover, it seems to me that the choice of a rightful end is that inner act of faith which Aquinas characterizes as an intel-lectual act of firm assent that does not depend upon clear knowledge, and thus, "to believe is that act distinguished from all acts of the intellect which are con-cerned with the true and the false."[626] Since the essential "object" of faith is beatitude and since beatitude is, first and foremost, the proper object of the will, that act of faith which does not require a clear intellectual apprehension must be the immediate intellectual assent to the singular essential identity between the true and the good.

Conclusion

The discussion of philosophical ethics, which was the first concern in this chapter, was limited to an investigation of the manner in which both Maimonides and Aquinas sought to disclose simultaneously the excellence and the limits of philosophical, predominantly Aristotelian, ethics. Ironically, Aristotle's distinction between nature and habit and Aristotle's recognition of the tension between ontologically grounded possibility and temporal actual-ization—the proper realm of ethics—made possible the argument that natural human reason is limited not only in relation to the final, extra-natural, human end but also in relation to the natural human end. Drawing upon yet another aspect of the distinction between the order of being and the order of knowing, a distinction that played a significant role in all the previous discussions, I examined how the relation between nature/reason and temporal habituation pertaining to ethics inverts or even subverts the priority of ontology/actuality and temporality/possibility for both Maimonides and Aquinas to such an extent that renders necessary divine revelation.

In the light of the inversion between the two causal orders it became clear why despite the substantial differences between their ontologies, espe-cially the difference between the ontological and noetic status of the good,

Maimonides and Aquinas reach strikingly similar conclusions about the limits of Aristotelian ethics. The same agreements and disagreements were disclosed in the discussion of divine law. Thus, although Maimonides asserts that Adam did not have the faculty to discern good and evil and that the intellect is not the proper subject of commandments, his concomitant assertion that Adam was given an intellectual commandment does not seem to me to differ substantially from Aquinas' explanation of the primary principles of natural law. These principles are the content of the immediate intellectual apprehension of being as both the true and the good. As (a) noetic principle(s), the identity between the true and the good indicate the possibility of understanding and action rather than their actuality, otherwise Adam could not have shunned the good. Likewise despite Aquinas' distinction between the old and the new law, Maimonides' and Aquinas' interpretation of the progressive ascent constituting the human relation to the law, Aquinas' emphasis upon its a-temporal nature, and Maimonides' distinction between love and fear as principles of obedience exhibit greater similarity than dissimilarity both with respect to the nomothetic status of divine law and with respect to epistemic role in human perfection. Where they differ, their difference is predominantly one of emphasis rather than substance and, in my opinion, their only substantial difference is based upon a theological rather than a philosophical consideration. The remnant of grace that is in every human being and the possibility of justification through an implicit act of faith posited by Aquinas, which extends the real possibility of human perfection beyond the very limited number of the elite posited by Maimonides, can best be explained by the belief in Christ's incarnation. Notwithstanding, since grace is the condition for, rather than the confirmation in, perfection, right order in the soul has to be actualized through understanding. According to both thinkers, the best means for achieving this understanding is divine law. The existential possibilities consequent upon divine law will be discussed in the following, concluding chapter.

7

HUBRIS, KNOWLEDGE, AND PROVIDENT PARTICIPATION

Introduction

The conclusion reached in all the previous chapters concerning the limitations of human reason and the consequent necessity for divine revelation may lead to the mistaken impression that once such limits are posited philosophy must cede to theology. Such a conclusion also may confirm the contemporary philosopher in the belief that neither Maimonides' nor Aquinas' writings are of great significance to contemporary thought, especially in view of the very constitution of many topics explored in my inquiry. For if the "knowledge" rendered possible by a recognition of the limitations of human reason requires that we reaffirm creation, evil, original sin, providence, and divine law, and since these notions have fortunately long been discarded by all philosophers and many theologians, such post-rational knowledge is either dogma or some mystical nonsense. In any event, whatever "it" is, it is best left outside the academy. Notwithstanding, since I opened this study with the assertion that Maimonides' and Aquinas' expositions on these matters are philosophically still interesting, not only do I wish to reaffirm this assertion, but also, in the following, I propose to explain the manner in which the subjects constituting the unity of this study give rise to a notion of human knowledge that opens-up rather than closes-off discussions concerning what is and is not philosophically admissible and ethically possible.

Since I began this study with an examination of Maimonides' and Aquinas' expositions on Job in order to draw out some of the essential questions that exhibit the limits of a narrowly defined rationality as inherited by both thinkers from philosophy and revelation, I shall conclude it with an explanation of the nature of the transformation consequent upon the true understanding of providence attributed to Job, or the perfect human being. I shall begin with a brief summary of the discussion of Job in order to recall the notion of *hubris* introduced there. In turn, *hubris* will be briefly rethought in the light of what followed in order to show how it is the contradictory of "prophetic" understanding whose consequence is a different mode of provident agency/freedom, of which a significant aspect is speaking/teaching. Before proceeding, it is advisable to recall my assertion in Chapter 1 that Maimonides' and Aquinas' writings are exemplary manifestations of prudent/provident teaching and that their relation to their respective traditions are exemplary manifestations of interpreting canonical texts. For any philosophical conversations with one's forebears must open their thought to, rather than close it off to further reflection and questioning. As Aristotle pointed out so poignantly after his review and critique of his forebears, "It is just to be grateful not only to those with whose opinions we might agree, but also to those who have expressed rather superficial opinions; for the latter, too, have contributed something, namely they have handed down to us the habit of thinking . . . for some of them handed down to us certain doctrines, but there were other before who caused them to be what they are."[627] The critical comportment towards one's forebears thus exhibits due ethical respect.

The Problem of Job

Two distinct problems emerged from the review in Chapter 2 of the scholarship on Maimonides' and Aquinas' writings on providence and Job; namely, a predominant concern with the possibility of affirming human freedom in view of eternal divine knowledge and the radical juxtaposition of the philosophical and theological approaches to the question. My concern in this concluding chapter will be limited to the first question, since all the preceding chapters should suffice as a response to the second. In Chapter 2, I argue that, since human choice is a consequence of human knowledge, since divine knowledge can be understood only by a remote analogy to human knowledge (if at all), and since the human relation to providence is a consequence of the human place in the order of being, an investigation of the ontological and noetic aspects constituting such a relation to providence must precede the examination of the relations between the human will and divine knowledge. Apart from following the order of priority and posteriority in the order of knowing, limiting the investigation to providence as it pertains to human existence provides the additional advantage for an investigation more compatible with traditional philosophical ones. In the conclusion, I shall return to what can and cannot be said about divine knowledge, in the light of what has preceded.

Of the three significant differences between Maimonides' and Aquinas' investigations of the Job narrative, two appear in their introductory remarks, namely, the interpretative level of the exposition and the determination of the historical reality of the narrated events. Whereas Maimonides argues that the story is a parable that requires a figurative interpretation, Aquinas defines the exposition as *ad litteram* and argues that the events narrated represent historical facts. In view of Aquinas' understanding of the interdependency between the literal-historical level and all other levels of interpretation and in light of his repeated explicit interpretations of numerous biblical expressions as metaphorical, I conclude that Aquinas' initial emphasis upon the literal nature of his commentary is aimed at drawing a distinction between his work and the Gregorian tradition rather than indicating a real difference between himself and Maimonides.[628] In a similar manner, since Maimonides explicitly disengages the question of historical reality from that of parable and explains that the significance of the story is trans-historical and reflects a perennial situation and since Aquinas defines the distinction as one between "something in the nature of things" and "a fictitious parable," I conclude that their respective designations do not indicate a dissimilarity, but rather a great similarity of purpose. My conclusion also can be supported by the significant similarities between the expositions on the central issues constituting Job; namely, the human place in the metaphysical order and the limitations of human knowledge.

Both Maimonides and Aquinas construct their expositions on Job around the figure of Satan and the influence he has on the human soul. In addition to occupying one of the central roles in the biblical drama, the figure of Satan, according to both thinkers, discloses the structure of the metaphysical order and, thus, makes manifest the manifold relations between God and the creatures, especially human beings. The status of the human soul as it is manifest through its essential activities and Satan's relative power over them constitutes the focus of both the biblical drama and Maimonides' and Aquinas' expositions. By emphasizing Satan's place in the created order, both thinkers eliminate the possibility of interpreting evil either as something real that possesses an independent existence, willed by God, or as something 'permitted' by Him through indifference to the sublunar realm.[629] Like the other angels to whose rank in the ontological order he belongs, Satan has an assigned role in the perfection of the order of generation and corruption. However, unlike other angels, his role is restricted to the sublunar realm, does not extend to any permanent existent, and hence, has no essential rule over the human soul. In this light, Satan's influence bears greater similarity to the influence of the heavenly bodies than to that of any of the other angels. It is as though Satan's punishment is to participate divine government in a "lower" realm, as human punishment is a participation in a lower realm.

It is noteworthy that, although both Maimonides and Aquinas underline the fact that Satan has no dominion over the human soul, the major difference between their respective understanding of the nature of the soul does not come to light in the context of their commentaries. Whereas Maimonides alludes to what he considers the nature of the soul to consist in, when he states that the term *soul* refers to "the thing that remains of man after death,"[630] Aquinas states only that *soul* here refers to the preservation of life. Insofar as the thrust of

Aquinas' commentary is to emphasize the limitations of human knowledge due to the low status of the human soul in the order of self-subsistent beings and insofar as Aquinas uses the drama of Job, first and foremost, to address the contingent part of human existence, his primary aim is to emphasize the necessity for supranatural help in order to avoid human ills.[631] Moreover, without benefit of his other writings, Aquinas' repeated assertions that human beings cannot overcome Satan, or shun evil, by their natural powers provides no indication that he understood the human soul to be self-subsistent. Consequently, on the basis of the exposition alone, Aquinas' psychology seems almost identical to Maimonides'.

In this manner, the seeming similarity between Maimonides' and Aquinas' psychologies indirectly reveals a major difference between the orders of discourse to which their commentaries belong. Maimonides' commentary, which occurs in the *Guide* after the elaborate expositions on creation, the angels, matter, and evil and assumes knowledge of philosophical metaphysics discusses the human being as a potentially active participant in divine providence.[632] The limitations of human knowledge emphasized here are not those consequent upon a deliberate human failure to actualize the natural powers of the soul, but rather those rooted in the very nature of the human soul and its proper place in the universal order. Maimonides' text is addressed to philosophers who have attained natural perfection. It presents a concept of providence that supplements and corrects the philosophical. Aquinas' commentary, on the other hand, assumes no philosophical knowledge in its audience; it is propaedeutic to philosophy and habituates the audience to the necessity of philosophical practice in biblical interpretation. Indeed, Aquinas' exposition begins with the letter in order to demonstrate its significance to understanding at any level.[633] Since the audience has no understanding of the nature and scope of natural perfection and since they do not understand the significance of its necessary conjunction with a material body, the greater part of the exposition is limited to a discussion of passive human relation to providence. Despite these limits, since the final chapters of Aquinas' exposition focus upon the possibility of overcoming Satan's temptation strictly in terms of the human soul and its essential intellectual activities and since the discussion clearly indicates that natural perfection is an intermediate state only, these chapters provide the audience with a preliminary account of every subject essential for understanding providence fully.[634]

The third apparent difference between Maimonides' and Aquinas' commentaries, which is discussed in Chapter 2, is also shown to be accidental to Aquinas' understanding of the nature of providence. Although Maimonides attributes greater perfection to Elihu and Aquinas attributes it to Job, their presentations of the nature of the distinct degrees of perfection and of possible human relations to providence are almost identical. Elihu's and God's speeches are the occasion to demonstrate that the acquisition of both natural science and philosophical metaphysics is a necessary, but insufficient, condition for ultimate perfection, since reason cannot attain adequately the first causes and true reality of intellectual objects. Relative lack of perfection manifests a disorder in the soul that cannot be overcome, nor sustained, without revelation. Although the psychological disorder pertains primarily to the perfection of moral virtue and of practical reason, clearly any disorder must affect the soul as a whole; and, in fact, the most significant consequence emerging from Maimonides' and Aquinas' interpretation of Job is the perennial danger of intellectual hubris. In addition, the human inability to recognize, or reluctance to admit, the natural limitations of human reason constitute a barrier to the attainment of full perfection—practical, speculative, and final.

Even though neither commentary addresses the precise nature of the psychological disorder, nevertheless, both Maimonides and Aquinas indicate clearly that it is a direct consequence of the human place in the ontological order. The necessary dependence of the human intellect upon sensible objects renders it incapable of knowing the intelligibles as they are. Consequently and ironically, the very means to perfection, the natural human inclination to material (i.e., sensible) objects, is also the barrier to proper human perfection. Inasmuch as both Maimonides and Aquinas argue that the limitations of the human intellect extend not only to metaphysical, but also to physical, reality, it is clear that *hubris* is a perennial possibility, which can affect human beings at any state of relative perfection. The assumption that one possesses perfect knowledge of any given object, be it an object known through revelation or one known through philosophical reasoning, is not only an indication of relative ignorance, but also a barrier to further understanding at any level.

Although, initially, Aquinas seems to deem Job's shortcomings less grave than Maimonides does, a close study of his explanation of God's response discloses that Aquinas considered Job neither perfectly just nor perfectly wise. Indeed, Job's acts of worship were reverent and his opinions correct when judged in proportion to his natural capacity and the knowledge available to him. Nevertheless, his disordered mode of speaking[635] indicates a disorder in the soul that cannot be corrected by human reason alone. Moreover, given Job's superior knowledge and given that his disordered speeches produced error in his audience, the psychic disorder was communicated to others. In a manner of speaking, Job's seemingly light transgression is more weighty than those of his interlocutors, whose knowledge was inferior, because his superior intellect renders him morally more responsible for the effects of his actions.[636]

Job's intellectual pride is a manifestation of ignorance concerning both theoretical and moral matters. In fact, it is his theoretical ignorance that gives rise to moral transgressions. By their own powers, human beings can not attain to full knowledge of divine government, the *ratio* of the universal order and, hence, no one can worship God fittingly by assuming his or her proper place as participant. God's government over every aspect of being is the unifying premise of Job and of the two commentaries. Failure to recognize this premise, according to both Maimonides and Aquinas, is the cause of all errors concerning not only providence but also the nature of human existence. Consequently, the function of these commentaries on Job is to outline the constitutive elements necessary for the correct understanding of providence and the human place within it, namely, the understanding of the metaphysical order, its ontological and existential manifestations, and the nature and activities of the soul. Nevertheless, biblical commentaries do not constitute philosophical studies *per se*.

The "question" of Job emerging from both Maimonides' and Aquinas' presentations consists of two problems, the ontological status of things in *rerum natura* and the scope of natural human understanding of such things. The figures of Satan and the angel appearing to Elihu are the two contrary poles of human possibility within a universe understood as perfectly ordered. The inaccessibility to natural knowledge of the origin of that order is equally problematic for contemporary thought as it was for the ancient and medieval philosophers. More precisely, with the exception of Enlightenment thought and its various progeny, it remained and remains a problem. For irrespective of any hypothetical premise a physicist, philosopher, or theologian may propose, the status of that premise remains as shaky as its proponent *knows* it to be invented or *constructed*. What is at issue then for any discourse based upon such a premise is its entailment; that is, what can be known and said about things in *rerum natura*, to what extent is what is affirmed or denied open to questioning, to what extent does it "better" disclose what is seen, and so forth. From the perspective of Job, *hubris* becomes a barrier to knowing precisely insofar as the human knower refuses to acknowledge the fact that what he or she affirms is based not upon knowledge, but upon the pretense of knowledge or relative ignorance. As the final chapters of Job indicate, human ignorance is, first and foremost, ignorance of first principles of which the first is the origin of the universe.

The exile of metaphysics does not seem to have diminished the central importance of the question of origin to inquiries into the nature of existence. Irrespective of the conclusions they reached concerning the ultimate human end, immanent or transcendent, most premodern traditions were agreed that a first, necessary, and impassible principle of all beings was demonstrable and hence beyond doubt. However, the nature of the relation between the first unifying principle and all other beings, especially the impermanent beings, which was determined by the nature of the act bringing all these beings into existence, was highly disputed. Not only did the philosophers disagree among themselves about these issues and not only did many philosophical doctrines conflict with the revealed traditions, there was also no agreement within the revealed traditions or between them about the relation between God and creatures. That is why both Maimonides and Aquinas underline the fact that Job's errors concerning providence are reducible to his ignorance of the origin of the universe. Where the desire for understanding originates in a recognition of ignorance, the medieval philosopher could follow either the Platonic position, which did not seem to conflict with revelation, or the Aristotelian, which did.

On the basis of Aristotelian logic, both Maimonides and Aquinas reach the same single conclusion, namely, the indemonstrable nature of the first act. It is precisely because Aristotle already suggested that the question does not lend itself to demonstration but only to probable reasoning that Maimonides and Aquinas can first challenge his conclusions and then posit an alternative explanation. Aristotle's position could be questioned because he, or rather his followers, violated Aristotle's own principles, inferring what is possible about a unique singular metaphysical act from the multiplicity of sensible existents for which it is the logical and ontological ground or, more precisely, for which it provides the measure (*ratio oridinis*). Conversely, on the basis of "eternity" Aristotle concluded that the divine is indifferent to all changeable entities.

Since both Maimonides and Aquinas repeatedly assert that with respect to physics Aristotle's teachings were not only most correct, but also most consonant with revealed teachings, the need for a long excursus on creation, prime matter, and similar metaphysical topics may well be questioned in an inquiry of which the stated purpose is its pertinence to human existence. That is, if the nature of what exists is both the grounds of human knowledge and the criterion for validation of any discourse, then questions about the nature of human existence need, indeed can, be answered strictly on the basis of sensible experience; speech, or discourse, itself is sensible. Conversely, if sensible experience cannot provide certain knowledge about unique acts and things, then, irrespective of their alleged significance, they cannot be investigated.

Notwithstanding, for both Maimonides and Aquinas, the absence of certain knowledge, which exhibits the limits of demonstrative reason, is an impetus to further questioning rather than to skepticism, which is nothing other than *hubris*. The more the philosopher understand the nature of the existing universe as it is, the more he or she understands what is and is not possible. That existing universe as it is, or the perfect necessary order—which no imaginative possibility can change—determines what is and is not possible of becoming, of knowing, and of acting. The question of the possibility of creation ultimately determines what can be said about human beings, especially about the limits of free human agency. In asking what kind of agency can be affirmed of God,[637] absolutely free, relatively free, or necessarily determined, we also determine the nature of human perfection and freedom, or possibility, of attaining it. For if we affirm either of the latter premises, not only is divine freedom questionable so that perfect order is compromised but also, and more radically, is human freedom. When Maimonides states that, philosophically—although not theologically—the Platonic position is identical to the Aristotelian, he is not so concerned with what can be said about God, since, for him what we say about God is by pure equivocation, as he is concerned with what can be said about human beings. The Aristotelian and Platonic positions philosophically amount to the same thing because the co-eternity of motion and of time are accidental to the co-eternity of prime matter. Since time and motion require a substratum in which to inhere, their necessity is relative to the fundamental necessity of the substratum. Moreover, since natural laws derive from determinate matter, its motion, and its duration and since they require the perpetuity of generation and corruption, their validity must be relative to the absolute validity of "metaphysical laws" governing the substrata of change that guarantee their perpetuity.[638] Consequently, to the extent that prime matter or radical indeterminacy is claimed to be independent of the divine order, to that same extent it would constitute a primary and fundamental determinant of the order of the universe. From the perspective of the relation between principles of determinacy (order, necessity) and indeterminacy (choice, possibility), human ignorance coupled with *hubris* is the greatest hindrance to knowledge and freedom. Since an *understanding* of first principles (as they are) exceeds natural reason proportionately as they precede determinate nature, only an a-natural impetus can disclose them. Likewise a recognition of their excess or of the insufficiency of reason is the condition for knowledge insofar as a determinate end (hindrance) set by reason is removed.

Modes of Participating Providence

The actual possibility of attaining perfection through the law and the sense in which divine law is the medium/measure through which human beings are related to providence directly remains to be indicated. Whereas divine government is best understood as the full manifestation of the *ratio* of the universal order, divine providence is its execution through the active preservation of universal order. Insofar as divine providence is effected through the mediation of intellectual beings, human beings can be related to it either as a subjects who are maintained in their proper order by the intellects or as both subjects and participating intellects. Clearly, so long as they do not become the actual governing principles of their own operations, human beings cannot become the governing principles of the operations of others. From the perspective of the providential order, divine law is the full articulation of the rule and measure necessary for an effective transformation from subjects to participants. It makes manifest the nature of the providential order and its preserving operations as they pertain to diverse human being. Thus, the promulgation of divine law renders the law as a whole, in principle, equally accessible to all human beings, and in principle renders human beings free to choose the nature of their relation to the law.

Two questions still require elaboration: How is the transformation from mere subjects to active participants effected?[639] And what is the nature of the participative activity? In light of the conclusion reached in the previous chapter that both Maimonides and Aquinas understood the human relation to the law as a progressive ascent from fear through reason to love, the answer to the first question is neither difficult nor does it require an elaborate explanation. The emphasis placed by both thinkers upon the natural limitations of human knowledge indicates clearly that unless and until each individual recognizes these limitations, he or she will remain merely subject to providence. Such response, however, raises a different and more difficult question: Can the human being who is related to the law through reason alone reach final perfection?

Before attempting to respond, it is important for me to point out that the rational individual should not be confused with one who has received personal revelation only, whose status will be addressed later. Strictly on the basis of the arguments presented, Maimonides' response must be negative. On the other hand, with the qualifications stated below, Aquinas' response may be positive. That is, since Maimonides held that (1) obedience to all the commandments was a prerequisite to final perfection, and (2) reason alone cannot attain to the rationale for, and the necessity of, observing some commandments, it follows that the objects of ratiocination are not identical with the understanding of which final perfection consists. More precisely, Aristotle's prime mover does not represent the true reality of the provident creator. On the other hand, since Aquinas argues that (1) the human intellect is immaterial, (2) that the will is a part of the immortal soul, (3) each individual possesses an agent intellect, (4) natural law is the participation of the eternal law in the rational creature, and (5) divine law is the full articulation of natural law precepts of which the derivation is difficult but not impossible after the fall, it is possible to conclude that some human beings can reach final perfection through reason *and will*. It is important to recognize, however, that although this conclusion may hold true for some individuals with respect to law, it is not true with respect to grace, which is always necessary for the attainment of final perfection. Moreover, given the temporal/existential hindrances to human perfection, given the necessity for universal perfection, and given the supra-natural, supra-rational human end, prophetic revelation is as necessary for human perfection and may indeed be understood as an act of grace.[640]

Apart from a rather brief descriptive statement in the *Guide* 3. 18, where Maimonides outlines the human relation to providence as an overflow of the divine intellect that is proportionate to the matter and prior intellectual perfection of the one affected and that is manifest in prophetic speech, in righteous actions, and in superior knowledge, the only discussion of the nature of the participative activity occurs in the final chapters of the text. The "non-philosophical" character of these chapters and Maimonides' statement that they do not constitute a discussion of new topics have led to doubt concerning their philosophical relevance or Maimonides' sincerity. Notwithstanding, these doubts seem unfounded in view of Maimonides additional qualification that the final account "is only a kind of a conclusion, at the same time explaining the worship as practiced by one who has apprehended the true realities peculiar only to Him after he has obtained an apprehension of what He is; and it also guides him toward achieving this worship, which is the end of man."[641] And in addition to the worship proportionate to final perfection, Maimonides states that he will explain the nature of providence as it pertains to the perfect person. That is, precisely because Chapters 51-54 are the conclusion to a long treatise, they in fact draw out the significant implication of all that preceded them explicitly. Although careful and prepared readers may be able to arrive at this conclusion after long study and reflection, nevertheless, Maimonides considers it important to assist them, clearly because he considers proper worship (i.e., action) and true understanding of providence to be absolutely necessary for attaining final perfection. Here, for the first time, Maimonides explains the nature of the commandment to love God and its relation to, and distinction from, all other commandments. True worship is manifest as a passionate love of God by the one who has apprehended the true reality of providence after having attained the true apprehension of God from the overflow of the agent intellect.[642]

Before I address the nature of the passionate love and the actions consequent upon it, it is necessary to outline the nature and quality of the true apprehension of the whole of Being since it has been argued that this type of cognition is weaker than that achieved through demonstrative reasoning.[643] Admittedly, in light of Maimonides' explanation that apprehension consists in the identity between the intellect, the intellectually cognizing "subject" and the intellectually cognized "object" and since there can be little doubt that in apprehending God and other metaphysical "objects" the human intellect does not become identical with its "objects," the apprehension in question is different in kind from demonstrative apprehension, be it of first principles or of the middle term.[644] However, although, unlike demonstrative apprehension, participative apprehension neither originates in the natural/sensible order nor is it acquired in the same manner, nevertheless, not only can it not be maintained that this type of apprehension is weaker than the demonstrative, but also the text indicates clearly that it is, without qualification, the most certain knowledge we can possibly acquire. Indeed, the "non-scientific" nature of such apprehension of metaphysical truths manifests the limitations of natural human reason, or the disproportionality between the rational "subject" and the extra-rational "object" of knowledge, but in no way does this reflect the quality of the apprehension itself, especially since this knowledge is said to render "perfect the act of the *rational* faculty (*al-kuwwah al-natiqa*), so that its act brings about its knowing things that are real in their existence, and it achieves this apprehension (*al-'idrak*) as if it has apprehended it by starting from speculative premises."[645] Consequently, Maimonides seems to suggest that participative knowledge not only can be verified by the degree of its congruence with what exists, but also that it enters into existence, the domain of demonstrative reason, and perfects it. This suggestion is not surprising insofar as the apprehension is an apprehension of the true reality of the "speculative premises" of natural science. It is important to recall and to emphasize that participative apprehension requires the prior natural perfection of the intellect as well as the acquisition of great moral perfection and that, apart from brief moments, it is not independent of sensible knowledge in this life.

Throughout the *Guide*, Maimonides consistently designates the human apprehension of metaphysical objects by *al-'idrak*, the same term he uses for referring to all acts of intellection, divine, angelic, and human.[646] With respect to human intellection, the same term is used to designate both demonstrative and participative apprehension. Despite the evident equivocity of the term, it neither reflects nor determines the quality of the knowledge acquired, but rather signifies the very nature of intellection, "for the very being and true reality of the intellect is apprehension."[647] With respect to the human intellect, the equivocity of the term results from the distinction between two modes of knowing a single object that occur in a single faculty of the soul, one reflecting its proper act, the other being disproportionate to its act. Indeed, the quality of the one apprehension is superior to that of the other, the participative, but this is not reflected by the term *al-'idrak* either.[648] More important, the human being should not be understood merely as a passive participant in its acquisition, since the very desire for true and certain knowledge of metaphysical objects manifest in the activity of demonstrative reasoning and in the recognition of its boundaries is the necessary, but not sufficient, condition for attaining the second and superior mode of cognition. The recognition of the limits of demonstration is a manifestation of the re-ordering of the desire for knowledge.

The existential consequences of the essentially metaphysical mode of cognition becomes manifest in both the speculative and the practical domains. In the sublunar realm, participation as a speculative pursuit transforms Aristotle's indifferent first cause into the provident creator and, consequently, overcomes the radical dichotomy between the supra- and sublunar realms, insofar as provident participants passionately "direct all the acts of their intellect toward an examination of the beings with a view to drawing from them proof with regard to Him, so as to know His governance of them in whatever way it is possible. . . . This is the rank of the prophets."[649] Subsequent to participative intellection, the aim of speculation is the apprehension of the nature of divine government so as to imitate it, or actively participate in it, by assimilation to God's actions and, especially, to His overabundance of loving kindness (*ḥesed*), righteousness (*ṣedaqah*), and judgment (*mishpat*).[650]

Since Maimonides maintains that the apprehension of divine government, which gives rise to the recognition that divine providence extends over the sublunar realm, is always manifest in specific activities, since these activities are what human beings understand as and name ethical activities, and since Maimonides characterizes these activities by excess (i.e., reflecting divine overabundance or excess), it is evident that Maimonides' understanding of the perfect person constitutes a radical departure from Aristotle. However, since prior to the apprehension of the whole of being, the good was merely a conventional category, the understanding of the act of being as good must constitute a radical break from all previous moral knowledge since it presents something entirely new, namely, the good as an intellectual actuality from which a new "ethics" (both as character and conduct) emerges. Clearly, at this point Maimonides breaks away from the Aristotelian tradition. Given that Aristotle's philosopher, like the first cause, is utterly indifferent to the practical realm, on the one hand,[651] and given that Maimonides understands the new mode of practical activity to be a *necessary* consequence of true knowledge, on the other, it follows that (like Job) the Aristotelian philosopher possesses neither perfect theoretical virtue nor perfect moral virtue. This is not an indictment against Aristotle, but rather a recognition of the respective boundaries of Maimonides' and Aristotle's philosophical teachings.

Following Maimonides, I am using Aristotle as the exemplar of natural perfection in order to emphasize the fact that, for Maimonides, true perfection has necessary external manifestations in ethical activity characterized by excess rather than by moderation. Since writing, too, is a public rather than a private activity, Aristotle's ethical writings manifest, for Maimonides, the great, but still partial, degree of perfection achieved by him. In fact, at the same time as he radically departs from Aristotle, Maimonides accepts his definition of ethical activity as that activity made manifest in the act of the righteous person. Indeed, the order of knowing, possibility, and becoming is directly related to the order of being or actuality and necessity. That is why Maimonides can maintain that true law can be distinguished from conventional law by their ends and by means of the activities exercised by the lawgiver.[652] Thus, those who have received participative apprehension, even if it was personal or sufficient for their own perfection only, like the prophets, must be 'compelled' by it to act in a certain manner, since the activity is but the existential manifestation of their being.

If Maimonides' doctrine of participation has to be carefully elicited from his writings, Aquinas' is not only explicit but also all-encompassing. The most succinct, and perhaps most accurate, reflection of Aquinas' understanding of divine providence will be its definition as the efficient communication of divine goodness. Nor is Aquinas' emphasis on divine goodness surprising when we recall that it is the overabundant emanation of divine goodness which communicates being to all things. Since the good in, and for, things consists in their preservation in the order of being, Aquinas repeatedly underlines the relation between providence and government; the former is but the execution of the latter. By focusing upon the primacy of the good in Aquinas' metaphysics throughout this study and by repeatedly referring to the discussions of good and of evil in *De Divinis Nominibus*, I intend to emphasize the fact that, for Aquinas, the *ratio* of the creative act and of the order of creatures is the good. And since divine providence is, first and foremost, a communication of divine goodness, *imitatio Dei*, provident participation, too, is the communication of goodness to other creatures. Thus, for Aquinas, the very possession of being, the expression, even the involuntary expression, of *esse* constitutes an active participation in the divine goodness. However, in contradistinction to other corporeal creatures, the proper participation of rational creatures communicated to them by the divine overflow consists "not only in this that they are good in themselves, but also in this that they should be the cause of goodness in others who possess the lowest form of participation in divine goodness."[653] Moreover, provident activity is *imitatio Dei* precisely because it is by means of a voluntary act that human beings communicate their actualized goodness to other human beings and to the irrational creatures. In this manner, only if rational creatures actualize their rational faculty, only if rational desire is ordered in accordance with the *ratio* of the universal order, can they assume their proper place as provident participants in this order. Conversely, so long as human beings do not apprehend the nature of the order of being and do not recognize their proper place within it, they participate in a lower order of being and in the mode of irrational creatures, that is, they are maintained in it out of necessity through the governing activities of others. Participation in the order proper to brutes is evil for human beings since it is the privation of the intellectual perfection proper to them.

Most studies of Aquinas' doctrine of participation focus upon the causality of being, since their primary concern is to demonstrate the centrality and novelty of his particular distinction between *esse* and *essentia* in order to establish a direct relations between God and creatures.[654] In contrast, I wish to emphasize the importance of the causality of the good since my primary concern is with the progressive ascent to God, rather than the order of descent from Him. More precisely, since the language of causality is the language through which reason ascends to God—since, *qua* causal, it is unidirectional and speaks strictly of possible human relations to God—my concern is with understanding the extent and limit of such "rational" language. It cannot be overlooked that even though Aquinas repeatedly insists that God is the first, the efficient, and the final cause, he also repeatedly insists that divine government and communication is mediated by the angels. With the exception of Moses (perhaps), all other prophets receive prophecy through the angels.[655]

When we begin with the actual order of human existence, the efficient causality of the will is temporally prior to the final causality of the intellect in the motion toward the object. Unless the motion of the will is understood to be the expression of a desire for the good that inheres in all beings by participation, it would be impossible for Aquinas to argue that perfection is a universal possibility even after the fall, since the desire for true good indeed would require the prior apprehension of the whole of being consequent upon an intellectual perfection beyond the capacity of many individuals. In order to overcome the Aristotelian problematic, Aquinas argues that the very understanding of God as the cause of things originates in the good since "the good is a more universal and higher cause than being because its causality extends to more things."[656] Likewise, the secondary causality of creatures is, first and foremost, a causality of the good, since the impetus to motion manifesting the *actus essendi* of creatures originates in the will's inclination to the good communicated to things in the creative act.

The apprehension of the identity between the good and the true by means of divine law that renders the law an internal principle of action is manifest as *imitatio Dei*. Since the fall resulted in the loss of the *order* of original justice, the restoration of the order consists in the possession of the rule and measure of the universal order as the principle of all acts. Participative activity, which is described by Aquinas as the imitation of divine and angelic government, is the provident communication of proper order to the sublunar realm in which human beings, as the most proximate self-subsistent beings, can communicate their actual goodness to other beings and conserve them in being. The restoration of the rule and measure to the human soul renders all voluntary desire intellectual so that all objects are judged simultaneously as good and true. Thus, every rational desire for an object is also the desire to preserve it, or communicate actual existence in a measure proportionate to its status in the order of being. Since God's actions are but manifestations of his overabundance or excess, the activities manifesting *imitatio Dei* cannot be measured by the Aristotelian mean. Indeed, there exists a due measure proportionate to each moral act, a measure deriving from the degree of participation in being rather than from a measure imposed by conventional accord.

Inasmuch as the metaphysical primacy of being forces Maimonides to posit the communication of the excess of being received from the divine overflow as necessary for the provident participant, the primacy of the good permits Aquinas to posit, in fact to demand, that the communication of goodness be a voluntary activity. Since the human will as a rational will is self-subsistent, since all human beings possess an individuated agent intellect, and since they possess the good as well as being as a primary principle, despite the fall, they can become active participants through reason, will, and law, through their own powers. Moreover, because he maintains that the good is a proper object of the intellect, Aquinas is not confronted with the difficulty faced by Maimonides of reconciling contemplation and action.[657]

Since participative ethical activity is only the actualization of the rational creature's proper place in the order of justice, indifference to practical activity manifests a disorder, rather than perfect order in the human soul. To that extent that any creature expresses its proper nature, it, and its activity, is good. Thus, Aquinas' departure from Aristotle is far more radical than Maimonides', originating in the ontological status of the human soul. Unlike Maimonides, for whom the transformation from subject to participant requires that there would be an ontological distinction between the two states and, hence, that it would affect only the few, for Aquinas, participation is but the expression of proper human nature as intellectual.

Conclusion: Excess and Reticence

The emphasis placed by Maimonides and Aquinas upon the limitation of human knowledge, limitations that extend as far as the understanding of first principles of natural science, when coupled not only with the grounding of knowledge but also with its ultimate validation in the nature of what exists, would be worthy of a Humean skeptic. However, unlike the Humean skeptic, both Maimonides and Aquinas argue that the recognition of natural human limitations is also the condition both for greater knowledge, irrespective of its source, and for human freedom. When both thinkers warn us against the perennial danger of *hubris* inherent in all intellectual pursuits, philosophical and theological, speculative and practical, and at every level of inquiry, they are, in fact, warning us against dogmatic reverence to set rules or "certain" philosophical conclusions. Ironically, their philosophical reflections disclose an identity between *hubris* and dogma. They also disclose that the consequences of *hubris* are manifold and affect both the soul of the individual and the souls of others.[658] With respect to the individual the imposition of set rules upon an "object" of inquiry not only misrepresents the object, but also misrepresents the complex order in which the object emerges. Moreover, since conclusions serve as premises for subsequent inquiries, errors are inherited and compounded. The most significant consequence of *hubris*, then, originates in the public nature of speech that necessarily results in the imposition of one's error upon others and their habituation to an uncompromising resistance to questioning. Intellectual pride is but the manifestation of the enslavement to the arbitrary limiting conditions one has placed upon further inquiry.

When the "name" *Torah* is understood literally as guidance, the ascent within the law from fear through reason to love can be understood as an exemplary rather than a single manifestation of the manifold possible relations to that which exists.

If knowledge exceeds what has traditionally been circumscribed by reason, and if discursive language is what has traditionally been taken to safeguard against "unlikely stories" and extravagant fantasies, how can such knowledge be communicated? And how can it be distinguished from poetry?[659] On the other hand, if such language cannot be distinguished from poetry, whose mimetic nature embodies a greater danger than the dogmas of philosophers, is the alternative silence? Very briefly, the answer to these questions is both affirmative and negative. In this brief conclusion, I will simply indicate how Maimonides and Aquinas responded to these questions in the light of divine excess.[660]

Given that for both Maimonides and Aquinas biblical language is paradigmatic communication of revealed truth, given that revealed truth is a manifestation of the highest form of human knowledge, prophetic knowledge, and given the apparent similarity between biblical and poetic language, the implications of Maimonides' and Aquinas' reflections upon biblical language clearly exceed those discussions and, I submit, are still relevant. Although a part of the following discussion will address the *via negativa*, I will avoid a proper comparative study of the degree of congruence between Maimonides and Aquinas on negation and so also avoid the fray of the secondary literature. Briefly, my justification is as follows.

Despite their excellence, most studies of Aquinas' understanding of divine names take their departure from his rejection of Maimonides' too radical a negative theology, arguing that for Aquinas some names can be positively attributed to God and that analogous predication is entirely unlike pure equivocation. But, although it is true that Aquinas prefers analogy to pure equivocation, three considerations lead me to regard the comparative starting point problematic. First, these studies are not preceded by a comparison of Maimonides' and Aquinas' general theory of language and, hence, assume an identity between the two thinkers' understanding and use of analogy, equivocation, and pure equivocation, a presupposition whose accuracy remains rather questionable, especially in the light of the facts that (1) the development of Aristotelian logic (which includes what today is assigned to philosophy of language) by the Islamicate philosophers does not follow the same path as the Latin Western one, (2) that the good for Maimonides has neither ontological nor rational status, and (3) that metaphor, being poetic, has no place in his discussion of divine attributes. Second, these studies do not consider the notion of analogy problematic despite Pierre Aubenque's and Joseph Owens' repeated counsel that Aquinas' use of analogy departs significantly from its Aristotelian provenance and is entirely unlike its contemporary English use and can be employed only with great caution and in a very restricted way.[661] Third, these studies seem to ignore the very different problems that divine names presented to the Jewish Maimonides and the Christian Aquinas.

Whereas Maimonides' major concern is to eradicate any trace of belief in divine corporeality, a belief that, for him, renders impossible "a portion in the world to come" and of which the prohibition is manifest in radical Jewish iconoclasm, for Aquinas the very fact of the incarnation, the Roman permission of iconography, and the Mass do not necessitate such austerity.[662] Aquinas' concern, then, is not primarily to deny the efficacy of all language in relation to God, but rather to determine what language would escape the boundaries of logical predication and how, without thereby undermining the significance of logic and of language.

Biblical language, for Maimonides, overcomes difficulties encountered by anyone attempting to communicate "true beliefs" about intelligible objects.[663] These difficulties originate in the disproportionality of language to its "objects" and is evident in the three types of discourse giving rise to the discursive contradictions discussed in Chapter 1. The first two are less "problematic" and do not give rise to genuine perplexity since they use amphibolous terms. These discourses, the dialectical or rhetorical and one using the language of similitude and metaphor, are not unique to biblical narratives. The third and most problematic is that type of parabolic discourse where language and objects are so disproportionate as to render all attempts at consistent accounts impossible and at coherent ones possible only exoterically in virtue of the absence of conditions restricting any term or part of the parable to a direct relation with a given object. Rather, the parable in its entirety renders the object(s) knowable in some way. The latter is the only articulation adequate to strictly intellectual, as opposed to imaginative, prophecy. Although the account must be translated into language by means of the imagination, the prophecy is about objects that are not, nor can be, communicated to the imaginative faculty precisely because they are immediate. This type of discourse is strict equivocal.

It is in virtue of the perfection of the prophet's imaginative faculty that the intimate relation between the imaginative faculty and language is disclosed as the cause of the inadequacy of language to translate the immediate apprehension of *real*, intelligibles as they are. The critical distinction to be made here is one between the knowledge and communication of objects that do not have a real existence outside the mind and those that do.[664] The paradigmatic example of the first category are mathematical objects; of the second, God. Since mathematical objects are understood by a process of discursive reasoning, that is, since they are known through internal mediation, their apprehension can be communicated perfectly through a perfectly corresponding, albeit arbitrary or conventional, linguistic mediation. Once they have been abstracted from matter and have become proper mathematical objects, no external quality or accident can conceal their "true reality." The diametrical opposite is the case with the understanding of God. As the perfect, absolutely simple being in whom no distinction can be found, not even between essence and existence, God cannot be known through 'regular' modes of discourse. And yet knowledge of God is the perfection proper to human beings. According to Maimonides, there are only two modes of discourse that are least inadequate to communicating some understanding of God, the one parabolic and the other *via negativa*; the former communicates true opinions by means of the imagination and is addressed to the masses as well as to the pre-philosophical elite; the second brings the philosophical elite closer to true knowledge insofar as "[t]he negative attributes only acquire meaning when their negation is a necessary truth."⁶⁶⁵ It should be noted, however, that what is negated is also an object of the imagination insofar as it is some quality or accident that inheres in a body. The statement "x is not a body" is said of Number and of God by pure equivocation.

Since language is the temporal intermediary par excellence, it must *necessarily* translate the incorporeal, a-temporal object into a temporal, corporeal one by means of the imagination. As intermediate, any instance of disclosing something about the object necessarily also hides all else and, thus, misrepresents the real object. The less composite the object is, the more inadequate the account, since the qualities and accidents by which it is translated into language in no way belong to the object. Consequently, negation is indeed the only manner in which the true knowledge consequent upon the immediate apprehension can be communicated. When such communication is unfitting to the intellectual capacity of the audience, parabolic discourse is least deceptive.

> Know that whenever one of the perfect wishes to mention either orally or in writing, something that he understands of these *secrets*, according to the degree of his perfection, he is unable to explain with complete clarity and coherence even the portion that he has apprehended, as he could do with the other sciences whose teaching is generally recognized. Rather there will befall him when teaching another that which he had undergone when learning himself. I mean to say that the subject matter will appear, flash, and then be hidden again, as though this were the nature of this subject matter, be there much or little of it.⁶⁶⁶

Thus, submitting to the necessity of the subject matter, a necessity that manifests actual prophetic necessity or compulsion, Maimonides does not attempt to provide a full coherent account of any of the mysteries of the Torah within a single discourse. Rather, in one chapter he "hint[s] at one of the meanings of an equivocal term," in another, he "hints at the fact that a certain story is a parable."⁶⁶⁷ By using the biblical parables themselves for explication, beginning with the explication of terms, Maimonides teaches the student how to understand the manifold meaning of biblical language. He does not change the terms nor does he replace a biblical term with a 'better', more scientific, one. He does not believe that scientific language can be used in metaphysical discourse, let alone divine science. In fact, Maimonides clearly states that, with respect to divine subjects, scientific language is more obscure than the parabolic. Both in the Introduction and throughout the *Guide* Maimonides underscores the fact that "scientific" language, insofar as it purports to provide a clear explanation that is proportionate to the objects, in fact misrepresents them, whereas parabolic language, precisely because it does not attempt to point directly at its referent, deliberately discloses its own inadequacy and thereby, points beyond itself.

Since parabolic biblical discourse presents the understanding of all prophets other than Moses—no parable is directly attributed to Moses[668]—each parable is a manifestation of the particular degree of knowledge of the named prophet at that particular time.[669] Insofar as the conjunction with the agent intellect of all the prophets except Moses is said to be intermittent, every instance of conjunction is distinct from any other in degrees both among the different prophets (proportionate to their intellectual perfection) and between instances of particular conjunctions. Consequently, each instance of prophetic revelation, each parable, must be unique and, thus, excludes the possibility of drawing general conclusions from it. Rather each parable is a whole that must be studied independently of all others.

Given the disproportionality of all language to objects of immediate apprehension, I cannot overemphasize the fact that all prophetic communication will appear to the philosopher as paradoxical or contradictory. As has been pointed out in Chapter 1, these contradictions are necessary and exhibit the singular nature of the apprehension or the radical difference between "universals," which are true because they exist only in the mind, and the singular, non-repeatable manifestation of an aspect of "true reality." Para-doxically, the more perfect the apprehension, the less adequate can its communication be. The superiority of the parable to "unlikely tales," poetry, and rhetoric consists precisely in its clear exhibition of its own inadequacy by *indication*, pointing beyond itself to the *via negativa*; the positive affirmations demanded by prophetic-parabolic pedagogy indicate the cognitive necessity for their negation. Thus, it is not surprising that Maimonides' brief explanation of Mosaic apprehension is followed by a lengthy discussion of negative attribution. The cognitive value of all parabolic expressions of prophetic apprehensions is measured by their capacity to disclose the superiority of Mosaic prophecy of which the substance can best be understood as their negation.

As Nuriel[670] points out, what is common to all discourses about God, whether they follow the prophetic parabolic way or the philosophic *via negativa*, is their status as true belief rather than as demonstrated or even intellectually apprehended *truth*. Whereas the latter consist in the identity of the intellect, the intellectually cognizing subject, and the intellectually cognized object, and hence is a cognition of the true reality of an "object," neither the parable nor the *via negativa* can be said to give rise to knowledge of the true reality of any object. Notwithstanding, true belief is a special kind of knowledge and with respect to some objects, at least, it consists in "the affirmation that what has been represented is outside the mind just as it has been represented in the mind."[671] However, according to Maimonides, beliefs can be ranked into those that are held without intellectual inquiry and are affirmed only on the basis of authority and those that are consequent upon inquiry and whose affirmation is strictly intra-mental. More precisely, such "affirmation" is simply the being or actuality of the intellect. Although even uncritical belief, if it is to be true, must consist of more than mere nominal affirmation, since it is an affirmation of the identity of the content of a proposition with its actually existing referent, nevertheless it can still be designated as conventional and hence cannot be understood to constitute a cognitional act. On the other hand, "If, together, with this belief one realizes that a belief different from it is in no way *possible* and that no starting point can be found in the mind for a rejection of this belief or for the supposition that a different belief is *possible*, there is certainty."[672] Consequently, this kind of belief can be designated a cognitional act, but of a special kind since unlike intellectual apprehension (*al-'idrak*), belief (*i'tiqad*) does not arise from the conjunction with the cognized object. But, although Nuriel argues that the contents of beliefs, even of certain ones, cannot be understood to be "the eternal constituents that bring about the immortality of the soul,"[673] in the light of the fact that Maimonides not only designates some beliefs intellectual (*i'tiqadat 'aqliya*) but also states that the first of these is "His apprehension . . . according to our capacity,"[674] it seems to me that he does hold intellectual beliefs to constitute the actuality, hence immortality of the soul. This is precisely the sense in which "a belief different from it is in no way possible." Conventional true beliefs are those communicated in biblical parables when understood literally; intellectual ones originate in intellectual reflection upon parables and culminate in the discourse communicated in the *via negativa*. Notwithstanding, it is important to emphasize that the two beliefs are closely related as are the two modes of communication, namely, as apples of gold to their settings of silver filigree.

　　Parabolic discourse is generically distinct from conventional rhetoric and poetry insofar as the mimetic nature of rhetoric and poetry both prohibits questioning and renders repulsive all discourse that appears contradictory to it. In contrast, insofar as the knowledge communicated in parables already embodies, however succinctly, the negative distinction between God and the world, it calls forth questioning. In addition to undermining the *mimesis* demanded by rhetoric and poetry, parabolic language also undermines the *mimesis* demanded by philosophical *hubris* insofar as, when it denies the possibility of inference of any truth concerning God from the nature of his effects, it denies the "absolute validity" of universals. Consequently, excluding error that is the result of inadequate instruction, however inadequate parabolic language is, even at the literal level, the affirmation of its propositions precludes the possibility of understanding divine attributes to indicate a real relation between God and the world. Nevertheless, understood literally, that is, as positive predications of qualities belonging to God, it does lead to belief that there exists an actual identity between the content of the affirmed belief and an external reality. Whereas the superiority of parabolic language over rhetoric and poetry consists in the fact that it safeguards the vulgar from idolatry, its superiority over propaedeutic philosophical discourse consists in the fact that it embodies the principles of its own displacement, pointing, as it does, to inquiry into the nature of language that is capable of designating by the same word objects among which there is no relation. This inquiry, in turn, gives rise to the first premises of divine science as distinct from philosophical metaphysics. These premises, however, are all articulated as negations.

Although, initially, it may be objected that negative principles are no principles at all, it should be noted that the three primary principles of theoretical science are themselves negations. Consequently, it is indeed possible to argue that, for Maimonides, divine science proper is distinct from the science of philosophical metaphysics, possessing as it does its own primary principles, which it receives indirectly from prophetic revelation and which, like the three primary principles of *theoria*, are not immediately evident. But, unlike *theoria*, where inductive intuition (*epagoge*) gives rise to positive affirmations, prophetic intuition denies the validity of these affirmations, not only to God, but also to metaphysics proper. That is, the knowledge that no relation between God and the world is possible, a knowledge that, nonetheless, does not result in the philosophical affirmation of the Aristotelian first co-eternal cause of the universe, also leads to the denial of the validity of Aristotelian metaphysics. But, it is only as a consequence of the perfection of natural reason, of the validity of demonstration in Aristotelian physics that one can recognize the real contradictions found in Aristotelian metaphysics. Consequently, according to Maimonides, the more attributes one knows *by demonstration* ought to be denied, the closer one comes to God.[675] That is, demonstrative knowledge—the most perfect natural knowledge of all things other than God—is the necessary condition for true denial of any similitude between God and his effects. And, demonstration, it should be remembered, is the proper domain of mathematics and natural science. Thus understood, the *via negativa* brings one nearer to God precisely in the order of cognition since it indicates clearly the radical difference not so much between the discourses of physics and metaphysics, between which some relation obtains, but rather between both orders of discourse and the *via negativa* that denies any relation between God and His effects. Consequently, the negation involved in the *via negativa* is of a different kind than a logical contradiction since in no way is it related to the philosophical understanding of necessity, possibility or impossibility,[676] an understanding based upon the eternity of the world as a first premise.

Finally, in contrast to all attributes predicated of God that can be "justified" by philosophy, such as wise, Maimonides "justifies" the three positive attributes of action as epistemic means to perfection. These are unique insofar as their very excess points beyond philosophy to the radical difference between the order of nature and that of God and, thereby, call to knowledge of God or "the deity's wily graciousness and wisdom, as shown in the creation of living beings."[677] Concomitant with the necessity by which the prophet (guide and teacher) is compelled to communicate to others the excess of the actual understanding/perfection he or she receives, that is, concomitant with the active participation in providence, is a recognition of the inadequacy of all language. That is why in relation to God "silence is praise."[678] It is not without irony that I note that the reticence or silence in relation to God is, philosophically, also the contradictory of the excess of teaching.

Aquinas' clearest reflection on the superiority of biblical language over all non-revealed ones occurs in the context of discussions of divine names. As was shown in the discussion of the distinction between names and definitions in Chapter 1, names do not communicate anything *per se*; consequently, the context in which names are employed is the only place where their disclosive capacity can be decided. The two preeminent, at times seemingly conflicting, contexts in which divine names are employed are either philosophical or biblical. Whereas Aristotelian philosophy would restrict the divine name(s) to one or two,[679] the biblical employs a multiplicity restricted only by the insistence upon divine singularity, a singularity that does not *ipso facto* deny complexity nor require univocity. That is, the insistence upon divine simplicity is already a philosophical one, even if only implicitly. Considered independently, each context presupposes a different audience. For whether a name is essential or accidental; whether it is univocal, equivocal, or analogical; whether it is also a definition is problematic only to the philosopher or, more precisely, to the religious philosopher who is also a teacher. That is, the question of names for Aquinas is not primarily a logical one, but rather pedagogic and noetic. Thus, notwithstanding their excellence, the commentaries on Aristotles' logical works cannot be understood to represent his only, let alone most significant, discussions on language, although they may help clarify other discussions.[680]

Given that the problem of divine names arises from the biblical context, I shall first address the two modes of biblical signification that seem to fall outside philosophical consideration, before I turn to the two primary philosophical analogues. The first question of the *Summa* provides a most convenient, because succinct, account of the first type of extra-philosophical designation. In Iᵃ Pars, Q. 1, a. 9, Aquinas first addresses the appropriateness of biblical language, more specifically of metaphor. Having explained both the necessity and fittingness of sensible similitude owing to the nature of the knower in the body of the Response, Aquinas makes what seems to be an astonishing statement in the reply to the third objection,

> it is more fitting that divine matters be taught in scripture under the figures of base bodies than of noble bodies. And this on account of three things. First, since thereby the human soul would be more free of error. For it seems clear that these are not said of the divine according to a quality, which may be doubtful, were they to be described under the figures of noble bodies, especially among those who would not wish to discover any other thing from noble bodies. Second, since this mode is more fitting to the cognition that we have of God in this life. For concerning God, what he is not is more manifest to us than what he is. And therefore, a similitude of those things which are more distanced from God render a truer judgment to us which should be beyond what we say or think about God. Third, since through such [similitudes] divine matters are more hidden from the unworthy.[681]

Apart from the fact that, for Maimonides, this explanation would, at first, be apologetics, and despite its linguistic clarity, the assertions made by Aquinas are far from self-evident. For what are the base corporeal metaphors to which Aquinas is referring? And it is not insignificant that no example whatsoever is given in a. 9. That is, Aquinas seems to be indicating that any sensible similitude, or a similitude to any entity that is corporeal, is a base one. Thus, it may be, most probably is, the case that the discussion of metaphors refers equally to ones derived from human qualities, even essential ones, as they do to any other sublunar entity. Moreover, since the most common attributes predicated of God are similes of human ones and since the question focuses on the cognitive role of metaphor or its efficacy to communicate something true about God, the question seems to be what and how names can be attributed to God in a manner such that they would not be taken as definitions or as signifying "*secundum proprietatem*" but, nevertheless, would not communicate something false. In the following article, as in the commentary on Job, Aquinas includes parable within the literal sense of Scripture and explains that a figurative literal voice never signifies the figure from which it derives but always that which is figured. Here he does use a corporeal figure, an arm, as a figure for divine operative power.

In a similar manner, it is far from clear whose cognition is questioned in the reference to those who would be unwilling to consider anything exceeding what is nominally disclosed about noble bodies. Although, initially, the reference seems to indicate a vulgar or non-philosophical audience, the second reason given for the fittingness of metaphor may in fact indicate that it includes philosophers as well. For, after all, with respect to knowledge, even metaphysical knowledge, Aristotelian metaphysics, which recognizes no other life nor any source of knowledge other than that originating in sensation, is concerned with degrees of knowledge about what and how being can be, rather than cannot be, said. In addition, in the previous reply (*ad 2ᵘᵐ*), Aquinas clearly states that "the hidden nature of figures is useful for "*exercitium studiosorum.*"

The rather brief discussions of the appropriateness of biblical language and especially of the relation between the literal figure and its signified object seem to indicate that, in his view, no attribute, no name, appears to be transparent, not even to the vulgar;[682] that is, the very nature of names is self-displacing. Moreover, the obscurity inherent in words, as names, does not originate from the obscurity of the signifying figure, but rather from the lack of proportionality between the signifier and the signified. Thus, precisely because it is sensible, precisely in its radical disproportionality to any intelligible object, let alone God, the metaphorical is a most fitting language about God because, by its very nature, it functions as negation.

The second extra-philosophical mode of naming God receives the briefest possible mention by Aquinas in two related articles of the *Summa*. For reasons that will become clear, I shall begin with the second. In Iᵃ Pars, Q. 13, a. 11, in the context of the discussion whether *Qui Est* is the most appropriate divine name, in the reply to the first objection, Aquinas states: "But with respect to that to which a name is given for signifying, this name God which is given for signifying the divine nature is more proper. And a still more proper name is Tetragrammaton which is given for signifying the very incommunicable substance of God, and, so that it may permissible to express the singular."[683] The incommunicability of the divine name, its very singularity, its ineffable nature, is likewise the focus of Aquinas' only other reference to the Tetragrammaton. In the body of the response to article 9, in an equally hesitant manner, Aquinas mentions that among the Jews the Tetragrammaton perhaps is an incommunicable name. One cannot overemphasize the great caution, the hesitancy, manifest in the two very brief references to the Tetragrammaton, the one mention preceded by *forte est*, the other succeeded by *ut sic liceat loqui*. This ineffable name, about which Aquinas says nothing, is the one name, even more appropriate than *Qui Est*, because it clearly exceeds being.

The two extra-philosophical discussions of names, thus, suggest that the less a name can be related to a being, even a being in act, the more appropriate it is to serve as a divine name, since the less likely it will be to result in error. For the Tetragrammaton, in its incommunicable singularity can in no way be understood to signify being in act, since being is the most common shared characteristic and notion of any thing that is.[684] It is only once the two polar extreme modes of naming God is clarified that we can begin to understand the place and limit of philosophical naming by analogy, a place that in the order of discourse is intermediate. Nor is the intermediate order of philosophical theology surprising in the light of the discursive nature of natural human cognition. Thus, in the first article of the question on divine names in the *Summa*, which asks whether any name is fitting to designate God, Aquinas first recalls Aristotle's definition of words as signs of the intellect that is itself a similitude of things, and then claims that "thus it is clear that words are referred to things which signify by a mediating concept of the intellect."[685] But, unlike intellectual concepts that, although they are arrived at by intermediate similitudes and phantasm, nevertheless can be transformed into purely intelligible entities through the agent intellect, words/names have a sensible dimension by their very nature; that is, they are similes of sensible object, they are sensually expressed, and their very function is intermediary. Language is the unique human characteristic presupposing motion, time, and a material substratum and incapable of exceeding these in its own order.

In all the discussions of divine names, Aquinas repeatedly emphasizes that no direct relation can be established between the name and what is named since names follow upon intellectual concepts derived from creatures. Thus, with respect to analogy, the name is never proportionate to the thing named, but rather the proportion is an intellectual representation of the relation between the intellect and the sensible objects whence the name is derived. "It ought to be said that God is not a proportionate measure in things measured"[686] and, again, "but in God there does not exist some real relation of him to creatures, but only according to reason (*rationem*) inasmuch as creatures are referred to him."[687] Properly understood, with respect to God, analogy, for Aquinas, is an affirmation of a unidirectional relation of creatures to their principle, rather than of cause to effect. This conclusion is reached as a critique of both Maimonides and Allanus ab Insulis, where he argues that neither signification merely by negation nor the common causal one make possible a distinction between more and less fitting divine names. The conventional use of causal predication (proportionate or *pros hen* analogy) would render possible naming God a body as much as good, since He is the cause of bodies. It also always can name God only *per posterius*. Conversely, the negation of corporeality would deny only that God is a being in potency. In such cases, both affirmation and negation place God in a direct relation of efficient causality with creatures and, hence, include God and creatures in the same genus.

In this light, Aquinas' concern with language, with affirmation, negation, and excellence, from the very beginning is ontological rather than logical; his use of the term *remotion* for negation, properly speaking, removes God from the order of *esse commune* in order to signify *esse tantum*, which exceeds being. That is why in the orders of cognition and of language remotion succeeds common negation and precedes the mode of excellence, whereas in the order of being the perfection clearly precedes rather than succeeds the predication. Attributes considered as names are said of creatures *per prius*, considered as perfections, they are said of God *per prius* in whom they preexist in a most excellent way and thus absolutely exceed knowledge and language.

Only now, and as a very brief conclusion, can I turn to the significance of the ontological distinction underlined throughout this study between Being and Good. Briefly stated, the discussions of Being are already philosophical discussions within the orders of knowledge and of language; it is in Being that analogy has its greatest extension and can serve as the *ratio* for all subsequent predication. But, at the same time and for the same reason, it is in the order of Being that these predications can be negated and removed. Conversely, the discussion of the Good is, above all, ontological. It is the Good that can explain creation or the procession of creatures from God. But, this is also why it is in the order of the Good that whatsoever relation obtains between creatures and God can be understood, and hence, it is the order wherein negation and *remotion* are least appropriate. That is, in the order of understanding the relation between the Good and Being is inverse. That is why in the philosophical contexts Aquinas can claim in one context that Being is the most fitting name of God and in another that the Good is.

Whereas, initially, the Good better explains the order of descent from God, Being better explains the order of ascent. The latter begins with determinate particulars and ascends through progressive differentiation to less determinate "universals" culminating in the least determinate substance, that is, in *esse commune*. But, in the order of ascent, including that of negation, the human intellect remains limited by the order of efficient causality so that the negation of all determination leads only as far as, but no further than, infinity and indifference. But, if *being* is the most universal, least determinate name, if it is indifferently related to particular beings, it cannot explain any other orders of causality, least of all final causality or the convergence of all particular efficient causality, nor can it account for the order as a whole. As simultaneously the most common and most diverse characteristic of all things, Being is infinitely and indifferently changeable and radically other than any essence. Indeed, in the order of being, *Qui Est* is the most appropriate divine name since it is in no way related to the essential predication of any temporal entity. And as permanent presence, the name also functions as remotion from the spatio-temporal order of change. Paradoxically, whereas all other definitional names misrepresent the subject as present and as fully actual, and hence the copula cannot refer to any real particular being, *Qui Est*, as *esse tantum*, simply is. It is thus that the name *esse* and other subsequent names have their origin in the divine names, an origin that is absolutely beyond the order of efficient causality, an order that, excluding the first and only real actuality that exceeds it, is secondary.

So long as the "Good" is understood within the order of efficient causality, it is a predicate that, properly speaking, cannot extend to, let alone determine, anything except as it is already determinate. Moreover, *esse commune* cannot in itself explain either the indeterminacy that precedes the diversity within it nor that exceeds it. Likewise, *esse tantum* cannot account for the communication of being or for *ens potentia*. Thus, *remotion* displaces *esse tantum* to the realm of excellence or excess. And what is excessive is the Good. It is precisely as excessive that the Good, for Aquinas, is a perfect divine name as the perfection that comprehends all other things and is self-diffusive. In an order of discourse that exceeds demonstrations and replaces rhetorical and poetic *mimesis*, the name *Good* is the perfect significative divine name because it is the *ratio/metron* of all causality; as self-diffusive, it is the origin of all things; as perfect, it is the final perfection that all desire. Whatever "form" the imitations ensuing from it may take, they express singular, intrinsic possibilities rather than common, extrinsic, conventionally imposed ones. But, and perhaps most significantly, the Good can account for the order of material causality and potency, to which language belongs, as an integral part of the causal order so that material causality, too, is gathered into the universal causal order.

The reality, to which the name *Good* refers, allows Aquinas to overcome the natural limitations of human reason in a manner such that free, rationally ordered human agency is extended to all human beings. Ironically, despite the philosophical discomfort (repulsion) it may cause, Maimonides' greater "pessimism" about human knowledge, language, and consequently, the "real" freedom of the many, may better facilitate thinking "in accordance with the nature of that which exists."

The Disaster (*Shoah*) that disrupted the progressive course of history in this century renders this conclusion all the more poignant. As Walter Benjamin acutely observed the "angel of history" shortly before his death,

> His face is turned toward the past. Where we perceive a chain of events, he sees one single catastrophe which keeps piling wreckage upon wreckage and hurls it in front of his feet. The angel would like to stay, awaken the dead, and make whole what has been smashed. But a storm is blowing from Paradise; it has got caught in his wings with such violence that the angel can no longer close them. This storm irresistibly propels him into the future to which his back is turned, while the pile of debris before him grows skyward. This storm is what we call progress.[688]

("Thesis on the Philosophy of History IX")

ENDNOTES

1. The term *understanding* will be used throughout this study to designate *intellectus* or the Arabic *al-'idrak* as distinct from *ratio*. It is important to note that the Arabic, Judaeo-Arabic and Latin traditions reduce the Greek *nous* and *epagoge* to a single name or term.

2. For an excellent study of the radical differences between the pre-Modern and Modern philosophical *ethe*, see David Rapport Lachterman, *The Ethics of Geometry: A Genealogy of Modernity* (New York and London: Routledge, 1989). I use the term "Modern" in the strict sense to designate the radical conceptual change that began in the seventeenth century.

3. It should be noted that I do not use the term *metaphysics* in its Modern, or post-Cartesian sense, as *mathesis universalis*. Like *providence*, to the moderns, the medieval understanding of *metaphysics* is strange and remains to be thought.

4. Harmony should not be confused with simple unity. Rather, it is the sameness that underlies and renders possible diversity.

5. Aristotle, *Posterior Analytics*, 1, 71a1-2. I apologize to the reader for the graceless "abuse" of the English language here. However, I want to preserve not only the noetic sense but also the sense of "going through."

6. Whether this relationship is bi- or unidirectional, whether it takes one or many forms remains to be understood.

7. As will become evident in the last three chapters, attraction and repulsion play a significant role in Maimonides' and Aquinas' noetics.

8. Rather than note all the thinkers to whom Maimonides and Aquinas are indebted, which will result in excessive footnotes, the bibliography will provide their significant sources. The most obvious example of a debt shared by both Maimonides and Aquinas is to Ibn-Sina (Avicenna). And as this study attempts to show, one of the most significant influences upon Aquinas' thought is that of Maimonides.

9. *Dalalat al ha-'Irin*, ed. and trans. Solomon Munk, 3 vols. (Osnabrück: Otto Zeller, 1964). Hebrew: *More Nevukhim*, trans. Samuel Ibn Tibbon (Jerusalem, 1960). All English references will be to *Guide of the Perplexed*, trans. Shlomo Pines (Chicago: University of Chicago Press, 1974), henceforth cited as *Guide*. The question of esotericism is another instance where Maimonides is said to be, and is to some extent, indebted to Alfarabi whose significant writing, again, will be cited in the bibliography.

10. *Summa Theologiae*, Iᵃ-IIᵃᵉ, Q. 90, a. 2 (Ottawa, 1941), henceforth cited as *Summa*.

11. The term *hermeneutics* is used throughout this text to refer to an approach to interpretation that is fully aware of the radical ambiguity of historical texts and, hence, in the spirit of Plato's *Phaedrus*, is always suspicious of the written word.

12. In the light of contemporary debates about the canon of philosophy, I consider the philosophical consequences of the differences between Maimonides and Aquinas of great significance. Paradoxically, both exponents and opponents of *the* canon presuppose a single, fixed canon, which is a chimera.

13. The number of comparative discussions of Maimonides and Aquinas are surprisingly few, and their scope is generally limited in the light of the centrality of each thinker to his respective tradition. The only significant book-length comparative study of both thinkers is Avital Wohlman's, *Thomas d'Aquin et Maimonide: un dialogue exemplaire* (Paris: Cerf, 1988). The bibliography provides a full list of other relevant studies. Nonetheless, precisely in virtue of the existing studies, I do not believe that it is still necessary to demonstrate the extent of Aquinas' familiarity with Maimonides.

14. "Strange" as this claim may initially appear to be, it can and should be understood in the light of *paradoxa*. Thus, the paradoxes and contradictions of which the Moderns accused the pre-Moderns are reversed when the Modern "biases" concerning knowledge are questioned or become *paradoxa*.

15. David Burrell, "Maimonides, Aquinas and Gersonides on Providence and Evil," *Religious Studies* 20, no. 3 (1984): 335-51.

16. This order is inverse in the *Summa* since, as will emerge out of this study, for Aquinas, the study of theology should succeed the study of philosophy, and hence, it ought to be undertaken after the apprehension that actual being is ontologically prior to all finite acts of becoming.

17. Again, I prefer the term *intellectual* to *rational* since one of the major justifications for undertaking this study is to show that reason's domain is far more restricted than that of the intellect.

18. Versions of parts of Chapters 1, 2 and 4 have appeared in print. Their presentation in the context of a larger inquiry modifies them significantly.

19. Neither Job nor any of the friends is said to have received divine law either in the form of personal revelation or in the form of external law.

20. The denial of purpose is itself a judgment about the purpose of human existence.

21. The philosopher here is the religious philosopher who often departs from the Aristotelian account of causality in one, highly significant way. Whereas for Aristotle (and Maimonides) the first cause is radically distinct from the plurality of final causes, for Christian philosophers the first and final cause are identical.

22. All references to Plato's and Aristotle's thought will be to their medieval versions, which underwent some significant modifications in their transmission. For example, in this context, the explicit affirmation of divine indifference is an Epicurean accretion rather than Aristotle's stated position.

23. Dante Alighieri, *The Divine Comedy*, trans. Charles S. Singleton, 3 vols. (Princeton, N.J.: Princeton University Press, 1970), vol. 1, *Inferno*, Canto 4, l. 41-2.

24. As a dialectical problema in the sense articulated in *Topics* 1, "creation" is, to borrow from Plato, an equally or even a more "likely story" than the eternity of the world.

25. *Topics*, 1. 1. 104b14-18,

26. As will become evident, the radical ambiguity of these attributes, their inappropriateness, itself contributes to the ambiguity inherent in the question of cosmogenesis.

27. Although for Aquinas the good has an ontological and an epistemic status, whereas for Maimonides it does not, as will become evident, after the Fall, its ontological and hence its epistemic status is occluded so that "will as appetite" and will as "rational choice" are existentially separated. The term *will* is used very loosely here. The distinction between "will" and "choice," which is most significant to understanding the human relation to providence, will be discussed in some detail in Chapters 5 and 6.

28. "A man who is . . . so self-sufficing that he has no need to do so is no part of the *polis* so that he must be either a lower animal or a god." *Politics*, trans. H. Rackham, The Loeb Classical Library (Cambridge, Mass.: Harvard University Press, 1934) 1. 1253a14.

29. The term *political* is used in its broadest sense here to refer to all activities that affect common life.

30. The relationship between the two approaches to interpretation, and especially the degree of compatibility between them, has been subject to a long debate and is beyond the scope of this study. For a limited review of scholarship on the topic see the Bibliography.

31. A brief glance at early Jewish writings reveals this unexpected absence of a doctrinal unification of biblical interpretation. For systematic and thematic reviews of these works, see Israel Efros, *Ha-Filosofia ha-Yehudit ha-'Atika* (Jerusalem, 1959); idem, *Ancient Jewish Philosophy*, (Detroit: Wayne State University Press, 1964), passim (the first part of the English edition is a revised version of the Hebrew text). Ephraim E. Urbach, *The Sages: Their Concepts and Beliefs*, 2d ed. (Jerusalem: Magnes Press, 1982).

32. Georges Vajda, *L'amour de Dieu dans la théologie juive du Moyen Âge*, Études de philosophie médiévale 46, (Paris: Vrin, 1957). In part one, Vajda outlines the early emphasis in the Jewish tradition on the relation between disinterested study of the Torah and love of God, the manifestation of human perfection.

33. Irrespective of the typology, rabbinic or philosophical, all systems of biblical interpretation are rooted in the prior understanding that "the Torah has many faces." For a comprehensive analysis of the medieval tradition of Jewish interpretation and its divergence from the Christian tradition, see Frank Talmage, "Apples of Gold: The Inner Meaning of Sacred Texts in Medieval Judaism," in Arthur Green, ed., *Jewish Spirituality I* (New York: Crossroad Publications, 1985), pp. 313-55.

34. I apologize to my readers for the noninclusive use of language in contexts referring to particular male figures. To do otherwise would be misleading. Where it is, at all, possible, I use inclusive language.

35. For details of Sa'adia's life and works, see Henry Malter, *Saadia Gaon, His Life and Works* (Philadelphia: Jewish Publication Society of America, 1921). Throughout this study, I deliberately retain the inconsistencies in spellings in order to preserve the difficulties of the transmission of living traditions.

36. Julius Guttman, *Philosophies of Judaism* (New York: Schocken Books, 1973), pp. 134-36. Ibn-'Ezra is the only biblical exegete praised by Spinoza whose alleged pantheism gave rise to vitriolic debates in eighteenth century Germany. It is highly likely that Julius Guttman's assessment of Ibn-'Ezra is influenced by these discussions.

37. "Quand il commente un texte scripturaire verset par verset, l'éxègete est porté à limiter son horizon au texte ou au contexte immédiat, surtout si son dessein est, du moins en principe, de faire dire a son texte ce que, à son avis, il signifie littéralement" (Vajda, *L'amour de Dieu*, p. 113, n. 1). Unless noted otherwise, translations into English are my own.

38. The refraining of philosophically inclined, pre-Maimonidean, Jewish thinkers from philosophical exegesis on biblical texts that beg for philosophical interpretation, such as Job, is a subject still unexplored. (Although Sa'adia's commentary on Job should not be overlooked, its philosophical merit remains to be questioned.)

39. Urbach, *The Sages*, Chap. 1, pp. 1-14.

40. Beryl Smalley, *The Study of the Bible in the Middle Ages* (1964; Notre Dame, Ind.: Notre Dame University Press, 1978), Chap. 1, i. 1-26; Cf. Smalley modifications of her conclusions in "William of Auvergne, John of la Rochelle and St. Thomas Aquinas on the Old Law," *St. Thomas Aquinas: 1274-1974 Commemorative Studies.* (Toronto: PIMS, 1974), pp. 11-71; Talmage, "Apples of Gold," p. 313.

41. Smalley, ibid.

42. Ibid., p. 23.

43. St. Augustine, *De Doctrina Christiana*, CCSL 32 (1962), Bk. 3.

44. Ibid., Bk. 2, x-xv.

45. Charles H. Haskins, *The Renaissance of the Twelfth Century* (Cambridge, Mass.: Harvard University Press, 1927), Chap. 9, pp. 278-302; Marie-Thérèse

d'Alverny, "Translations and Translators," *Renaissance and Renewal in the Twelfth Century*, ed. Robert L. Benson and Giles Constable, with Carol D. Lanham (Cambridge, Mass.: Harvard University Press, 1982), pp. 421-62; Smalley, *Study of the Bible*, passim.

46. Smalley, ibid., pp. 33 and 281-92.

47. Ibid., p. 83.

48. Ibid., p. 93.

49. Ibid., pp. 292-328.

50. On the relations between the *intentio auctoris* and the commentator, see M.-D. Chenu, *Nature, Man and Society in the Twelfth Century*, ed. and trans. Jerome Taylor and Lester K. Little (1968; Chicago: University of Chicago Press, 1983), Chap. 9, pp. 310-30; idem, *Toward Understanding St. Thomas*, ed. and trans. A. M. Laudry and D. Hughes (Chicago: University of Chicago Press, 1964), passim. Whereas Chenu maintains that the medieval expositor often appropriates the text as his own (*Toward Understanding*, pp. 207-8), the opposite opinion is put forth by P. O'Reilly, "Expositio super librum Boetii *De Hebdomadibus*: An Edition and Study," diss., University of Toronto, 1960, pp. 387-88.

51. Although this specific articulation is taken from Aquinas' *In librum Beati Dionysii De Divinis Nominibus Expositio* (Rome: Marietti 1950), Chap. 4 1.4, the same understanding is common to the Western philosophical tradition that identifies unity and unicity with God, and hence with simplicity and truth, and degrees of multiplicity with progressive distance from God and truth. The question of error will be discussed in Chapter 5.

52. Smalley, *Study of the Bible*, p. 293.

53. Other examples abound. To name but a few: William of Auvergne, Roland of Cremona, Albertus Magnus, in the Christian tradition; Sa'adia Gaon, Abraham Ibn 'Ezra, Samuel Ibn Tibbon, in the Jewish tradition. Each of these writers, as well as others, combined the tools available to them and most fitting for their topic.

54. I shall return to the tension between the multiplicity belonging to "fitting modes of interpretation" and that evident in error in the final chapters.

55. *Guide*, see the [Epistle Dedicatory], the general introduction to Bk. 1, the introduction to the proofs of the existence of God (1, 71-73), etc.; *Summa*, Iᵃ Pars, *prologus*, Q.1, especially aa. 9-10, and the statements preceding each question in the work.

56. The paucity of comparative studies of their thought is in itself an indication of an implicit judgment concerning an incompatibility between Maimonides and Aquinas, given the stature and historical proximity of the two thinkers, and given the numerous references to Maimonides by Aquinas. Apart from a very small number of articles, the majority of comparative studies have been partisan. The most notable exceptions can be found in the collection edited by Jacob I. Dienstag, *Studies in Maimonides and St. Thomas Aquinas*, Biblioteca Maimonidica, vol. 1 (New York: Ktav

Publishing House, 1975) in David Burrell's comparative articles (see Bibliography) and in the most recent study by Avital Wholman, *Thomas d'Aquin et Maimonide: un dialogue exemplaire.*

57. It should be noted that in addition to the two main secrets of the Torah, the Account of the Beginning or Genesis and the Account of the Chariot or Ezekiel, all the prophetic books contain secrets, the elaboration of which requires great caution: "and I saw that you are one worthy to have the secrets of the prophetic books revealed to you so that you would consider in them that which perfect men ought to consider. Thereupon I began to let you see certain flashes and to give you certain indications" (*Guide*, 3). Cf. *Guide*, 5-20.

58. It should be noted that my critical comments have nothing to do with the philosophical justification of the skeptics et al. concerning their own position but rather with their attribution of such "Latin-Averroism" to Maimonides. The most notable advocates of this position are Leo Strauss and his students. See "The Literary Character of the *Guide for the Perplexed*," *Persecution and the Art of Writing*, (Westport, Conn.: Greenwood Press, 1952), pp. 38-94; Introductory Essay to Shlomo Pines' translation of the *Guide*, xi-lvi, reprinted in Leo Strauss, *Liberalism Ancient and Modern* (New York: Basic Books, 1968), pp. 140-84.

59. See Lawrence Berman, "Maimonides the Disciple of Alfarabi," *Israel Oriental Studies* 4 (1974): 154-78. What *prudent dissimulation* means in the context of al-Farabi's thought requires reevaluation as well.

60. "He appears as the commentator, the lawyer, the jurisprudent, the theologian, the communal leader, and the physician, but not the philosopher. . . . In his role as theologian, Maimonides accepts the fundamental principles of a particular tradition. . . . In fact, Maimonides is stating that his book is necessarily dialectical, rather than being demonstrative" (Berman, ibid., p. 163). In a footnote appearing at the end of the last sentence quoted here, Berman's own philosophical 'bias' explains why he arrived at his judgment of the *Guide*. After glossing his depiction of the text as dialectical, Berman states: "[o]ne is tempted to say sophistical"(p. 164, n. 33). He then adds, however, that Maimonides may have defended dialectics as a way to truth, although Berman clearly does not consider it a method proper to philosophy.

61. See Marvin Fox, "Maimonides and Aquinas on Natural Law," *Dinei Israel* 3 (1972): 5-36; and "The Doctrine of the Mean in Aristotle and Maimonides: A Comparative Study," *Studies in Jewish Religious and Intellectual History* (presented to Alexander Altmann), ed. Sigfried Stein and Raphael Loewe (University, Ala.: University of Alabama Press, 1979), pp. 93-120, henceforth, *Studies*. Despite the seeming moderation of the latter article, Fox minimizes the role of practical philosophy in Maimonides to an extent such that it is fully replaced by the Torah. See also David Hartman, *Maimonides: Torah and Philosophical Quest* (Philadelphia, 1976).

62. Cf. Norbert M. Samuelson, "The Problem of Free Will in Maimonides, Gersonides, and Aquinas," *CCARJ* 17 (1970): 3-13. The appropriateness of Neo-Kantian categories for understanding Maimonides, even if they are adopted by Jewish Neo-

Kantian interpreters of the *Guide*, e.g., Solomon Maimon and Herman Cohen, remains to be clearly justified. This is equally true of all premodern philosophers. I doubt that either Maimonides' Islamicate-Aristotelian logic or his Neoplatonic noetics and cosmology could be easily or charitably accommodated to a post-Cartesian model. Suffice it to point out that the development of, and attempt to apply, infintesimal calculus to the question of the origin of the universe undertaken by Jewish Neo-Kantians, such as Solomon Maimon and Herman Cohen, irrespective of their other merits, are in tension with Maimonides' resistance to such attempts, as will become clear in Chapter 3.

63. Cf. Charles Touati, "Les Deux Theories de Maimonide sur la Providence," *Studies*, pp. 331-41; Georges Vajda, "La Pensée religieuse de Moise Maimonide: unité ou dualité?" *Cahiers de Civilisation Médiévale* 9 (1966): 29-49. I do not assume that in interpreting the thought of another, especially an historically remote writer, it is possible to avoid 'bias', nor do I consider it desirable. I do, however, hold that greater awareness of one's own 'prejudice' provides some safeguards against anachronistic misappropriations of premodern thought. For a thoughtful discussion of the concomitant necessity and danger inherent in 'prejudice', see Hans-Georg Gadamer, *Truth and Method*, ed. and trans. Garrett Barden and Jon Cumming (New York: Seabury Press, 1975).

64. Cf. Charles Raffel, "Maimonides' Theory of Providence," diss. Brandeis University, 1983.

65. Cf. Alfred L. Ivry, "Maimonides on Possibility," *Mystics, Philosophers, and Politicians: Essays in Jewish Intellectual History* (in honour of Alexander Altmann), ed. Jehuda Reinharz and Daniel Swetchinski (Durham, N.C.: Duke University Press, 1982), pp. 67-84. Ivry's conclusion that Maimonides is not "a mystic in any formal or traditional sense" and that he "attempts to work within that rational and scientific framework which he regards as both necessary and inevitable for man" (pp. 83-84) can be developed further if mystical and philosophical knowledge are contradistinguished as, respectively, the negation and the affirmation of reason. Consequently, Maimonides' affirmation of an apprehension which exceeds demonstrative reasoning only *seems* to fall short of the philosophical rigor promised by him.

66. See Maimonides' discussion of the indemonstrability of either the creation or the eternity of the world, *Guide*, 2, 15-17; Maimonides' explanation of the manner whereby he arrived at his own knowledge of providence, *Guide*, 3, 17, 471, a subject that will be investigated in some detail in the following chapter as well as in the final chapter.

67. *Mishneh Torah, Sefer ha-Madda'* (Jerusalem: Mosad ha-Rav Kook, 1961).

68. In fact, a review of Thomistic bibliographies reveals a paucity in studies of Aquinas' biblical commentaries, which is rather surprising amidst the wealth of other studies.

69. The late James A. Weisheipl is known for his oft-repeated exclamation: "non loquamur metaphysice." It should be noted that by Christian Neoplatonist I des-

ignate a modified Neoplatonism, of which some essential elements will emerge out of this study.

70. In fact, one of my conclusions will be that, when treating metaphysical questions, no thinker who accepts the truth of revelation can follow Aristotle. In the *proemium* to *De Divinis Nominibus*, Aquinas states: "Haec igitur Platonicorum ratio fidei non consonant nec veritati, quantum ad hoc quod continet de specibus naturalibus separatis, sed quantum ad id quod dicebant de primo rerum Principio, *verissima est eorum opinio et fidei christianae consona*," 2 (my emphasis). All Latin quotations will follow the medieval spellings as they appear in the cited text.

71. I understand Aquinas' constant references to biblical passages in the *Summa*, especially, in the *sed contra* and the *respondeo*, to indicate his instruction to the reader to consult his treatment of a given subject elsewhere. For an outline of all direct references to the *Platonici*, see R. J. Henle, *St. Thomas and Platonism: A Study of Plato and the Platonici*, Texts in the Writings of St. Thomas (The Hague, M. Nijhoff, 1956). It should be noted, however, that I disagree with Henle's conclusions.

72. Cf. O'Reilly, "Expositio super librum Boetii," pp. 387-88.

73. Chenu, *Toward an Understanding*, p. 257.

74. It is my opinion that Martin Yaffe's conclusion that both Maimonides' and Aquinas' Aristotelianism leads them to offer "an Averroistic account of their meaning" is based upon an a priori conclusion about their philosophical orientation, rather than upon their commentaries on Job. As will become clear in the following chapter, I believe that this prior conclusion also leads Yaffe to an erroneous reading of the texts. Martin Yaffe, "Providence in Medieval Aristotelianism: Moses Maimonides and Thomas Aquinas on the Book of Job," *Hebrew Studies* 20-21 (1979-80): 62-74.

75. ". . . dicendum, quod varietas sensuum, quorum unus ab alio non procedit, facit multiplicitatem locutionis; sed sensus spiritualis *semper* fundatur super litteralem, et procedit ex eo" (*Quaestiones Quodlibetales* [Rome: Marietti, 1956], VII, Q. 6, a. 1, ad 1m; it should be noted that Marietti's edition differs from earlier editions designating this section of Q. VII as a. 14). Cf. *Summa*, I^a Pars, Q. 1, aa. 9-10.

76. "Non enim cum Scriptura nominat Dei brachium, est litteralis sensus quod in Deo sit membrum huiusmodi corporale, sed id quod per hoc membrum significatur, scilicet virtus operativa" (*Summa*, I^a Pars, a. 10, ad 3^{ium}).

77. "Scripsit . . . super Job ad litteram, quem nullus Doctor litteraliter tentavit exponere propter profunditatem sensus litterae, ad quem nullus potuit invenire" (Guillelmus de Tocco, 'Vita S. Thomae Aquinatis'. *Fontes Vitae S. Thomae Aquinatis*, ed. D. Prummer, O. P. [Toulouse: Privat, Bibliopolam, 1912-37], p. 88). Cf. "Scripsit quoque super Job ad litteram, quem nullus doctor litteraliter sic sicut ipse exponere attemptavit" (Bernardus Guidonis, "Vita S. Thomae Aquinatis," *Fontes*: 219). William's testimony is far from accurate. As Smalley points out both in the *Study of the Bible* and in the "Old Law," a number of other Christian thinkers have attempted to write literal commentaries.

78. Biblical exegesis exhibits only one aspect of the limits of linguistic expression. These are manifest most fully in Divine Science since there the limitations of human knowledge, especially of demonstrative reasoning, are brought into the sharpest focus. Cf. *In librum Beati Dionysii De Divinis Nominibus Expositio*, (Rome: Marietti, 1950); *De Trinitate*. The limitations of human, corporeal, expression will be addressed later. It will also be re-thought in the final chapter.

79. In the preliminary remarks to this section, I am greatly indebted to Hans-Georg Gadamer, especially to "Hermeneutic as Practical Philosophy," *Reason in the Age of Science*, trans. Frederick G. Lawrence (1981, Cambridge, Mass.: MIT Press, 1984), pp. 88-112.

80. Ibid., p. 89.

81. The differences indicated by *respective traditions* refer not only to those found between the Jewish and Christian traditions of biblical interpretation but also to the different forms in which the classical philosophical tradition was appropriated in respectively, the Judaeo-Arabic and Western Chrisian milieux.

82. *Guide*, 3-4.

83. *Guide*, 4. Emphases on lines 3 and 4 are mine. Line 5 is a quotation in Hebrew from Ecclesiastes 12:10. A more accurate and more fitting translation would read "find desirable words," or as the Munk French translation renders it: "de trouver les objets de ton désir," especially since Joseph's "unruly desire" for knowledge is the psychic disorder that occasions the composition of the *Guide*. For the reader unfamiliar with Maimonides' original work, it should be noted that, although the *Guide* is written in Judaeo-Arabic, all the biblical and rabbinic quotation are in Hebrew.

84. The significance of Joseph's natural ability to grasp the concomitant necessity and inadequacy of language for knowledge will, first, be discussed below. Its greater extension and depth will emerge as this study progresses. It should be noted, however, even at this early stage, that the language of desire and repulsion plays a significant role in Maimonides' pedagogy, and in his understanding of language.

85. *Guide*, 4.

86. Even if Joseph was not a Rav, Maimonides' form of address indicates a certain degree of respect for his student.

87. See *Guide*, 3, 51, 619, 87, 2.

88. *Guide*, 3.

89. The term *virtue* is used in its medieval sense, as an habitually acquired capacity of the soul. I am deliberately avoiding terms such as *skill* and *method* since it is my claim that philosophical interpretation cannot be acquired passively as a skill nor applied as a method.

90. In what follows I shall address only instances of error about language. The discussion of language as the origin of perplexity and error will be resumed in the final chapter.

91. Given Maimonides' endeavors on behalf of the vulgar—the *Mishneh Torah*, correspondence, etc.—it seems to me more reasonable that his caution in the *Guide* manifests a prudence exercised for their sake rather than his own.

92. "I know that, among men generally, every beginner will derive benefit from some of the chapters of this Treatise, though he lacks even an inkling of what is involved in speculation" (*Guide*, 16).

93. *Guide*, 18.

94. *Guide*, 19.

95. See Maimonides' *Treatise on [the Art of] Logic* (*al Makalah fi-Sina'at al Mantiq*, ed. and trans. Israel Efros (New York: American Academy for Jewish Research, 1938; and *PAAJR* 34 [1966]), where Maimonides' states that the art of rhetoric that derives at least one of its premises from tradition uses analogical syllogisms and that sometimes in rhetorical syllogisms "one premise appears while the other is, for various reasons, suppressed" (C. 8, 48-49).

96. Aristotle, *Posterior Analytics*, 71a1-72b32, especially, 72b25-32; *Nicomachean Ethics*, 1094a1-1095a14 and 1138b19-1139b35; and *Metaphysics*, 980a1-983a23.

97. It should be recalled that the apparent contradictions referred to here are deliberate and hence both their discovery and their dissolution presuppose full knowledge of the methods and rules of logic.

98. For example, psychological and epistemological discussions that, properly speaking, belong to a single order of discourse since Maimonides, like all other medieval thinkers, does not elaborate an epistemology independent of his psychology.

99. *Guide*, 1, 34, 73.

100. *Guide*, 19.

101. *Guide*, 12.

102. *Guide*, 1, 69, 168-69.

103. Herbert Davidson raises the possibility that the *Guide* may contain unintended contradictions, or contradictions, that in Maimonides' classification will belong to the sixth type. See Herbert Davidson, "Maimonides Secret Position on Creation," *Studies in Medieval Jewish History and Literature*, ed. Isadore Twersky (Cambridge, Mass.: Harvard University Press, 1979), pp. 16-40. This suggestion will be addressed in detail in Chapter 3, in the discussion of creation.

104. "Know that with regard to natural matters as well, it is impossible to give a

clear exposition when teaching some of their principles as they are" (*Guide*, Introduction, 7). Cf. Sara Klein-Braslavi, *Maimonides' Interpretation of the Story of Creation* (Jerusalem, 1987), pp. 29-31.

105. Aristotle, *Nicomachean Ethics*, trans. Sir David Ross (Oxford: Oxford University Press, 1925), 1. 3. 1094b12-1095. See *Metaphysics*, trans. Hugh Tredennick (Cambridge, Mass.: Harvard University Press, 1933), 2. 3. 994b32-995a19, for a brief but poignant discussion of the relation between the ethos of the audience and tropos of instruction; see also *De Anima*, trans. W. S. Hett (Cambridge, Mass.: Harvard University Press, 1936) 1. 1. 402a1-23.

106. *Guide*, 1. 31. 66.

107. *Guide*, 2. 22-23. 317-22.

108. The superiority of prophetic knowledge to natural/rational knowledge will be discussed in detail in Chapters 5-7.

109. *Guide*, 2. 23. 321. The relation between "political" and individual perfections will be discussed in Chapters 6-7.

110. "The second condition [for evaluating one's doubts] is to have knowledge of the natural sciences and to apprehend their truth so that you should know your doubts in their true reality" (*Guide*, 2, 23, 321).

111. Although it may be objected that as, "prince of the philosophers," Aristotle's opinion is superior to that of the prophets since their authority extends only to the moral perfection of the species, whereas his pertains to the intellect, as will be shown in the last two chapters, noetic perfection requires prior moral perfection, the principles of which cannot be discovered by philosophy.

112. *Guide*, 2. 40. 382. I shall discuss these two modes of cognition and their interrelation in the last two chapters.

113. See note 50.

114. "Quia catholicae veritatis doctor non solum provectos debet instruere, sed ad eum pertinet etiam incipientes erudire, . . . propositum nostrae intentionis in hoc opere est, ea quae ad Christianam religionem pertinent eo modo tradere secundum quod congruit ad eruditionem incipientium." *Summa*, I\u1d43 Pars, Prologus, 1a.

115. Leonard E. Boyle, "The Setting of the *Summa Theologiae* of Saint Thomas," *Etienne Gilson Series 5* (Toronto: PIMS, 1982). Fr. Boyle's lecture, in fact challenges the traditional assumption that the *Summa* was written for students at the universities and *studia generalia*. This assumption is amply evident throughout Chenu's *Towards Understanding*, a text singled out by Fr. Boyle to exemplify his worthy opponents, p. 18.

116. Boyle, ibid., pp. 18-19. Aquinas may well be using the general deficient state of Dominican education in order to illustrate a specific point.

117. The far greater circulation of the II^a-II^{ae}, recorded by Fr. Boyle (p. 29), may explain the tendency still in evidence to divide the books of the *Summa*, see pp. 00-00. In fact, in a private discussion with Fr. Boyle about his conclusions, he informed me that his conclusions about the audience of the *Summa* may be valid for the II^a-II^{ae} only. Indeed, by being rather vague in the Prefaces to the books of the *Summa*, Aquinas must have compounded unwittingly an already "lopsided system of theological education" (Boyle, ibid., p. 30). Despite the greater circulation, the *cura animarum* outlined in the II^a-II^{ae} demands of its reader not only an understanding of the two preceding books, but also previous study in philosophy exceeding the level of education available to most members of the Dominican order.

118. Boyle, ibid., p. 9.

119. ". . . tentabimus . . . ea quae ad sacram doctrinam pertinent breviter ac dilucide prosequi, secundum quod materia patietur" (*Summa*, I^a Pars, *prologus*).

120. For a detailed and provocative discussion of the duality or "doubling" of metaphysics articulated by Aquinas, see Jean-Francois Courtine, "Philosophie et théologie: Remarque sur la situation aristotélicienne de la détermination thomiste de la 'theologia' (*S. Th.*, Ia, qu. 1, a. 1 et 5)," *Revue philosophique de Louvain* 84 (1986): 315-44.

121. Aristotle, *Categoriae, Categories and Propositions (De Interpretatione)*, trans. Hippocrates G. Apostle (Iowa: The Peripatetic Press, 1980), 1b1-25, 6a37-8b24.

122. *Summa*, I^a Pars, Q. 1, a. 8. See *In duodecim libros Metaphysicorum Aristotelis Expositio* (Rome: Marietti, 1964). Bk. III, l. 5. 387-92; henceforth, *In Meta.*

123. "Dicendum quod poeta utitur metaphoris propter repraesentationem; repraesentatio enim naturaliter homini delectabilis est. Sed sacra doctrina utitur metaphoris propter necessitatem et utilitatem, ut dictum est" (*Summa*, I^a Pars, Q. 1, a. 9, ad 1um). The necessity for metaphorical language will be examined in the final chapter. Note Aquinas' agreement with Maimonides about the appetitive aspect of language and pedagogy, see above n. 84.

124. "Quia vero sensus litteralis est, quem auctor intendit; auctor autem Sacrae Scripturae Deus est, qui omnia simul suo intellectu comprehendit" (*Summa*, I^a Pars, Q. 1, a. 10). The Plotinian or Proclean tenor of this 'thesis' is rather striking, especially since the Aristotelian divinity comprehends only itself.

125. This general statement will be modified considerably in the final chapter, when I discuss non-demonstrative modes of knowing and speaking. My concern here is limited to eliciting general "principles" governing Aquinas' approaches to interpretation.

126. See pp. 20-21.

127. *In Aristotelis libros Peri Hermeneias et Poteriorum Analyticorum Expositio* (Rome: Marietti, 1955); henceforth, *De Interpretatione* and *In Post. An.*

128. Aquinas explanation of Aristotle's brief statement is not only much longer than the Philosopher's text, but also develops the statement of procedure into an expla-

nation of the nature of language and the role it plays in philosophical inquiry. *De Interpretatione*, Bk. I, l. 4-10. 74-142.

129. It should be noted that, although this "ignorance" is eminently true of God and all "things" that do not exists *per se*, e.g., prime matter, it is equally true of "things" that can be known by natural reason but are not *known*, e.g., that human being *is* a rational animal.

130. "Dicitur enim scientia divina sive *theologia*, in quantum praedictas substantias considerat. *Metaphysica*, in quantum considerat ens et ea quae consequuntur ipsum. . . . Dicitur autem *prima philosophia*, in quantum primas rerum causas considerat" (*In Meta.*, *proemium*, 2). The emphasis of the term *divine science* in the translated text is mine.

131. *Guide*, 1. 3; 8-9; Bruno Decker ed. *Expositio super librum Boethii De Trinitate* (Leiden: E. J. Brill, 1959), Qs. V-VI.

132. Rather than referring to the particular curricula used at their time, I am repeating Maimonides' and Aquinas' own recommendations. Consequently, both are concerned with preserving the spirit of their traditions, precisely when they are critical of the manner and methods of teaching.

133. As noted previously, my general understanding of contemporary hermeneutics is informed primarily by Hans-Georg Gadamer. On some particular issues it is also informed by Paul Ricoeur. For a comprehensive general introduction to hermeneutics and its practice, see Richard E. Palmer, *Hermeneutics: Interpretation Theory in Schleiermacher, Dilthey, Heidegger, and Gadamer*, Northwestern University Studies in Phenomenology and Existential Philosophy (Evanston, Ill.: Northwestern University Press, 1969).

134. Hans-Georg Gadamer, *Truth and Method*, ed. and trans. Garrett Barden and John Cumming (New York: Seabury Press, 1975), pp. 274-341; "Hermeneutics as Practical Philosophy," and "Hermeneutics as Theoretical and Practical Task," *Reason in the Age of Science*, trans. Frederick G. Lawrence (Cambridge, Mass.: MIT Press, 1981), pp. 88-138.

135. *Truth and Method*, pp. 274-78, 305-41, and 378-87.

136. Although the terminology I employ is borrowed from Paul Ricoeur, "Explanation and Understanding," *Interpretation Theory: Discourse and the Surplus of Meaning* (Fort Worth, Texas: Texas Christian University Press, 1976), pp. 71-88, I do not follow Ricoeur's structuralist analysis of interpretation.

137. As I have tried to illustrate throughout this chapter, the demand for an historical situating of texts is not a uniquely contemporary one. Rather, both Maimonides and Aquinas are acutely aware of historical transformations, linguistic as well as disciplinary, and hence develop theories of language and approaches to interpretations that underline the disjunction between "universal truth," on the one hand, and understanding and explanation, on the other. Properly speaking, universal truth is unattainable in lan-

guage, if at all. Understanding and explanation must always remain intermediate and indeterminate. In this light, it is especially significant to render explanation fitting (*conveniens*) to the audience's capacity to understand, let alone tolerate ambiguity and *aporiae*. The caution exhibited and counseled is as, perhaps more, significant to the philosophers as it is to the "vulgar," since, in addition to historical and disciplinary changes, their ignoring of distinctions in *media* and *foci* while treating a single topic (e.g., metaphysics, divine science, theology, first philosophy) is simultaneously detrimental to them and to their audiences.

138. Again the term *Modern* is used here strictly to designate the period beginning with the seventeenth century.

139. See Karl Löwith, *Meaning in History* (Chicago: University of Chicago Press, 1949). Although Löwith's interpretation is clearly "Augustinian," and although the Augustinian understanding of the *eschaton* is strictly Christian in origin, the 'identity' between the Jewish and Christian Bible created by the powerful and pervasive Judaeo-Christian "myth" has successfully covered over the radical difference between the Jewish and Christian interpretation of the Genesis' *incipit* and subsequent views of temporality, time and finitude.

140. My critique of modern methodologies extends to any approach that treats as secondary the importance of the belief in the divine origin of Scripture. The accidental quality of the specific variants evident in biblical language is pertinent equally to literary forms of biblical expression, and so on. Rather than undermining the significance of philological and literary studies of the Bible, my criticism aims at recovering their full significance in biblical narrative.

141. The subject merits a full study, in the absence of which it would be vain to speculate about the possible reasons for this 'silence'. Notwithstanding, thinkers, such as Ibn 'Ezra, exhibited greater prudence than Maimonides in their biblical commentaries. See Colette Sirat, *Hagut Filosofit bi-Yemei ha-Beynayim* [*Jewish Philosophical Thought in the Middle Ages*] (Jerusalem: Keter Publishing House, 1975), p. 113. Cf. Chap. 1, p. 14, n. 38 above, and Baruch (Benedict) Spinoza, *Tractatus Theologico-Politicus*, passim.

142. As noted in the introduction, pp. 6-7, the question of human freedom in relation to divine knowledge (or what is erroneously termed *foreknowledge* (*praevidens*) can be raised only after we understand the nature of providence, especially in relation to *human* knowledge.

143. Israel Efros, "Shitato ha-filosofit shel R. Saadia Gaon," *Medieval Jewish Philosophy: Systems and Problems* (Jerusalem: Merkaz Press, 1965), pp. 155-58.

144. Ibid., pp. 156-57.

145. It should be noted that the absence of suffering results from (a) lack of desire for material goods and (b) the possession of the true good, namely, the apprehension of the true, single, final end.

146. St. Gregory the Great, *Moralia in Iob*, CCSL 143-44 (1979).

147. "Aliquando vero exponere aperta historiae verba negligimus, ne tardius ad obscura veniamus; aliquando autem intellegi iuxta litteram nequeunt, quia superficie tenus accepta nequaquam instructionem legentibus sed errorem gignunt" (*Expositio*, 25-26), quoted in the Preface to the Leonine edition of Aquinas. Given the profusion of *hapax legomena* in Job and given that the Septuagint translators, unable to understand many of its verses, paraphrased rather than translated the text, St. Gregory's difficulties are explicable. (As an aside, it may be helpful to note that the modern Hebrew student of the text often encounters like difficulties.) The preceding quoted text, too, is highly ambiguous. Were it not seriously distorting in this context, especially the context of the St. Gregory of the *Moralia* as he has influenced subsequent interpretations of Job, this text would call for "dis-construction." For, how are we to understand the "*obscura*" here, let alone the "*superfecie*" that undermines instruction and leads to error?

148. Smalley, *Study of the Bible*, pp. 34-35. In the context of present debates about deconstruction and in the light of Smalley's "credentials" as an interested defender of the canon, Smalley's exasperation with St. Gregory are themselves highly instructive.

149. According to the Leonine editors of Aquinas' exposition on Job, Roland of Cremona had emphasized the importance of the letter of the text of Job "une génération avant saint Thomas." However, they add that "le commentaire de Roland de Cremone, lourd et confus, était resté dans l'oubli. Au contraire, celui de saint Thomas devint très tôt célèbre et connut une grande diffusion" (*Expositio* 25).

150. *Expositio*, Preface, 33-34.

151. All references to St. Albert will be to the *Commentarii in Iob*, ed. Melchior Weiss (Freiburg: Herder, 1904). Albert's commentary is much more expansive than Aquinas'. Although he is attempting to provide an *ad litteram* commentary, his commentary is less sober than Aquinas' and thus more in keeping with the preceding tradition, a continuity evident also in his constant reference to Gregory. In addition, Albert's refers to Maimonides' *Guide* rather frequently and favorably even when he criticizes Maimonides' "heretical" position. See p. 48, n. 191.

152. Both Smalley and the Leonine editors of the *Expositio*, repeatedly emphasize Aquinas' radical break from the Gregorian tradition and the novel character of his work. Note that in the "Old Law" Smalley modifies her position.

153. Marcos F. Manzanedo, O.P., "La antropologia filosofica en el comentario tomista al libro de Job," *Angelicum* 62 (1985): 419-71; Martin D. Yaffe, "Providence in Medieval Aristotelianism," pp. 62-74. Manzanedo's article is a somewhat scanty summary of the text.

154. See, respectively, Introduction, p. 6, n. 15, and Chap. 1, p. 18, n. 62.

155. Henceforth, *knowledge*, since foreknowledge implies time whereas divine knowledge is eternal. The use of the term *foreknowledge*, inadvertently, predicates time, an accident inhering in motion (another accident) of God. The application of the

prefix *fore-* to divine knowledge has produced some of the confusion about its relation to freedom of choice. Irrespective of the conclusion reached, most questions addressed to God's knowledge of *future* events fall, to some extent, into the same trap. Although, in *Thomas d'Aquin et Maimonide*, Avital Wohlman discusses both aspects of providence, the existential and metaphysical, she, too, considers the question of divine knowledge to constitute the primary and preliminary question: "Du côte de Dieu, d'abord. . . . Du côte de l'homme, ensuite" (p. 208).

156. It should be noted that any positive predication applied to God is used to refer to human understanding only, except when directly addressing the question of divine attributes. From the perspective of human knowledge, I wish to emphasize, at the outset, a distinction between divine providence and divine knowledge as belonging to different kinds of attributes, an attribute of action (known as an effect) and an essential attribute.

157. Since for Maimonides, following the Islamicate tradition, the human will is not a rational faculty of the soul, and since for Aquinas, *liberum arbitrium* occurs only when the will is informed by reason or *chooses* to be informed by reason, I will, henceforth, prefer *choice* to *will*, except when discussing Maimonides' and Aquinas' respective psychologies.

158. Although the Leonine editors of the *Expositio* admit that Maimonides' *Guide* had some influence on Aquinas, in fact that "[l]'inspiration initiale de *l'Expositio* vient incontestablement de la lecture de quelques chapitres du *Dux neutorum* de Moyses Maimonide," they conclude that it did not have a significant influence on Aquinas, since "trop de divergences separent les points de vue respectif" (pp. 26-27). Although, in her very brief treatment of Maimonides' and Aquinas' commentaries, Wohlman recognizes a greater affinity bettween Maimonides' and Aquinas' works, her substantial conclusions still echo the Leonine editors' judgment. See Wohlman, *Thomas d'Aquin et Maimonide*, pp. 256-66, especially pp. 257-59.

159. *Guide*, 3, 22-23.

160. The most notable, 'substantial' dissimilarity between Maimonides and Aquinas is their interpretation of Elihu's speech. Whereas Maimonides considers Elihu's opinion to represent a profound truth exceeding Job's preprophetic understanding, Aquinas considers his understanding superior to that of the other interlocutors, but inferior to Job's. See *Expositio*, 38-42, and the discussion of the nature of Elihu's knowledge that follows.

161. The operations of divine providence with respect to the irrational creatures in the sublunar realm belongs to a discussion of the nature of divine knowledge, and especially of God's knowledge of singulars that, as stated previously, is beyond my intention and scope.

162. Chenu, *Toward Understanding*, 233-63; Preface passim. Both Chenu and the Leonine editors see a complete congruence between Aquinas' philosophical and theological enterprise. Yaffe's assertion about the primacy of the religious community's

needs over the integrity of the text in fact implies that Aquinas accepted and adopted the Gregorian method.

163. Following the tradition of the *Nicomachean Ethics* that "amicus Plato magis amica veritas."

164. Yaffe, "Providence in Medieval Aristotelianism," p. 62.

165. *Guide*, 3-4. See discussion in Chapter 1 of the audience of the *Guide*.

166. See the discussion of the *prologus* to the *Summa* in the previous chapter and especially Aquinas' designation of the readers of the *Summa* as *incipientes*. Since the reader of the *Expositio* cannot be assumed to be *more* advanced in learning than that of the *Summa*, attributing perfect wisdom to him seems somewhat hasty. See Chapter 1, pp. 30-32, especially n. 117.

167. The former designation is that of Aquinas, the latter that of Maimonides.

168. See my discussion of philosophical prudence in Chapter 1. Conversely, were we to understand the term *wisdom* here as equivocal, following the Arabic language philosophical tradition, wisdom would refer to *phronesis* only.

169. ". . . he is kept away by a barrier from the soul. This is the meaning of its saying: *Only spare his soul.* I have already explained to you that in our language the term *soul* is equivocal and that it is applied to the thing that remains after death; this is the thing over which Satan has no dominion" (*Guide*, 3, 22, 488). However equivocal the term *soul* may be then, Maimonides here insists on the singular status of immortality.
"pro anima sua, idest pro vita sua conservanda" and ff. (*Expositio*, 2. 95-99). It is noteworthy that although many Christian commentators on Job, apart from Aquinas and Albert, comment on this verse, no other Christian commentator in the *Glossa Ordinaria* explains the term *soul*.

170. It cannot be overemphasized that *Aristotelian* and *Platonic* refer to their varied Hellenistic-medieval versions.

171. The relation between natural and supra-natural knowledge or, in the language of philosophy, *episteme* and *nous*, will be discussed in Chapters 5 and 6.

172. "The story of *Job*, which is extraordinary and marvellous, belongs to the kind of things we are discussing now. I mean to say that it is a parable intended to set forth the *opinions* of people concerning providence" (*Guide*, 3. 22, 486). The opening statement clearly refers back to the final statements in the previous chapter where, after discussing the inaccessibility of divine to human knowledge, Maimonides states: "For I say that this is something most extraordinary and a *true opinion*; if it is carefully studied, no mistake or distortion will be found in it. . . . No demonstration at all can be obtained with regard to these great and sublime notions, either for our opinion—that of the community of those who adhere to a Law—or for the opinions of the philosophers, . . ." (*Guide*, 3. 22, 485). Emphases upon opinion(s) are mine. See Chapter 1, pp. 23-29 and Chapter 7, pp. 187-192, where I discuss Maimonides general explanation of the nature of biblical parables.

173. See ibid.; and *Guide*, 1, 31. 66.

174. See ibid.; and *Guide*, 1, 12. As already noted, further discussion of the nature of parabolic language, especially in relation to conradiction and negation, will be resumed in the final chapters.

175. See *Guide*, 3, 23, 494, where Maimonides states that the opinions expressed by the interlocutors might have been expressed "in true reality if this is a story that has happened." Note the disruption of a linear notion of redemptive time implied by the distinction between historical facticity and recurrent manifestations of truth. This distinction will be essential for understanding Maimonides' distinction between the soul's permanence or "immortality" and temporal rational perfection.

176. Both Aquinas and Albert preface God's conversations with Satan with the explanation that the reference to God's speech is "modo respondendi." See *Expositio*, 38. 20-37; *Commentarii*, 38.

177. *Guide*, 3, 22, 486.

178. See Chapter 1, pp. 21-29.

179. See ibid. and the concluding statement to the explication of Job, *Guide*, 3, 23, 497.

180. Maimonides uses a quotation from Isaiah. 8:10 to corroborate his reading, "Uṣu 'Eiṣa" ("Take counsel together"). St. Albert repeats Maimonides' interpretation of Uz, as counsel as well as a place name, although he does not identify Maimonides as the source of his reading. *Commentarii*, 1. 26-28. The variant spellings reflect variations between the respective texts.

181. *Guide*, 3, 22, 487. Although the Hebrew term *ḥakham* used here (and its cognate Arabic *ḥakhim*) is equivocal and often refers to skill or practical rather than theoretical knowledge, the tenor of the discussion indicates that in relation to Job's virtues, Maimonides employs it strictly to refer to wisdom.

182. Raffel maintains that Maimonides contradicts even this modified understanding at the end of the *Guide*, asserting that the truly wise man experiences no suffering whatsoever. I will address this alleged contradiction in Chapter 6.

183. See the preceding discussion of Sa'adia's position and the bulk of *Guide*, 3, 23.

184. See especially the discussion of trials and actions in the two chapters immediately following that on Job, *Guide*, 3, 24-25.

185. At the end of the chapter, Maimonides indicates that the disorder in the explanation of Job should be overlooked. See outline for causes of contradictory statements, especially the third and fourth causes, *Guide*, 1, 17. Discussion of the relation between parabolic language and contradicion will be undertaken in the final chapters.

186. *Guide*, 3, 22, 488.

187. The distincion alluded to by Maimonides is reminiscent of Plato's ironic discussion of Cephalus' "piety," in *Republic* 1.

188. *Guide*, 3, 22, 488.

189. Note Maimonides' claim that he understood these notions through something akin to prophetic vision. *Guide*, 3. 22. 488.

190. *Guide*, 3, 22, 488.

191. *Guide*, 3, 22, 488. See *Guide*, 1. 41, 91-92, where Maimonides discusses the equivociy of the word *soul*. St. Albert states that although Maimonides is correct in emphasizing the immortality of the soul in this context, nevertheless his opinion "is heretical, since the whole soul remains after death," rather than the intellect alone. See *Commentarii*, 2. 27-35.

192. *Guide*, 3, 22, 489 [Babylonian Talmud (henceforth, B.T.), Baba Batra, 16a].

193. See *Guide*, 3, 22, 488.

194. *Guide*, 3, 22, 489-90.

195. I deliberately refer to the Account of the Beginning as metaphysics and ontology rather than physics since physics addresses the created universe after it came to be. As will become evident in Chapter 3, a part of Maimonides' 'refutation' of Aristotle is based upon his denial of the validity of an inference to an unknown, inaccessible originary state strictly on the basis of perceptions of the nature of what exists.

196. It is unclear whether Maimonides accepted the rabbinic opinion that Job denied the resurrection of the dead since he presents it as "they say," neither affirming nor denying it. Maimonides does not shy away from either strong affirmations or strong denials of rabbinic opinions. In fact, in the same context (B.T., Baba Batra, 16a-b) he does both.

197. It is noteworthy that Maimonides uses the term *Shari'a* rather than Torah here.

198. *Guide*, 3, 23, 493.

199. In *Guide*, 3, 17, 477, Maimonides ascribes this opinion to some of the later Gaonim, possibly having Sa'adia in mind. See pp. 39-40.

200. *Guide*, 3, 23, 494. Maimonides' earlier statement concerning the 'virtues' of the friends whom he describes as "men famous *at that time* because of virtue and knowledge" (p. 494). (The same Arabic term, *'ilm*, most often used to translate *episteme*, is used to designate knowledge in both contexts. Note that the statement does not reflect Maimonides' own opinion.

201. Note the similarity between Maimonides' praise of the true Sages just mentioned and Elihu.

202. See Chapter 1 passim.

203. *Guide*, 3, 23, 494.

204. *Guide*, 3, 23, 495.

205. *Guide*, 1, 49; 2, 1-12; 3, 1-8.

206. *Guide*, 3, 23, 496; my emphasis.

207. The relation between providence and government will be discussed in Chapter 6.

208. *Guide*, 3, 17, 471; my emphasis. Although the term *al-qiyas* is equivocal, the predication by *al-ʿaql* indicates that Maimonides here is refering to demonstration or other modes of syllogistic reasoning.

209. "Fuerunt autem aliqui . . ." (*Expositio*, Prologue, 72).

210. Aquinas' refraining from quoting a specifically Christian source and his exclusive use of biblical quotations to support his argument can lend support to a conclusion that his refutation was directed at a non-Christian source, i.e., Maimonides.

211. See Aquinas' explanation for the necessity of biblical parables: "Christus quaedam turbis loquebatur in occulto, parabolis utens ad annuntianda spiritualia mysteria ad quae capienda non erant idonei vel digni" (*Summa*, IIIª Pars, Q. 42, a. 3). Msgr. Synan suggests that Aquinas' reluctance to accept some biblical stories as parables may originate in his identification of some unacceptable Platonic positions as parables. See Edward A. Synan, *Thomas Aquinas: Propositions and Parables*, The Etienne Gilson Series 1 (Toronto: PIMS, 1979).

212. "Quo autem tempore fuerit vel ex quibus parentibus originem duxerit, quis etiam huius libri fuerit auctor, utrum scilicet ipse Iob hunc librum conscripserit, de se quasi de alio loquens, an alius de eo ista retulerit, non est praesentis intentionis discutere" (*Expositio, prologus*, 91-96). As I pointed out in Chapter 1, St. Gregory held the same opinion.

213. ". . . ad intentionem libri non multum differat utrum sic vel aliter fuerit . . ." (*Expositio, prologus*, 77-78).

214. See the introductory discussions both in Chapter 1 and in this chapter.

215. See Ezekiel 14:14; 20.

216. See *Guide*, 3, 17, 464-69. Maimonides' list is more comprehensive and includes not only the philosophical but also the Kalam positions. Among the philosophical opinions, he mentions only the opinions of Epicurus (which in the Jewish tradition is synonymous with the denial of providence) and of Aristotle.

217. It is highly likely that Aquinas intentionally refrained from drawing his audiences attention to the Aristotelian origin of this opinion. The only thinkers men-

tioned by name in the Prologue are Democritus and Empedocles.

218. The implications of the conflict between the Aristotelian and revealed tradition concerning providence for Aquinas' noetics and metaphysics (even *primary principles* of physics) will be explored in subsequent chapters.

219. "Unde eorum qui divinu spiritu sapientiam consecuti <sunt> ad aliorum eruditionem, primum et praecipuum studium fuit hanc opinionem a cordibus hominum amovere" (*Expositio, prologus*, 48-51).

220. "ut per *probabiles rationes* ostendatur res humanas divina providentia regi" (*Expositio, prologus*, 56-57, my emphasis).

221. ". . . quasi quoddam thema" (*Expositio, prologus*, 69).

222. Whereas Aristotle and the Aristotelian tradition, especially following Boethius' transmision of the *Topics*, recognize the limits of demonstration, for Aristotle, there is no extra-natural source for principles of human knowledge. That is why I think that Aquinas' claim here extends much further than to limit demonstration.

223. On the relation between the book of history and the book of nature, see Chenu, *Nature, Man and Society*; Jesse M. Gellrich, *The Idea of the Book in the Middle Ages: Language Theory, Mythology, and Fiction* (Ithaca, N.Y., and London: Cornell University Press, 1985.)

224. Since Aquinas' depiction of the variety of opinions concerning providence has been outlined previously and since both Maimonides and Aquinas outline errors only to refute them, it would be superfluous to outline Aquinas' interpretation of the opinions of Eliphaz, Bildad, and Zophar, which both consider erroneous. For despite a number of differences in their respective interpretations of the friends' opinions owing to differences in their traditions, these are of little philosophical consequence. Disagreements that may have philosophical significance will be discussed later.

225. The significance of this difference between Maimonides and Aquinas, both for evaluating the thought of each thinker in the light of all his works and for comparing their works, will be discussed in the final chapter.

226. Whether in this instance the remarks are meant to recall previous teachings or to constitute an indication of the appropriate context for further investigation cannot be determined from the commentary.

227. Aquinas uses *spiritus* rather than *intellectus* to designate the general category and *animae* to refer to humans specifically.

228. It is unclear why Aquinas considers it necessary to support his discussion of celestial beings with authority. It is possible that he wishes to establish a certain agreement between Christianity and philosophic cosmology, on the one hand, and to explain the divergence with respect to evil spirits, on the other, since, for philosophy, evil, a privation, cannot be attributed to incorporeal entities.

229. "Mali autem spiritus quidam sunt, non per naturam aut per creationem cum cuiusque naturae auctor sit Deus nec summum bonum potest esse causa nisi bonorum, sed sunt mali per *propriam culpam*" (*Expositio*, 1. 249-53, my emphasis). See 1. 316-22, where Aquinas explains that their will deviates from the divine will. In the discussion of evil, in Chapter 4, the distincion between "nature" and proper act will be elaborated.

230. As will become evident in Chapter 4, to angelic knowing there still belongs an ignorance, and it is that ignorance which makes possible a proper (*proprium*) choice to act contrary to the divine will. A certain obscurity, or lack of certainty, thus still pertains to angelic vision.

231. A similar distinction is also drawn by Albert. See *Commentarii*, 1. 21-41.

232. As will become evident later, Satan's ignorance is culpable because he *can* choose otherwise.

233. The natural human incapacity for understanding clearly should be read in relation to the presence or absence, scrutiny or vision, of God to creatures.

234. In the absence of a detailed study of the respective positions of the Jewish and Christian traditions regarding the wisdom of Job and detailed comparative philological studies of the respective Jewish and Christian textual traditions of the biblical book, it is not possible to arrive at a conclusive judgment of the possible doctrinal origins for Maimonides' and Aquinas' discrepant readings of the speeches. For a review of the pre-Maimonidean tradition, see the translator's introduction, *Saadiah ben Joseph al Fayyumi's Book of Theodicy, a Tenth Century Arabic Commentary and Translation of the Book of Job*, trans. Lenn E. Goodman, Yale Judaica Series 25 (New Haven, Conn.: Yale University Press, 1988). Nevertheless, we should recall, on the one hand, that there was no consensus in the Jewish tradition regarding either the justice or the wisdom of Job, and on the other, that St. Gregory, the Christian commentator dominating the medieval Christian exegetical tradition of the text, asserted Job's moral and intellectual superiority. It is also important to note that the attribution of a specific opinion to someone is irrelevant to the general teachings on providence.

235. ". . . omnes adversitates praesentis vitae pro peccatis provenire" (*Expositio*, 37. 381-82).

236. The claim here is not that all partial understanding is *ipso facto* erroneous, but rather that conclusions based upon such an understanding are invalid.

237. ". . . unde subdit *per somnium in visione nocturna*: quod quidem potest referri ad propheticam revelationem, secundum illud Num. xii <Si quis fuerit inter vos propheta Domini per somnium aut in visione loquar ad eum>" (*Expositio*, 38. 155-59). The Leonine editors point out to a discrepancy between Aquinas' Bible and the Jerome tradition, the latter reads "Si quis fuerit inter vos propheta Domini, in visione apparebo ei, vel per somnium loquar ad illum."

238. ". . . et sumitur hic disciplina pro instructione eorum quae homini occurunt agenda vel vitanda, non pro cognitione scientiarum speculativarum quae non consueverunt in somnio revelari" (*Expositio*, 33. 188-92).

239. "... principium peccatorum est superbia qua Dei praecepta contemnuntur" (*Expositio*, 33. 195-96).

240. "... per deordinationem potentiarum animae" (*Expositio*, 33. 201-3). In *Expositio*, 38, especially, 38-53. 76-77, Aquinas explains that inexpert speeches manifest that "every disorder proceeds from a defect of reason (omnis inordinatio ex defectu rationis procedere videtur)."

241. All that can be learned from the *Expositio* is that, although pride is the cause of ignorance, its recognition can occur only once the limitations of human knowledge are encountered. God's speech is said to confront human beings with their ignorance (38. 76-77). Thus, it seems that proper obedience to the divine precepts can occur only after human beings acknowledge their rational limitations. Since this is not a philosophical inquiry, the question of the proper order of the sciences does not arise in this context.

242. "[S]ed quia humana sapientia non sufficit ad veritatem divinae providentiae *comprehendendam*, necessarium fuit ut praedicta disputatio divina auctoritate determinaretur; sed quia Iob circa divinam providentiam recte *sentiebat*, in modo autem loquendi excesserat intantum quod in aliorum cordibus exinde scandalum proveniret dum putabant eum Deo debitam reverentiam non exhibere, ideo Dominus, tamquam quaestionis determinator, et amicos Iob redarguit de hoc quod non recte sentiebant, et ipsum Iob de inordinato modo loquendi, et Eliud de inconvenienti determinatione" (*Expositio*, 38. 5-17, my emphasis).

243. See n. 240.

244. "... quia scilicet divinam inspirationem in hac vita non possumus clare percipere sed cum quadam obumbratione sensibilium similitudinum" (*Expositio*, 38. 31-34). Note reference to Dionysius in this passage; and see previously p. 57 and n. 237.

245. It should be noted that according to Aquinas an opinion can be said to be held by faith only when it succeeds an intellectual apprehension and that faith precedes hope and charity in the temporal order of the theological virtues. "Per fidem autem apprehendit intellectus ea quae sperat et amat. Unde oportet quod ordine generationis fides praecedat spem et caritatem" (*Summa*, Iᵃ-IIᵃᵉ, Q. 62, a. 4).

246. "Ubi considerandum est quod Dominus operationem suam quam exercet in malos circa superbos manifestare incepit et in superbis narrationem terminat, ut ostendat hoc praecipue Iob fuisse timendum ne diabolus, qui eum expetierat ad tentandum, praecipue eum ad superbiam inducere conaretur ut sic transferretur in regnum ipsius, et ideo cavere debebat affectum et verba quae superbiam saperent" (*Expositio*, 41. 448-57).

247. See p. 56, n. 233 and p. 57, n. 241.

248. St. Albert's conclusion is similar to those of both Maimonides' and Aquinas'.

249. The distinction between *min 'adam* and *ba'd al-'adam* will be addressed further on in this chapter.

250. It is not surprising that in the Latin West no ambiguity is recognized in Plato's account since the *Timaeus* (in the form of Calcidius' translation and commentary) was the only available Platonic text at least until the twelfth century (and little else was in circulation until much later). It is less clear why no mention is made in the Arabic-language tradition of the tension between the *Timaeus* account of origin and those presented in *Laws* X. It should also be noted that the tentative nature of the *Timaeus* account, or its presentation as a "likely story," does not render it ambiguous for the medieval reader, since metaphysics is a speculative rather than a precise science. This is one, exemplary instance where the radical dissimilarity between modern (epistemological) metaphysics and medieval (noetic) metaphysics is clearly manifest.

251. Plato, *Timaeus*, 27c-38c, trans. R. G. Bury, Loeb Classical Library (Cambridge, Mass.: Harvard University Press, 1966).

252. See William Dunphy, "Maimonides and Aquinas on Creation: a Critique of Their Historians, "*Graceful Reason: Essays in Ancient and Medieval Philosophy Presented to Joseph Owens*, ed. Lloyd P. Gerson (Toronto: PIMS, 1983), pp. 361-79; and "Maimonides' Not So Secret Position on Creation," *Maimonides and His Times*, Studies in Philosophy and the History of Philosophy, ed. Eric Ormsby (Washington, D.C.: Catholic University of America Press, 1989). Dunphy's article also traces the history of this debate.

253. As will become evident later, the juxtaposition between something and nothing requires further nuance, especially how "nothing" may be understood.

254. Whereas Maimonides argues that, since time is an accident inhering in motion, it is logically posterior to some preexistent substratum, Aquinas argues that it is created simultaneously with the universe. As will become evident, this difference is not substantial.

255. *Guide*, 2, 13, 285.

256. As was pointed out in Chapter 1, Maimonides' deliberately "strange," or dispersed style of writing contributes greatly to the interpretative difficulties and conflicts rendering their resolution impossible.

257. By *Maimonides esotericism*, I am designating the issue of his orthodoxy, especially since his alleged heterodoxy is a persistent theme in the scholarship concerning the origin of the universe. Despite the fact that *first*, rather than *prime matter* is commonly used by Maimonidean scholars, I prefer the latter term both because I consider it more accurate, or rather less likely to be interpreted temporally, and because it is consistent with the general scholarship in the history of philosophy and hence would render the comparison with Aquinas less awkward. Since my concern is with the interpretation of the concept as presented by Maimonides and since this study is not concerned with the nature of supralunar existence, I shall not address the disagreement between Maimonides and Aquinas with respect to celestial hylomorphism and, hence, shall use the singular to designate prime matter, although, properly speaking, as will become evident in the following chapters, Maimonides may be suggesting a distinction within prime matter, perhaps even a duality.

258. An examination of the sources available to either Maimonides or Aquinas on any of Plato's or Aristotle's teachings is beyond both the thematic and disciplinary scope of this study.

259. *Guide*, 7.

260. Sarah Klein-Braslavy, *Perush ha-Rambam le-Sippur Beri'at ha-'Olam* (Jerusalem: ha-Ḥebra le-Ḥeker ha-Mikra be-Yisrael, 1978), pp. 27-35.

261. See the discussion of Elihu's and God's rebuke of Job in Chapter 2, pp. 50-52.

262. Alhough the general distinction of possible knowledge is into "that" (*quod*) and "what" (*quid*) something is, it may well be the case that "how" (quo-modo) more closely approaches Maimonides' use of *true reality* (either *ḥaqiqah*, *dhah*, or even, as here, a term related to *mahiyya*).

263. The difficulties alluded to here will be addressed in some detail in the final chapters.

264. Maimonides' designation *Mutakallimun* is not limited to Islamic Kalam nor to Islamic and Jewish Kalam only. Rather the term is used to designate anyone within the revealed traditions, Jew, Christian, and Moslem, who follows a certain method of apologetics defending principles of belief, as will become evident in the following discussion. See *Guide*, 1, 71, 175-84.

265. Strauss, "The Literary Character," passim; Berman, "Maimonides the Disciple," p. 163.

266. Note the distinction in temporal priority between "those communities in which philosophy has first risen . . ." and "[w]hen thereupon the community of Islam arrived and the *books of the philosophers were transmitted to it* . . ." (*Guide*, 1. 71. 177). See Abu Nasr Alfarabi, *Alfarabi's Book of Religion and Related Texts*, ed. Muhsin Mahdi (Beirut: Dar El-Machreq, 1968), pp. 46-47; and *Alfarabi's Book of Letters*, ed. Muhsin Mahdi (Beirut: Dar El-Machreq, 1970), pp. 131-34, and compare Berman, ibid.

267. *Guide*, 1, 71, 178.

268. Ibid.

269. *Guide*, 1, 71, 179.

270. *Guide*, 1, 71, 175-84.

271. In a manner of speaking, the early Mutakallimun exhibit one mode of hubris discussed in the exposition on Job.

272. The expression *merely as a tool* is used here to distinguish between practice ignorant of the inherent integrity of the discipline and what I describe as prudent practice in the previous chapters. The use of philosophy "merely as a tool" denies *ipso facto* a possible harmony between reason and revelation as well as the unity of truth.

Expediency, independent of considerations of excellence, dictates such a practice. This is one example of the difference between the Sophistic and Socratic use of rhetoric.

273. *Guide*, 2, 7, 266.

274. Dunphy's articles, especially "Maimonides' Not So Secret Position . . ." take particular issue with the claim that the theological and philosophical positions are contradictory. Cf. Warren Harvey, "A Third Approach to Maimonides' Cosmogony-Prophetology Puzzle," *Harvard Theological Review* 74, no. 3 (1981): 287-301.

275. Davidson, "Maimonides Secret Position," p. 20.

276. Ibid., p. 36. Cf. Alfred L. Ivry, "Beri'at ha-'Olam le-fi ha-Rambam," Forthcoming in a Festschrift in Honour of Shlomo Pines (Jerusalem: University Press). Despite the different focus of Ivry's article, in my opinion, his conclusion is essentially identical with Davidson's. There is a shorter English version of this article entitled "Maimonides on Creation," in *Creation and the End of Days* (proceedings of the 1984 meeting of the Academy for Jewish Philosophy); eds. D. Novak and N. Samuelson, 1986. I refer to the Hebrew rather than the English version since the former includes a more thorough philological account.

277. Although few texs afford the reader the luxury of arriving at such a determination, Maimonides' own discussion of contradictions in the Introduction to *Guide*, 1, at the very least, facilitates precisely such a discernment.

278. Davidson, "Maimonides Secret Position," p. 19.

279. Although from an Aristoelian perspective the substratum precedes time and motion only *to logo* or *to einai* rather than *to chrono*, if Maimonides, in fact, believes the biblical position to affirm creation *ex nihilo*, then his is not only a logical or epistemic claim, but also an ontological one and will include priority of genesis or order.

280. It should be pointed out that Davidson's assertion that Aristotle's position denies that God is possessed of will represents his own interpretation rather than Maimonides'. In his outline of the Aristotelian position in *Guide*, 2, 13, 284, Maimonides interprets it to affirm a divine will, but not an unconditioned one. It seems to me that Maimonides' opinion that the Aristotelian position does not deny divine will is an additional factor in the explanation why he maintained that the Platonic and Aristotelian positions are identical.

281. Davidson, "Maimonides Secret Position," p. 21.

282. Davidson's use of necessity seems to follow Aristotle's (*De Interpretaione*) logical modal rather than Plato's *Timaeus*, whose demiurge may lack jelousy but is, without a doubt, bound by necessity. In fact, I am unaware of any ancient Greek thinker whose undersanding of divinity separates it from *anagke*.

283. Properly speaking, medieval Judaism has no theology, but rather, has a science of legal practices. Hence, it must be emphasized that the term may be used only for the sake of convenience and in order to facilitate translation into common idiom or

comparisons between the Jewish and Christian traditions. But, it should be remembered that the 'translation' is inaccurate and hence, that conclusions based upon it will always conceal more dissimilarities than disclose similarities. This is just one example of why I refrain from attempting a comparison between Maimonides' and Aquinas' understanding of providence in relation to divine knowledge.

284. If we apply Maimonides' conclusions in this context to the early Mutakallimun following the conclusions drawn previously, they can be grouped with the philosophers with respect to implications, even though they attempt to defend the biblical position.

285. The distinction between rational and natural possibility is a principle of Jewish biblical interpretation since Saʿadia Gaon outlined his canons of interpretation. Saʿadia argued that the class of rational impossibilities demands figurative interpretation of teachings of the Torah. Saʿadia Gaon, *The Book of Beliefs and Opinions (Kitab al Amanat wal I'tiqadat)*, trans. Samuel Rosenblatt (New Haven, Conn.: Yale University Press, 1948), especially Chapter 7.

286. *Guide*, 3. 8. 432. Although Maimonides' personal 'aversion' to matter can be gleaned in all discussions of matter, he valiantly attempts to disregard it. I shall return to this problem further on in this chapter.

287. Again one should recall that Maimonides' Plato is a florilegia composed of many accounts and misinterpretations. For example, no term for *matter* occurs in the *Timaeus*, although Aristotle, in *On Generation and Corruption*, III, 2, 329a23, identifies the "nursemaid" (*tithene*) with [*prote*] *hyle*. See J. Skemp, "*hyle* and *hypodoxe*," in *Aristotle and Plato in the Mid-Fourth Century* (Goteborgy, 1960), pp. 201-12.

288. Quoted by Shlomo Pines in "Translator's Introduction: The Philosophical Sources of *The Guide of the Perplexed*," *Guide*, lix. This statement will be discussed at some length in the final chapter.

289. The restriction of the domain of philosophy implied here will be discussed in the final chapter.

290. *Guide*, 2, 13, 285; my emphasis. It should be noted that, however "corrupt" Maimonides' Plato is, he is sensitive to the Ancient Greek concurrence beween divinity and necessity. Given that such a necessity is ontological, its consequences are simply unacceptable to Maimonides for whom nothing essential can be understood, let alone said, about God.

291. "My purpose in this chapter is to make clear that Aristotle possesses no demonstration for the world being eternal, as he understands this. Moreover he is not mistaken with regard to this" (*Guide* 2, 15, 289 ff).

292. For a study of Maimonides relations to Kalam with respect to 'possibility' see, Ivry, "Maimonides on Possibility," passim.

293. *Guide*, 2, 17, 297-98. It should be noted that here Maimonides is not deny-

ing inference from actuality to potentiality in the same *temporal* order. Rather, he is denying inference from the temporal to the ontological order.

294. See Aristotle, *Metaphysics* 995a1-6, for the strangeness and unintelligibility of the unfamiliar.

295. *Guide*, 2, 17, 294-98.

296. The use of *laws* here should not be confused with post-Newtonian notions of natural laws. See David Lachterman, "Laying Down the Law: The Theologico-Political Matrix of Spinoza's Physics," *Leo Strauss's Thought*, ed. Alan Udof (Boulder, Colo.: Lynne Reimer, 1991), pp. 123-58.

297. It should be emphasized, however, that at the same time as he underlines the distinction between the archeological and the temporal orders, Maimonides also insists that conclusions which conflict with the temporal order of being are strictly inadmissible.

298. *Guide*, 2, 17, 298.

299. *Guide*, 2, 21, 314-17.

300. Provided, of course, that we acknowledge that the universal abstract concepts forming the basis for theoretical knowledge are abstracted from initial sensible perceptions as well as primary intuitions.

301. See Ivry, "Maimonides on Possibility," especially pp. 78-84. As noted earlier, however, Ivry does not develop the argument but rather hesitates in his conclusion. In fact, in a later article, "Beri'at ha-'Olam," he honestly questions the conclusions reached here, notably, those distancing Maimonides from the philosophical tradition.

302. Emil Fackenheim, "The Possibility of the Universe in al-Farabi, Ibn-Sina and Maimonides," *PAAJR* 16 (1946-47): 39-70; reprinted in *Essays in Medieval Jewish and Islamic Philosophy*, ed. Arthur Hyman (New York, 1977).

303. Ibid., p. 62.

304. Ivry, "Beri'at ha-'Olam," p. 4. As Ivry points out, although Maimonides makes use of Aristotle's discussions of origin and cause in *Metaphysics* V, xxiv, 1023a26-b11, to draw a distinction between *min* and *ba'd* (from and after) in the sense of from nothing and after non-existence, he is not consistent in the use of either term. Notwithstanding, Ivry emphasizes Maimonides' special use of *after* in order to reach his conclusion.

305. Ivry, ibid., p. 17.

306. Ibid.

307. Ivry admits that great caution must be exercised in describing this 'condition', that it is inaccessible to human knowledge with the exception of the description offered by him, and that his arguments cannot be supported sufficiently by the actual terminology used since Maimonides' articulation is inconsistent.

308. *Guide*, 1, 28, 61.

309. See pp. 68-72.

310. I do not believe that God, for Maimonides, can be placed in, even if at the culminaion of, the order of Being. Hence, on the one hand, I doubt that Aristotle's *energeia* is a fitting term for Maimonides' God and, on the other hand, that the *steresis-energeia* contrariety is the most urgent question concerning God's creation of prime matter.

311. Note that this conclusion is consistent with Aristotle's claim that no science can prove its own principles.

312. *Guide*, 2, 17, 297.

313. For one example of the nature of the difficulty attendant upon the diversity of discussions of creation, see Anton C. Pegis, "A Note on St. Thomas, *Summa Theologica*, 1, 44, 1-2," *Mediaeval Studies* 8 (1946): 159-68.

314. It can be argued that the very wording of the question biases the outcome since *creatum* can designate nothing other than a created entity. This is not surprising since the *Summa* was written for a specifically Christian audience.

315. Again, note the ontological rather than logical status of Aquinas' claim. I hasten to add, though, that I do not believe that any of Aquinas' proofs for God's existence is an ontological proof.

316. Pegis, "A Note on St. Thomas," p. 166.

317. "Sicut igitur generatio hominis est ex non ente quod est non homo, ita creatio, quae est emanatio totius esse, est ex non ente quod est nihil" (*Summa*, Iᵃ Pars, Q. 45, a. 1). Earlier in the response, the text has "emanatio totius entis", rather than "emanatio totius esse." Although, in this context, prior to individuation, a distinction between *ens* and *esse* is irrelevant, the distinction becomes essential for understanding Aquinas' differentiation of matter from privation. This distinction will be discussed in some detail later. Note that Aquinas' explanation seems to follow Aristotle's distinction between contradiction and contrariety, i.e., between not being-a-man and being a non-man. Genesis in the natural order is always from contraries rather than contradictories.

318. It should be noted that the "activity" understood as emanation is a manifestation of an *energeia* that is, at the very least, a contradictory of *dunamis*. As will become clear in the discussion of prime matter later, Aquinas overcomes the difficulty of associating God, as the creator of matter, with evil, by drawing a very clear distinction between matter and privation.

319. See *Summa*, Iᵃ Pars, Qs. 44-45 and 65, especially aa. 3-4. It cannot be overemphasized that, properly speaking, no being other than God can *create*. As pointed out earlier, from an Aristotelian perspective, creation is the contradictory of generation. It should also be noted, however, that this is a rather crude, imprecise formulation since, properly speaking, creation is also the origin of the possibility of contradiction and,

hence, exceeds philosophical understanding and language.

320. For a history of the question see, Dunphy, "Maimonides and Aquinas on Creation," especially pp. 364-65.

321. Mark D. Jordan, *Ordering Wisdom: The Hierarchy of Philosophical Discourses in Aquinas*, (Notre Dame, Ind.: Notre Dame University Press, 1986). See especially, Part 2, 3.3-3.5, 98-113.

322. An inquiry into the nature and hierarchy of the sciences is beyond the scope of this study. My concern here is restricted to underlining the limits of demonstrative reason. It should be noted, however, that Aquinas is following the aforementioned Aristotelian claim that no science can demonstrate its own principles.

323. *Summa*, Iᵃ Pars, Q. 46, a. 1.

324. Aristotle, *Organon*, vol. 2, *Topica*, 104b1-20.

325. "Dicendum quod mundum non semper fuisse, sola fide tenetur, et demonstartive probari non potest; sicut et supra de mysterio Trinitatis dictum est" (*Summa*, Iᵃ Pars, Q. 46, a. 2); cf. ibid. a. 1. Aquinas position is far more radical than Maimonides' since the latter's position, at least in principle, does not exclude the possibility of some mode of 'understanding', or of providing a reasonable account of creation. This is but another example of the difference between the Christian notion of faith and the Jewish understanding of belief.

326. ". . . abstrahit ab hic et nunc; propter quod dicitur quod "universalia sunt ubique et semper" (*Summa*, Iᵃ Pars, Q. 46, a. 2).

327. Aquinas must be referring here to things pertaining to God alone.

328. "Unde mundum incoepisse est credibile, non autem demonstrabile vel scibile" (*Summa*, Iᵃ Pars, Q. 46, a. 2).

329. Given the tenuous "political" climate of the thirteenth century universities and given his familiarity with the Jewish and Islamicate philosophical traditions, it is clear that Aquinas is fully aware of the fact that the danger consequent upon improper use of philosophy in defence of the faith is two directional; namely, both ridicule on the part of nonbelieving philosophers and prohibition of the philosophical endeavor on the part of religious authority.

330. ". . . scilicet caelum empyreum, materia corporalis, quae nomine terrae intelligitur, tempus, et natura angelica" (*Summa*, Iᵃ Pars, Q. 46, a. 3). The change in tone between all previous discussions and the one in article three is rather striking.

331. *Quaestiones disputatae de potentia* (Rome: Marietti, 1953), vol. 2.

332. Since I think that Pegis has demonstrated sufficiently the consistency between the *Summa* and the *De Potentia*, I shall address neither the question of the seeming contradiction between these texts nor their respective dates of composition.

333. In *De potentia* it becomes clear why Aquinas claims that the angelic nature was created simultaneously with the empyrean heaven, corporeal matter, and time since secondary causality requires the preexistence of an actuality or beings in act who, nevertheless, are other than God.

334. "*Nos autem ponimus*, quod a Deo procedunt res per modum scientiae et intellectus, secundum quem modum nihil prohibet ab uno primo et simplici Deo multitudinem immediate provenire, secundum quod sua sapientia continet universa" (*De potentia*, Q. 3, a. 4, respondeo, p. 46).

335. Aquinas' understanding of the problematic relation between *esse commune* and *esse tantum* will be discussed in the final chapter.

336. See the discussion of natural and rational possibility on pp. 71-76.

337. Note that no contradiction is involved in the affirmation of miracle here since it is extra-rational and natural and since it does not alter the "laws" of nature. The entire discussion of possibility and the limits of demonstration also indicate that there are no grounds for arguing that Aquinas held that creation *ex nihilo* can be demonstrated.

338. "Dicendum quod firmiter tenendum est mundum non semper fuisse, sicut fides catholica docet. Nec hoc potest aliqua physica demonstratione efficaciter impugnari" (*De potentia*, Q. 3, a. 17, respondeo, p. 93).

339. The Peripatetic position used by Aquinas is identical to one of the arguments presented by Maimonides to refute the later Aristotelians' claims for demonstrability; namely, that the divine will cannot be understood as hindered from any activity without violating the rational concept of God.

340. *Opera Omnia, De Principiis Naturae ad fratrem Sylvestrum*, Editori di San Tommaso, Commissio Leonina (Rome: 1976), vol. 43; and *Opuscula philosophica* (Rome: Marietti, 1954), pp. 121-28.

341. "Causalitas autem entis non se extendit nisi ad entia. Sic igitur secundum eos causalitas entis non se extendebat ad materiam primam, ad quem tamen se extendit causalitas boni. Cuius signum est quod ipsa maxime appetit bonum. Proprium autem est effectus ut convertatur per desiderium in suam causam. Sic igitur bonum est universalior et altior causa quam ens, quia ad plura se extendit eius causalitas" (*De Div. Nom.*, Chap. III, l. u. 226).

342. ". . . id quod est primum subiectum in effectibus, id est materia prima, sit effectus solius primae causae quae est bonum, causalitate secundarum causarum usque ad hoc non pertingente" (*De Div. Nom.*, Chap. IV, l. 2, 296).

343. ". . . <non ens>, propter privationem adiunctam" (*De Div. Nom.*, Chap. IV, l. 2, 295).

344. ". . . unde materia prima desiderat bonum, secundum quod desiderium nihil aliud esse videtur quam privatio et ordo ipsius ad actum" (*De Div. Nom.*, Chap. IV, l. 2, 296).

345. It seems clear to me that Aquinas realized that an Aristotelian metaphysics of being necessarily led to a denial of sublunar providence.

346. ". . . proprie loquendo quod est in potentia ad esse accidentale dicitur subiectum, quod vero est in potentia ad esse substantiale dicitur *proprie* materia: Quod autem illud quod est in potentia ad esse accidentale dicatur subiectum, signum est quia dicuntur esse accidentia in subiecto" (*De Prin. Nat.*, Chap. 1, 20-25). Further on, in Chapter 2, Aquinas explains that "privatio non dicitur nisi de determinato subiecto" (Chap. 2, 30-31). The Marietti edition differs substantially from the Leonine in this paragraph. Although in other sections the different readings do not change the meaning of the text, in the first sentence quoted here the meaning emerging out of the Leonine edition is inaccurate. The Marietti edition reads: ". . . proprie loquendo, illud quod est in potentia ad esse substantiale, dicitur materia *prima*" (Chap. 1, 339). Clearly, when principles of generation and corruption are discussed, the matter in question cannot be "*proprie materia*," since this would indicate formed matter. It seems as if the Leonine editors read the abbreviation adverbially rather than as an adjective modifying *matter.*

347. "Ad hoc ergo quod sit generatio tria requiruntur: scilicet ens potentia quod est materia, et non esse actu quod est privatio, et id per quod fit actu, scilicet forma. . . . Sunt igitur tria principia nature, scilicet materia, forma et privatio, quorum alterum, scilicet forma, est id ad quod est generatio, alia duo sunt ex parte eius ex quo est generatio. Unde materia et privatio sunt idem subiecto, sed differunt ratione" (*De. Prin. Nat.*, Chap. 1, 342; Chap. 2, 343; Leonine edition, Chap. 1, 68-71, Chap. 2, 1-6). See *In octo libros Physicorum Aristotelis Expositio*, (Rome: Marietti, 1954), Bk. I: VII, l. 13, and Bk. IX, l. 15; and *In Meta.*, Bk. I, l. 12; Bk. VII, l. 2; Bk. VIII, l. 4; and Bk. XII, l. 2.

348. It is clear here that Aquinas, at the very least, modifies Aristotle's position that prime matter is the *contradictory* of form, privation its contrary. That is, in Aquinas' view, prime matter is constitutive of natural substance and hence of every mode of existence, privation a necessary accident concommitant with particular existence. Privation is indeed the contrary of a particular form, but that contrariety originates in an originary contrariety and is thus delimited by it. For designated matter, of which privation is a contrary, is an actuality.

349. However tempting it may be to draw further conclusions from *Metaphysics* X,x, Aristotle's *nous* is the good and *arche* of universal order strictly as the moving cause.

350. John M. Rist, "Plotinus on Matter and Evil," *Phronesis* 6 (1961): 154-66, quote on p. 160, my emphasis.

351. See in particular, *Nicomachean Ethics* 10. 8-9. 1178a8-1181b23; and David Ross' introductory essay.

352. The previous chapter has sufficiently demonstrated that, at least for Maimonides and Aquinas (if not for Ibn-Sina), an irreconcilable conflict existed between Aristotle and revelation on the question of cosmogenesis.

353. As will become evident later, Maimonides reinstitutes the tension at the

level of knowing, or reinscribes matter as a hinderance to that kind of perfection that constitutes the proper end of human life.

354. *Guide*, 1. 7. 32.

355. The question whether or not this statement is in tension with Maimonides' discussion of "a portion in the world to come" in "Pereq Heleq" (*Perush ha-Mishnah: Nezikin*, ed. Joseph D. Kafih [Jerusalem: Mossad ha-Rav Kook, 1964], "Sanhedrin," p. 10) is beyond the scope of the present inquiry. I should add, however, that, properly speaking, affirmations or denials of principles of the Torah requires some degree of intellectual perfection. Relative degrees of perfection in relation to principles of the Torah and immortality will be discussed in Chapter 6.

356. For the meaning of *devil*, see the discussion of Satan as the evil inclination in Chapter 2, pp. 48-49.

357. *Guide*, 1, 7, 33; my emphasis. Maimonides' use of the term *engendering* or *begetting* here suggests that he views the begetting of harm as the contrary of the begetting of knowledge. Conversely, absence of knowledge seems to necessarily entail here the 'begetting' of harm.

358. Given Maimonides' criticism of Plato's use of parables in the letter to Samuel Ibn Tibbon, his approbation of Plato's figurative designation of matter and form, respectively, as the male and female principles is striking, especially since the language used recalls Maimonides' previous discussions and judgments. (Maimonmides' source here for the Platonic position is clearly some version of Aristotle's *agrapha dogmata*.)

359. *Guide*, 3, 8, 431.

360. The importance of attraction and repulsion in Maimonides' moral psychology will be discussed in the following chapters.

361. The extent of Maimonides' admiration for the ascetic rejection of material pleasures is best exemplified by his disdain for communal dining. See his approbation of Phineas ben Yair's refusal to eat at Judah the Prince's house, *Guide*, 3. 8. 434. This attitude is especially striking in view of Jewish Law of commemorative celebrations. Although these types of discussion are clearly at odds with Maimonides' medical writings and counsel for moderation in the "Eight Chapters," all of which are more 'Aristotelian', it seems to me that the disdain for matter is taken to a greater length than would be necessary for pedagogic reasons. Coversely, the length to which Maimonides takes the admonitions against matter does seem to suggest that he may have believed that material potency was not impotant.

362. *Guide*, 3, 8, 433. Here again is an indication that Maimonides considered at least some matter potent over form. As will become evident later, few individuals are endowed with 'divine' matter, many with 'earthly' matter.

363. The distinction between necessary and unnecessary pleasures echoes Plato's *Republic* 8 as well as the *Philebus*, as is also the highly 'poetic' language used.

364. *Guide*, 3, 8, 433; my emphasis.

365. The quesion of Maimonides' departure from the Aristotelian counsel to moderation will be resumed in the final chapter when discussing prophetic excess.

366. *Guide*, 3, 8, 435.

367. As will become evident in the discussion of divine law in Chapters 5 and 6, in my opinion, Maimonides' pessimistic, non-Aristotelian, view of matter can explain his denial of a natural rational law.

368. This is one important and exemplary reason why I refrain from using the term *epistemology* and replace it either with *epistemic psychology* or with *noetic* (depending upon the context) throughout this study.

369. *Guide*, 3, 9, 436.

370. Although Maimonides is curiously silent about the nature of Mosaic prophecy, it is possible to draw out some conclusions about it, which will be outlined in the final chapter. See *Guide*, 2, 45, 402-3, which is ambiguous and, as Pines points out in n. 72, can be interpreted either way.

371. As will become evident, the basis of Maimonides' critique is identical to that used in his critique of the Mutakallimun's teachings on creation; namely, that they disregarded the nature of what exists. See Chapter 3, passim.

372. Note that Maimonides uses *al-'adam* to designate relative privation, *al-'adama l-mahda l-mutlaq* absolute privation. See Ivry's discussion of the problem in "Beri'at ha-'Olam," passim. I do not think that we can reach conclusions concerning Maimonides' actual views strictly on the basis of linguistic consistency. Nor, as I have indicated in a number of places and will explore further in subsequent chapters, do I believe that contradictions are used only for the purpose of concealment, on the contrary.

373. *Guide*, 3. 10. 439.

374. It should be noted that this claim does not necessarily contradict the claim about those who possess only the "external human form," whose "choice of doing harm" is not true human agency.

375. *Guide*, 3, 10, 440.

376. See *Guide*, 2, 30, 358. I shall return to the difficulties inherent in the predication 'good' both later on in this chapter and in the following chapters. It should be noted that, although *benei adam* is the common Hebrew term for human beings, Maimonides' repetition of the rabbinic statement concerning the polysemy of the Torah may also be read to signify specifically Adam's descendants and thus allude to his claim that knowledge of good and evil is the consequence of Adam's disobedience.

377. A conclusion identical with one of the possibilities suggested by Davidson regarding creation.

378. This view will be consistent with Straussian interpretations.

379. See *Guide*, Introduction, pp. 17-20; Chapter 1, infra. Chapter 7 will shed further light upon necessary contradictions.

380. *Guide*, 3, 11, 440.

381. *Guide*, 3, 12, 443.

382. *Guide*, 3, 12, 445; my emphasis.

383. The nature of true apprehension and its essential relation to the necessary (unchanging) will be discussed in the final chapter.

384. Note that the argument presents the "service of kings" as aiming at superfluous luxuries. *Guide*, 3, 12, 446.

385. I shall discuss human ends in great detail in the final chapter. See *Commentary on the Mishnah, Nezikin*, ed. and trans. Joseph D, Kafih, "Introduction to Avot,: Chap. Five," (Jerusalem: Mosad ha-Rav Kook, 1964). English: *The Ethical Writings of Maimonides*, "Eight Chapters," trans. Raymond L. Weiss and Charles E. Butterworth (New York: New York University Press, 1975), pp. 60-104.

386. I shall discuss the problem consequent upon the failure to develop an account of the relation between the will and the intellect in the following chapter. For an analysis of some of the difficulties related to this problem evident in Islamicate philosophy, see Alfred, L. Ivry, "Destiny Revisited, Avicenna's Concept of Determinism," *Islamic Philosophy and Theology: Studies in Honour of George F. Hourani*, ed. Michael E. Marmura (Albany: SUNY Press, 1984), pp. 160-304; and "The Will of God and the Practical Intellect of Man in Averroes' Philosophy," *Israel Oriental Studies* 9 (1979): 377-91.

387. *Guide*, 3, 12, 448.

388. The following chapter will address the nature of human knowledge and especially the relation between imagination and reason in some detail.

389. See *Guide*. 2, 40, 381-82.

390. *De Div. Nom.*, Chap. I, 1. 3, 87; Chap. III, 1. u, 227; Chap. 4, 1. 2, 295-96.

391. Aquinas' account is not without tension insofar as he clearly grounds the good as an ontological category and denies that 'privilege' to evil. That is, he does not seem to fully acknowledge evil as the *real* or ontological contrary of the good so that, whereas evil is granted a logical status, the status of the good is, first and foremost, ontological. This is not the place to develop a comprehensive inquiry into the difficulty, but the tension may be attenuated if we clearly distinguish between final and efficient causality. Nontheless, it is far from clear to me that Aquinas' cosmogeny can accomodate this distinction easily at the level of first order causality.

392. ". . . quia de ratione eius quod est contrarium virtuti est malum, nec inveni-

tur in alio genere quod aliquae species distinguantur per differentiam boni et mali, nisi in habitibus animae virtuosis et vitiosis" (*De Div. Nom.*, Chap. IV, l. 15, 486).

393. ". . . impressio divini luminis in nobis. Unde patet quod lex naturalis nihil aliud est quam participatio legis aeternae in rationali creatura" *Summa*, I^a-II^{ae}, Q. 91, a. 2).

394. For the relation between the good and the beautiful, and especially with respect to desire, see *De Div. Nom.*, Chap. IV, ll. 5-14. See *Scriptum super libros Sententiarum* (Paris: Mandonnet, 1929), Bk. I, d. 31, q. 2, a. 1, ad 4um, henceforth, *In I Sent.*; *De Veritate*, Q. 22, a. 1, ad 12um, where Aquinas states that the desire for the good is simultaneously a desire for beauty and peace.

395. See *De Div. Nom.*, Chap. IV, l. 1, especially 286, where Aquinas distinguishes between angelic and human ignorance, explaining that the former is unrelated to the stain of sin. Two types of ignorance ought to be distinguished; namely, culpable and non-culpable ignorance. The former pertains to human beings only and, as will become evident, designates a willful ignoring in the particular case of what one knows as a universal truth; the latter pertains to both angels and human beings designating a lack of knowledge that exceeds one's natural capacity.

396. Henceforth, ignorance.

397. Although it is clear that error, as the source of disunity, disrupts the natural order, Aquinas does not account for its consequences nor for its remedies in this context. As will become clear in the discussion of the will at the end of this chapter (pp. 107-117) as well as in the discussion of the relation between divine and natural law in Chaper 6, I believe that the only remedy for error 'open' to Aquinas is revelation. This will also be the locus that mitigates significantly the ontological disagreements between Maimonides and Aquinas.

398. *De Div. Nom.*, Chap. IV, ll. 19-22, especially l. 19, 541. See *Summa*, I^a Pars, Q. 83; I^a-II^{ae}, Qs. 27-28.

399. It is important to note, however, that although some features of the critique do not seem to be immediately relevant with respect to Maimonides, e.g., the separation between particular and universal natures, nevertheless the conclusions are. This seeming inconsistency, in my opinion, is due to the problems inherent in Maimonides' twofold ontology, as outlined previously.

400. ". . . vis activa primi corporis, quod est primum in genere causarum naturalium" (*De Div. Nom.*, Chap. IV, l. 21, 550). See *In I Sent.*, d. 8, q. 5, a. 1; *Quaestiones de Anima*, ed. J. H. Robb (Toronto: PIMS, 1968), Q. 1, ad 2; and J. Owens, C.Ss.R., "Diversity and Community of Being," *Mediaeval Studies* 22 (1960): 257-302. It should be noted that Aquinas' claim here pertains equally to a critique of 'Platonic' separate Forms and to any ontological discontinuity. For Aquinas, *analogia entis* is, first and foremost, ontological. In other words, whereas for Maimonides the fact that "being can be said in many ways" exhibits the radicaly eqivocal status of being, for Aquinas it exhibits its analogical, even though onesided, continuity.

401. ". . . posita enim causa ex necessitate sequitur effectus nisi aliquis impediat. Sed hoc videmus esse falsum: *multae enim* animarum respiciunt *ad bonum*, quod non posset esse si *materia* totaliter attraheret eas *ad malum*. Unde manifestum est quod *malum in animabus non est ex materia, sed ex inordinato* motu liberi arbitrii; quod est ipsum peccatum" (*De Div. Nom.*, Chap. IV, l. 21, 566).

402. See Owens, "Diversity and Community," passim; and idem "The Unity in the Thomistic Philosophy of Man," *Mediaeval Studies* 25 (1963): 54-82 (passim).

403. *De Div. Nom.*, Chap. IV, l. 21, 555.

404. If the two desires for disproportionate perfections are to constitute moral evils and if error, by definition, cannot be freely chosen, then, properly speaking, both desires must originate in ignorance. That is, error, as the cause of disunity or disruption of the natural order, must be reduced at the order of causaliy to some prior ignorance as its first and efficient cause and must formally resemble it, if the conserving order of providence is the order of nature or necessity. As will become evident at the end of this chapter and in Chapter 6, owing to the external nature of its origin, an external agent, i.e., divine law, would be needed to remedy error. And, see *infra.*, Chapter 5, the section on "Aquinas and the Harmony of the Soul."

405. I shall discuss these aspects of providence in some detail in the final chapter.

406. Since a discussion of grace is beyond the scope of a philosophical inquiry I shall not address its role in human perfection. It should be emphasized, however, that it forms an essential part of the divine gift, according to Aquinas. Notwithstanding, like law, as an extrinsic principle of action, grace requires rational assent.

407. *Opera Omnia*, "Quaestiones Disputatae De Malo," ed. Pierre-Marie Gils, Commissio Leonina (Rome: 1982), vol. 23.

408. *De Malo*, Q. 1, aa. 1-5.

409. ". . . quia anima non tenetur nec potest attendere ad huiusmodi regulam semper in actu" (*De Malo*, Q. 1, a. 3, 274-75).

410. ". . . de ratione culpe est quod sit secundum voluntatem, de ratione autem pene est quod sit contra voluntatem" (*De Malo*, Q. 1, a. 4, 108-10).

411. *De Malo*, Qs. 6-7.

412. ". . . forma rei naturalis est forma individuata per materiam; unde et inclinatio ipsam consequens est determinata ad unum, sed forma intellecta est universalis sub qua multa possunt comprehendi; unde cum actus sint in singularibus, in quibus nullum est quod adaequet potentiam universalis, remanet inclinatio voluntatis indeterminate se habens ad multa" (*De Malo*, Q. 6, a. 1, 284-92). It should be noted that *comprehended* here also, and quite precisely, means "gathered."

413. *Opera Omnia*, "Quaestiones Disputatae De Veritate," ed. Antoine Dondaine, Commissio Leonina (Rome: 1970), vol. 22.

414. "Respondeo. Dicendum quod voluntas et intellectus sunt diversae potentiae, et ad diversa genera potentiarum pertinentes" (*De Veritate*, Q. 22, a. 10, 49-51).

415. In the following chapter, I shall address the full range of relations existing between the will and the intellect in the perfection of the soul, especially, the role of judgment in practical intellection.

416. Aquinas uses these adverbs in the same manner as Maimonides uses *equivocally* and *univocally*. *Qua* appetite, whose motion is caused by an external object, the human will is indistinct from that of the animals or rather, more precisely, the will is not distinctly human. *Aliqualiter*, however, is not used as a radical or pure equivocation.

417. For an elaboration on *lex fomitis*, see *Summa*, I*-II*, Q. 91, a. 6; Q. 93, a. 3, ad 1.

418. Note that the disordered inclination constituting the *lex fomitis*, or concupiscence, is an ordered inclination belonging to all sensitive creatures, except human beings.

419. As already indicated in previous chapters, no medieval thinker can be said to have an epistemology since there is a plurality of *epistemai*, each appropriate to a different subject matter. Although both Maimonides and Aquinas discuss the ordering of the sciences in various contexts, these discussions do not in themselves amount to a theory of cognition. Neither Aquinas' commentary on Aristotle's *De Anima* nor Maimonides' discussion of the soul in the "Eight Chapters" can be considered to constitute theories of cognition, just as Aristotle's *De Anima* does not constitute such a theory.

420. I am referring to the perfection of reason manifest as choosing the good exclusively as an end in itself, rather than to the habituation in right conduct out of either fear of punishment or desire for reward, neither of which is based upon knowledge and, hence, neither of which stems from a real desire for the good. My claim extends only to the epistemic priority of speculative perfection, rather than to the temporal order of acquisition. That is, prior to knowing that the good is not a proper object of the intellect or that it is a relative rather than a universal notion, one has to have acquired speculative knowledge to the extent naturally possible. As is the case with all generalized statements, my introductory remarks can be open to dispute since they necessarily overlook differences between thinkers. For this, I beg the readers' forebearance. I hope that the following discussion of Maimonides will rectify the present oversimplified treatment of the relation between the two human perfections.

421. For an example, see, Ivry, "The Will of God," passim.

422. It is neither my intention nor within the scope of a philosophical inquiry to address the doctrinal differences between Judaism and Christianity that may account, in part, for the universalization of the attainability of perfection, made possible by the incarnate Christ.

423. The "Eight Chapters," p. 60; my emphasis.

424. Herbert Davidson argues that Maimonides is referring to a single source, namely, to al-Farabi, especially to his *Fusul al-Madani*. See Herbert Davidson, "Maimonides' *Shemonah Peraqim* and al-Farabi, *Fusul Al-Madani*," *Proceedings of the American Academy for Jewish Studies* 31 (1963): 33-50. Although al-Farabi's influences upon Maimonides are indisputable, I think that Maimonides' statement is more comprehensive and, at the very least, includes Aristotle as well. Maimonides' statement also anticipates the following discussions of the role of habituation in acquiring virtue as well as his discussion in *Guide* 1, 31, of hindrances to philosophical instruction, listing habit and upbringing (i.e., convention) as significant hindrances. I will return to a discussion of convention later.

425. The fact that the fullest discussion of the nature of the soul occurs in the context of a traditional text when coupled with the emphasis placed upon extra-traditional writings also undermines the arguments for a radical distinction between Maimonides' esoteric and exoteric writings. In addition, the absence of a full coherent discussion of the soul in the *Guide* supports my claim that Maimonides regarded the corpus of his writings as complementary, and hence, that the *Guide* cannot be viewed as a strictly esoteric text in the sense that it requires no supplement by other 'less philosophical' writings.

426. For the sake of convenience, and in order to avoid an archaic term, I shall henceforth use the term *faculty* for (*al-quwah, ha-khoah*) but it should be kept in mind that, properly speaking, all that the term signifies is a power or pure potentiality. The faculty is the specific *dunamis* made possible by a specific, determinate *entelechia* as the particular manifestation of the absolutely necessary *energeia* constituting the hierarchical order of the universe. That is why there is only a name in common between the *dunameis* of the palm's and the human souls.

427. Maimonides' claim in "Eight Chapters," 1, that the discernment between good and base actions belongs to the rational part of the soul *seems* to be in tension with his claim in Chapter 2 that moral virtues and vices are radically distinct from rational ones. The tension manifest in this context, which is characteristic of the entire 'ethical' account, will be addressed in some detail following the present summary of his psychology. At present, suffice it to emphasize the difference and consequent tension between "good" and "bad" as ontological and as moral categories.

428. The relation between the acquisition of the arts as the productive aspect of practical reason and its deliberative aspect concerning possibility clearly establish the relation between the so-called theoretical and practical reasoning as an internal, dynamic one. Thus understood, the question of the "good" and "bad" activity is a question of ontology or concerns the actual/existential possibility of bringing it into 'being' rather than its relation to some other, perhaps higher, and external moral end.

429. The "Eight Chapters," chap. 1, 64.

430. Since commandments and prohibitions are meant to habituate the human being into proper practice which may, or may not, become an acquired power of the soul and since their initial 'binding' force is rooted in an external power to punish or reward

a given practice, they cannot be effective with respect to activities intrinsic to the *human*, i.e., rational, soul that have no extrinsic expression. As will become evident in the discussion of divine law, the intellect can be said to 'obey a commandment' only if the commandment becomes an intrinsic principle of action.

431. Maimonides' account of the imaginative faculty follows Aristotle's *de Anima* III (428a12-13 and 19) quite closely. It also recalls Aristotle's *de Interpretatione*, II, 9 (18a28-19a23), where Aristotle underlines the fact that truth and falsity, necessity and possibility, must follow *actual existence*. After insisting upon the relation between actual existence and possibility, Maimonides severely criticizes the Mutakallimun who confused imaginative existence with possible existence. The "Eight Chapters," 63.

432. The "Eight Chapters," chap. 2, 65.

433. I intentionally refrain from rendering the term *al-Ḥikmah* by "wisdom" since, as will become evident in the final chapter, Maimonides emphasizes its equivocity, see *Guide*, 3, 54. The term is used in the medieval Islamicate and Jewish philosophical traditions to designate knowledge of the various sciences in a manner similar to the Latin use of *scientia*, in contradistinction to *sapientia*. The same term, however, is used generally in Hebrew to designate wisdom. It can also be used to designate phronesis.

434. A similar reticence is expressed at the end of Chapter 1 concerning a discussion of form, matter, the number of intellects, etc. One would be hard pressed to claim that this reticence is a mark of esotericism since all these topics are discussed in *Mishne Torah*: *Sefer ha-Mad'a*, an indisputably exoteric text, written in Hebrew.

435. Since, apart from the references to the material origins of the 'veils' to human knowledge, Maimonides does not address the imagination in the "Eight Chapters," I shall postpone further discussion of the imagination until the analysis of the *Guide*.

436. It should be noted that, strictly speaking, the realm of moral action is a-natural, since political existence, too, manifests human life in-between the divine and the beastly. As will become evident in the following chapters, this is one reason why Maimonides (like other Islamicate philosophers) considers the perfect city to be the one governed by divine law, and why he maintains that the perfect philosopher/legislator is the prophet.

437. The agent/patient relation clearly indicates the fact that the one acquiring moral habits is affectively or appetitively related to the one possessing reason.

438. Maimonides also claims that, properly understood, most of the commandments are aimed at disciplining the powers of the soul to the acquisition of the mean. Eight Chapters, Chap. 4, 72.

439. The "Eight Chapters," Chap. 4, 68, and Chap. 8, 83-95 passim.

440. The "Eight Chapters," Chap. 8, 84.

441. Since moral virtue is not a natural *habitus*, it seems inevitable that all conventional habituation would fail to some degree in the absence of the perfect legislator/prophet. As will become evident in the following chapter, one aspect or manifestation of the noetic perfection that is prophecy is the perfection of the imagination.

442. See Chapter 4, for a discussion of Maimonides' denial that good and evil are essential predicates or properties of things.

443. The "Eight Chapters," Chap. 5, 75.

444. Maimonides, here, is clearly blurring Aristotle's difference between virtue *simpliciter*, which, for Aristotle, too, is not a natural habit of the soul and continence and incontinence. It is possible that "the philosophers" discussed here do not include Aristotle. We shall return to this distinction in the following chapter in the discussion of 'ethics' proper.

445. The "Eight Chapters," Chap. 6, 79.

446. The "Eight Chapters," Chap. 6, 80.

447. Maimonides must be referring to Sa'adia Gaon and anyone who followed his division of the commandments and prohibitions of the Torah.

448. By concomitantly insisting that the mean is the manifestation of moral virtue and that moral virtue pertains only to the appetite, Maimonides is denying that the mean is a rational category. Since he also argues that most of the commandments aim at moderation, the explanation is internally consistent. Consistency, notwithstanding, none of the assertions provided by Maimonides are philosophically convincing, *inter alia*, because rational consistency does not enter into moral habituation, constancy does.

449. If no relation obtains between the rational and moral virtues, then Maimonides' failure to indicate that they have nothing but a name in common is, at best, an oversight. On the other hand, as will become evident in the following chapters, it may be possible that what is commonly understood by moral virtue, indeed, has only a name in common with rational virtue, whereas real moral virtue is, in fact, intellectual.

450. Since Maimonides does not attribute moral virtues to practical reason and, since, as will become evident in the following discussion of the *Guide*, he does not consider good and evil to be proper objects of reason, the objects of practical reason must be judgments about the necessity or contingency of past actions. These objects must serve as premises for discursive activity about future actions as either necessary, or possible, or impossible. Necessity and possibility with respect to actions, then, will have to constitute the ground for their goodness or baseness. As will become evident in the following chapter, the unruly desire for knowledge that Maimonides attributes to Joseph is "base" or "bad" precisely because it is a desire for what is actually or naturally impossible.

451. It also should be remembered that Maimonides states explicitly both in the "Eight Chapters" and in the *Guide* that he will not provide a full philosophical account

of the subject since the philosophers and the Sages have done it already. Thus, he draws the readers attention to the fact that the account has to be supplemented by other inquiries. His exegetical practice, which combines the teachings of both traditions, seems to indicate that neither the philosophers' teachings nor those of the Sages' suffice *per se*.

452. For a detailed discussion of the material intellect and of Maimonides' possible sources, see Alexander Altmann, "Maimonides on the Intellect and the Scope of Metaphysics," *Von der mittelalterlichen zur modernen Aufklärung*, Texts and Studies in Medieval and Early Modern Judaism 2 (Tubingen: J.C.B. Mohr (Paul Siebeck), 1987), pp. 60-129.

453. See "The Letter on Resurrection," *Crisis in Leadership: Epistles of Maimonides*, trans. Abraham Halcyon (Philadelphia: Jewish Publication Society of America, 1985), pp. 209-45. Original text: *Ma'amar Teḥiyyat ha-Metim*, ed. Joshua Finkle, *PAAJR* 9 (1939): 61-105 and 1-42.

454. *Guide*, 1, 72, 190.

455. For the history of the interpretations of Aristotle's distinction between the possible and actual intellect, see Altmann, "Maimonides on the Intellect"; cf. Herbert Davidson, "Averroes on the Material Intellect," *Viator* 17 (1986): 91-137. Rather than address it directly at this point (which I consider premature) Maimonides' own interpretation of the relation between possibility and actuality as it pertains to the human intellect will emerge from the following discussions. A direct discussion will be postponed to the final chapter.

456. *Guide*, 1, 40, 91. Note translator's note 22.

457. See *Guide* 1, 72, passim.

458. *Guide*, 1, 1, 22. Note Maimonides' identification of human apprehension (*al-'idrak al-ansani*), the true human reality or primary substance, with intellectual apprehension (*al-'idrak al-'aqli*), rather than with discursive ratiocination. The significance of this identification will be spelled out in the final chapter.

459. The notional status of the terms *image* and *likeness* indicate, for Maimonides, the immaterial status of the intellectual human form.

460. Note that Maimonides' example of an instance of a manifestly evil act is the uncovering of the genitals, *Guide*, 1. 2. 25. It should be noted that this example recalls Maimonides' distinction, in the "Eight Chapters," between acts designated as evil by the philosophers, such as murder and theft, and those that the Torah prohibits and that Maimonides described as being rationally and morally neutral in themselves. The significance of this distinction will be discussed in greater detail in the following chapter.

461. Adam's status, whether it is historical or parabolic, is not discussed in this context although later on in the *Guide* Maimonides states that the name *Adam* signifies the human form. It is ironic that material individuation not only distances human beings

from their proper intellectual form but also renders them less perfect than beasts *qua* natural beings since, unlike other natural entities, who attain their proper end unless some accidental cause intervenes, human beings do not posses by nature an appetitive faculty, a faculty of attraction and repulsion, of a kind proportionate to either their natural or their supranatural end.

462. Adam's imaginative desire may be akin to Joseph's unruly desire for knowledge and, as will become evident in the following chapters, may be an example of the intellectual *hubris* evident in Job. See Chapter 2.

463. Since the *act* of transgression originated in Adam's perfectly ordered human soul, Adam must be seen as the efficient cause of human knowledge of "good" and "evil" as well as all other conventional knowledge. In this light, unless Maimonides were to claim that there was some other beginning, prior to the beginning of time and history of creation, which he does not, the story of Adam, for Maimonides, must point to both the *aporia* of creation and to the paradox of human existence, of which both the "beginning" and "end" are a-natural or constitute radical breaks with the universe as it is or, more precisely, as it is known.

464. The radical distinction between modes of knowing will be discussed in the final chapter. Suffice it to point out, here, that there is a curious relation between the demand for certainty and adherence to external authority.

465. Although Maimonides does not state it clearly, it seems that the absence of desire applies both to the human species as a whole and to individuals. Viewed as a member of the human species, the human being lacks the desire for objects of knowledge entirely beyond her or his species' capacity to know; viewed as an individual, one lacks the desire for objects exceeding one's particular capacity to know.

466. *Guide*, 1, 21, 49.

467. As will become evident when I discuss the difference between human perfections in the final chapter, it is precisely the lack of identity between the object of longing and the true 'object' of worship that 'condemns' the multitude of believers, including some of the respected Mutakallimun, to their lowly 'perfections'. See "Letter on Resurrection."

468. Actual perfection cannot be understood mathematically or quantitatively, possibility can. The acquired human form is not *more* perfect than the acquired animal form since they differ substantially. A quantitative comparison is simply a category mistake. That is why Maimonides insists on the equivocity of names applied to different species, e.g., the power of nutrition possessed by the palm's and the human souls.

469. *Guide*, 1, 31, 66. Note that "certainty" properly pertains to mathematics, whose objects are not actual existents.

470. Cf. Aristotle's *Metaphysics* passim, where Aristotle repeatedly underlines the difference between what is most known to us and what is clearest by nature. Perhaps the most poignant example is given in A Elatton, where Aristotle states: "[f]or as the

eyes of bats are to the light of day, so is the intellect of our soul (*psyches o nous*) to the objects which in their nature are most evident of all (*pros ta te phusei phanerotata panton*)," 993b9-11.

471. Prophetic knowledge will be discussed in the final chapter.

472. See Altmann, "Maimonides on the Intellect," both for Maimonides' sources and for his departure from them.

473. *Guide*, 1, 73, 209.

474. *Guide*, 1. 68. 164. Munk's French translation reads ". . . car la véritable être de l'intellect, c'est la *perception*." *Guide des Égarés*, 1, 68, 308. Since *'idrak* is unique to the intellect and is analogous to perception only if perception is taken to indicate immediacy, i.e., only if there is no distinction between subject and object of perception, which is questionable in the case of sensible perception, I prefer the term *apprehension*. I shall return to a discussion of *'idrak* in the final chapter. It may be helpful to note that *perception* is the term used by Spinoza to designate knowledge of the third kind, which is, in fact, similar to Maimonides' notion of *'idrak*.

475. As will become evident in the final chapter, the extension and degree of "certainty" obtaining in apprehension has been doubted. Although I do not believe that certainty is the appropriate description of the *quality* or kind of knowing designated by *'idrak*, I certainly disagree with the assumption that demonstrative certainty is the highest form of knowledge.

476. See pp. 116-119.

477. *Guide*, 2, 36, 372.

478. See *Guide*, 1, 72 and 2, 10-12.

479. *Guide*, 1, 73, 209. The act of the imagination disregards actual existence, that of the intellect both derives from and exhibits actual existence.

480. As will become evident in the following chapter, however, appetitive relations to divine law will still be mediated through the imagination so that the latter's original disposition will continue to be a determinant aspect in the possibility of perfection.

481. For a full bibliographic enumeration, see, *Ordering Wisdom* 115-18.

482. See *Ordering Wisdom* 115 and ff.

483. The diverse and sometimes conflicting examinations of participation in the thought of Aquinas are too numerous to quote in this context, especially since I am not relying on a specific text or texts at present. Apart from direct references to relevant texts in context, under the heading "Secondary Sources: Aquinas," the Bibliography will provide reference to a few texts that I have consulted. The final chapter will address participation in some detail.

484. It is important to note that by *twofold ontology* I do not mean dual ontology,

but two aspects of a single actuality, since, properly understood, being and good are the same *arche* causally manifest in two ways, *qua* form and *qua* end, respectively, although they interact efficiently.

485. The most striking criticism is the one found in *Sententia Libri Ethicorum*, VI, 1, 1119-1123, *Opera Omnia* XLVII (Rome: Iussu Leonis, 1969), where Aquinas criticizes Aristotle's distinction between the possible and the actual intellect. The significance of this criticism will emerge in the following discussion as well as in the following chapter.

486. Although a discussion of the divergent opinions concerning the human intellect is well beyond the scope of this study, it should be noted that Aquinas' criticism of Aristotle's *Ethics* VI, 4, echoes his discussion in *De Unitate Intellectus contra Averroistas*, *Opuscula Philosophica* (Rome: Marietti, 1954), pp. 59-90, as well as that in *Quaestiones de Anima*, ed. James H. Robb (Toronto: PIMS, 1968), especially Q. 3, pp. 77-88. Although a speculation whether or not the appreciation of the "danger" inherent in a real distinction between the possible and the active intellect preceded Aquinas' development of his psychology is futile, the connection between the concern with individual immortality and the critique of Aristotle cannot be overlooked. It also explains the presence of Neoplatonic elements in Aquinas' 'more Aristotelian' texts.

487. On difficulties inherent in commentaries in general see, Chapter 1, pp. 19-20. Concerning debates among Thomistic interpretations of the difficulties encountered in Aquinas' discussion(s) of the soul's knowledge, see *Ordering Wisdom* 125, n. 7.

488. In this context, Aquinas uses *anima intellectiva* rather than *intellectus*, presumably because with respect to psychology he is anticipating the debate in the following question (76) with the Platonists, wherein he denies the plurality of souls. This denial has yet to account for the relation between the agent and the possible intellect within the intellective soul. The term *anima intellectiva* also recalls Aristotle's *psuches o nous*.

489. "Non enim est operari nisi entis in actu; unde eo modo aliquid operatur, quo est" (*Summa*, I* Pars, Q. 75, a. 2).

490. "Si igitur principium intellectuale haberet in se *naturam* alicuius corporis, non posset omnia corpora cognoscere. Omne autem corpus habet aliquam *naturam* determinatam. Impossibile est igitur quod principium intellectuale sit corpus.—Et similiter impossibile est quod intellegat per organum corporeum, quia si esset, *natura* determinata illius organi corporei prohiberet cognitionem omnium corporeum" (*Summa*, I* Pars, Q. 75, a. 2, respondeo; emphasis added).

491. It should be noted that, in this context, Aquinas does not distinguish between *knowing* (*cognitio*) and *understanding* (*intelligere*), since understanding which is the principle of operations, governs the possibilities of knowing. Although the two ways of knowing are distinct, from the perspective of natural possibility, actuality (understanding) governs the possibility of knowing.

492. See *Summa*, I*, Pars, Q. 75, a. 2, ad 3[ium].

493. For an illuminating discussion of the diverse views concerning the status of the soul, see Anton C. Pegis, *St. Thomas and the Problem of the Soul in the Thirteenth Century* (Toronto: PIMS, 1978 [1934]).

494. *Summa*, I^a Pars, Q. 75, a. 7, response and ad 3^{ium}.

495. "Obiectum autem comparatur ad actum potentiae passivae, sicut principium et causa movens" (*Summa* I^a Pars, Q. 77, a. 3). Cf. Aristotle, *Metaphysics*, 9, passim. E.g., [i]t is evident, then, that in a sense the potency of acting (*poiein*) and of being acted upon (*paschein*) is one (1046a19-20).

496. As will become evident later, and in the following chapters, it is in virtue of the twofold aspect of the soul's powers that Aquinas would be able to depart from Aristotle's and Maimonides's ethics and argue that practical reason possesses its own first principles.

497. *Summa*, I^a Pars, Q. 77, a. 8.

498. See *Opera Omnia: Sentencia libri "De Anima,"* ed. Rene A. Gauthier, Commissio Leonina (Rome, 1959). Although it is not our concern here to show the congruence between the discussions of the respective hierarchical importance of the appetitive and locomotive powers in the *Summa* (I^a Pars, Q. 78) and the *De Anima*, it should be noted that these differences reflect the different *foci* of concern, i.e., the order of ends and the natural order of the object.

499. Aquinas' discussion of the internal senses follows Avicenna quite closely. He both refers to Avicenna's discussion of the soul in the *sed contra* and reproduces Avicenna's example of the sheep's perception of the harmful intention in the wolf, a perception not given in the immediate sensible form of the wolf.

500. For the sake of consistency and clarity I shall render sensible apprehension as perception so as not to confuse it with intelligible apprehension.

501. *Summa*, I^a Pars, Q. 78, a. 4.

502. Given Maimonides' insistence upon creation and his discussions of the material intellect, it would be misleading to claim that such a relation is absolutely impossible. Nonetheless, with respect to sublunar existence, such a relation may obtain only in the case of human beings and, even then, only with respect to very few individuals.

503. *Analogy* is used here strictly as an ontological category. For the logical status of *analogy* in Aquinas' works in relation to his ontology, see E. J. Ashworth, "Analogy and Equivocation in Thirteen-Century Logic: Aquinas in Context," *Medieval Studies* 54 (1992): 94-135, especially 122-30.

504. "Non enim potest esse quod una et eadem virtus sit diversorum subiectorum" (*Summa*, I^a Pars, Q. 79, a. 5).

505. ". . . intellectus separatus, secundum nostrae fidei documenta, est ipse Deus, qui est creator animae" (*Summa*, I^a Pars, Q. 79, a. 4).

506. "Et quantum ad hoc, non differt utrum intellectus agens sit aliquid animae, vel aliquid separatum" (*Summa*, I* Pars, Q. 79, a.4, ad 3^{ium}).

507. *Summa*, I* Pars, Q. 79, a.5, ad 2^{ium}. Aquinas' discussion, here, both recalls Augustine's and anticipates later discussions of the *lumen naturale*. It also establishes the basis for his later claims that the practical intellect possesses its own primary principles.

508. See *Summa*, I* Pars, Q. 79, a. 4, ad 3^{ium}.

509. See *Summa*, I* Pars, Q. 79, a. 6.

510. The differences between Aristotle and Maimonides concerning the relation between practical and theoretical modes of knowing will be addressed in the following chapter.

511. Both the differences between *ratio* and *intellectus* and between abstractive and participative (or intuitive) knowledge will be discussed in some detail in the following chapters.

512. "Dicendum quod impossibile est intellectum secundum praesentis vitae statum, quo passibili corpori coniungitur, aliquid intelligere in actu, nisi convertendo se ad phantasmata" (*Summa*, I* Pars, Q. 84, a. 7).

513. For detailed discussions of composition and separation in Aquinas, see George P. Klubertanz, "St. Thomas and the Knowledge of the Singular," *The New Scholasticism* 26 (1952): 135-66.; Francis M. Tyrrell, "Concerning the Nature and Function of the Act of Judgement," *The New Scholasticism* 26 (1952): 393-423.

514. *Summa*, I* Pars, Q. 84, a. 7.

515. Ibid. and Q. 86, a.1.

516. "Unde manifestum est quod intellectus actu intelligat, non solum accipiendo scientiam de novo, sed etiam utendo scientia iam acquisita, requiritur actus imaginationis et ceterarum virtutum" (*Summa*, I* Pars, Q. 84, a. 7).

517. Klubertanz, "St. Thomas and Knowledge," p. 145. Throughout the discussions of the intellect and its knowledge in *Summa*, I* Pars, Qs. 84-88, Aquinas repeatedly underlines the positive role of the imagination in human knowledge.

518. "Et ideo necesse est ad hoc quod intellectus intelligat suum obiectum proprium, quod convertat se ad phantasmata, ut speculetur naturam universalem in particulari existentem" (*Summa*, I* Pars, Q. 84, a. 7).

519. See *Summa*, I* Pars, Q. 87, especially, a. 3.

520. "Et ideo id quod primo cognoscitur ab intellectu humano, est huiusmodi objectum [aliquid extrinsecum]; et secundario cognoscitur ipse actus *quo cognoscitur objectum*" (ibid., emphasis added).

521. Since I find no significant distinction in Aquinas' work between the singular (as immediate either in sensation or understanding) and the particular (mediated and the contrary of the universal), I will not draw such a distinction here.

522. "Sicut hoc ipsum quod est Socratem currere, in se quidem contingens est; sed habitudo cursus ad motum est necessaria; necessarium enim est Socratem movere, si currit" (*Summa*, Iᵃ Pars, Q. 86, a. 3).

523. See the general distinction drawn by Aquinas between will and intellect and the attribution of will to the angels as a distinct faculty, *Summa*, Iᵃ Pars, Q. 59, aa. 1 and 2.

524. ". . . actus voluntatis nihil aliud est quam inclinatio quaedam consequens formam intellectam, sicut appetitus naturalis est inclinatio consequens formam naturalem . . . Unde inclinatio naturalis est naturaliter in re naturali; et autem quae est appetitus sensibilis, est sensibiliter in sentiente; et similiter inclinatio intelligibilis, quae est actus voluntatis, est intelligibiliter in intelligente" (*Summa*, Iᵃ Pars, Q. 87, a. 4).

525. "Unde relinquitur quod voluntas sit potentia omnino immaterialis et incorporea" (*Summa*, Iᵃ-IIᵃᵉ, Q. 9. a. 5).

526. "Quinimmo necesse est quod, sicut intellectus ex necessitate inhaeret primis principiis, ita voluntas ex necessitate inhaeret ultimo fini, qui est *beatitudo*; finis enim se habet in operativis sicut principium in speculativis" (*Summa*, Iᵃ Pars, Q. 82, a. 1; my emphasis).

527. *Summa*, Iᵃ Pars, Q. 82, a. 2. See Iᵃ-IIᵃᵉ, Q. 51, a. 2; and *In I Post. An.*, lect. 3, 1. "Principia autem se habent ad conclusiones in demonstrativis, sicut causae activae in naturalibus ad suos effectus . . ."

528. *Summa*, Iᵃ Pars, Q. 82, a. 4; and see the discussion in Chapter 4, pp. 109-111.

529. "Unde manifestum est quod sicut se habet intellectus ad rationem, ita se habet voluntas ad vim electivam, idest ad liberum arbitrium, - Ostensum est autem supra quod eiusdem potentia est intelligere et ratiocinari, sicut eiusdem virtutis est quiescere et moveri. Unde etiam eiusdem potentia est velle et eligere" (*Summa*, Iᵃ Pars, Q. 83, a. 4). See the discussion of the will and free choice in the previous chapter, pp. 109-111.

530. See *Summa*, Iᵃ-Iᵃᵉ, Q. 9, a. 1.

531. It should be emphasized that the objects are not base in themselves but, rather, they are either disproportionate to the final end or understood as ends in themselves.

532. By *utility* I do not intend any utilitarian connotation. The relation between the two human perfections will be discussed in the following chapter.

533. See the discussion in Chapter 3, pp. 84-86 and Chapter 4, pp.102ff.

534. In the light of the intimate relation between moral and rational habituation, it should be evident why I argued in Chapter 2 that, *pace* some interpretations, Job could not be understood as either perfectly wise or as perfectly just.

535. The discussion of ethics will require the summary reiteration or "translation" of some of the previous discussions of epistemic psychology and pedagogy.

536. *Guide*, 1, 5, 30.

537. Aristotle, *De Caelo*, 291b24-28, trans. W. K. C. Guthrie, Loeb Classical Library (Cambridge, Mass.: Harvard University Press, 1971 [1939]), emphasis added and translation modified. See *Guide*, 1, 5, 29, for both Maimonides' paraphrase and Pines' translation in n. 1.

538. Maimonides' distinction between Aristotle's recognition of the non-demonstrative status of the origin of the universe and the ignorance of the later Aristotelians should be recalled here.

539. *Meta*, 995a1-6.

540. See the "Eight Chapters," 5, 75 and the discussion in the previous chapter of Maimonides' claim in Chapter 5 that it is irrelevant for moral training whether the habituation is pleasureable or repugnant.

541. *Guide*, 1, 34, 72-79. The fourth cause describes at length the necessity for preliminary moral habituation and impediments to it both natural and habitual; the fifth cause identifies the necessary temporal priority of corporeal perfection; and the third is a lengthy description of the necessity for a very lengthy preparatory habituation, moral as well as ethical. For an excellent study of Aquinas' debt to and departures from Maimonides, see P. Synave, "La révélation de vérités divines naturelles d'après St. Thomas d'Aquin," *Mélanges Mandonnet*, vol. 1 (Paris: Vrin, 1930), pp. 327-70; reprinted in Jacob Dienstag, ed., *Studies in Maimonides and St. Thomas Aquinas* (Hoboken, N.J.: Ktav, 1975), pp. 290-333.

542. *Guide*, 1, 10, 35.

543. The discussion in the *Guide* sheds a different light upon the discussion of speculative perfection in the "Eight Chapters," and requires a modification of the claim in the previous chapter that speculative perfection does not require moral virtue. Given the preceding statement about Aristotle's ethical metaphysics, it may, in fact, be claimed that it is not only as propaedeutic to divine science that philosophical metaphysics requires moral perfection, but also that, at the very least, 'natural' ethics is a prerequisite for metaphysics.

544. See Maimonides' scathing critique of the Bagdad Gaon, Samuel ben Ali, in the "Essay on Resurrection," *Crisis and Leadership: Epistles of Maimonides*, trans. A. Halkin (Philadelphia: Jewish Publication Society of America, 1985), pp. 209-45. Hebrew: *Qovetz Teshuvot ha-Rambam ve-Iggerotav*, 3 parts, ed. A. L. Lichtenberg (Leipzig: L. Schnauss, 1859).

545. *Guide*, 1, 31, 67.

546. *Guide*, 1, 34, 73.

547. The secondary literature on Maimonides' discussions of law, both halachic and philosophical, is too extensive to cite here. Specifically relevant works will be noted in context and the Bibliography will supply some additional references.

548. The distinction between all the teachings of the Torah and the Law is important for understanding the limits of the role of the Law as moral as well as epistemic guidance. It is also important for appreciating the limits of Maimonides' philosophical interpretations, limits indicated in the Introduction to *Guide* 1, where Maimonides clearly distinguishes between the apparent contradictions found in "commandments or precepts regarding conducts" (p. 19), which are discussed by the Sages, and the contradictions, which constitute the concern of the *Guide*. See Chapter 1.

549. *Guide*, 1, 2, 25.

550. For the difficulties in identifying the Mutakallimun in question, see Arthur Hyman, "A Note on Maimonides' Classification of the Law," *American Academy for Jewish Research: Jubilee Volume (1928-29/1978-79)*, ed. Salon W. Baron and Isaac E. Barzilay (Jerusalem: American Academy for Jewish Research, 1980), pp. 323-43, passim.

551. For discussions of divine action, will and possibility, see Ivry, "The Will of God" and "Destiny Revisited."

552. *Guide*, 3, 13, 448-56.

553. Maimonides earlier discussion of "trials" in *Guide*, 3, 24, undermines the understanding of divine commandments as "trials of love." See Chapter 2.

554. *Guide*, 3, 20, 480.

555. For the limitation of human understanding of divine action to the natural manifestations of divine acts, see *Guide* 3, 32, 524, where Maimonides states: "If you consider divine actions—I mean to say natural actions—the deity's wily graciousness, as shown in the creation of living beings . . . will through them become clear to you."

556. *Guide*, 3, 26, 509.

557. Ibid.

558. It must be emphasized, however, that the relative "neutrality" of particulars does not entail an ethical relativism, on the contrary. For an excellent, brief discussion of the relation and distinction between Maimonides' "relativistic" meta-ethics and his "realist" ethics, see Ze'ev Harvey, "Ethics and Meta-Ethics, Aesthetics and Meta-Aesthetics in Maimonides," in *Maimonides and Philosophy*, pp. 131-38.

559. For a thorough discussion of the relation between the epistemic and the historical aspects of the law, see Joseph Stern, "The Idea of Hoq in Maimonides'

Explanation of the Law," *Maimonides and Philosophy*, ed. Shlono Pines and Yirmiyahu Yovel (Dordrecht: Martinus Nijhoff, 1986), pp. 92-130. Both Hyman, "A Note . . . ," passim. and Stern, passim. provide some of the relevant bibliography on the relation between Maimonides' discussion of the epistemic neutrality of some choices, that of al-Ghazali and "Buridan's Ass."

560. See Chapter 2.

561. *Guide*, 3, 26, 507. For a discussion of the status of the *ḥuqqim* in Maimonides, see Joseph Stern, "The Idea of a *Hoq*."

562. Stern, ibid., p. 92.

563. On the Aristotelian origin of Maimonides' understanding of *endoxa*, see Aristotle, *Topics* I, 100a18ff. See Hyman, "A Note," pp. 336-38.

564. *Guide*, 3, 27, 510. For a discussion of end(s) of the law, see Alexander Altmann, "Maimonides' Four Perfections," *Israel Oriental Studies* 2 (1972): 15-24; Arthur Hyman, "Maimonides' 'Thirteen Principles'," in *Jewish Medieval and Renaissance Studies*, ed. A. Altmann (Cambridge, Mass.: Harvard University Press, 1967), pp. 119-44.

565. *Guide*, 2, 40.

566. Viewed from the perspective of the end, if rational perfection is attained in a society ruled by *nomos*, it is attained by chance in Aristotle's sense of chance (see *Physics*, 195b31-198a13). Since the formal cause is identical to the final cause and if these determine the nature and definition of a species, a perfection whose final cause is strictly corporeal belongs to a different species than the corporeal perfection whose final end is simultaneously intellectual.

567. *Treatise*, 8, 47. See Hyman, "A Note," pp. 14-16.

568. *Treatise*, 47.

569. *Guide*, 2, 40, 381.

570. All that is intended by the determination of the "flow" of nature is the actuality that determines the soul's motion. Whereas the *telos* of *nomoi* is the material intellect, that of divine Law is the acquired intellect.

571. *Guide*, 2, 40, 382.

572. *Guide*, 2, 40, 384.

573. This may well be the source of Spinoza's distrust of knowledge *ex auditis et signis*, especially, in relation to the Bible.

574. For lack of a better term, I use the term *intellectual commandments* to designate commandments that aim at intellectual perfection. My use of this designation should not be understood to contradict my claim that commandments and prohibitions

do not pertain to the intellect. Rather, it should be noted that without prior natural intellectual perfection, these commandments either lack binding force or do not pertain to the intellect directly. Although these commandments embody true rational principles, the multitude do not assent to them rationally, but rather obey them out of fear. For those capable of final perfection, the "intellectual commandments" can provide either certainty where reason stops short or perfect prior and partial understanding of principles, e.g., communicating that the true reality of the unmoved mover is to be the Creator. That is, properly speaking, as will become evident from the discussion of modes of participation in the following chapter, "intellectual commandments" can function either as intellectual or as commandments, but not as both.

575. For the sake of convenience, I shall henceforth designate the commandments according to their respective ends, although Maimonides not only refrained from doing so, but also can be understood to enjoin against such practice when he criticizes Sa῾adia. Thus, *intellectual commandments* will be used to designate commandments that aim at final perfection *conventional commandments*, those that aim at corporeal and some moral perfection.

576. *Guide*, 3, 28, 512.

577. See the "Eight Chapters," Chap. 5.

578. For a discussion of the distinction between "love" (*mahabba*) and "passionate love" (*'ishq*), see also Shlomo Pines, "The Philosophical Purport of Maimonides' Halachic Works and *The Guide of the Perplexed*," *Maimonides and Philosophy*, pp. 1-14, especially pp. 8-9. As the following quotation from the *Guide* makes evident, however, Maimonides' use of this terms is not always consistent, most likely because he is restricted by the language of the biblical text upon which he is commenting, Deut. 6:5 and cf. 10:12; 11:1, 13 and 22; 19:9; 30:6, 16 and 20. The discussion of active participation in the following chapter would shed further light upon the nature of *'ishq*.

579. *Guide*, 3, 28, 512-13.

580. It is interesting that Aquinas does not identify "*superbia*," such as that of Satan, as simultaneously an intellectual and sensitive vice, especially since he posits an intellectual appetite distinct from sensitive appetites. Nonetheless, as will become evident later, Aquinas' discussion of *superbia* suggest such a possibility at least in the post-lapsarian state.

581. St. Thomas Aquinas, *Opera Omnia: Sententia Libri Ethicorum*, vol. 47 (Rome: Commissio Leonina, 1969); heneceforh, *Sent. Lib. Eth.* All English refernces will be to *Commentary on the Nicomachean Ethics*, trans. C. I. Litzinger (Chicago: Henry Regency Co., 1964), 2 vols.; henceforth, *Com. Nic. Eth.*

582. "Cum autem amicitiam habeamus ad ambo, scilicet ad veritatem et ad hominem, magis debemus veritatem amare quam hominem, quia hominem praecipue debemus amare propter veritatem et propter virtutem, . . . est etiam veritas quiddam divinum, in Deo enim primo et principaliter invenitur . . ." (*Sent. Lib. Eth.* 1, 6, 22).

583. *Sent. Lib. Eth.*, 1, 4, 73.

584. ". . . in intellectu autem vel ratione consideratur speculativum et practicum, in appetitu autem rationali cosideratur electio et executio, omnia autem ista ordinantur ad aliquod bonum sicut in finem, nam verum est finis speculationis. Quantum ergo ad intellectum speculativum ponit doctrinam, per quam transfunditur scientia a magistro in discipulum; quantum vero ad intellectum practicum ponit artem, quae est recta ratio factibilium...quantum verum ad actum intellectus appetitivi ponit electio; quantum vero ad executionem ponit actus" (*Sent. Lib. Eth.*, 1, 1, 4). Aquinas identifies "right reason" with "prudence." I will not discuss "prudence" directly in this study since in this context (a) as a philosophically understood moral virtue, it is "right reason" and (b), as a fully actual ethical virtue, it is provident participation. Moreover, since, for Maimonides, the closest cognates of *prudence* are either "practical reason," or *al-ḥikhmah*, which is generally translated by "wisdom" but which Maimonides identifies as an equivocal term, contextually limited discussions of practical reason and providence will render the comparison between Maimonides and Aquinas less cumbersome and less misleading.

585. Whatever interpretation we may come to of *Nicomachean Ethics*, 6, 2, 1139a18-b6, what Aristotle names *orektikos nous* or *orexis dianoetike* is neither an efficient cause that moves the intellect nor an *actual* power of the intellective soul. Since the intellect itself has no exernal motion, desire provides its external motion, rather than moves it.

586. See the discussion of reason and will in Chapters 4 and 5 passim.

587. It cannot be overemphasized that it is in this text, a text whose concern is action, that Aquinas criticizes Aristotle for positing too sharp a distinction between the possible and agent intellect. See Chapter 5.

588. Throughout the commentary Aquinas identifies the *telos* of all natural inclinations as God, a teleology that is clearly not Aristotelian. For Aristotle, the *telos* of all strictly natural entities is their *proper* form and *no more*. Note Aquinas' gloss on Aristotle's opening statement that all things aim at the good, "Quod autem dicit": "quod omnia appetunt," non est intelligendum solum de habentibus cognitionem, quae apprehendunt bonum, sed etiam de rebus carentibus congnitione, quae naturali appetitu tendunt in bonum, non quasi cognoscant bonum, sed quia *ab aliquo cognoscente* moventur ad bonum, scilicet *ex ordinatione divini intellectus*." Fully aware of the change, Aquinas adds, "Non autem est unum bonum in quod omnia tendunt . . . et ideo non describitur hic aliquod unum bonum, sed bonum communiter sumptum; quia autem nihil est bonum nisi in quantum est quaedam similitudo *et participatio* summi boni" (*Sent. Lib. Eth.*, 1, 1, 5 [1094a2], emphases added). Aristotle's discussion of the greater nobility of the common than the individual good does not extend further than the *polis*.

589. See Aquinas comments on the relation between the actuality that is virtue and the habituation to it in his gloss on the Greek *ethos* and *ηthos* in *Sent, Lib. Eth.*, 2, 1, 247.

590. See Chapter 3, pp. 84-85.

591. ". . . sed secundum *rei* veritatem bonum cum ente convertitur" (ibid., emphasis added). I believe that Aquinas' use of language is deliberate and that it does not contradict the statements in the *De Div. Nom.* (see Chapter 4 passim.) that the good extends further than the act of being, since the discussion here is of primary entities rather than of principles. The language used supports this reading since *secundum veritatem* is perfectly good Latin and less cumbersome than *secundum veritatem rei*. The discussion following this "correction" supports this reading further insofar as it concerns knowledge and insists that knowledge of primary entities is possible only through their posterior effects. Later, in 1, 2, 9, in a language highly reminiscent of the *De Div. Nom.*, Aquinas states that as a final cause "tanto potius est quanto ad plura se extedit." A discussion of the relation between "good" and "being" will be resumed in the conclusion.

592. "verum necessarium et verum contingens videntum se habere sicut perfectum et imperfectum in genere veri; eadem autem potentia animae cognoscimus perfecta et imperfecta in eodem genere. . . ." (*Sent. Lib. Eth.*, 6, 1).

593. It should be noted that no contradiction is entailed by the claim that the natural appetitive powers are passive, on the one hand, and that there exists a rational appetite, on the other, since the two claims belong to two distinct orders of discourse so that in the ontological order actuality is underlined, in the temporal/existential order potency and possibility are explored.

594. "multototiens agimus secundum rationem imprimitur forma rationis in vi appetitiva, quae quidem impressio nihil aliud est quam virtus moralis" (*Sent. Lib. Eth.*, 2, 1, 77).

595. Following Aristotle, Aquinas' discussion of the distinction between natural and acquired habit directly precedes the discussion of continence. The first discussion occurs in *Sent. Lib. Eth.*, 6, 11, the second begins in 7, 1.

596. "Sed si huiusmodi inclinatio coaccipiat in operando intellectum, ut scilicet cum discretione operetur, tunc multum differet secundum excellentiam bonitatis, et habitus qui erit similis tali operationi cum discretione factae, erit proprie et perfecte virtus, quae est moralis" (*Sent, Lib. Eth.*, 6, 11, 376).

597. The importance of this distinction for Aquinas will emerge in the discussion of active participation, where the difference between Aristotelian and revealed "ethics" will emerge. At this point, suffice it to note that, from the perspective of philosophical ethics, the theological virtues are either excessive or defective.

598. Qua principles of potency and act neither the intellect nor the appetites are causes of diversity; rather, the composition constituting this or that human being is. Recall that there is no "universal" human being except as an abstraction from individuals. See the discussion of matter and form as principles and thus, as existing only *in alio*, in Chapter 4.

599. The entire discussion of incontinence in book 7, and especially 1, 10, 422, seems to imply the reversibility of acquired a-natural habit. "Et dicit quod illi qui sunt incontinentes per consuetudinem sunt sanabliores illis qui sunt incontinentes per natu-

ram, scilicet corporalis complexionis ad hoc inclinantis, quia facilius potest transmutari consuetudo quam natura." He adds, however, that custom, too, is difficult to change *"quia assimulatur naturae."*

600. St. Thomas Aquinas, *In duodecim libros Metaphysicorum Expositio* (Rome: Marietti, 1964); henceforth, *In Meta.*

601. "quia consuetudo vertitur in naturam; unde et habitus ex consuetudine generatur, qui inclinat per modum naturam" (*In Meta.*, 2, 5, 92).

602. "quae homines a puerita audientes magis approbabant quam veritatis cognitionem" (*In Meta.*, 2, 5, 93).

603. "Sed lex divinitus data ordinat hominem ad veram felicitatem cui omnis falsitas repugnat. Unde in lege Dei nulla falsitas continetur" (ibid.).

604. "Consequenter considerandum est de principiis exterioribus actuum. Principium autem exterius ad malum inclinans est diabolus, de cuius tentatione in Primo dictum est. Principium autem exterius movens ad bonum est Deus, qui et nos instruit per legem et iuvat per gratiam" (*Summa*, I^a-II^{ae}, Q. 90).

605. ". . . potest dici lex non essentialiter, sed quasi participative" (*Summa*, I^a-II^{ae}, Q. 90, a. 1, ad 1um).

606. See R. A. Armstrong, *Primary and Secondary Precepts in Thomistic Natural Law Teaching* (The Hague: Martinus Nijhoff, 1966).

607. It should be noted that both aspects of natural law belong to human beings in virtue of the agent intellect in a manner such that the "passive" aspect is a determinate immanent possibility to become agent.

608. As should be evident from the preceding discussion, the common good should be understood both as the good of the community and as the good of each individual comprising the diversity of the species since understanding the nature of the species connotes the understanding of its causes and ends, which is a prerequisite for the perfection of all human virtues, individual as well as common.

609. I cannot overemphasize the fact that it is only the nomination of the *lex fomitis* as law which Aquinas deems derivative or equivocal rather than its status as a quasi-natural, determinate inclination.

610. ". . . potest dici lex non essentialiter, sed quasi participative" (*Summa*, I^a-II^{ae}, Q. 90, a. 1, ad 1um).

611. "Video legem aliam in membris meis, repugnantem legi mentis meae" (Romans 7:23, quoted in the *sed contra* to *Summa*, I^a-II^{ae}, Q. 91, a. 6).

612. "Non enim homo propriis viribus potest liberari a corporis corruptione, nec etiam animae, quamvis consentiat rationi contra peccatum, sed solum per gratiam Christi" (*Super epistolas S. Pauli Lectura*, "Ad Romanos" 7:25, 2 vols. [Rome: Marietti,

1953], vol. 1). See *Opera Omnia: In Psalmos Davidis* (Paris: Vives, 1876), vol. 18, 48: 19-21, where Aquinas identifies the person under the law of brutes with one who "introibit usque in progenies patrum suorum, et usque in aeternum non videbit lumen."

613. *Posterior Analytics*, 1, 2ff. 71b10ff. See *In Posteriorum Analyticorum*, 1, 5, 166ff.

614. My concern here is limited to the discussion of law. For a succinct and clear discussion of a broader range of issues involved in Aquinas' appeal to knowledge according to the mode of the knower, see John F. Wippel, "Thomas Aquinas and the Axiom 'What Is Received Is Received According to the Mode of the Receiver,'" *A Straight Path: Studies in Medieval Philosophy and Culture, Essays in Honor of Arthur Hyman*, ed. Ruth Link-Salinger, Jeremiah Hackett, Michael Samuel Hyman, R. James Long, and Charles H. Manekin (Washington, D.C.: Catholic University Press of America, 1988), pp. 279-89.

615. The example given by Aquinas of propositions understood by the wise but not by the vulgar (*rudis*) is that angels are not bodies because they are not circumscribed by place.

616. See *Summa*, Iª-IIªᵉ, Q. 94, a. 1.

617. "... aliqui habent depravatam rationem ex passione, seu ex mala consuetudine, seu ex mala habitudine naturae" (*Summa*, Iª-IIªᵉ, Q. 94, a. 4). Note the emphasis upon both custom and habit as obstacles to knowledge.

618. *Summa*, Iª-IIªᵉ, Qs. 94-95, especially Q. 94, a. 4.

619. It should be noted that, for Aquinas, as for Maimonides, insofar as divine law contains positive legal precepts necessary for the governance of cities, it replaces imperfect human law. See Iª-IIªᵉ, 173, a. 1.

620. See especially *Romans* 10:4 on Christ as the *telos* of the law and "Ad Romanos," ad loc.

621. "... gratia Spiritus Sancti, quae datur per fidem Christi" (*Summa*, Iª-IIªᵉ, Q. 106, a. 1).

622. It should be noted that insofar as the new law assists in the *actualization* of proper human action it reestablishes the original, proper order between potency and act within the intellect.

623. "Unde etiam littera Evangelii occideret" (*Summa*, Iª-IIªᵉ, Q. 105, a. 2).

624. "... nondum est praedictum Evangelium in universo orbe; sed hoc facto, veniet consummatio mundi" (*Summa*, Iª-IIªᵉ, Q. 106, a. 4, ad 4m).

625. *Summa*, Iª-IIªᵉ, Q. 89, a. 6.

626. "... distinguitur iste actus qui est credere ab omnibus actibus intellectus qui sunt circa verum vel falsum" (*Summa*, IIª-IIªᵉ, Q. 2, a. 1).

627. *Metaphysics*, Alpha elatton, 993b12-20.

628. What I consider the significance of the literal level of the commentary to consist in will emerge in the following summary.

629. My concern here is with the status of "evil," exemplified by Satan's influence rather than the status of Satan. In conversation, Joseph Stern has correctly pointed out to me the dissimilarity between Maimonides and Aquinas on the status of Satan. I believe that this difference arises strictly from a doctrinal one and has little significance in this context. It should also be noted that even from a strictly theological perspective, for Christianity, Satan presents the same problem found in Job except to a higher degree. In fact, the problem of "how one possessing as perfect a knowledge as is possible for a created being can choose otherwise?" is not that dissimilar to the problem presented to Maimonides by Adam.

630. *Guide*, 3, 22, 488.

631. Since Satan belongs to the realm of permanence, it follows that overcoming his influence requires the aid of other permanent beings, such as God or the angels.

632. The continuous postponment of a discussion of active participation is deliberate. In fact, although later I will briefly indicate what such active participation may look like, the outline would remain tentative and indicative precisely because I believe that it may take many forms or, like the Torah, have many faces.

633. See Chapter 2, pp. 43-45, where I outline and question Yaffe's opposite claim that the audience to whom Aquinas addressed the commentary were perfectly wise but unjust.

634. In this light, Aquinas's exposition bears greater similarity to Maimonides' *Commentary on the Mishnah* and *Mishneh Torah*, especially, the "Book of Knowledge." See Chapter 1, pp. 17-19.

635. See Chapter 2, pp. 56-59.

636. It should be recalled that the disordered speech produced by Aquinas's predecessors is the primary reason he offers for writing the *Summa.* See Chapter 1, pp. 30-37. Although Aquinas does not explicitly identify the disordered speech with a disordered desire for knowledge, the similarity between Maimonides' Joseph and Aquinas' Job is striking.

637. God here need not (indeed cannot) refer to any particular determinate entity. One can replace it with Spinoza's *Natura Naturans*, or with any ontological first principle that determines all subsequent possibility.

638. See Chapter 3, especially Fackenheim's argument, pp. 72-75.

639. As will become evident later, this formulation is somewhat imprecise with respect to Aquinas since through their *esse* all creatures can be said to participate in divine providence. However, this participation is neither voluntary nor theoretical.

640. See *Summa*, II^a-II^{ae}, Q. 171-74. In my opinion, a comparative analysis of Aquinas' understanding of the role of grace in human perfection with Maimonides' explanation of personal prophecy may prove to be not only a fruitful subject for further research, but also a means to demonstrate a greater harmony between their conceptions of human perfection, especially since like grace, prophecy assists but does not preserve human beings in perfection. See *Guide*, "Translator's Introduction," p. lxxii, n. 32.

641. *Guide*, 3, 51, 618.

642. See Pines, "Maimonides' Halachic Works."

643. See Shlomo Pines, "The Limitations of Human Knowledge according to Al-Farabi, Ibn Bajja, and Maimonides," *Studies in Medieval Jewish History and Literature*, ed. Isadore Twersky (Cambridge, Mass.: Harvard University Press, 1979), pp. 82-109. It should be noted that in "Maimonides' Halachic Works," Pines modifies the conclusions reached in this article. Henceforth, I shall designate knowledge gained from the overflow of the agent intellect *participative apprehension*.

644. Clearly, in the light of the threefold identity constituting understanding, the terms *subject* and *object* are highly inappropriate and are used simply (to borrow from Spinoza) because of the "poverty of language."

645. *Guide*, 2, 38, 377; my emphasis.

646. For some significant examples, see *Guide*, 1, 53 and 68; 2, 4-5, and 36, especially p. 369; 3, 51-54, 618-38.

647. *Guide*, 1, 68, 164.

648. Although I fully agree with Maurer that for Maimonides' the "little old woman" (*vetula*) can in no way be said to have *knowledge* whereas for Aquinas she can, I disagree with his conclusion that, for Maimonides, there is no distinction between the knowledge involved in philosophical metaphysics and that involved in "divine science." See Armand A. Maurer, "Maimonides and Aquinas on the Study of Metaphysics," *A Straight Path, Studies in Medieval Philosophy and Culture, Essays in Honor of Arthur Hyman*, ed. Ruth Link-Salinger et al. (Washington, D.C.: Catholic University Press of America, 1988), pp. 206-15, especially, pp. 214-15.

649. *Guide*, 3, 51, 620.

650. *Guide*, 3, 51-54, 618-38.

651. Although this claim is disputable with respect to Aristotle, it represents the way in which he was read by the Islamicate philosophers, e.g., al-Farabi, especially, *Taḥsil al-Sa'adah* and *Al-Siyasah al-Madaniyah*.

652. *Guide*, 2, 40, 384; and see Chapter 6, pp. 150-153.

653. ". . . non solum quod in seipsis bonae sunt; sed etiam quod sint causa bonitatis aliorum, quae extremum modum participationis divinae bonitatis habent" *De Veritate*, Q. 5, a. 8, 213-17).

654. A partial list of important interpretations of participation in Aquinas is provided in the bibliography.

655. See *Summa*, Iª-IIªᵉ, Q. 174, a. 4 and Q. 172, a. 2, respectively. Whereas Moses received revelation "face to face," according to Aquinas, the other prophets received illumination and revelation through the angels.

656. "Sic igitur bonum est universalior et altior causa quam ens, quia ad plura se extendit" (*De Div. Nom.*, Chap. 3, 1, 1, 226).

657. See *Summa*, IIª-IIªᵉ, Q. 45, a. 3.

658. Whether or not we accept Aristotelian epistemic psychology is irrelevant to these conclusions since the effects of authorial speaking and of teaching upon the hearers remain the same. One need only recall here Spinoza's criticism of "knowledge *ex auditis et signis*" in the *Tractatus de Intellectus Emendatione*, a discussion that also makes manifest the dogmatic nature of skepticism. Benedict (Baruch) Spinoza, *Tractatus de Intellectus Emendatione*, *Spinoza Opera*, vol. 2, ed. Carl Gebhardt (Heidelberg: Carl Winter, 1925).

659. I need not belabor the point that it is highly likely that such questions will be raised at this point. They should be immediately evident to anyone familiar with the contemporary anatagonism between "analytic" and "continental" philosophy.

660. Given its indicative mode, the account will be neither comprehensive nor "scholarly." Its success will depend upon whether, and to what extent, it will provoke further discussion. It should be noted, however, that the discussion here depends to a large measure upon the discussion of language and interpretation in Chapter 1, in particular, as well as throughout the various chapters.

661. The Bibliography will provide a number of relevant texts. Although she does not refer directly to Aristotle, E. J. Ashworth's recent work shows clearly that Aquinas' use of analogy bears greater similarity to "equivocation," than to some proportionate relation. E. J. Ashworth, "Analogy and Equivocation in Thirteen-Century Logic," pp. 94-135.

662. It should be noted, however, that the incarnation *as* mystery exceeds logical-rational determinations and renders impossible "correct" linguistic access.

663. It should be recalled that these difficulties are the ones that give rise to the contradictions, both real and apparent, enumerated in the Introduction to the *Guide*.

664. For an important distinction between these objects respectively as objects of mind and of intellect, see Abraham Nuriel, "Remarks on Maimonides' Epistemology," *Maimonides and Philosophy, Papers Presented at the Sixth Jerusalem Philosophical Encounter, May 1985*, ed. Shlomo Pines and Yirmiyahu Yovel (Dordrecht: Martinus Nijhoff, 1986), pp. 36-51.

665. Ibid., p. 41.

666. *Guide*, Introduction, 8.

667. *Guide*, Introduction, 10.

668. Since the purpose of the "law as a whole" is to render possible knowledge and love of God, since Moses received the "law as a whole" immediately, and since, *qua* immediate knowledge, it is the negation of discursive adequacy, the closest we can come to a discussion of Mosaic prophecy is in the discussion of the *via negativa*.

669. A thorough evaluation of the respective "adequacy" of a parable, then, will have to take into account Maimonides' particular rankings of that prophet or instance of prophecy.

670. Despite my disagreement with Nuriel's conclusion, the following discussion is highly indebted to his outstanding article.

671. *Guide*, 1, 50, 111.

672. *Guide*, 1, 50, 111; my emphases.

673. Nuriel, "Remarks on Maimonides' Epistemology," p. 49.

674. *Guide*, 9.

675. *Guide*, 1, 60, 144.

676. *Treatise on [the Art of] Logic*, C. 4, pp. 38-39.

677. *Guide*, 3, 32, 525. As Pines notes in the "Translator's Introduction," lxxii, n. 32, the term *talattuf* that is translated "wily graciousness," resembles Hegel's *List der Vernuft* to which I would add Spinoza's *natura naturans*.

678. Psalms, 65:2; and *Guide*, 1, 59, 139.

679. Aquinas seems to indicate that two names are used by Aristotel*ian* philosophy, namely, *first efficient cause* and *necessary cause*. See, *Summa*, Iᵃ Pars, Q. 2, a. 3. I am restricting the name to two since the "first way" does not claim that "everybody *calls* God" moving cause but only that they "understand (*'intelligunt'*) God as moving cause." The second and third ways use *nominant* and *dicunt*, respectively. The fourth and fifth ways restrict those naming God by "we," which I take to refer to believers.

680. It should be noted that Aquinas is by far less concerned with rhetoric and poetry as "pretenders" to revealed truth than Maimonides is. This is simply another reason for the caution counseled previously against a comparison between Maimonides' and Aquinas' understanding of logic and language at this time.

681. ". . . magis est conveniens quod doctrina in Scripturis tradantur sub figuris vilium corporum quam corporum nobilium. Et hoc propter tria. Primo, quia per hoc magis liberatur humanus animus ab errore. Manifestum enim apparet quod haec secundum proprietatem non dicuntur de divinis; quod posset esse dubium, si sub figuris nobilium corporum describerentur divina; maxime apud illos qui nihil aliud a cor-

poribus nobilius excogitare noverunt.—Secundo, quia hic modus convenientior est cognitioni quam de Deo habemus in hac vita. Magis enim manifestatur nobis de ipso quid non est, quam quid est; et ideo similitudines illarum rerum quae magis elongantur a Deo veriorem nobis faciunt aestimationem quod sit supra illud quod de Deo dicimus vel cogitamus.—Tertio, quia per huiusmodi divina magis occulantur indignis."

682. I cannot help but wonder how fundamentalist solfidianism may have modified the possibilities of understanding Aquinas' views of language, especially of divine names.

683. "Sed quantum ad id ad quod imponitur nomen ad significandum, est magis proprium hoc nomen Deus, quod imponitur ad significandum naturam divinam. Et adhuc magis proprium nomen est Tetragrammaton, quod est impositum ad significandam ipsam Dei substantiam incommunicabilem, et, ut sic liceat loqui, singularem."

684. See Owens, "Diversity and Community of Being in St. Thomas Aquinas," pp. 257-302.

685. "Et sic patet quod voces referuntur ad res significandas mediante conceptione intellectus." *Summa*, Iᵃ Pars, Q. 13, a. 1.

686. "Dicendum quod Deus non est mensura proportionata mensuratis" (*Summa*, Iᵃ Pars, Q. 13, a. 5, ad 3m).

687. ". . . sed in Deo non est aliqua realis relatio eius ad creaturas, sed secundum rationem tantum, inquantum creaturae referuntur ad ipsum" (ibid., a. 7).

688. Walter Benjamin, *Illuminations: Essays and Reflections*, Harry Zohn, trans. (New York: Schocken Books, 1969), pp. 257-258.

BIBLIOGRAPHY

Primary Sources: Maimonides

Crisis and Leadership: Epistles of Maimonides. trans. A. Halkin. Philadelphia: Jewish Publication Society of America, 1985.

Dalalat al-Ha'irin. ed. Solomon Munk, 3 vols. Osnabrück: Otto Zeller, 1964; reprint of 1856-88 ed.

The "Eight Chapters." In *Ethical Writings of Maimonides.* trans. Raymond L. Weiss and Charles E. Butterworth. New York: New York University Press, 1975.

The Guide of the Perplexed. trans. Shlomo Pines, 2 vols. Chicago: University of Chicago Press, 1963.

Maimonides' Treatise on [the Art of] Logic. ed. and trans. Israel Efros. New York: American Academy for Jewish Research, 1938.

Al Makalah fi-Sina'at al Mantiq. ed. Israel Efros. *PAAJR* 34 (1966).

Mishneh Torah: The Book of Knowledge. ed. and trans. Moses Haymson. Jerusalem: Boys' Town, 1965.

Mishneh Torah: Sefer ha-Madd'a. ed. M. D. Rabinowitz. Jerusalem: Mossad ha-Rav Kook, 1958.

Moreh Nevukhim. trans. Samuel Ibn-Tibbon. Jerusalem, 1960.

Perush ha-Mishnah: Nezikin. ed. Joseph D. Kafih. Jerusalem: Mossad ha-Rav Kook, 1964.

Qovetz Teshuvot ha-Rambam ve-Iggerotav. 3 parts, ed. A. L. Lichtenberg. Leipzig: L. Schnauss, 1859.

Primary Sources: Aquinas

De Principiis Naturae ad fratrem Sylvestrum. Rome: Marietti, 1954.

Expositio super librum Boetii "De Trinitate." ed. Bruno Decker Leiden: E. J. Brill, 1959.

In Aristotelis Libros Peri Hermeneias et Posteriorum Analyticorum. Rome: Marietti, 1955.

In duodecim libros Metaphysicorum Aristotelis Expositio. Rome: Marietti, 1964.

In librum Beati Dionysii "De Divinis Nominibus" Expositio. Rome: Marietti, 1950.

In octo libros Physicorum Aristotelis Expositio. Rome: Marietti, 1954.

Opera Omnia: De Principiis Naturae ad fratrem Sylvestrum. vol. 43. Editori di San Tommaso, Commissio Leonina. Rome, 1976.

Opera Omnia: Expositio super Iob ad litteram. vol. 26, ed. Antoine Dondaine. Commissio Leonina. Rome, 1965.

Opera Omnia: In Psalmos Davidis. vol. 18. Paris: Vives, 1876.

Opera Omnia: Quaestiones disputatae de malo. vol. 23, ed. Pierre-Marie Gils. Commissio Leonina. Rome, 1982.

Opera Omnia: Quaestiones disputatae de potentia. vol. 2. Rome: Marietti, 1953.

Opera Omnia: Quaestiones disputatae de veritate. 3 vols., vol. 22, ed. Antoine Dondaine. Commissio Leonina. Rome, 1970-1976.

Opera Omnia: Sentencia Libri "De Anima." vol. 45, ed. Rene-A. Gauthier. Commissio Leonina. Rome, 1984.

Opera Omnia: Sententia Libri Ethicorum. vol. 47, 1-2, ed. Rene-A. Gauthier. Commissio Leonina. Rome, 1969.

Quaestiones de Anima. ed. James H. Robb. Toronto: PIMS, 1968.

Scriptum super libros Sententiarum. Book I. Paris: Mandonnet, 1929.

Summa Theologiae. 4 vols. Ottawa, 1941.

Super epistolas S. Pauli: Lectura: Ad Romanos. 2 vols., vol. 1. Rome: Marietti, 1953.

Primary Sources: General

St. Albert. *Comentarii in Iob.* ed. Melchior Weiss. Freiburg: Herder, 1904.

Al-Farabi, Abu Nasr. *Aphorisms of the Statesman (Fusul al-Madani).* ed. and trans. D. M. Dunlop. Cambridge: Cambridge University Press, 1961.

———. *Alfarabi's Political Regime (Al Siyasa al-Madaniyya).* ed. Fauzi M. Najjar. Beirut: Imprimerie Catholique, 1964.

———. *Alfarabi's Book of Religion and Related Texts (Kitab al-Millah wa Nusus Ukhra).* ed. Muhsin Mahdi. Beirut: Dar El-Marchreq, 1968.

———. *Alfarabi's Book of Letters (Kitab al-Huruf).* ed. Muhsin Mahdi. Beirut: Dar El-Machreq, 1969.

————. *Tahsil al-Sa'adah*. ed. Jafar Al Yasin. Beirut: Al-Andaloss, 1981.

Alfarabi's Philosophy of Plato and Aristotle. trans. Muhsin Mahdi. Ithaca, N.Y.: Cornell University Press, 1969.

Alfarabi on the Perfect State: Abu Nasr al-Farabi's Mabadi' Ara' Ahl al-Madina al-Fadila. ed. and trans. Richard Walzer. Oxford: Oxford Clarendon Press, 1985. See also the collections of medieval translations.

Aristotle. *Politics*. ed. and trans. H. Rackham. Loeb Classical Series. Cambridge, Mass.: Harvard University Press, 1934.

————. *Nicomachean Ethics*. trans. H. Rackham. Loeb Classical Series. Cambridge, Mass.: Harvard University Press, 1934.

————. *Metaphysics*. 2 vols., trans. T. Tredennick. Loeb Classical Series. Cambridge, Mass.: Harvard University Press, 1936.

————. *De Anima*. ed. and trans. W. S. Hett. Loeb Classical Series. Cambridge, Mass.: Harvard University Press, 1936.

————. *Categories and On Interpretation*. trans. H. P. Cooke and H. Tredennick. Loeb Classical Series. Cambridge, Mass.: Harvard University Press, 1949.

————. *Physics*. 2 vols., trans. P. H. Wicksteed and F. M. Cornford. Loeb Classical Series. Cambridge, Mass.: Harvard University Press, 1957 and 1935.

————. *Posterior Analytics and Topica*. ed. and trans. H. Tredennick and E. S. Forster. Loeb Classical Library. Cambridge, Mass.: Harvard University Press, 1960.

St. Augustine. *De Doctrina Christiana*. Corpus Christianorum Series Latina 32. Brepols, 1932.

Averroes. *Averrois Cordubensis Commentarium Magnum in Aristotelis De Anima Libros*. ed. F. S. Crawford. Cambridge, Mass.: Medieval Academy of America, 1953.

Avicenna. *Al-Shifa; al-Mantiq; al-Taba'iyyat; al-Riyadiyyat; Illahiyyat*. 23 vols., general ed. I. Madkour. Cairo: Al-Hay'a al-Misriyya al-'Amma li al-Kitab, 1953-82.

————. *Kitab al-Isharat wa al-Tanbihat*. 3 vols., ed. S. Dunya. Cairo: Dar al-Ma'arif, 1958.

————. *Al-Najat*. ed. M. Fakhry. Beirut: Dar al-Afaq al-Jadida, 1985.

Avicenna's Psychology: An English Translation of Kitab al-Najat, Book II, Chapter VI. trans. Fazlur Rahman. London: Oxford University Press, 1952.

The Metaphysics of Avicenna (Ibn Sina): A Critical Translation-Commentary and Analysis of the Fundamental Arguments in Avicenna's Metaphysics in the Danish Nama-i Ala'i. trans. Parviz Morewedge. New York: Columbia University Press, 1973.

————. *Ibn Sina Remarks and Admonitions Part One: Logic.* trans. Shams C. Inati. Toronto: PIMS, 1984. See also collections of medieval translations.

Glossa Ordinaria et postilla Nicolai Lyrani. Job, vol. 3. Paris, 1590.

St. Gregory. *Moralia in Iob.* Corpus Christianorum Series Latina 143-44. Brepols: 1979-85.

Plato. *Timaeus.* ed. and trans. R. G. Bury. Loeb Classical Series. Cambridge, Mass.: Harvard University Press, 1966.

Sa'adia Gaon. *The Book of Beliefs and Opinions.* trans. S. Rosenblatt. New Haven, Conn.: Yale University Press, 1948.

Saadiah ben Joseph al Fayyumi's Book of Theodicy, a Tenth Century Arabic Commentary and Translation of the Book of Job. trans. Lenn E. Goodman. Yale Judaica Series 25. New Haven, Conn.: Yale University Press, 1988.

Collective Translations of Primary Sources

Medieval Philosophy: The Christian, Islamic and Jewish Traditions. ed. Arthur Hyman and James J. Walsh. Indianapolis: Hackett, 1973.

Medieval Political Philosophy: A Sourcebook. ed. Muhsin Mahdi and Ralph Lerner. Ithaca, N.Y.: Cornell University Press, 1963.

Secondary Sources

Altmann, Alexander. "Maimonides' 'Four Perfections'." *Israel Oriental Studies* 2 (1972): 15-24. Reprinted in Altmann, *Essays in Jewish Intellectual History*, pp. 65-76. Hanover, N.H.: published for Brandeis University Press by the University Press of New England, 1981.

————. "Free Will and Predestination in Saadia, Bahya and Maimonides." *Religion in a Religious Age*, ed. S. D. Goitein, pp. 25-51. Cambridge, Mass.: Association for Jewish Studies, 1974. Reprinted in Altmann, *Essays in Jewish Intellectual History*, pp. 35-64.

————. "Maimonides and Thomas Aquinas: Natural or Divine Prophecy?" *Association for Jewish Studies Review* 3 (1978): 1-19. Reprinted in: Altmann, *Essays in Jewish Intellectual History*, pp. 77-96.

————. "Maimonides on the Intellect and the Scope of Metaphysics." *Von der mittelalterlichen zur modernen Aufklärung*, pp. 60-129. Texts and Studies in Medieval and Early Modern Judaism 2. Tubingen: J. C. B. Mohr, 1987.

Armstrong, R. A. *Primary and Secondary Precepts in Thomistic Natural Law Teaching.* The Hague: Martinus Nijhoff, 1966.

Ashworth, E. J. "Analogy and Equivocation in Thirteenth-Century Logic: Aquinas in Context." *Medieval Studies* 54 (1992): 94-135.

Aubenque, Pierre. *Le probleme de l'etre chez Aristote: essai sur la problématique aristotélicienne.* Paris: Presses universitaires de France, 1977 [1962].

Berman, Lawrence. "Maimonides the Disciple of Alfarabi." *Israel Oriental Studies* 4 (1974): 154-78.

Booth, Edward. *Aristotelian Aporetic Ontology in Islamic and Christian Thinkers.* Cambridge: Cambridge University Press, 1983.

Boyle, Leonard E. "The Setting of the *Summa Theologiae* of St. Thomas." *Etienne Gilson Series 5.* Toronto: PIMS, 1982.

Brague, Remi. *Aristote et la question du monde: essai sur le contexte cosmologique et anthropologique de l'ontologie.* Paris: Presses universitaires de France, 1988.

Brague, Remi, and Jean-Francois Courtine, eds. *Hermeneutique et ontologie: melanges en hommage à Pierre Aubenque, phronimos aner.* Paris: Presses universitaires de France, 1990.

Joseph A. Buijis. "Negative Language and Knowledge About God. A Critical Analysis of Maimonides' Theory of Divine Attributes." Ph.D. dissertation, University of Western Ontario, 1976.

————. "Comments on Maimonides' Negative Theology." *The New Scholasticism* 49 (1975): 87-93.

————. "The Philosophical Character of Maimonides' Guide—A Critique of Strauss' Intrepretation." *Judaism* 27 (1967-68): 448-457.

Burrell David. "Aquinas' Debt to Maimonides." *A Straight Path. Studies in Medieval Philosophy and Culture: Essays in Honor of Arthur Hyman.* ed. Ruth Link-Salinger et al., pp. 37-48. Washington, D.C.: Catholic University of America Press, 1988.

————. *Knowing the Unknowable God: Ibn Sina, Maimonides, Aquinas.* Notre Dame, Ind.: Notre Dame University Press, 1986.

————. "Maimonides, Aquinas, and Gersonides on Providence." *Religious Studies* 20, no. 3 (1984): 335-51.

Chenu, M.-D. *Toward Understanding St. Thomas.* ed. and trans. A. M. Landry and D. Hughes. Chicago: University of Chicago Press, 1964.

————. *Nature, Man, and Society in the Twelfth Century.* ed. and trans. Jerome Taylor and Lester K. Little. Chicago: University of Chicago Press, 1968.

Courtine, Jean-Francois. "Philosophie et théologie: Remarque sur la situation aristotélicienne de la détermination thomiste de la 'theologia' (S. Th., 1a qu. 1, a. 1 et 5)." *Revue philosophique de Louvain* 84 (1986): 315-44.

d'Alverny, Marie-Thérèse. "Translations and Translators." In *Renaissance and Renewal in the Twelfth Century*. ed. Robert L. Benson and Giles Constable with Carol D. Lanham, pp. 421-62. Cambridge, Mass.: Harvard University Press, 1982.

Davidson, Herbert. "Maimonides' Secret Position on Creation." In *Studies in Medieval Jewish History and Literature*. ed. Isadore Twersky, pp. 16-40. Cambridge, Mass.: Harvard University Press, 1979.

———. "Maimonides' *Shemonah Peraqim* and Alfarabi's *Fusul Al-Madani*." *PAAJR* 31 (1963): 33-50.

Dienstag, Jacob I. *Studies in Maimonides and St. Thomas Aquinas*. Biblioteca Maimonidica vol. 1, ed. J. I. Dienstag. New York: Ktav Publ. House, 1975.

———. "Biblical Exegesis of Maimonides in Jewish Scholarship." *Samuel K. Mirsky Memorial Volume: Studies in Jewish Law, Philosophy, and Literature*. ed. Gersion Appel, pp. 151-90. New York: Yeshiva University Press, 1970.

———. "Christian Translators of Maimonides' *Mishneh Torah* into Latin." *Salo Wittmayer Baron Jubilee Volume on the Occasion of his 80th Birthday*. 3 vols., ed. Saul. Lieberman, vol. 1, pp. 287-309 Jerusalem: American Academy for Jewish Research, New York: Columbia University Press, 1974.

Dunphy, William. "Maimonides and Aquinas on Creation: A Critique of Their Historians." *Graceful Reason: Essays in Ancient and Medieval Philosophy Presented to Joseph Owens*. ed. Lloyd P. Gerson, pp. 361-79. Toronto: PIMS, 1983.

———. "Maimonides' Not So Secret Position on Creation." *Moses Maimonides and His Time*. Studies in Philosophy and the History of Philosophy, vol. 19, ed. Eric Ormsby, pp. 151-72. Washington, D.C.: Catholic University of America Press, 1989.

Efros, Israel. *Ha-Filosofyah ha-Yehudit ha-'Atikah*. Jerusalem, 1959.

———. *Ancient Jewish Philosophy*. Detroit: Wayne State University Press, 1964.

———. "Shitato ha-filosofit shel R. Sa'adia Gaon." In *Medieval Jewish Philosophy: Systems and Problems*. Chap. 6. Jerusalem: Merkaz Press, 1965.

———. *Studies in Medieval Jewish Philosophy*. New York: Columbia University Press, 1974.

Fackenheim, Emil. "The Possibility of the Universe in Alfarabi, Ibn Sina, and Maimonides." *PAAJR* 16 (1946-47): 39-70.

Fox, Marvin. "Maimonides and Aquinas on Natural Law." *Dinei Israel* 3 (1972): 5-36.

———. "The Doctrine of the Mean in Aristotle and Maimonides: A Comparative Study." In *Studies in Jewish Religious and Intellectual History*. ed. Sigfried Stein and Raphael Loewe, pp. 93-120. University, Ala.: Alabama University Press, 1979.

Gadamer, Hans-Georg. *Reason in the Age of Science.* trans. Frederick G. Lawrence. Cambridge, Mass.: MIT Press, 1984.

———. *Truth and Method.* ed. and trans. Garrett Barden and Jon Cumming. New York: Seabury Press, 1975.

Gellrich, Jesse M. *The Idea of the Book in the Middle Ages: Languages, Theory, Mythology, and Fiction.* Ithaca, N.Y., and London: Cornell University Press, 1985.

Guttman, Julius. *Philosophies of Judaism.* New York: Schocken Books, 1973.

Harvey, Ze'ev Warren. "Maimonides and Aquinas on Interpreting the Bible." *PAAJR* 55 (1988): 59-77.

———. "A Third Approach to Maimonides' Cosmogony-Prophetology Puzzle." *Harvard Theological Review* 74, no. 3 (1981): 287-301.

———. "Ethics and Meta-Ethics, Aesthetics and Meta-Aesthetics in Maimonides." *Maimonides and Philosophy: Papers Presented at the Sixth Jerusalem Philosophical Encounter, May 1985.* ed. Shlomo Pines, and Yirmiyahu Yovel, pp. 131-38. Dordrecht: Martinus Nijhoff, 1986.

Haskins, Charles H. *The Renaissance of the Twelfth Century.* Cambridge, Mass.: Harvard University Press, 1982.

Henle, R. J. *St. Thomas Aquinas and Platonism: A Study of Plato and the Platonici.* Texts in the Writings of St. Thomas. The Hague, 1956.

Hyman, Arthur. "Maimonides' 'Thirteen Principles'." *Jewish Medieval and Renaissance Studies.* ed. A. Altmann, pp. 119-44. Cambridge, Mass.: Harvard University Press, 1967.

———. "Interpreting Maimonides." *Gesher* 6 (1976): 46-59.

———. "A Note on Maimonides' Classification of Law." *PAAJR,* pp. 323-43. Jerusalem: American Academy for Jewish Research, 1980.

———. "Maimonides on Causality." *Maimonides and Philosophy: Papers Presented at the Sixth Jerusalem Philosophical Encounter.* ed. Shlomo Pines and Yirmiyahu Yovel, pp. 157-72. Dordrecht: Martinus Nijhoff, 1986.

Ivry, Alfred L. "Maimonides on Possibility." In *Mystics, Philosophers, and Politicians: Essays in Jewish Intellectual History.* ed. Jehudah Reinharz and Daniel Swetchinski, pp. 67-84. Durham, N.C.: Duke University Press, 1982.

———. "Beri'at ha-'Olam le-fi ha-Rambam." In a forthcoming Festschrift in Honour of Shlomo Pines. Jerusalem: Hebrew University Press.

———. "Maimonides on Creation." *Creation and the End of Days: Judaism and Scientific Cosmology. Proceedings of the 1984 Meeting of the Academy for Jewish Philosophy.* ed. David Novak and Norbert Samuelson, pp. 185-213. Landam, Md.: University Presses of America, 1986.

————. "Providence, Divine Omniscience and Possibility: The Case of Maimonides." *Divine Omnisicence and Omnipotence in Medieval Philosophy: Islamic, Jewish and Christian Perspectives.* ed. Tamar Rudavsky, pp. 143-59. Boston: Dordrecht, 1985.

————. "Destiny Revisited, Avicenna's Concept of Determinism." In *Islamic Philosophy and Theology: Studies in Honour of George F. Hourani.* ed. Michael E. Marmura, pp. 160-71. Albany: SUNY Press, 1984.

————. "The Will of God and the Practical Intellect of Man in Averroes' Philosophy." *Israel Oriental Studies* 9 (1979): 377-91.

Jordan, Mark D. *Ordering Wisdom: The Hierarchy of Philosophical Discourses in Aquinas.* Notre Dame, Ind.: Notre Dame University Press, 1986.

Kaplan, Laurence. "Maimonides on the Miraculous Element in Prophecy." *Harvard Theological Review* 70 (1977): 233-356.

Kellner, Menachem M. "Maimonides and Gersonides on Mosaic Prophecy." *Speculum,* 52 (1977): 62-79.

————. "Maimonides' Thirteen Principles and the Structure of the 'Guide of the Perplexed'." *Journal of the History of Philosophy* 20 (1982): 76-84.

Kendzierski, Lottie H. "Maimonides' Interpretation of the 8th Book of Aristotle's Physics." *The New Scholasticism,* 30 (1956): 37-48.

Klein-Braslavy, Sarah. *Perush he-Rambam le-Sippur Beri'at ha-'Olam.* Jerusalem: ha-Ḥebra le-Ḥeker ha-Mikra be-Yisrael, 1978.

Klubertanz, George P. "St. Thomas and the Knowledge of the Singular." *The New Scolasticism* 26 (1952): 135-66.

Kraemer, Joel L. "Alfarabi's *Opinions of the Virtuous City* and Maimonides' Foundations of the Law." *Studia Orientalia D. H. Baneth Dedicata* (Jerusalem, 1979): 107-53.

Lachterman, David R. *The Ethics of Geometry: A Genealogy of Modernity.* New York and London: Routledge, 1989.

————. "Laying down the Law: The Theological-Political Matrix of Spinoza's Physics," *Leo Strauss's Thought,* ed. Alan Udof (Boulder, Colo.: Lynne Riemer, 1991), pp. 123-158.

Löwith, Karl. *Meaning in History.* Chicago: University of Chicago Press, 1949.

Malter, Henry. *Saadia Gaon, His Life and Works.* Philadelphia: Jewish Publication Society of America, 1921.

Manzanedo, Marcos F. "La antropologia filosofica en el comentario tomista al libro de Job." *Angelicum* 62 (1985): 419-71.

Maurer, Armand. "St. Thomas on the Sacred Name 'Tetragrammaton'." *Mediaeval Studies* 34 (1972): 275-86.

―――. "Maimonides and Aquinas on the Study of Metaphysics." *A Straight Path. Studies in Medieval Philosophy and Culture, Essays in Honor of Arthur Hyman.* ed. Ruth Link-Salinger et al., pp. 206-15. Washington, D.C.: Catholic University of America Press, 1988.

McMullen, Ernan, ed. *The Concept of Matter in Greek and Medieval Philosophy.* Notre Dame, Ind.: Notre Dame University Press, 1963.

Nuriel, Abraham, "Remarks on Maimonides' Epistemology." *Maimonides and Philosophy: Papers Presented at the Sixth Jerusalem Philosophical Encounter, May 1985.* ed. Shlomo Pines and Yirmiyahu Yovel, pp. 36-50. Dordrecht: Martinus Nijhoff, 1986.

O'Reilly, P. "Expositio super librum Boetii *De Hebdomadibus*: An Edition and Study." Diss., University of Toronto, 1960.

Owens, Joseph. "Diversity and Community of Being." *Mediaeval Studies* 22 (1960): 257-302.

―――. "The Unity in a Thomistic Philosophy of Man." *Mediaeval Studies* 25 (1963): 54-82.

―――. "Metaphysical Separation in Aquinas." *Mediaeval Studies* 34 (1972): 287-306.

Palmer, Richard E. *Hermeneutics: Interpretation Theory in Schleiermacher, Dilthey, Heidegger, and Gadamer.* Evanston, Ill.: Northwestern University Press, 1969.

Pegis, Anton C. "A Note on St. Thomas, *Summa Theologica*, 1, 44, 1-2." *Mediaeval Studies* 8 (1946): 159-68.

Pines, Shlomo. "Notes on Maimonides' Views Concerning Human Will." *Scripta Hierosolymitana* 6 (1960): 195-98.

―――. "Some Traits of Christian Theological Writing in Relation to Moslem *Kalam* and to Jewish Thought." [Appendix II: "Adams Disobedience in Maimonides' Interpretation and a Doctrine of John Philoponus"], *Proceedings of the Israel Academy of Sciences and Humanities* 5 (1971-76): 105-25.

―――. "The Limitations of Human Knowledge according to Al-Farabi, Ibn Bajja, and Maimonides." *Studies in Medieval Jewish History and Literature.* ed. Isadore Twersky, pp. 82-109. Cambridge, Mass.: Harvard University Press, 1979.

―――. "The Philosophical Purport of Maimonides' Halachic Works and the Purport of *The Guide of the Perplexed." Maimonides and Philosophy: Papers Presented at the Sixth Jerusalem Philosophical Encounter, May 1985*, ed. Shlomo Pines and Yirmiyahu Yovel, pp. 1-14. Dordrecht, Martinus Nijhoff, 1986.

Prummer, D., ed. *Fontes Vitae S. Thomae Aquinatis.* Toulouse: Privat Bibliopolam, 1912-37.

Raffel, Charles. "Maimonides' Theory of Providence." Diss., Brandeis University, 1983.

Ricoeur, Paul. *Interpretation Theory: Discourse and the Surplus of Meaning.* Fort Worth, Texas: Texas Christian University Press, 1976.

Rist, John M. "Plotinus on Matter and Evil." *Phronesis* 6 (1961): 154-66.

Samuelson, Norbert M. "The Problem of Free Will in Maimonides, Gersonides, and Aquinas." *CCARJ* 17 (1970): 3-13.

Sirat, Colette. *Hagut Filosofit bi-Yemei ha-Beynaim.* Jerusalem: Keter, 1975.

———. *A History of Jewish Philosophy in the Middle Ages.* Cambridge: Cambridge University Press, 1985.

Smalley, Beryl. *The Study of the Bible in the Middle Ages.* Notre Dame, Ind.: Notre Dame University Press, 1978.

———. "William of Auvergne, John of la Rochelle and St. Thomas Aquinas on the Old Law." *St Thomas Aquinas: 1274-1974 Commemorative Studies.* pp. 11-71. Toronto: PIMS, 1974.

Stern, Joseph. "The Idea of *Hoq* in Maimonides' Explanation of the Law." *Maimonides and Philosophy: Papers Presented at the Sixth Jerusalem Encounter, May, 1985.* ed. Shlomo Pines and Yirmiyahu Yovel, pp. 92-130. Dordrecht: Martinus Nijhoff, 1986.

Strauss, Leo. "The Literary Character of the *Guide for the Perplexed.*" In *Persecution and the Art of Writing.* pp. 38-94. Westport, Conn.: Greenwood Press, 1952.

———. "On the Plan of *The Guide of the Perplexed.*" *Harry Austyn Wolfson Jubilee Volume on the Occasion of his Seventy-fifth Birthday.* vol. 2, English section, ed. S. Lieberman, pp. 775-92. Jerusalem, 1965.

———. "Notes on Maimonides' Book of Knowledge." *Studies in Mysticism and Religion Presented to Gershom G. Scholem on his Seventieth Birthday by Pupils, Colleagues and Friends.* ed. E. E. Urbach, R. J. Zwi Werblowsky, and C. Wirszubski, pp. 269-83. Jerusalem: Magnes Press and Hebrew University Press, 1967. Reprinted in *Studies in Platonic Political Philosophy.* ed. T. Pangle, pp. 192-204. Chicago, 1983.

———. "Note on Maimonides' *Treatise on the Art of Logic.*" *Studies in Mysticism and Religion Presented to Gershom Scholem.* pp. 208-9. Jerusalem: Magnes Press and Hebrew University Press, 1967.

Synan, Edward A. "Thomas Aquinas: Propositions and Parables." *The Etienne Gilson Series* 1. Toronto: PIMS, 1979.

Synave, P. "La révélation de vérités divines naturelles d'après saint Thomas d'Aquin." *Mélanges Mandonnet.* vol. 1, pp. 327-70. Paris: Vrin, 1930. Reprinted in *Studies in Maimonides and Aquinas.* ed. J. Dienstag, pp. 290-333. New York: Ktav, 1975.

Talmage, Frank. "Apples of Gold: The Inner Meaning of Sacred Texts in Medieval Judaism." In *Jewish Spirituality I.* ed. Arthur Green, pp. 313-55. New York: Crossroad Publications, 1985.

Touati, Charles. "Les Deux Theories de Maimonides sur la Providence." *In Studies in Jewish Religious and Intellectual History.* ed. Sigfried Stein and Raphael Loewe, pp. 331-41. University, Ala.: Alabama University Press, 1979.

Tyrrell, Francis M. "Concerning the Nature and Function of the Act of Judgment." *The New Scholasticism* 26 (1952): 393-423.

Urbach, Ephraim E. *The Sages: Their Concepts and Beliefs.* 2nd ed. Jerusalem: Magnes Press, 1982.

Vajda, Georges. *L'amour de Dieu dans la théologie juive du Moyen Âge.* Études de Philosophie Médiévale 46. Paris: Vrin, 1957.

————. "La Pensée religieuse de Moise Maimonide: unité ou dualité?" *Cahier de Civilisation Médiévale* 9 (1966): 29-49.

Wippel, John F. *Metaphysical Themes in Thomas Aquinas.* Studies in Philosophy and the History of Philosophy. Vol. 10. Washington, D.C.: The Catholic University of America P., 1984.

————. "Thomas Aquinas and the Axiom "What Is Received Is Received According to the Mode of the Receiver." *A Straight Path: Studies in Medieval Philosophy and Culture. Essays in Honor of Arthur Hyman.* ed. Ruth Link-Salinger et al., pp. 279-89. Washington D.C.: Catholic University of America Press, 1988.

Wohlman, Avital. *Thomas d'Aquin et Maimonide: un dialogue exemplaire.* Paris: Cerf, 1988.

Wolfson, Harry A."Amphibolous Terms in Aristotle, Arabic Philosophy and Maimonides." *Studies in the History of Philosophy and Religion.* 2 vols., ed. Harry A. Wolfson, vol. 1, pp. 455-77. Cambridge, Mass.: Harvard University Press, vol. 1, 1973; vol. 2, 1977.

————. "Maimonides and Gersonides on Divine Attributes as Ambiguous Terms." *Mordecai M. Kaplan Jubilee Volume.* ed. Moshe Davis, pp. 515-30. New York: Jewish Theological Seminary of America, 1953. Reprinted in *Studies in the History and Philosophy of Religion.* vol. 2, ed. H. A. Wolfson, pp. 231-46. Cambridge, Mass.: Harvard University Press, 1977.

————. "Maimonides on the Unity and Incorporeality of God." *Jewish Quarterly Review* 56 (1965): 112-36. Reprinted in *Studies in the History and Philosophy of Religion.* vol. 2, ed. H. A. Wolfson, pp. 433-57. Cambridge, Mass.: Harvard University Press, 1977.

———. "Maimonides on Modes and Universals." *Studies in Rationalism, Judaism and Universalism in Memory of Leon Roth.* ed. R. Loewe, pp. 311-21. London: Routledge and Kegan Paul; New York: Humanities Press, 1966.

———. "St. Thomas on Divine Attributes." *Melanges offerts à Etienne Gilson.* pp. 673-700. Toronto: PIMS; Paris: Vrin, 1959. Reprinted in *Studies in Maimonides and St. Thomas Aquinas.* ed. J. Dienstag, pp. 1-28. New York: Ktav, 1975.

Yaffe, Martin. "Providence in Medieval Aristotelianism: Moses Maimonides and Thomas Aquinas on the Book of Job." *Hebrew Studies* 20-21 (1979-80): 62-74.

Sources on Participation

Fabro, Cornelio. "The Intensive Hermeneutic of Thomistic Philosophy: The Notion of Participation." *The Review of Metaphysics* 27, no. 3 (1974): 449-91.

Geiger, L.-B. *La Participation dans la Philosophie de S. Thomas.* Paris: Vrin, 1942.

Wippel, John F. "Thomas Aquinas on the Distinction and Derivation of the Many from the One." *Review of Metaphysics* 38, no. 3 (1985): 563-89.

Other Sources

Alighieri, Dante. *The Divine Comedy.* trans. Charles S. Singleton, 3 vols. Princeton, N.J.: Princeton University Press, 1970.

Benjamin, Walter. *Illuminations: Essays and Reflections.* trans. Harry Zohn. New York: Schocken Books, 1969.

Spinoza, Benedict. *Spinoza Opera.* 4 vols., ed. Carl Gebhardt. Heidelberg: Carl Winter, 1925.

NAME INDEX

al-Farabi, 17, 64, 199, 223, 237, 256
Albertus Magnus, 41, 203, 213, 216,
    217, 220, 221
Alexander of Aphrodisias, 143
Altmann, Alexander, 240, 241, 249
Aristotle, 1, 9, 12, 15, 16, 19, 20, 28-29,
    31, 34-35, 43, 45, 49, 61, 62-63, 66,
    69, 71, 76, 80, 82, 85, 86, 90, 91, 117,
    127-128, 130, 131, 133, 141-143,
    148, 155, 156, 157, 158, 160, 165,
    168, 172, 177, 179, 181, 182, 195,
    199, 200, 201, 206, 208, 210, 218,
    219, 225, 226, 227, 230, 236, 237,
    238, 241, 243, 244, 245, 247, 251,
    257
Armstrong, R. A., 253
Ashworth, E. J., 244, 257
Augustine, 14-16, 41, 129, 202
Averroes. See Ibn-Rushd
Avicenna. See Ibn-Sina

Benson, Robert L., 203
Berman, Lawrence, 204
Boethius, 54
Boyle, Leonard E., 209, 210
Burrell, David, 42, 200, 204

Chenu, M. D., 29, 43, 203, 214
Christ, 13
Cohen, Herman, 205
Constable, Giles, 203
Courtine, Jean-Francois, 210

d'Alverney, Marie-Therese, 202-203
Dante, 9, 201
Davidson, Herbert, 66-68, 71, 208, 224,
    232, 237, 240

Democritus, 219
Descartes, 2
Dionysius, 84, 104, 105, 221
Dunphy, William, 222, 224, 228

Efros, Israel, 201, 212
Empedocles, 219
Epicurus, 218

Fackenheim, Emil, 72, 226, 255
Fox, Marvin, 204

Gadamer, Hans-Georg, 19-20, 205, 207,
    211
Gaon Sa'adia, 14, 40, 202, 203, 225
Gellrich, Jesse M., 219
Goodman, Lenn, 220
St. Gregory, 15, 40, 41, 213, 218, 220
Gui, Bernard, 19
Guttman, Julius, 202

Hartman, David, 204
Harvey, Warren, 224
Harvey, Ze'ev, 248
Haskins, Charles H., 202
Hegel, 258
Henle, R. J., 206
Hyman, Arthur, 248, 249

Ibn Ezra, Abraham, 14-15, 202, 203
Ibn Rushd, 133
Ibn Sina, 131, 199, 230, 244
Ivry, Alfred L., 71-72, 76, 205, 224, 226,
    235, 236, 248

Jerome, 14
John of la Rochelle, 202
Jordan, Mark D., 79

Klein-Braslavi, Sara, 63, 209, 223
Klubertanz, George, 244

Lachterman, David, 199, 226
Lowith, Karl, 212

Maimon, Solomon, 205
Malter, Henry, 202
Mansanedo, Marcos, 42, 213
Maurer, Armand, 256
Munk, Solomon, 199

Nietzsche, 1
Nuriel, Abraham, 189, 257

O' Reilly, P., 85, 203, 206
Owens, Joseph, 186, 235, 259

Palmer, Richard, 211
Pegis, Anton C., 77, 227, 228, 244
Philo, 13, 15
Pines, Shlomo, 199, 204, 225, 250, 256
Plato, 1, 16, 17, 19, 61, 62, 63, 66, 68,
    69, 77, 82, 85, 86, 155, 156, 200, 201,
    217, 222, 224, 225, 231
Plotinus, 90, 92

Rachham, H., 201
Raffel, Charles, 205, 216

Ricoeur, Paul, 211
Rist, John M., 90
Roland of Cremona, 203
Ross, David, 230

Samuelson, Norbert M., 42, 204
Sirat, Colette, 212
Skemp, J., 225
Smalley, Beryl, 16, 17, 202, 203, 206,
    213
Socrates, 1, 155, 156
Spinoza, 2, 202, 242, 249, 255, 257
Stern, Joseph, 149, 248
Strauss, Leo, 204, 233
Synan, Edward A., 218
Synave, P., 247

Talmage, Frank, 202
Tibbon, Samuel Ibn, 69, 199, 203, 231
Touati, Charles, 204
Tyrrell, Francis, 244

Urbach, Ephraim, 201, 202

Vajda, Georges, 201, 202

Weispheipl, James A., 205
William of Aurverge, 202, 203
William of Tocco, 20
Wippel, John F., 254
Wohlman, Avital, 200, 204, 214

Yaffe, Martin, 42, 43-45, 206, 214, 215,
    255

SUBJECT INDEX

act/potency, 68, 70, 71, 72, 73, 74, 75,
79, 82, 84, 85, 86, 91, 93, 94, 101,
116, 117, 119, 122, 123, 132, 147,
148, 151, 157, 159. *See* human soul
and perfection, and understanding.
See also creation and matter
Adam, 91, 92, 96, 108, 113, 123-124,
146, 153, 154
Ash'arite, 40, 44, 50, 147
attraction/repulsion, 119, 144, 157, 160,
199
Averroism, 44, 127, 130, 132-133

being. *See* good and other headings
biblical exegesis, 8, 13-37, 175. *See also*
biblical interpretation
biblical interpretation (early Christian),
body, soul, and meaning, 15, 16;
early culmination in Augustine, 15-
16; effect of Aristotle on, 15-16; first
principle of; 15, interest in interpretation itself, 14-15, 16, levels of meaning, 15-16; literal and spiritual meaning, 14-15; origins and development
of, 14-16; secular knowledge and
truth, 16; as tradition and Aquinas'
relation to, 16
biblical interpretation (early Jewish),
levels of meaning, 13-14; major
currents of, 15-16; and
Maimonides, 14; origins and development of, 13-14; pre-systematic
tradition, 13, 14
body. *See* human soul and perfection

cause (causality), 4, 8, 63, 77, 81, 82, 83,
84, 85, 147, 179, 181, 182, 183-184;

good as, 84-85. *See* human soul, perfection, and understanding. *See also*
creation and matter
creation, 10, 15, 17, 49, 56, 61-87, 132,
133, 174; act of, 71, 78, 85, 96, 147-
148; act/potency, 68, 70, 71, 72, 73-
74, 75, 78, 79, 81, 82-83, 85; analogy, 71, 78-79; Aquinas, 76-87;
causality, 77, 81-82, 83, 84-85; con-
creation, 79; "*de novo*" ("*huduth*"),
61, 62, 65, 67; demonstration of
(extent and limits), 62, 63-64, 65,
70, 71, 79-81, 82-83, 176-177; emanation, eternal necessity, and divine
free-will, 65, 66, 67, 68, 72, 73, 75,
76, 77, 79-80, 83, 132-133, 177;
eternity of, 18, 61, 66, 70-71, 77,
79, 83, 133; and evil, 76, 78, 84, 86;
"*ex nihilo*" ("*min 'adam*"), 61-62,
65-66, 67-68, 70, 72-73, 75, 77-79;
form, 70, 73, 75, 77, 78, 79, 83-84,
85-86; good, 83-85, 86;
Maimonides, 63-76; matter, 62, 66-
68, 69-70, 72-74, 75-76, 77, 78-79,
83, 84-85, 89, 90-91, 92, 95-96, 98,
177; modes of existence ("*quod*,"
"*quid*," and "*quo modo*") 64, 77;
modes of knowing, 64, 79; necessity, possibility, and impossibility,
62, 67-68, 69, 70-71, 72, 74, 75, 79-
80, 83, 147-148, 168, 177; participation, 77, 81; perfection, 70, 77, 85,
86-87; philosophy and revelation,
61, 63, 64, 65-66, 67-68, 76, 82-83;
privation, 73-74, 75-76, 78, 83-86;
proofs in relation to God, 65; providence, 63, 66-67, 68, 83-84. *See
also* matter

DATE DUE

FEB 10 1997			
			Printed in USA

HIGHSMITH #45230